# Out of Egypt

## A Devotional Study of Exodus

WARREN HENDERSON

Out of Egypt – A Devotional Study of Exodus
By Warren Henderson


Cover Design by Rachel Brooks

Published by Gospel Folio Press
304 Killaly Street West
Port Colborne, ON, L3K 6A6, Canada

ISBN 978-1-926765-07-5

ORDERING INFORMATION:
Gospel Folio Press
Phone 1-905-835-9166
E-mail: order@gospelfolio.com

Printed in Canada

# Acknowledgements

The author greatly appreciates all those who assisted the publishing of *Out of Egypt*. I thank the Lord Jesus Christ for each of the following individuals and for their contributions to this work: Colin Anderson and Randy Amos for technical editing. Kathleen Henderson for the enormous task of general editing. Matthew Henderson and David Lindstrom for proofreading assistance.

# Preface

Commencing with the dawn of time, the book of Genesis reveals the birth pangs of the world, testifies of the fall of man, and then unveils God's plan of redemption for humanity in "seed" form. The closing chapter of Genesis contains Jacob's funeral – one of the most elaborate processions and burials in the Bible. In contrast, the record of Joseph's death and burial contained in the final two verses of Genesis is relatively brief.

The last verse of Genesis reiterates a main theme of the book: *"So Joseph died ...and they embalmed him, and he was put in a coffin in Egypt."* This verse reminds us of the fact that man is under a sentence of death in the world, as pictured by Joseph "in a coffin in Egypt." The key words in Genesis 50 are "mourning," "weeping," and "lamentation," which occur seven times. These words capture the anguish of God over the fallen spiritual condition of humanity.

Thankfully, the Bible does not end with the book of Genesis; God's plan of salvation unfolds with more detail in each subsequent book of the Bible. The Pentateuch, for example, is one continuing storyline which reaches its typological climax in Joshua. Notice how the following conjunctions form a bridge between each of these six books. In Genesis, sin brought man *down*. In Exodus, he is redeemed by blood and brought *out* of the world. In Leviticus, man is permitted to come *nigh* (but not too near) God to worship by substitutional sacrifices. In Numbers, man is brought *through* trials and is refined for service. In Deuteronomy, which means "Second Law," man is *reminded* of his responsibility to the Lord and the consequences of rebellion. In Joshua, a redeemed people are led by Joshua through the Jordan River and *into* victorious living and seize their promised possession.

It was fitting that Moses should die before the Israelites entered the Promised Land (Deut. 34) and that the very next chapter records

Joshua's commission to lead the Israelites into Canaan (Josh. 1). Moses brought the Law, which could never bring spiritual life; the Law only condemned the Jews because they could not keep it. Consequently, Law-keeping, which centers in human effort alone, can never result in victorious living, which depends solely on God's infusing power. Joshua pictures Jesus Christ of the New Testament; both of their names mean "God's Salvation." Israel's trip through the Jordan River represents the receipt of the resurrection life of Christ. It is only by this infusing power that a believer can have victory over the enemy, lay hold of spiritual possessions, and please God.

The book of Exodus reveals two central qualities of God's salvation for man: redemption by blood through substitutional death and consecrated living apart from the world. Exodus records God's work to deliver His people from Egypt as well as His labors to remove Egypt from His people. The book can be divided into three major sections: Israel in Egypt (1:1-12:36), Israel in the Wilderness (12:37-18:37), and Israel at Mt. Sinai (19:1-40:38). Key words in Exodus include: bondage, deliverance, heart, sacrifice, sanctuary, sign, son, tabernacle, and wilderness.

As in *Seeds of Destiny: A Devotional Study of Genesis*, I have endeavored to include some of the best gleanings from other writers in this book. *Out of Egypt* is a "commentary style" devotional which upholds the glories of Christ while exploring Exodus within the context of the whole of Scripture. *Out of Egypt* contains over 100 brief devotions. This format allows the reader to use the book as either a daily devotional or a reference source for deeper study.

— Warren Henderson

# Types

God understands our natural limitations to comprehend spiritual and eternal matters. As a declaration of grace to us, He exercised various literary forms in the Old Testament, including word-pictures, prophecies, shadows, types, allegories, symbols, and plain language, to anticipate the revelation of His supreme gift of love to the world – His own Son. These word pictures prepared humanity to both recognize Christ and freely accept His offer of salvation when He arrived. Consequently, a thorough study of Exodus, which has its center in the theme of redemption, cannot fail to display these literary forms of revelation. Of particular interest throughout the book is the Holy Spirit's usage of *types*.

By the word *type*, we simply mean a picture, figure, or pattern that reflects something or someone in reality (which is the antitype). The word "type" or "print" comes from the Greek word *tupos*. It is used to speak of the nail "print" in the Lord's hand (John 20:25) and of the tabernacle furniture which was to be fashioned according to the "pattern" given Moses in the mount (Heb. 8:5). Thomas said he would not believe that the Lord had been raised up unless he saw and felt the print of the nails in the Lord's hands. In other words, the pattern left in the Lord's hand would match the nail, yet it was not the nail. However, the print furnished evidence of what the nail was like (size and shape). Likewise, Scripture is saturated with "types" of Christ. These offer evidence of Christ, but are not Christ. There is no perfect "type" or "pattern," or it would be the real thing. Therefore, all types, foreshadows, symbols, analogies, and patterns are inadequate to express fully and completely every aspect of His person and work.

Biblical *typology* and *numerology* have perhaps suffered more at the hands of overzealous theologians than by those who would undermine their proper use. Though a hermeneutical defense of these interpretative methods is beyond the scope of this book, some fundamental definitions are appropriate. *Numerology* focuses its attention upon the symbolic meaning of numbers beyond their normally understood numerical significance. In biblical study, numerology forms a portion of the broader study called *typology*. Concerning *typology*, John Walvoord offers a concise definition:

> A *type* may be defined as an exceptional Old Testament reality which was specially ordained by God effectively to prefigure a single New Testament redemptive truth.[1]
>
> Typology is thus a form of prophetic statement. It differs from prophecy in that it may be discerned as typological only after its fulfillment is known. Once this antitype is revealed, one may look back and see that certain expressions and images have meanings besides the historical experience.[2]

F. W. Grant acknowledges the proper use of and, indeed, need for typology to understand the fullness of what God has revealed to mankind through Scripture:

> Some would have us stop where the inspired explanation stops. But in that case, how large a part of what is plainly symbolical would be lost to us! – the larger part of the Levitical ordinances, not a few of the parables of the Lord himself, and almost the whole of the book of Revelation. Surely none could deliberately accept a principle which would lock up from us so large a part of the inspired Word.
>
> Still many have the thought that it would be safer to refrain from typical applications of the historical portions where no inspired statement authenticates them as types at all. Take, however, such a history as that of Joseph, which no direct Scripture speaks of as a type, yet the common consent of almost all receive it as such; or Isaac's sacrifice, of the significance of which we have the merest hint. The more we consider it, the more we find it impossible to stop short here. Fancy, no doubt, is to be dreaded. Sobriety and reverent caution are abundantly needful. But so are they everywhere. If we profess wisdom, we become fools: subjection to the blessed Spirit of God, and to the Word inspired of Him, are our only safeguards here and elsewhere.

> When we look a little closer, we find that the types are not scattered haphazardly in the Old Testament books. On the contrary, they are connected together and arranged in an order and with a symmetry which bear witness to the divine hand which has been at work throughout. We find Exodus thus to be the book of redemption; Leviticus, to speak of what suits God with us in the sanctuary of sanctification, then Numbers, to give the wilderness-history – our walk with God (after redemption and being brought to Him where He is,) through the world. Each individual type in these different books will be found to have most intimate and significant relation to the great central thought pervading the book. This, when laid hold of, confirms immensely our apprehension of the general and particular meaning, and gives it a force little if at all short of absolute demonstration.[3]

Though most numbers in Scripture have a literal meaning (e.g. Christ arose from the grave on the *third* day), some numbers serve a figurative purpose. The Lamb with *seven* horns in Revelation 5:6 symbolically represents the Lord's omnipotence (*Seven* being the number of perfection, and a *horn* representing *power* in Scripture.). Sometimes both a figurative and a literal meaning may be understood, especially when the obvious literal sense is within a personal narrative and the figurative sense conveys a future meaning verified elsewhere in Scripture. For example, the seven-year famine in Joseph's day was both an actual devastating famine that affected the whole land and also a forewarning of a yet future seven-year Tribulation Period that would devastate the entire planet. It is noted that *Egypt* figuratively speaks of "the world" in Scripture.

Numbers *one* through *forty* and many numbers above forty are used in a repeated figurative manner in the Bible to show a particular meaning. This figurative repetition is one of many evidences which demonstrates that all Scripture comes from one Mind – it is God-breathed (2 Tim. 3:16). For example, in Genesis 2:1-3, we are first introduced to the number "seven." From the beginning, the number *seven* is God's number and a fundamental building block which speaks of "perfection" or "completeness." The word "sanctified," also appearing for the first time in these verses, means "set apart" or "holy." The week of creation ended on the seventh day with a day of rest for the Lord. This rest was a divine response to His satisfaction with His creative work, not to weariness (Isa. 40:28). God declared literally seven times in Genesis 1 that what He had created was *good*, but also declared through the use of the number seven that it was *perfect*.

# *Devotions in Exodus*

# "These are the Names"
## Exodus 1:1-7

Genesis records the covenants between Jehovah and the Patriarchs, some of these promises were unconditional, while others were contingent upon human faithfulness. Some promises pertained to individuals and others had national ramifications. It is the latter, which forms the bedrock of the Exodus narrative. Accordingly, this covenant dynamic, as Arthur Pink notes, creates a number of contrasting features between the books of Genesis and Exodus:

> In the book of Genesis we have the history of a family, in Exodus the history of a nation. In Genesis the descendants of Abraham are few in number, in Exodus they are to be numbered by the million. In the former we see the Hebrews welcomed and honored in Egypt, in the latter they are viewed as feared and hated. In the former there is a Pharaoh who says to Joseph, *"God hath showed thee all this"* (41:39); in the latter there is a Pharaoh who says to Moses, *"I know not the Lord"* (5:2). In Genesis there is a "lamb" promised (22:8); in Exodus the "lamb" is slain (chap. 12). In the one we see the entry of Israel into Egypt; in the other we behold their exodus. In the one we see the patriarchs in the land "which flowed with milk and honey;" in the other we behold their descendants in the wilderness. Genesis ends with Joseph in a coffin; while Exodus closes with the glory of the Lord filling the tabernacle. A series of more vivid contrasts could scarcely be imagined.[1]

The names of those composing the initial seed of Abraham, from which God would build a great nation, are contained in Exodus 1. The Hebrew name of the second book in the Bible is drawn from the first two Hebrew words of the text, *twmv hlaw* ("these are the names"); sometimes it has been shortened to just "names." However, in the Septuagint the book is named "Exodus" to emphasize the departure of

Israel from Egypt.[2] Exodus begins by *naming* Jacob and his family members who trekked from Canaan to Egypt to be preserved by Joseph, the second in command of Egypt, during the great famine.

While Jacob was journeying to Egypt to embrace his previously lost son Joseph, he stopped at Beersheba to offer sacrifices to God for miraculously safeguarding and honoring his son. It was at Beersheba that God spoke to Jacob in a vision to reaffirm His presence, to promise his preservation while in Egypt, and to promise that He would create a great nation from them while they sojourned there (Gen. 46:3).

Genesis 46 provides a roster of Jacob's wives, sons, and grandsons that traveled with him to Egypt – in all, sixty-six sons and grandsons are named. Counting Joseph, his two sons, and Jacob, the total number of males composing the nation of Israel at this time was seventy (v. 5). The number seventy is associated with the nation of Israel in a special way through the remainder of Scripture. There were seventy elders of Israel (Num. 11:16), seventy years of Babylonian captivity (2 Chron. 36:21), seventy prophetic weeks determined upon Israel before their restoration (Dan. 9:24-27), and during New Testament times, there were seventy members of the Sanhedrin, and seventy witnesses sent out to Israel by Christ (Luke 10:1). Could God, using seventy souls, build the Jewish nation?

Yes, God kept His promises to Jacob. First of all, the nation was marvelously preserved in Egypt, although most of its latter years there were spent in bondage. Secondly, God greatly multiplied Jacob's family into a great nation. Exodus 1 records the initial seed of the nation, while Numbers 1:46 documents its fantastic growth. From seventy males, the nation had grown to 603,550 men who were twenty years of age and older, which meant the entire population of Israel (including women and children) was likely between two and three million people at the time of the exodus. Yes, God kept His promise to Jacob, a covenant that had been previously affirmed with Isaac and was originally made with Abraham.

Exodus records the direct fulfillment of God's promise to Abraham as recorded in Genesis 15. God had identified three events which would come upon Israel in association with Egypt: they would *sojourn* there as strangers, they would *serve* the Egyptians there, and then they would suffer in *slavery* there (Gen. 15:13). Not only does God foreknow all things, but the Exodus narrative demonstrates that God is in complete control of all things at all times: *"For Whom are all things, and by Whom are all things"* (Heb. 2:10). Every detail of every moment for every person is in His control.

Secondly, the prophetic fulfillment of God's visage, as He passed through the midst of the animal pieces, was fulfilled: *"A smoking furnace and a burning lamp that passed between those pieces"* (Gen. 15:17; KJV). The story of Israel from the time of Abraham can be summed up in these two figures – the "smoking furnace" and the "burning lamp." The *smoking furnace* represents those dark periods of time when Israel was being refined through suffering and fiery trials (Jer. 11:4). The *lamp* pictures those bright spots in Israel's history when Jehovah directly intervened to deliver a repentant Israel from aggression, captivity, and evil (Isa. 62:1). The thicker and darker the smoke, the brighter the lamp would seem during times of restoration. Certainly this would characterize the Israelites' experience in Egypt and their awesome deliverance.

In application for the present day, we might think upon Paul's attitude concerning suffering for Christ's sake: *"For our light affliction, which is but for a moment, is working for us a far more exceeding and eternal weight of glory, while we do not look at the things which are seen, but at the things which are not seen. For the things which are seen are temporary, but the things which are not seen are eternal"* (2 Cor. 4:17-18). Let this be an encouragement to all believers – the darker the threatening cloud overhead, the brighter the dawning of our future in Christ. From our vantage point shadows loom, but from the throne of heaven the same cloud reflects the brilliance of God's grace. Let us cling to His promises and hope for His imminent deliverance, if permitted, and if not, for His sustaining grace to weather the storm!

> God moves in a mysterious way His wonders to perform;
> He plants His footsteps in the sea and rides upon the storm.
>
> Deep in unfathomable mines of never failing skill
> He treasures up His bright designs and works His sovereign will.
>
> Blind unbelief is sure to err and scan His work in vain;
> God is His own interpreter, and He will make it plain.
>
> — William Cowper

# Oppressed in Egypt
## Exodus 1:8-22

While Joseph was alive, the Israelites fared well in Egypt, but after his death several factors led to their oppression. First, there was a new leadership in Egypt that was not familiar with Joseph, or perhaps did not favor him (v. 8). Does the *"new king over Egypt"* refer only to a new Egyptian Pharaoh or to the demise of a foreign power that had been ruling over Egypt? Because Scripture does not record the actual names of Egyptian Pharaohs until the days of Ruth, it is difficult to precisely correlate the events of the Exodus with other historical records.

Biblical scholars have placed the date of the Exodus from as late as 1230 B.C. to as early as 1580 B.C. Archeological evidence has been used to bolster various dates in this range. Recognizing that the Exodus occurred 480 years before Solomon began constructing the temple (1 Kgs. 6:1) and that the temple work was initiated in about 960 B.C., a date in the mid-fifteenth century B.C. for the Exodus seems appropriate. Note: The 1 Kings 6:1 reference may include 93 years in which Israel was in service to foreigners during the era of the judges (Acts 13:18-21). An exodus date of 1446 B.C. is approximately placed.[1]

The king mentioned in verse 8 probably relates to Egypt's 18$^{th}$ dynasty, perhaps Amenhotep I (1545–1526 B.C.) or Thutmose I (1526-1512 B.C.). Amenhotep II (1450-1425 B.C.) was involved with building projects in northern Egypt and may have been Pharaoh at the time of the Exodus. History records that an Asiatic people called the Hyksos captured and ruled Egypt from around 1720 to 1580 B.C. (corresponding to the time of the Patriarchs and to the 15$^{th}$ and 16$^{th}$ Egyptian dynasties).

Some historians believe that the Hyksos, like the Hebrews, were a nomadic people. They were also Semitic (i.e. descendants of Shem), as were the Israelites. If the date of 1446 B.C. is correct for the exodus, then the available historical information aligns well with the biblical account. For example, it seems logical to conclude that the migration of the Israelites to Egypt and the rise of Joseph to power corresponded with the Hyksos' control of Egypt. Semitic rulers would have been more favorable than the Egyptians to allow a Semitic "foreigner" to be the second in command of Egypt and to permit a migration of other Semitic people to Goshen. The "new king" who did not know Joseph would correspond with the expulsion of the Hyksos from Egypt after the 16th dynasty. With the removal of Joseph and the Hyksos, the Egyptians regained political control and enslaved the Israelites, perhaps in retaliation for Semitic rule.[2]

The Egyptians feared the growing population of Hebrews and were concerned that they might align themselves with Egypt's enemies, perhaps a reference to the Hyksos. The solution was to enslave the Hebrews and to start whittling down their numbers by killing their baby boys. This action would certainly minimize the availability of male soldiers for a future army.

Though their main task was to build the royal storage cities of Pithom and Rameses (v. 11), the Egyptians forced the Hebrews to work in the fields and anywhere else they could find work for them to accomplish (v. 14). Not only were the Jews Egypt's construction labor force, they also had to create their own building supplies (bricks). The narrative paints a bleak picture of their plight, including the following descriptions: "with vigor," "hard bondage," "lives bitter," "afflicted," and "burdens."

As did the children of Israel, all of us will face troubling times during our sojourn on a sin-cursed planet. Paul teaches us in Philippians 1 that even during the most dismal of situations there is always a mental escape from depression for the believer called rejoicing, and *rejoicing is a choice*. Though a prisoner in Rome, the apostle focused his mind on what great things God had accomplished through his imprisonment: Some in Caesar's household had come to Christ, timid brethren had become bold in the preaching of Christ, and even though some were preaching against Paul, he could still say, *"Christ is preached; and in this I rejoice, yes, and will rejoice"* (Phil. 1:18). If Paul had focused his thoughts on his difficulties he would have been overcome with despair. Instead, he chose to concentrate on the positive outcomes of his suffering: *"But I want you to know, brethren, that the things which happened to me have actually turned out for the furtherance of the gospel"* (Phil. 1:12).

1 Thessalonians 5:16, *"rejoice evermore,"* is the shortest verse in the Greek New Testament, but one of the most important. Joy removes life's burden. God's family should be a happy family, meaning we all must contribute to the atmosphere of joy. There is no room for a "doom and gloom" attitude. *"Yet if anyone suffers as a Christian, let him not be ashamed, but let him glorify God in this matter"* (1 Pet. 4:16). As a believer chooses to rejoice in the Lord while in the midst of a dire situation, God often chooses to glorify Himself by working a miraculous solution to end the trial. This is why, though constantly threatened, Paul could write, *"As sorrowful, yet always rejoicing"* (2 Cor. 6:10).

For the Hebrews there were at least two things mentioned in Exodus 1 that they could rejoice in. First, the more they were afflicted the more *they multiplied and grew* (v. 12); in fact, *the people multiplied and grew very mighty* (v. 20). God's expressed desire for His people throughout the Bible is that they would be fruitful and multiply. The Lord Jesus expressed His desire for His disciple's *fruitfulness* the night before His death (John 15). Note the progression of His appeal to them to be fruit-bearing: He seeks *"fruit"* (v. 2), then *"more fruit"* (v. 2), then *"much fruit"* (v. 5). Yet, fruit-bearing is only possible for those who abide in Christ (John 15:4-5) and are pruned (John 15:2). Pruning doesn't feel good at the time, but the action stimulates fruit production in trees, and no less in Christians, if they choose to yield to and abide in Christ.

The Lord Jesus also spoke of them *multiplying* after His resurrection: *"Go therefore and make disciples of all the nations, baptizing them in the name of the Father and of the Son and of the Holy Spirit, teaching them to observe all things that I have commanded you; and lo, I am with you always, even to the end of the age"* (Matt. 28:19-20). All believers are to be actively proclaiming the gospel message and to teach new converts so that they also will make new disciples of Christ. The Lord's plan to build His Church would be by making and mentoring one disciple at a time. May God's people "be fruitful and multiply!"

The second matter the Hebrews could rejoice in was the brave conduct of the midwives. These women refused to obey Pharaoh's command to kill the Hebrew baby boys because the midwives feared God more than they did Pharaoh (v. 17). Their bold testimony has now been remembered for 3,500 years. The names of these women are interesting: *Shiphrah*'s name means "beauty" and the meaning of *Puah* is "splendor." What does God find beautiful in a woman? Chaste conduct, godly fear, and a meek and quiet spirit, says Peter (1 Pet. 3:2-4). It was not their outward appearance that Scripture recalls as beautiful, but the inward reality of their godliness as witnessed in their conduct. This is a beauty which can be enriched with years: "*Even though our outward man is perishing, yet the inward man is being renewed day by day*" (2 Cor. 4:16). All believers (not just women) should understand that the outward appearance perishes and that each of us should long for an inner beauty that only gets better with time!

The midwives feared God more than they feared Pharaoh and God rewarded their courage by bestowing them families of their own. How should we understand their lying to Pharaoh in order to cover up their disobedience to his command? Though lying is never condoned in Scripture, God has repeatedly shown that He is quite able to work His will despite human falsehoods. Rahab lied to the officials in Jericho in order to preserve the two spies from being discovered. Mistreated Tamar lied to Judah in order to have children. David acted insane before Achish to escape death. Is God capable of accomplishing His purposes without human deception? Absolutely! So let us put away all lying (Eph. 4:25), and if necessary, suffer honestly for saying the truth in love, or in some cases, for saying nothing at all. Lying does not honor God, and in fact, demonstrates a lack of faith in His Word.

What is the real agenda associated with the slaughtering of Hebrew babies? God told Satan in the Garden of Eden that the seed of the woman would crush his head in a future day (Gen.3:15). Later divine covenants with humanity would also reveal that the future Messiah would be a descendant of Abraham (Gen. 12:3), of Isaac (Gen. 17:19) and of Jacob (Gen. 25:23). Still later, Judah would be named in the Messianic line (Gen. 49:10). Satan also knew of the Genesis 15 prophecies to Abraham which foretold of Jewish deliverance from Egypt and when this would take place. Yes, the slave workforce had become enormous, but every Hebrew boy killed would lessen the possibility of the deliverer appearing.

Since the first prophecy concerning the coming victor in Genesis 3, Satan's primary mission has been against Messiah (more specifically the person of Jesus Christ). This attack has come on three main fronts:

(1) Satan tried to destroy the family line through which the Deliverer would come. Examples include: Effort to pervert the godly line of Seth in Genesis 6 and Athaliah's attempt to kill the entire royal seed to obtain the throne (2 Chron. 22:10-12). However, Jehoshabeath protected the only remaining son of Ahaziah – Joash, who is listed in the genealogy of Christ (Matt. 1).
(2) When the prevention of the birth of Messiah was unsuccessful, direct attempts on the life of the Lord Jesus were made. When He was a child in Bethlehem, Herod attempted to kill Him by murdering all the boys two years old and younger in the vicinity (Matt. 2). Later, attempts would be made on the Lord's life as an adult in Nazareth, when distraught Jews tried to push Him over a cliff (Luke 4:29) and when the religious leaders sought to stone Him (John 8:59, 10:31) for His alleged blasphemies.
(3) Having failed to stop Christ from completing His redemptive work, Satan now concentrates on casting doubt on the Person of Christ, on slandering His name, and seducing worshippers into idolatry or heresy.

Pharaoh's plan to slaughter the Hebrew babies was only temporarily foiled by the midwives bravery, for verse 22 records his charge to all Egyptians to cast the newborns into the river. The *river* pictures Satan's power: the source of life to the Egyptians, but in reality it is the realm of death to God's people. In a not too distant day, Moses would turn the water of the Nile into blood (illustrating death) and prove to all the Egyptians that all power originates from the God of the Hebrews.

The situation in Egypt was desperate for the Israelites. Their bitter slavery paled in comparison to the murdering of their children. But the stage is set; God has heard the wailing of His people, His deliverer is coming, and salvation is near.

While we tread the vale of sorrow, may we in Thy love abide;
Keep us O our gracious Saviour cleaving closely to Thy side:
Still relying on our Father's changeless love.
Saviour, come! We long to see Thee, long to dwell with Thee above;
And to know, in full communion, all the sweetness of Thy love:
Come, Lord Jesus! Take Thy waiting people home.

— William Williams

# The Birth of the Deliverer
## Exodus 2:1-2

A certain Levite named Amram married his Aunt Jochebed (Ex. 6:20) and had three children. Their daughter Miriam (Ex. 2:4, 15:20) was their oldest child, and their second child, Aaron, was three years older than Moses (Ex. 6:20, 7:7). If the Exodus occurred in 1446 B.C., when Moses was 80 years of age, then Moses' birth would have been in 1526 B.C. which correlates with the end of Amenhotep I's reign and the beginning of the reign of Thutmose I. The fact that Moses was threatened with death and not Aaron indicates that the decree to kill baby boys must have been issued about the time of Moses' birth, perhaps aligning with the change of Pharaohs.

During Stephen's historical dissertation to the Pharisees, he notes that Moses was no ordinary newborn, but was *well-pleasing* to God (Acts 7:20). The Exodus narrative also confirms that Moses entered the world as a beautiful baby (v. 2). The Hebrew word used to describe baby Moses is translated as "good" seven times in Genesis 1 to speak of God's satisfaction with His work of creation. His parents, seeing his *goodliness*, determined to ignore Pharaoh's command and hide the child. The consequence of a slave rebelling against Pharaoh is not specified; however, judging from the harsh manner in which the Egyptians treated the Hebrews, the punishment would be severe (likely the penalty of death).

So why did Amram and Jochebed risk their lives to protect Moses? The writer of Hebrews answers this question: *"By faith Moses, when he was born, was hidden three months by his parents, because they saw he was a beautiful child; and they were not afraid of the king's command"* (Heb. 11:23). They hid Moses by faith. But faith must have a promise and an object to trust in order to be faith. The Egyptians considered Pharaoh to be a god, yet Moses' parents were willing to reject his command because their allegiance was to One higher than Pharaoh – the God of Abraham.

The promise that Moses' parents were contemplating was, as previously discussed, likely the one God extended to Abraham concerning their plight and deliverance. This prophecy states that Abraham's offspring *"shall be a sojourner in a land that is not theirs, and shall serve them; and they shall afflict them four hundred years"* (Gen. 15:13). These events occurred in the order they were revealed to Abraham – sojourning to serving to suffering. Certainly, the Hebrews suffered verbal abuse in those early years in Egypt because the Egyptians despised shepherds. The cruelty of the Egyptians towards the Jews increased over time. Ultimately, the Egyptians enslaved the Hebrews and murdered their babies in an attempt to reduce their growing numbers.

This prophecy spanned 400 years (Gen. 15:13; Acts 7:6) and four generations (Gen. 15:16). How should we understand the meaning of this prophecy? Some believe that the 400 years began with Jacob's arrival at Goshen, where the descendants of Abram sojourned in peace for a time and then were placed in bondage for a total of 430 years before being delivered (Ex.12:40-41); therefore Genesis 15:13 and Acts 7:6 speaks of this period in the round figure of 400 years.

Yet, Paul states that there were 430 years from the covenant with Abraham to the giving of the Law on Sinai (Gal. 3:17). Also, the above interpretation does not explain the deliverance and return of the Jewish nation in the fourth generation of captivity unless one assumes that some generations were not named. This is very unlikely considering these were the glory days of Israel's expansion and the ages of the fathers were recorded when the subsequent generations were born. The four generations relate to those who sojourned in Egypt: Levi to Moses, the deliverer. We read that Kohath, the son of Levi, was already born when Jacob's family arrived in Egypt (Gen. 46:11). Kohath had a son named Amram, and Amram was the father of Moses. Kohath lived only 133 years, Amram lived 137 years (Ex. 6:18-20), and Moses was 80 years old when he was sent as God's deliverer (Ex. 7:7). It is noted that Amram was the first of four sons born to Kohath. So, even if Kohath and Amram had both married late in life and had children late in life (which is not likely because each had several children), it would "practically speaking" be difficult to have more than 275 years between Kohath's coming into Egypt and Moses' delivering of the children of Israel.

So how long were the Israelites actually in Egypt if the 430 years does represent the time from the covenant with Abraham to the Exodus? Abraham was 75 years old when the covenant was made (Gen. 12:4). Then, 25 years later, Isaac was born (Gen. 21:5); 60 years later Jacob was born to Isaac, and we know that Jacob was 130 years old when he went to Egypt (Gen. 47:9). The addition of these years equals 215 years and reflects the time between the covenant and Jacob's entrance into Egypt. By subtracting this figure from the overall time period of 430 years, we can ascertain that the total time the descendants of Jacob were in Egypt was also 215 years (430 – 25 – 60 – 130 = 215).

This figure aligns well with the "fourth generation" prophecy. It is recorded that Isaac's age was 60 when Jacob was born (Gen. 25:26), and Jacob was in his mid-eighties before he had children. If we assume that Kohath and Amram were about halfway through their lifespan before they had children (ages 65 and 70, respectively), 215 years between arriving at Egypt and deliverance from Egypt would be the result (133 – 65 {for Kohath} + 137 – 70 {for Amram} + 80 {for Moses} = 215 years).

How long were the Israelites slaves in Egypt? We cannot say definitely, but we do know that they were not slaves while Joseph was alive. Joseph was 39 years old when Jacob came to Egypt (Gen. 41:45-53, 45:6), and Joseph died at 110 years of age (Gen. 50:26). Therefore, we can subtract another 71 years (110 – 39) from the 215 number to represent the time between Joseph's death and the exodus. The result is 144 years. Therefore, the maximum time the Israelites were enslaved was 144 years. This also puts the death of Joseph in 1590 B.C., which aligns with the end of the Hyksos rule over Egypt and the rise of the new Egyptian regime which chose to enslave the Jews.

Is it possible for the nation of Israel to have grown from 70 males, plus a number of unnamed wives and daughters to a population, say of 2.5 million in 215 years? Assuming that the number of males and females were initially equal, an annual population growth rate of only 4.65 percent is required to obtain the exodus population described in Scripture (140 souls x $1.0465^{215}$ = 2.46 million people). Initially, the population would have grown by only six or seven individuals each year, but as the years passed the nation of Israel would have reached a population size reported in Exodus and Numbers in 215 years. This type of growth is possible; in fact, some countries are even now experiencing an annual population growth rate between four and five percent: Afghanistan, for example, has an annual growth rate of 4.77 percent.[1] Assuming a population growth of five percent per year, the nation of Israel would have numbered about 51,000 souls at the time of Moses' birth and about 2.5 million at the exodus.

It is *my opinion* that the 400-year, or more specifically, the 430-year prophecy initiated with the sojourn of Abraham in Egypt (Gen. 12) and concluded with the exodus of his descendants from there. If this interpretation is correct, Moses' parents may have known of the 400-year prophecy, and more certainly of the fourth generation prophecy of deliverance from a foreign land. Moses was a beautiful child of the fourth generation; could this baby boy possibly be connected to the fulfillment of this prophecy? Apparently, his parents discerned God had a special plan for their son and in faith they risked their lives to preserve his life.

> A man who has faith must be prepared not only to be a martyr, but to be a fool.
>
> — G. K. Chesterton

# Rescuing the Deliverer
## Exodus 2:3-10

The situation apparently became too dangerous for the family to keep baby Moses in their home any longer. Perhaps Jochebed was inspired to build a little ark for her son after pondering God's means of delivering Noah, His "preacher of righteousness," from death. She built an ark of bulrushes and daubed it with slime to keep the waters of death out. Acting by faith, and ironically in accordance with Pharaoh's command, she took the ark which she had constructed and her beautiful baby to the Nile River. Jochebed placed her son in the ark and situated it among the reeds of the river. The fact that Miriam remained behind to monitor the ark was proof that Jochebed was constructing not a coffin, but rather a means by which God would direct the life of her son. God honored her faith, for Pharaoh's own daughter found the ark among the reeds at the river's edge. Just as she was opening the ark, the precious contents within let out a cry. The infant's plea struck a maternal chord in her heart and she felt compassion for him.

According to Pharaoh's law she should have pushed the ark under the water, but instead she determined to save the baby's life. Young Miriam, seeing the opportunity, offered to get Pharaoh's daughter a Hebrew woman to nurse the child. She consented and Miriam brought Jochebed to meet Pharaoh's daughter, who instructed her to nurse and care for the baby, which she had now adopted as her own. She agreed to pay Jochebed wages in return for properly caring for the child. Can you imagine the exuberant delight of Jochebed? She had returned to the river to find the very son she had abandoned was now under royal protection and – to top it off – she would be paid for fulfilling what she longed to do – to be a mother to her son. To protect her family from dire consequences she had obeyed Pharaoh's command – she put her baby boy in the river. But Moses had not been tossed into the waters of death, he had been protected from death by his mother's faith in God, and she had been wonderfully rewarded.

We cannot pass over this death-life presentation without reflecting on the developing pattern in Scripture to call attention to God's Son. In type, the Old Testament contains many previews of that which the Gospels ultimately reveal – life comes to us through death. Isaac was near death, but an unblemished ram took his place on his father's altar – Isaac later inherited all that his father had. Joseph had been thrown into a pit and his brothers contemplated his murder, but his life was spared and he was later raised up to rule over them in Egypt. As we have been contemplating, Moses was laid in the waters of death, but he was miraculously snatched out and ushered into Pharaoh's house; later he would be admired by all in Egypt. These situations may suggest how God would be able to righteously offer salvation to sinners: His Son, a sinless substitute, would die in place of fallen humanity – His life comes to us through His death. The deaths of Isaac, Joseph, and Moses, could not accomplish this feat, but their life experiences preface various aspects of what God would eventually accomplish through the death and resurrection of His Son.

Pharaoh's daughter's royal command reflects the high-calling Christian parents have to train up their children for God (2 Cor. 12:14; Eph. 6:1-4). God does not desire merely morally-sound children; *"He seeks godly offspring"* (Mal. 2:15). God longs for spiritually-minded people in the world and He knows this training begins in the home. To those Christian parents who take His command seriously He rewards their faith with *wages* (speaking of various forms of divine blessing). What a deal! Parents are rewarded by God for godly parenting, not merely for raising good children (for some children will go their own way despite the best parenting).

There are often unique circumstances related to the births of those God calls to perform, naturally speaking, the impossible. Isaac, Samson, Samuel, and John the Baptist were all born according to prophetic announcement and from previously barren wombs. The Lord Jesus Christ's birth was unique; He was born of a virgin. Although Moses' conception and birth were normal, the life-threatening situation at his birth, his miraculous escape from death, and the fact that he was nursed by own mother and then inducted into the house of Pharaoh all speak of God's guiding hand in the situation.

As affirmed in verse 10, Moses' name means, "he who draws out (from the water)." His name would be a reminder of his humble beginning, of God's intervention in his life, and of his divine calling. Every believer in Christ also has a name that reminds him or her from what he or she has been called out of and called into. We read in Acts 11:26 that *"the disciples were first called Christians in Antioch."* "Christian" simply means "Christ-one" and refers to those who have trusted Christ alone for salvation and have thereby become His disciples. To completely identify with Christ, to learn of Christ (Matt. 11:29), and to be like Christ (Matt. 10:25) is the essence of biblical discipleship. The extent that this identification occurs will directly reflect how well believers manifest the nature of Christ to the world and fulfill their calling in Christ.

To declare the name of Christ our Deliverer is a high honor, but to associate with His name is the highest call to honor Him. This aspiration is reflected in Paul's prayer for the believers at Thessalonica: *"That the name of our Lord Jesus Christ may be glorified in you, and you in Him, according to the grace of our God and the Lord Jesus Christ"* (2 Thess. 1:12). To be identified as a Christian is to acknowledge Christ's call to live as He did and to not return to that which He has called believers out of. This reality is pictured in God's dealings with Moses and the Israelites. In order to bear God's name Moses was drawn from Nile, which was the life of Egypt but death to the children of Israel. God's plan of redemption would draw the Israelites out of the death of Egypt and into new life with Him.

Rejoice ye saints, rejoice in Christ, your glorious Head;
With heart, and soul, and voice, His matchless honours spread;
Exalt His love, proclaim His name, and sweetly sing the Lamb once slain.

— Gadsby's Selection

# Rejected by Egypt
## Exodus 2:11-25

There are forty years of silence between the events of Exodus 1 and Exodus 2; Moses was now a grown man (v. 11). He has had a privileged upbringing in the house of Pharaoh. Moses enjoyed social status, the riches of Egypt, higher education, and all the things that made life easy, but the time of moral decision loomed over his head as a threatening storm. He was a Hebrew by blood and by Pharaoh's own decree he should have died at birth. His people were suffering under the brutality of Egyptian rule; how long could he sit still and do nothing?

One day Moses witnessed an isolated Egyptian smiting a Hebrew slave. This was the breaking point: after ensuring there were no witnesses, he slew the Egyptian and buried his body in the sand. When he went out the following day, he saw two Hebrew slaves fighting; while attempting to break up the squabble, one of the slaves rejected Moses' leadership and asked if he would kill him as he had the Egyptian the day before. Moses was stunned on two counts: first, that his brethren had rejected his efforts to deliver them from oppression and, second, that the matter of the dead Egyptian was known. C. H. Mackintosh identifies Moses' error in this matter:

> He [Moses] supposed his brethren would have understood how that God by his hand would deliver them. All this was true; yet he evidently ran before the time, and when one does this, failure must be the issue. And not only is there failure in the end, but also manifest uncertainty, and lack of calm elevation and holy independence in the progress of a work begun before God's time. Moses "looked this way and that way." There is no need of this when a man is acting with and for God, and in the full intelligence of His mind, as to the detail of His work. If God's time had really come, and if Moses was conscious of being divinely commissioned to execute judgment upon

> the Egyptian, and if he felt assured of the divine presence with him, he would not have "looked this way and that way."[1]

The death of the Egyptian was not a secret and Moses feared what would happen when Pharaoh heard about it. Pharaoh did learn of the murder and rightly sought to slay Moses. Fleeing Egypt for his life, Moses came to the land of Midian, which would be his home for the next forty years.

The book of Hebrews provides insight as to why Moses chose to identify with God's covenant people instead of with the Egyptians:

> *By faith Moses, when he became of age, refused to be called the son of Pharaoh's daughter, choosing rather to suffer affliction with the people of God than to enjoy the passing pleasures of sin, esteeming* ***the reproach of Christ*** *greater riches than the treasures in Egypt; for he looked to the reward. By faith he forsook Egypt, not fearing the wrath of the king; for he endured as seeing Him who is invisible* (Heb. 11:24-27).

First of all, Moses understood who he was and he chose to identify with God's people. Moses was willing to forsake great riches and high status to suffer *the reproach of Christ* in the world. Notice the text does not say Moses suffered *reproach for Christ*. Christ departed heaven to take up a lowly existence upon the earth in order to identify with those He came to save. Though Moses didn't suffer because of his testimony for God, he did honor God by foreshadowing Christ's suffering by identifying with God's people. Somehow he understood that there was a day of reckoning with God, and he determined that it would be better for him to identify with God's people and forsake the splendor of Egypt rather than to be associated with a dismal system of rule which brutalized God's people.

What is meant when referring to the "world?" The world has different forms: political, artistic, musical, religious, entertainment, business, etc. Biblically speaking, the "world" may refer to the world we live on (Earth), the world of things, the world of people, or the world system controlled by Satan. In the latter instance, the world represents a human society built up apart from God; it is human civilization with base motives and desires, the outworking of mankind's depraved state.

Worldliness, then, is any sphere from which the Lord Jesus is excluded. Ponder for a moment how the world's standard of success is in direct opposition to what the Lord Jesus taught:

*The world* wants to be served, but Christ says humble yourself and serve others.
*The world* says save your life, but the Lord says lose your life to gain one worth living.
*The world* exclaims "live for the moment," but Christians are to live for eternity.
*The world* says live for self, but the Lord says lose your life for Him.
*The world* is into power, but the Lord uses weak things to confound the mighty.
*The world* permits greed to rule distribution, but Christians are to give according to need.
*The world* says acquire wealth, but God teaches us not to seek to be rich.
*The world* uses money and power to rule, but Christians are to pray and to use Scripture in love to serve others.
*The world* says retaliate and get even, but the Lord teaches us to repay evil with good and be forgiving.
*The world* uses violence, but Christians are to turn the other cheek.

So why is it that the world stands in opposition to Jesus Christ and His message? Why does the world exclude Christ from conversational, educational, and professional realms, but talk about world religions is permissible? It is because Satan is behind the scene, controlling the various systems of the world, and he despises Christ and those who identify with Him. Paul identifies Satan as *"the god of this age"* (2 Cor. 4:4) and *"the prince of the power of the air"* (Eph. 2:2). On three occasions the Lord Jesus said that Satan is *"the prince of this world"* (John 12:31, 14:30, 16:11). The world is Satan's delegated domain, but he must function within divine boundaries. God is holy, and He cannot tempt anyone to sin (Jas. 1:13), but Satan is allowed to test man's resolve to obey God.

Consequently, the believer's thinking must be aligned with Christ's because he or she has been called out of the vain philosophies, human traditions, and the moral corruption of the world (Col. 2:8). The believer does not want to be under Satan's control or agenda as these are in direct conflict with Christ. For this reason the Christian's motto should be: We are in the world, but not of the world (John 17:11, 16).

Christians compose the Church, the body of Christ, which positionally is affixed in heaven (Eph. 2:6), but presently exists physically on earth. The Greek word for church is *ekklesia,* which combines the preposition *ek*, meaning "out of," with a form of the Greek word *kaleo*, which means to "to bid" or "to call forth." Literally, "Church" means "a calling out" or by implication a "called out company." As part of the Church, a true Christian's allegiance is to the Lord Jesus and not the world; he or she is part of a *called out company* which has its sole identity and life in the Lord Jesus Christ.

Salvation is an eternal gift of God which He does not take away. But how much we enjoy our salvation in Christ is dependent upon our separation from the world and our consecration to God. Pain and suffering are "inevitable," but shame is "optional." If we sanctify ourselves from filth, He promises to use us as a vessel of honor for His glory (2 Tim. 2:20-21). At this time, Moses did not know his calling, but he had made a choice to separate from the world and to identify with God's covenant people. God blessed him for it and the world would hate him for it. Nothing has changed; the world continues to hate those who choose to identify with God and His people rather than to engage in its pleasures and ideologies.

This separation from the world's thinking, power, and prestige answers the question as to why God did not use Moses' political clout to affect better living conditions for the Hebrews in Egypt. Commenting on this matter, J. N. Darby writes:

> How many reasons might have induced Moses to remain in the position where he was; and this even under the pretext of being able to do more for the people; but this would have been leaning on the power of Pharaoh, instead of recognizing the bond between the people and God: it might have resulted in relief which the world would have granted, but not in a deliverance by God, accomplished in His love and in His power.[2]

Is it possible that Moses could have used his political influence to help the Jews? Perhaps, but even if this had been possible the outcome would have been accomplished through an extension of Pharaoh's authority over the people, and thus would have promoted Pharaoh's glory. Secondly, God's people would have still been subject to Pharaoh's rule and therefore could not receive the blessings which would flow down through God's authority. Thirdly, God's people would still be in Egypt and under the control of the world's thinking; God desired complete separation from Egypt so that He could enjoy unhindered communion with them.

In verse 11, God's people were identified as "Hebrews" for the fifth time in Exodus. As there is only one more reference to "Hebrew" in the remainder of Exodus, the significance of this name particularly relates to the Israelites' captivity in Egypt. We first read of the name "Hebrew" in Genesis 14: shortly after Lot's capture, *"There came one that had escaped, and told Abram the Hebrew"* (v. 13). The wonder of Abram's power is revealed in the word *Hebrew*. The meaning of the word, "the passenger," beautifully encapsulates the pilgrimage of Abram and his strangership in a world estranged from God. Likewise, "Hebrew" signified the calling of Abram's descendants to be delivered out of Egypt and into God's presence. To be a Hebrew meant that you were a stranger in the world; thus, Egypt could never be the resting place for God's people.

God's salvation, His redemption of Israel by lamb's blood, would be a complete deliverance; it would not only save from judgment but would include deliverance from bondage and from Egypt. Yet, God's fellowship with the Israelites would depend on how much His people were willing to part with Egypt (i.e. how well they would live up to their name "Hebrew").

> Worldliness is excluding God from our lives and, therefore, consciously or unconsciously accepting the values of a man-centered society. …Worldliness is not only doing what is forbidden but also wishing it were possible to do it. One of its distinctives is mental slavery to illegitimate pleasure. Worldliness twists values by rearranging their price tags.
>
> — Erwin W. Lutzer

# The Burning Bush
## Exodus 3:1-6

Moses abode with the Midianites who, like him, were descendants of Abraham. Midian was the son of Abraham by his wife Keturah. Because they were monotheistic and not pagans, Moses felt comfortable enough to dwell with them and he married Zipporah, the daughter of a Midianite priest named Reuel (also called Jethro). By Egyptian standards, Moses had slid to the bottom of the social scale; he forsook the upper crust of Egypt to live among nomadic shepherds, and *"every shepherd is an abomination to the Egyptians"* (Gen. 46:31). God would use forty years of character-building on the backside of a desert to prepare Moses for the arduous work ahead. Moses learned to care for lambs, to protect helpless sheep from vicious animals, and to be satisfied with a simple life. These and other experiences prepared Moses for a new commission – he was to be God's appointed deliverer for Israel.

One day while tending his flock at the foot of Mt. Horeb, Moses noticed a spectacular sight in the mount – a bush that appeared to be burning, yet was not consumed by the flames. The text reads, *"The Angel of the Lord appeared unto him in a flame of fire out of the midst of a bush"* (v. 2). God was drawing and Moses was responding, the result of which is always beneficial for man.

We understand the appearance of "the Angel of the Lord" to be a *theophany*. A theophany is a pre-incarnate visit of Christ, the second person of the Godhead, to the earth as His Father's messenger. Normally, He appeared as a man, but His presence was also made known in a pillar of cloud or, in this case, a burning bush. He is called "the Angel of the Lord," not to be confused with "an angel of the Lord," which could be any one of the millions of the holy angels.

The English word translated "angel" in Scripture means "messenger" in both Hebrew and Greek. The role of the Son in the Trinity is to do the Father's will; therefore, part of that activity is to communicate the Father's will to humanity. When the Son does this in the Old Testament, He is referred to as "the Messenger (Angel) of the Lord." In the New Testament, the Son of God is called the Word (John 1:1; 1 Jn. 1:1); the Son became a man to bring the ultimate message of God to humanity. The Lord Jesus was a living message – He was both the message and the messenger of God. In addition to the title of "the Angel of the Lord," the context of Scripture can be used to identify a theophany. The Angel of the Lord is worshipped as God by others (Josh. 5:14; Judg. 6:18-20), initiates covenants and makes promises that only God can keep (Gen. 16:10, 22:16-17), and in most occurrences, clearly identifies Himself as God (Gen. 31:11-13; Ex. 3:2-6). These temporary theophanies are not needed now to do the Father's will. The Son of God became flesh over 2000 years ago (John 1:14) and has completed the Father's will on earth up until the moment comes when He will bodily return to judge wickedness and to rule and reign in righteousness forever.

God called to Moses by name and as he neared the bush commanded him: *"Do not draw near this place. Take your sandals off your feet, for the place where you stand is holy ground."* We are not told why Moses was to remove his sandals while in God's presence; so we can only speculate. Moses' shoes would have been hand-made and thus would represent the *works* of his hands. His feet would take him where he wanted to go, thus picturing his *will*. The stains in the soles of his shoes would have provided a record of all his past missteps. Furthermore, shoes protect one's feet and God wanted Moses to understand that He would be Moses' shield and protection. Perhaps, in God's presence Moses was to be made aware of the uncleanness of the works of his hands, his selfish will, the mistakes of the past and also of Who would safeguard him in times of trouble. He had murdered a man with his hands in Egypt and had escaped justice by fleeing Egypt on foot. Moses could not approach the self-existing and unchanging God of the universe on the basis of human effort and be accepted. Nor could Moses acceptably serve God, without adopting God's will for his life, which also meant laying aside the failures and disappointments of the past. By stepping out of his shoes and standing upon holy ground, Moses became available to enter into his divine calling – God's purpose for his life.

Moses, with shoes removed, stood before the burning bush. As William Kelly comments, the burning bush conveys two critical aspects of God's nature to Moses:

> Jehovah here appears in … a bush in a desert burning but unconsumed. It was no doubt thus that God was about to work in the midst of Israel. Moses and they must know it. They too would be the chosen vessel of His power in their weakness, and this for ever in His mercy. Their God, as ours would prove Himself a consuming fire. Solemn but infinite favor! For, on one hand, as surely as He is a consuming fire, so on the other the bush, weak as it is, and ready to vanish away, nevertheless remains to prove that whatever may be the siftings of judicial dealings of God, whatever the trials and searchings of man, yet where He reveals Himself in pitifulness as well as in power, He sustains the object and uses the trial for nothing but good – no doubt for His own glory, but consequently for the very best interests of those that are His.[1]

The fact that God is holy, a consuming fire (Heb. 12:29), and righteous in all His ways is portrayed in the fiery glow of the bush. Because He is holy, God hates sin; because He is righteous, God must punish sin. Yet, in the midst of this spectacular scene of God's holiness stands a mundane bush. The bush pictures the frail and fragile things God chooses to shape our destiny and bring honor to His name. In the matter of the deliverer, Moses was the selected "bush;" he was a lowly shepherd in a remote wilderness and *"was very humble, more than all men who were on the face of the earth"* (Num. 12:3). The Jews were a nation of distraught slaves; they had no strength against their oppressors, and no hope of affecting an escape. Both Moses and the nation of Israel were but fragile bushes in which God would show forth His glory in flaming vengeance upon the wicked.

Apparently, after Moses removed his shoes, the Angel of the Lord introduced Himself to Moses as the God of Abraham, Isaac and Jacob. Moses responded by turning away and hiding his face. God purposely identifies Himself as the God of the patriarchs; this would cause Moses to ponder the unique manner in which Almighty God made Himself known to Abraham, Isaac, and Jacob. Stephen states that *"the God of Glory appeared unto our father Abraham"* in Ur (Acts 7:2). Isaac first heard the voice of the Lord on a mount in the land of Moriah just moments before his father was to sacrifice him to God (Gen. 22). Later, God visibly appeared to Isaac to provide direction during a distressing famine (Gen. 26:2). Jacob was fleeing for his life to Paddanaram when, in the seclusion of a solitary place near Bethel, God presented Himself as the Ladder to heaven in Jacob's dream. Each divine introduction was uncanny and spectacular, and Moses' first encounter with God would be no less unique. Each time God spoke to the patriarchs it was to affirm His promises; Moses would be aware of these and likewise of His faithfulness to keep them.

In response to Moses' humility, God informs him of the distressing condition of His people in Egypt. God had seen their affliction and heard their cries, and the time had now come for their deliverance. Notice that each time Moses responds to the revelation of God there is blessing and further disclosure. Humility before God and reverence for His Word result in blessing and further understanding of God's will. The Lord Jesus offered this promise to His disciples the night before He was crucified: *"He who has My commandments and keeps them, it is he who loves Me. And he who loves Me will be loved by My Father, and I will love him and manifest Myself to him"* (John 14:21). Love for the Lord Jesus will be communicated to Him by trusting in His Word and obeying it. The outcome of this is the fulfillment of Christ's promise to show more of Himself to those who obey His Word. Willful ignorance, rebellion, or compromise should be unheard of responses to Scripture, that is, for those who truly long to know and experience God.

> When we walk with the Lord in the light of His Word,
> What a glory He sheds on our way!
> While we do His good will He abides with us still,
> And with all who will trust and obey.
> Trust and obey, for there's no other way,
> To be happy in Jesus, but to trust and obey.
>
> — John H. Sammis

# "Come"
## Exodus 3:7-12

Not only did God reveal to Moses His plan to deliver His people from Egypt, He summoned Moses to be the deliverer. Notice that God commissioned Moses only to deliver the Israelites from Egypt, not to lead them into the Promised Land (v. 10). God told Moses that *He* would lead the Israelites into the Promised Land (vv. 8, 17); He foreknew that Moses would not enter it.

What was Moses' response to God's command, *"**Come now**, therefore, and I will send you to Pharaoh"* (v. 10). He replied, *"Who am I that **I should go** to Pharaoh"* (v. 11)? Moses had a two-fold identity crisis: first, he was unsure of who he was and, second, he didn't know who God was (v. 12). The following discussion focuses on God's answer to these questions. Moses would be brought to understand that doing the will of God did not depend on who he was, but rather on who God is.

God initiates meetings with man to reveal Himself and to declare His will. After introducing Himself to Moses, the Lord made known His resolve: *"I have **come down** to deliver them out of the hand of the Egyptians"* (v. 8). God had personally come to earth to speak to him and the only acceptable response for Moses was to immediately draw near to Him. Moses had to be willing to *come to God* before he would be willing to *go for God*. This explains his initial objection about going to Egypt; without knowing the Lord, such a venture would be impossible.

The word "come" formed the first heeded gospel message recorded in Scripture. God commanded Noah and his family to *come* into the ark to avoid destruction and they readily obeyed. God said "come," not "go," into the ark, which meant He was waiting in the ark for them. After they were shut into the ark and the flood commenced, Noah and his family journeyed with the Lord – wherever the Lord went, they went also. Likewise, God did not tell Moses to "go" to Egypt; he had to first "come" to God or there would be no "going." Moses needed to personally know God before he would be effective in co-laboring with Him in service. God's invitation to humanity to "come" always precedes His commissioning to "go." Service for God without personal knowledge of Him cannot be based in truth or motivated by love, and thus, is meaningless for eternity.

Once Noah and his family were sealed in the ark by God and with God, their deliverance from God's wrath over wickedness was secure, but that was not all that God was accomplishing by the great flood. Certainly the deluge destroyed life upon the earth, but it also lifted the ark off the earth to symbolize the separation that God's people were to have from the world. Salvation from hell and deliverance from the wickedness of the world are not independent realities with God. When God calls man *out of* something it is in order *to enter* something else.

God's salvation for man is a complete salvation from sin and thus guarantees a consecrated people to God. Consequently, He warns both Old Testament and New Testament saints: *"Be holy, for I am holy"* (Lev. 11:44; 1 Pet. 1:16). Moses needed to know that God's plan to deliver the Israelites from Egypt also included separating Egypt from the Israelites. God presented Moses with His four-stage plan to bless the Israelites:

> *So I have come down to deliver them out of the hand of the Egyptians, and to bring them up from that land to a good and large land, to a land flowing with milk and honey, .... Come now, therefore, and I will send you to Pharaoh that you may bring My people, the children of Israel, out of Egypt. ... I will certainly be with you. And this shall be a sign to you that I have sent you: When you have brought the people out of Egypt, you shall serve God on this mountain* (Ex. 3:8-12).

God desired to deliver the Israelites first from bondage and second from Egypt itself. In allegory, slavery describes the terrible bondage of sin we are born into and Egypt reflects a world system apart from God. These two agencies have caused man's misery since his fall in Eden. Paul explains that God continues to work to deliver humanity from these two agents of death: *"Grace to you and peace from God the Father and our Lord Jesus Christ, who gave Himself for our sins, that He might deliver us from this present evil age, according to the will of our God and Father"* (Gal. 1:3-4). The Lord Jesus not only delivers believers from the bondage of sin, but He also liberates them from the corruption of Egypt.

Thirdly, God desired to bless His people with a spacious *"land flowing with milk and honey,"* but this blessing would be contingent upon their exercise of faith in God's command conveyed by Moses to come to Mt. Sinai. Lastly, they would come to Sinai to serve the Lord. Clearly, obedience to the calls of deliverance and sanctification would precede the opportunity to serve God and to be blessed by Him. Paul summarizes these aspects of salvation for believers in the Church Age:

> *For the grace of God that brings salvation has appeared to all men, teaching us that, denying ungodliness and worldly lusts, we should live soberly, righteously, and godly in the present age, looking for the blessed hope and glorious appearing of our great God and Saviour Jesus Christ, who gave Himself for us, that He might redeem us from every lawless deed and purify for Himself His own special people, zealous for good works* (Tit. 2:11-14).

Deliverance from the bondage of sin and from the worldliness of Egypt leads to a life of divine blessing and the opportunity to please God through service.

God's plan was not just to deliver the Jews from slavery and from Egypt, but *"to bring them up from that land to a good and large land."* There is nothing in God's plan about remaining between Egypt (the world) and Canaan (victorious Christian living); journeying to Mt. Sinai was merely a necessary step towards their ultimate destiny in Canaan. But, as Edward Dennett notes, the limiting factor of arriving in Canaan expeditiously was not God's power, but the Israelites' faith, or better put, their lack of it:

> There is nothing here between Egypt and Canaan. The wilderness does not appear. In like manner, in Romans we read, "Whom He justified, them He also glorified." We thus learn, as has been often remarked, that the wilderness is not part of the purpose of God. It belongs to His ways, and not to His purposes; for it is in the wilderness that the flesh is tested, that we learn what we are as well as what God is (see Deut. 8). But as far as God's purposes are concerned, there is

> nothing between redemption and glory. So in the actual fact, there were only eleven days' journey from Horeb to Kadesh-barnea (Deut. 1: 2), but the children of Israel were forty years through their unbelief in accomplishing the distance.[1]

The phrase "a land flowing with milk and honey" is not a contemporary expression which we can readily identify with; however, as John Hannah explains, it had great symbolic ramifications for the Israelites, a nation of herdsmen and farmers:

> The phrase a land flowing with milk means that Canaan was ideal for raising goats and cows. Feeding on good pastureland the goats, sheep, and cows were full of milk. Flowing with honey means that the bees were busy making honey. Milk and honey suggested agricultural prosperity.[2]

Goshen had been God's provision for sustaining His people during the great famine and the place where He could multiply them and assemble a nation. Yet, the time had now come for His people to come out of Egypt and to inherit a full land, a land of milk and honey, a place where God could commune with His covenant people unhindered by Egypt.

God's answer to Moses' objection was *"Certainly I will be with you"* (v. 12). When called by God to action, Moses initially focused on his own inabilities, rather than trusting in God's capabilities. We will find satisfaction in life by accepting and fulfilling our divine calling; preoccupation with our abilities, inadequacies, or personal interests is time-consuming and only hinders our availability to be used by God. Consequently, each of the personal inadequacies Moses identified as an excuse as to why he was not fit to be the deliverer only served to highlight the very reasons God had selected him for the task. Paul explains why God chooses to accomplish His purposes in this manner:

> *For you see your calling, brethren, that not many wise according to the flesh, not many mighty, not many noble, are called. But God has chosen the foolish things of the world to put to shame the wise, and God has chosen the weak things of the world to put to shame the things which are mighty; and the base things of the world and the things which are despised God has chosen, and the things which are*

> *not, to bring to nothing the things that are,* ***that no flesh should glory in His presence*** (1 Cor. 1:26-39).

After twenty years of verbal silence, the Lord spoke to Jacob in the same way, saying, *"Return to the land of your fathers and to your family, and I will be with you"* (Gen. 31:3). Whether the child of God is commanded "to come," "to go," or "to return," the same solace of peace is enjoyed – God's abiding presence. The prophet Jeremiah depended on it (Jer. 1:8), and so did Paul (Acts 18:10). For centuries, suffering saints have found comfort in the presence of God during the most difficult of times. Living for Christ in a sin-cursed world is challenging, but the believer's calling in Christ is not burdensome because he or she is yoked with the Lord:

> *Come to Me, all you who labor and are heavy laden, and I will give you rest. Take My yoke upon you and learn from Me, for I am gentle and lowly in heart, and you will find rest for your souls. For My yoke is easy and My burden is light"* (Matt. 11:28-30).

Every true disciple of Christ is to be a learner of Christ. This is the only passage in the New Testament in which the Lord personally informs His disciples of what He is like and tells them that they should learn of Him. The believer learns of the Lord's gentle and humble spirit when yoked with Him and he or she enjoys the peace of His presence in service when resting in Him. The goal of discipleship emphasizes again that the Holy Spirit's work of sanctification is critical in a believer's life if he or she is to effectively serve the Lord. To learn and to know Christ are integral to the sanctification process.

Consequently, doing important tasks in the name of Christ without bringing honor to His name is hypocrisy, not biblical discipleship. Profitable service to the Lord occurs as we learn Him. Not only does the believer learn Christ by spending time in His Word, but the believer is also increasingly transformed into Christ-likeness by the same activity (2 Cor. 3:18). John N. Darby poetically expresses this truth:

> And is it so – I shall be like Thy Son?
> Is this the grace which He for me has won?
> Father of glory, thought beyond all thought!
> In glory, to His own blest likeness brought!

Is the Lord beckoning you to come and know Him and learn of His calling for your life? The promise of His abiding presence will safeguard your mind in times of trouble: *"'I will never leave you nor forsake you.' So we may boldly say: 'The Lord is my helper; I will not fear. What can man do to me?'"* (Heb. 13:5-6). Moses found God's abiding presence to be a wonderful source of comfort during the many difficulties he faced in the remainder of his life. This provision of peace only resulted from his earlier obedience to the Lord's command, "Come."

Abide with me – fast falls the eventide,
The darkness deepens – Lord, with me abide,
When other helpers fail and comforts flee,
Help of the helpless, O abide with me!

Swift to its close ebbs out life's little day,
Earth's joys grow dim, its glories pass away;
Change and decay in all around I see
O Thou who changest not, abide with me!

— Henry F. Lyte

# A Forever Name
## Exodus 3:13-15

Moses' first question to God after being commissioned as the deliverer was, *"Who am I?"* His second question was, *"What is your name?"* or by implication, Who are you? Usually, the first thing a person learns about someone he or she has just met is his or her name, and Moses needed to know who he was to represent in Egypt. Moses' request indicates a shift in mental focus from his own lack of ability to God's power and authority; this is the first step in understanding the purposes of God in our life.

God's response to Moses' question was *"I AM that I AM."* In preparation for their deliverance from Egypt and the wilderness experience to follow, God wanted His covenant people to know Him as "I AM." The Hebrew word *hayah* is used here to mean "I will be," and is a wordplay on *Yahweh* (Jehovah) in verse 15, which means "to be." Moses was to tell the children of Israel that I AM had sent him to them.

In the Old Testament, great significance is attached to personal names, for a name reveals not just the identity of a person but also their features, nature, or character. For example, Jacob lived up to his name "supplanter" – he was a trickster and a schemer. Esau's name related to the hairy appearance of his body at birth. Likewise, God's names in Scripture reveal information about Him. The prophetic rendering of divine names in the Old Testament had substantial importance to His people, for many of God's names pertained to His relationship with them.

*Yahweh*, "the self-existent One," is found 6,828 times in the Old Testament; it may be translated as "Jehovah," but normally it is rendered as "the Lord" or "O Lord" (often "Lord" is in upper case font - LORD). *Yahweh* is derived from the Hebrew tetragrammaton YHWH. As there are no vowels in the Hebrew written language, no one is quite sure how God's covenant name is to be pronounced.

The affirmation of God's personal name would be a divine invitation for His people to draw near and have communion with Him. Knowing God's personal names is really a prerequisite of knowing God Himself. To fabricate one's concept of God through mental images, humanly ascribed names and earthly forms is nothing less than pernicious idolatry. To approach God by any other name or way than what He has revealed in Scripture is vain religion. May we know and esteem God's various names, for in them He beckons us to draw near and know Him more deeply.

In the Old Testament, God is addressed by several names and titles. *Elohim* is normally rendered "God" in the English translations and emphasizes God's transcendence and majesty: God is preeminent above all creation and certainly above all humanly contrived deities. *Elohim* is the plural form of *Eloah. Eloah* is a generic Old Testament name for deity. It is interesting that it is only found fifty-seven times in the Old Testament (mostly in the book of Job) as compared to its plural form *Elohim*, which is found some 2600 times. The Hebrew language has singular, dual, and plural forms. *Elohim* is the form used to express an association of three or more and, thus, reflects the triune nature of God as revealed from the whole of Scripture.

The root meaning of *Adonai* is "Lord" or "master." *Adonai* is normally translated "Lord" in English Bibles. Of the 449 times *Adonai* occurs in the Old Testament, it is used in conjunction with *Yahweh* 315 times. Besides the frequently used references to God that were just mentioned, a number of compound forms of the name of God involving the words *El* (or *Elohim*) and *Yahweh* may be found throughout Scripture. *El Shaddai* is translated "God Almighty," and conveys the idea of the power and strength of God. *El Elyon* is rendered "God Most High," and emphasizes the supremacy of God. "Everlasting God" is derived from the Hebrew *El Olam*, which stresses the unchanging character of God.

Other compound names or descriptions of God in Scripture include:
*Yahweh-Jireh*, "The Lord Will Provide" (Gen. 22:14)
*Yahweh-Rapha,* "The Lord Who Heals" (Ex. 15:26)
*Yahweh-Nissi*, "The Lord Our Banner" (Ex. 17:15)
*Yahweh-Maccaddeshcem*, "The Lord Your Sanctifier" (Ex. 31:13)
*Yahweh-Shalom*, "The Lord is Peace" (Judg. 6:24)
*Yahweh-Sabbaoth*, "The Lord of Hosts" (1 Sam. 1:3)

*Yahweh-Tsidkenu*, "The Lord Our Righteousness" (Jer. 23:6)
*Yahweh-Shammah,* "The Lord is Present" (Ezek. 48:35)[1]

These names for God are but a culmination of the "I AM" expression, explains C. H. Mackintosh:

> All these gracious titles are unfolded to meet the necessities of His people; and when He calls Himself "I AM," it comprehends them all. Jehovah, in taking this title, was furnishing His people with a blank check, to be filled up to any amount. He calls Himself "I AM," and faith has but to write over against that ineffably precious name whatever we want.... If we want life, Christ says, "I AM the life;" if we want righteousness, He is "The Lord Our Righteousness;" if we want peace, "He is our peace;" if we want "wisdom, sanctification, and redemption," we may travel through the wide range of human necessity, in order to have a just concept of the amazing depth and fullness of this profound and adorable name, "I AM."[2]

It is of no surprise that the New Testament reveals the Lord Jesus Christ as the great I AM of Exodus; He is the only One who can satisfy all human need. Seven is the number of perfection and completeness and John presents in his gospel account the seven I AM statements of Christ: "The Bread of Life," "The Light of the World," "The Door," "The Good Shepherd," "The Resurrection and the Life," "The Way, the Truth, and the Life," and "The True Vine." The perfect self-existent One declared in His own words the fullness of I AM. Unfortunately, as in Moses' day, many of the Lord's people today fail to know and thus to appreciate the fullness of who Christ is as revealed in Scripture. Moses had an excuse; God had not fully revealed Himself yet. You and I have no excuse, for God has revealed Himself to us through His Son (Heb. 1:2-3); if we want to know the Father, we must first know the Son, and then the Spirit of God will assist us every step of the way (John 16:13-15).

Not only was Moses to go to Egypt in the name of *Yahweh,* the Self-Existing One, but he was to inform the Israelites that this was God's name forever and it was to be remembered by them forever. The Self-Existing One was eternal, thus, His name would remain the same. God told the prophet Malachi, *"I change not"* (Mal. 3:6). Correspondingly, the writer of Hebrews proclaims, *"Jesus Christ the same yesterday, and today, and forever"* (Heb. 13:8). Jesus Christ is Jehovah God, the great I AM!

Many more Old Testament names and expressions for God are applied directly to the Lord Jesus in the New Testament, all of which affirm His deity and also demonstrate the unique importance of each of God's names in representing His overall essence. The evening before His crucifixion, while speaking to His Father, the Lord Jesus said *"I have manifested Your name unto the men..."* (John 17:6). May each believer follow the example of the Lord Jesus, who was committed to declaring God's great name before men, that they might know Him, have their needs meet, and long to honor His name forever.

> The God of Abraham praise, Who reigns enthroned above;
> Ancient of everlasting days, and God of love.
> Jehovah, great I AM, by earth and heaven confessed;
> I bow and bless thy sacred Name, forever blest.
>
> — Thomas Olivers

# "Go"
## Exodus 3:16-22

The first word in verse 16 is "go." God had invited Moses to come near to Him and Moses responded. Moses learned of the holiness of God and that his own lack of ability would be used to bring honor to the Lord. Through the disclosure of God's personal name Moses discovered something of God's essence and character. As a result of coming to God and having contact with His nature, Moses was made ready to "go."

It is significant that God told Moses the general game plan, but did not include the specifics of how He would use him. God grows people as He grows ministries and, spiritually speaking, Moses was just getting started. Serving God before knowing Him translates into worthless busyness. Moses had a few more objections as to why he was not the right person for the job, but he was going to Egypt nonetheless. Each answered objection provides Moses with greater understanding of God's plan.

Can you imagine what would have happened to poor Moses if God had told him at the burning bush all that would befall him: ten devastating plagues in Egypt, the opening up of the sea to secure passage into the wilderness, all the events that would transpire at Sinai, and then the following forty years of wandering because of Jewish rebellion? All that Moses needed to know at present was that he was going to Egypt and God was with him. God desires His children to walk with Him by faith and He ensures that each step of the way is not more cumbersome than His grace makes possible. At times, the Lord may illuminate the shadowy path of life we tread, but in general, it is the next step of faith, the next decision, the next moment with the Lord which defines our lives.

The Lord longs for us to rely on His grace as we learn to walk with Him. In doing so, we do not fall prey to temptation and we are not overcome by daunting trials. Paul encourages the believers at Corinth with this aspect of God's provisional care: *"No temptation has overtaken you except such as is common to man; but God is faithful, who will not allow you to be tempted* [or tested] *beyond what you are able, but with the temptation will also make the way of escape, that you may be able to bear it*" (1 Cor. 10:13). Each step we take in obedience to God's design for our life will be upheld by His grace; we can rest assured of that. We may not know where we are going as we walk with the Lord, but each step of the way is secured by grace.

Though Paul exhorted the Church at Philippi to follow his example of pressing on *"toward the goal for the prize of the upward call of God in Christ Jesus"* (Phil. 3:14), he also realized that many younger saints would not understand what he was talking about, so he continues, *"Therefore let us, as many as are mature, have this mind; and if in anything you think otherwise, God will reveal even this to you. Nevertheless, to the degree that we have already attained, let us walk by the same rule, let us be of the same mind"* (Phil. 3:15-16).

It is quite possible that you do not understand where the Lord is leading you at this present moment, but keep pressing on for the upward calling of God in Christ Jesus. Be faithful to what you know to be true; maturity will come and the confirmation of your calling with it. Remember, God grows ministries as He grows people. In the growing interim, be faithful to what you know God has asked you to do and long for what is yet to come.

When the Lord opens the doors of a ministry, no one can close them (Rev. 3:7). When the Lord closes doors of ministry, He usually opens others (unless sin or foolishness is involved). But in any case, we can be *"confident of this very thing, that He who has begun a good work in you will complete it until the day of Jesus Christ"* (Phil. 1:6-7). *"For we are His workmanship, created in Christ Jesus for good works, which God prepared beforehand that we should walk in them"* (Eph. 2:10). God is sovereign and will preserve believers in this world until their homecoming. Until that time, may we diligently co-labor with Him (1 Cor. 3:9) in those things He has prepared for us to do to honor Him.

Each segment of God's progressive plan to deliver the Israelites from Egypt contains the word "go:" Moses was first to *"go and gather the elders of Israel together"* to notify them that God was aware of their plight in Egypt, had heard their petitions, had sent Moses to rescue them from Egypt, and would lead them into the Promised Land (v.16). Secondly, Moses, with the elders, was to go to Pharaoh and communicate God's request on behalf of His people, saying, *"let us go ... three days into the wilderness that we may sacrifice to the Lord"* (v. 18). Thirdly, God informed Moses that initially Pharaoh would not heed the request and would *"not let you go"* (v. 19) until He had smitten Egypt with great plagues, but that afterwards *"he will let you go"* (v. 20). Fourthly, when the Egyptians finally did agree to release their slave population, the Hebrews were to plunder Egypt before leaving: *"When you go, you shall not go empty"* (v. 21). This plan prompts a few questions for consideration.

Why did God ask Pharaoh to grant the Israelites a leave of absence to journey three days into the wilderness (beyond Egypt) to worship Him instead of requesting full release for the Israelites? We are not told why He did this, but please note that Moses never said anything about returning to Egypt, and the Hebrews (and I believe Pharaoh did also) understood that. Perhaps God was using this less exigent measure as a means of demonstrating the hardness of Pharaoh's heart to the idea of relinquishing his labor force. However, in type, F. W. Grant explains why three days were significant in pointing to a future event:

> Not in Egypt, however, can that feast be held; for on the ground of nature no true joy in God or worship in the Spirit is possible. From this there must be three days' removed – the distance between death and resurrection alone can carry us into our place of blessing and intimacy with God. But this will be developed hereafter.[1]

Why did God want the Hebrews to despoil Egypt after it would be decimated by divine judgments? Judging wickedness in the world is only a part of God's righteous work, another part is rewarding His people for obedience and faithfulness. In the case of the Egyptians, God was not going to deliver His people from slavery without giving them a provision to worship Him in the wilderness. The spoil of Egypt would present the Israelites with an opportunity to return to God in adoration what God had bestowed to them in grace. Besides this, the Jews deserved back-wages for their many years of blood, sweat, and tears in Egypt without any compensation.

God providing His people with the wherewithal to freely return to Him in worship is a pattern that is witnessed throughout Scripture. In Genesis 14, Abram, upon returning victorious from battle, was moved to give Melchizedek a tenth of the spoil as an offering to the Lord. Abram could have kept the spoil, but instead he saw it as God's provision for him to worship. Noah was commanded to bring seven pairs of "clean" beasts and fowls on the ark; these would be used for food during the voyage and for sacrifice once their journey was over. Scripture tells us that the ascending smoke from Noah's offering was a sweet savor in the nostrils of God. Why? Because it was an offering that cost Noah something – he had to care for those animals for over a year just to have a provision to worship God in the future.

Today, we do not offer animals to God as burnt sacrifices because that dispensation (stewardship of accountability) has been put away by the finished work of Christ. There are few commandments under the new covenant which Christ sealed with His own blood; God has given the Church a great deal of freedom to work out acceptable conduct (Phil. 2:12) and the liberty to praise and worship Him to the extent to which we desire. Returning to God what He has first granted to us is a spiritual matter, not a material one; God amply supplies a heart that beats for Him. Hoarding God's goodness is evidence of spiritual stagnation.

Man is required to give God his first fruits of time, finances, and energy. Yet, God desires another sacrifice; one that requires laboring in Scripture, learning of the beauties of His Son. We carefully arrange what we have gleaned throughout the week for a sacrifice of adoration to be laid at His feet when the assembly gathers for the Lord's Supper. This is a spiritual activity that every man, woman, and child should engage in, though not all will share audibly. In this way, the spiritual worship of all God's people, who have come with an offering in the beauty of holiness, mingles together and ascends up to God's throne. One brother at a time, guided by the Spirit of God, audibly leads the assembly to align and center everyone's thoughts on an aspect of God's goodness or character. God has given the verbal role of leading and teaching in the local assembly to the men as part of His overall order for the Church (1 Cor. 14:34, 11:7; 1 Tim. 2:8-12). Yet, the entire Christian assembly joins together in offering sacrifices of praise as well as uniting together in song (Heb. 13:15).

After coming in contact with the nature of God, there is only one proper response for the child of God: to serve and worship the Lord. May we accept our availability, abilities, and assets from God as His provision for us to worship Him no matter how difficult the situation we may find ourselves in.

Go, heralds of salvation, forth; go in your heavenly Master's Name;
From east to west, from south to north, the glorious Gospel wide proclaim.

Go forth to sow the living seed; seek not earth's praise, nor dread its blame;
Nor labors fear, nor trials heed; go forth to conquer in His Name.

— Samuel F. Smith

# The First Objection
## Exodus 4:1-9

In presenting his objections, Moses was not protesting going to Egypt; he had already acknowledged that he was going. Rather, his doubts center in his own inabilities to adequately do God's bidding. The Lord already knew all about Moses' strengths and weaknesses and that His grace would overcome both, especially his strengths. Concerning our self-perceived abilities Oswald Chambers notes, "Unguarded strength is double weakness."[1] As the great I AM, the command to go should have been sufficient to settle Moses' quandaries, yet, God graciously answered each of his objections.

The first objection Moses voiced was that the Jews would not believe that he had been commissioned by God and, therefore, they would ignore his message. God responded to this objection by personally involving Moses in the working of two miracles.

The Jews, by nature, have always been a people that must see to believe. Paul acknowledged this tendency in his day with the statement *"For Jews request a sign, and Greeks seek after wisdom"* (1 Cor. 1:22). God was willing to work miracles to prompt the Jews to do His will, but He knew that faith based on sight would be shallow and thus liable to falter when tested. Accordingly, we read *"for without faith it is impossible to please God"* (Heb. 12:6). God-pleasing faith takes God at His Word apart from full sensual or intellectual validation. This type of faith rises above natural experiences to connect with supernatural power.

The Lord Jesus stated that it was the unrighteous who wanted to see a *"sign or a wonder"* in order to believe in Him. He called these *"sign seekers"* an evil generation and spiritual adulterers (Matt. 12:38-39). Even those Jews who witnessed the miracle of the feeding of over 5000 pestered the Lord the very next day, asking, *"What sign will You perform then, that we **may see it and believe You**?"* (John 6:30). Did they not recall the miracle from the day before? Had they not filled their bellies with a boy's multiplied sack lunch? The Israelites saw miracles every day in the wilderness for forty years, yet this did not increase their spirituality, for they constantly murmured against God and His leadership.

Peter shows us that true faith in God opens our eyes to understand the mysteries of God. When the Lord asked His twelve disciples if they, also, would turn away from Him, as many had done, Peter responded, *"Lord, to whom shall we go? You have the words of eternal life. Also we have come to* ***believe and know*** *that You are the Christ, the Son of the living God"* (John 6:68-69). The unrighteous want a sign to believe, but the righteous believe, then understand. Thus, until we exercise faith we will not understand from where we came: *"Through faith we understand that the worlds were framed by the Word of God, so that things which are seen were not made of things which do appear"* (Heb. 11:3).

The human mind cannot rationalize the operation of faith, because it requires a living trust in an unseen God that cannot be confirmed through the senses. This is not to say that we cannot render a logical decision to trust Christ, for indeed God has revealed Himself through creation, conscience, changed lives, miracles, and His Word. The mind logically evaluates what is observed, but *"faith is the substance of things hoped for, the evidence of things not seen"* (Heb. 11:1). This is the kind of faith that pleases God, not an experientially-based confidence: *"But without faith it is impossible to please Him, for he who comes to God must believe that He is, and that He is a rewarder of those who diligently seek Him"* (Heb. 11:6). Those who don't want to see Christ by faith will not know Him. Conversely, a believer's dedication to Christ will be directly proportionate to how much he or she really believes His gospel message. If we truly believe the gospel, our belief is evident in our lives – we practically live out the truth.

The Lord's school was now in session; Moses being the student and God the instructor. In the first lesson the Instructor demonstrated His power by performing a few miraculous signs. Moses would have used his hands earlier to remove his shoes, and in so doing he must have put aside his shepherding rod. Apparently, after removing his shoes he picked the rod up again and continued to hold it while talking with I AM. The training session began with an easy question, *"What do you have in your hand?"* Moses answers correctly, *"a rod."* The Lord then instructed Moses to cast the rod to the ground, which he did. The familiar rod became a threatening serpent and Moses fled from it. God then instructed Moses to pick up the safe end of the serpent, its tail. Moses obeyed and after grasping the serpent it became his shepherding rod again.

A rod speaks of *power* in Scripture (Rev. 12:5). Egyptian power had become satanic in nature, as pictured by the serpent (Gen. 3), and God was going to reclaim that power to accomplish His purpose, as symbolized by Moses grasping the serpent and its transformation back into his rod. God had shown Moses that he would not be overcome by the Egyptians, who viewed snakes as a symbol of their power. Moses' shepherding rod had now become the "rod of God" (v. 20) to work great signs (v. 17).

Throughout the exodus and the wilderness experience that followed the shepherd's rod in Moses' hand would be a symbol of God's authority and a tool of His power. God's rod was a sign of wrath to the rebel, but to God's people it was a symbol of His love in action. F. W. Grant explains:

> All power belongeth unto God, and this shepherd's rod shows us how He uses it. Power with Him waits always upon love. Do you doubt this? Do you ask, "Is the rod of iron, with which He will crush His enemies – is that love? I answer that in all the passages where this is spoken of, the exact rendering is, "He shall shepherd them with a rod of iron;" for, severely as it may smite, loves guides it. Woe to those indeed whom everlasting love has thus to smite! Still the hand that wields the scepter of the universe is guided by the heart of Him who has revealed Himself, not as power, nor even as righteousness, but as Love.[2]

In a second demonstration of His power, God instructs Moses to put his hand, the one that was not holding the rod, into his bosom. God never told Moses to pull it out, but Moses did and found it leprous. Moses was told to put his leprous hand again into his bosom. When he removed his hand the second time it was found to be normal.

Leprosy is a picture of sin in Scripture. It was an incurable disease that rotted one's flesh from the inside out, meaning that an individual was a leper long before there were visible signs of the disease. We are all born in sin (Ps. 51:5; Rom. 5:12), and in time our rotten nature becomes apparent in works of the flesh (Gal. 5:19-21). The only remedy for leprosy is divine cleansing, and other than this miracle and Miriam's healing after seven days of chastening, there is no example in Scripture of a Jew being healed of leprosy until the Lord Jesus Christ came to the earth. By His cleansing power many lepers were healed and according to the Law had to return to the temple, the place in which they had been previously declared unclean, in order to be inspected and ceremonially purified by the priests (Lev. 14). The cleansed lepers brought the gospel message of Jesus Christ and the evidence of supernatural healing to the temple; consequently, many of the priests who verified these miracles later trusted Christ as Saviour (Acts 6:7).

Until an individual experiences regeneration and receives the Holy Spirit the deadly disease of sin is uncontrollable (Rom. 8:2-4). Furthermore, a child of God cannot righteously serve the Lord with leprosy (sin) in his or her bosom (heart). Sin in our flesh must be supernaturally put to death *"because they that are in the flesh cannot please God"* (Rom. 8:8). One cannot rightly exercise the power of God without being under His moral authority (Luke 7:6-9). Concerning Moses' leprous hand miracle, C. I. Scofield offers this observation:

> The bosom (heart) stands for what we are, the hand for what we do. What we are, that ultimately we do. It is the sign of Luke 6:43-45. The two signs, rod and hand, speak of preparation of service: (1) consecration – our capacity taken up for God; and (2) the hand that holds the rod of God's power must be a cleansed hand swayed by a new heart (Isa. 52:11).[3]

In order to exercise God's authority we must first be under His rod (His loving authority). Serving the Lord requires more than knowing what we are supposed to do for Him, it also requires abiding within God's framework of approved conduct while serving Him. Otherwise, like the disciples, we may be tempted to call down fire from heaven upon those who oppose us. God's authority is to be used to affirm His glory, not to obtain personal gain; consequently, the human heart must be cleansed to maintain clean hands for service. Without a divine work of grace in our hearts there can be no acceptable service offered to God. This is why the Lord Jesus rebuked the Pharisees, saying, *"Brood of*

*Vipers, how can you, being evil, speak good things? For out of the abundance of the heart the mouth speaks"* (Matt. 12:34). Moses would need to know the heart of God in order to rightly wield the rod of God.

If the Jewish elders did not believe Moses' story after these first two signs, then he was instructed to perform a third. He was to pour out water from the Nile and it would turn to blood upon the ground. In Moses' day, Egypt was mainly a desert with a narrow strip of fertile land which bordered both sides of Nile. The Hebrew word for Egypt is *Mitsrayim* (or *Mizraim*), which means "double straitness," and undoubtedly refers to the two straits of land on either side of the Nile. It was these irrigated strips of sand that gave Egypt her prominence. Because the Nile brought life to Egypt, the river was honored. The miracle of turning the Nile's water into blood would prove that the God of heaven was superior to the Nile of the earth.

The Egyptians were looking down and revering creation instead of looking up and worshipping the Creator. Paganism develops naturally when man ignores the testimony of God in creation (Rom. 1:19-23). The blood in this miracle signified the forthcoming judgment on and death of the Egyptians; the Nile would become a river of death, it would not be able to save the Egyptians from Jehovah's wrath.

> Lord, now indeed I find Thy power and Thine alone,
> Can change the leper's spots, and melt the heart of stone.
> Jesus paid it all, all to Him I owe;
> Sin had left a crimson stain, He washed it white as snow.
>
> — Elvina M. Hall

# More Objections
## Exodus 4:10-17

Moses' next objection was that he was not an eloquent speaker, but was in fact, slow in speech. How could he possibly be the best man to face off against Pharaoh? The comment was an affront to the Creator who had fashioned Moses as a unique vessel to serve Him as He deemed best. God answered Moses' objection, *"I will be with your mouth and teach you what you shall say"* (v. 12). Moses did not need to be anxious about the matter; he was to repeat to Pharaoh only what God told him to say. Moses spoke as if everything depended upon his persuasive speech before Pharaoh, but as Edward Dennett notes, this is not God's way, neither before pagans nor in the Church:

> How common the mistake, even in the Church of God! Hence eloquence is that which even Christians desire – giving it a place beyond the power of God. The pulpits of Christendom are thus filled with men who are not of a slow tongue, and even the saints who in theory know the truth are beguiled and attracted by splendid gifts, and take pleasure in their exercise apart from the truth communicated. How different was the thought of Paul. "And I, brethren, when I came to you, came not with excellency of speech or of wisdom, declaring unto you the testimony of God." And again, "my speech and my preaching was not with enticing words of man's wisdom, but in demonstration of the Spirit and of power" (1 Cor. 2:1, 4). It is on this account that God often uses the "slow of speech" far more than those who are eloquent; for there is no temptation in such cases to lean upon the wisdom of men, all beholding that it is the power of God.[1]

The Lord Jesus extended similar counsel to His disciples. He was preparing His disciples for their arduous task of apostleship, a commission which would commence shortly after He had returned to heaven:

> *Now when they bring you to the synagogues and magistrates and authorities, do not worry about how or what you should answer, or what you should say. For the Holy Spirit will teach you in that very hour what you ought to say* (Luke 12:11-12).

Christ promised that all those who were brought into hardship because of their testimony for Him would be issued special enlightenment from the Holy Spirit in order to answer questions and accusations with the wisdom of God. Believers would do well to remember this today when engaged in evangelism – we don't talk lost souls into "getting saved." Christians are merely facilitators of God's word; we say no more than what God has commissioned us to speak.

This point is illustrated by the Lord Jesus in His response to a lawyer who was testing Him concerning how someone could inherit the kingdom of heaven. The Lord answered the lawyer's question with two of His own: *"What is written in the law?"* and *"What is your reading of it?"* (Luke 10:26). The Lord Jesus caused the man to personally consider what the Word of God stated about the matter of salvation. Clearly, an individual cannot repent and receive Christ as Saviour without first understanding the Word of God; *"faith comes by hearing, and hearing by the word of God"* (Rom. 10:17). Secondly, conversion is impossible without the work of the Holy Spirit to convince the sinner of his or her sin, the need for a righteous standing before God, and of forthcoming judgment for those who rebel (John 16:7-11; 1 Cor. 2:8-15). If Christians would follow the Lord's example of asking questions and referring their listeners to God's Word, they would avoid almost all arguments. It is the injection of our words, feelings, traditions, and methods into conversations which hinder the work of God.

Moses was to learn that it would not be his fanciful words or eloquent speeches that would pry the Jews from Pharaoh's clutches. He was to convey to Pharaoh only the words that God put in his mouth. It would be God's word of power alone which would defeat the enemy.

Sensing the overwhelming nature of what he was being asked to do, Moses pleads, *"O my Lord, please send by the hand of whomever else You may send"* (Ex. 4:13). This self-centered frankness angered God, but His wrath was tempered by mercy and His foreknowledge had already provided the solution – Aaron, who even then was already en route to Moses. God's gracious response to Moses' lack of faith resulted in a sign with which to enrich his faith. Arthur Pink explains:

> To strengthen his weak faith, the Lord grants him still another sign that He would give him success. As Moses returned to Egypt he would find Aaron coming forth to meet him. What an illustration is this that when God works, He works at both ends of the line! The eunuch and Philip, Saul and Ananias, Cornelius and Peter supply us with further illustrations of the same principle.[2]

The coming of Aaron would be another sign to Moses of God's wisdom and control. God did not choose to send someone else to Egypt, nor did He give Moses a persuasive tongue, but He did transfer some of the honor offered to a hesitant Moses to a willing Aaron.

The Lord Jesus told the Church at Philadelphia, *"Behold, I am coming quickly! Hold fast what you have, that no one may take your crown"* (Rev. 3:11). His reward, which He bestows at His Judgment Seat, will be with Him when He comes to the clouds to snatch away His Church from the earth (1 Thess. 4:13-18; Rev. 22:12). In light of the Lord's imminent return, the saints at Philadelphia were to be attentive and faithful, lest they lose their reward (crown); this would allow someone else to earn it. This is what happened to Moses: God had given him a service opportunity, but he complained and wavered, so the Lord transferred part of the prospect, and the accompanying honor, to Aaron. God has a work to do and it will be accomplished by those who are willing to serve Him, and God shall recompense them accordingly.

Because Moses balked, fluent Aaron was brought into the work as Moses' spokesman; later, he would become God's high priest. God would speak to Moses and he would convey God's words to Aaron who then would speak to the people. Moses was to be the deliverer and Aaron was to be his helper, for this reason, except in the genealogies (because Aaron was Moses' older brother), Moses' name always precedes Aaron's name when they are mentioned together. Ministry can be grueling without a co-laborer and the enlistment of Aaron in the work seemed to quell Moses' apprehensions.

Moses' faith in Jehovah was but in infancy; it would be refined and developed in the coming years, but presently Moses received more consolation in having along a feeble mortal like himself than in the abiding presence of the invisible God of the universe. Like Moses, we too, when facing a daunting situation, are prone to rely on that which is visibly tangible rather than on the vast resources of an infinite God. As C. H. Mackintosh notes, this tendency serves as a reality check as to the quality of our faith.

> Oh! My reader, does not all this hold up before us a faithful mirror in which you and I can see our hearts reflected? Truly it does. We are more ready to trust anything than the living God. We move along with bold decision when we posses the countenance and support of a poor frail mortal like ourselves; but we falter, hesitate, and demur when we have the light of the Master's countenance to cheer us, and the strength of His omnipotent arm to support us. This should humble us deeply before the Lord, and lead us to seek a fuller acquaintance with Him, so that we might trust Him with a more unmixed confidence, and walk on with a firmer step, as having Him *alone* for our resource and portion.[3]

When God first summoned Moses to deliver His people from bondage and from Egypt, Moses rejected the idea. He argued that the Israelites would not believe that he was from God, that the Egyptians would not release their slave force, and that, beside all this, he was not an eloquent speaker. A few moments later, after God demonstrated His power and affirmed Aaron as his helper, Moses surrendered to God's call.

Over the following years Moses' faith in and devotion to Jehovah steadily grew. After Moses death Joshua recorded sixteen times in his book that Moses was "the servant of the Lord." In fact, the New Testament attributes a special honor to Moses' service to the Lord. The Greek word *therapon*, translated "servant" in Hebrews 3:5, is used to describe the type of servant Moses was. *Therapon* is not the typical word used in the New Testament to describe a servant or a slave. This word conveys the idea of a voluntary servant who is motivated by devotion for his superior. At first, Moses was hesitant to accept the call of God for his life, but when he did, he did so of his own free will because he loved the Lord.

Accordingly, I understand Moses' statement this way: "Lord, isn't there some other person better fit for this task than me?" Moses didn't want to go to Egypt for he knew such a mission would cost him personally, so, as a last-ditch effort, he asked if someone else could go instead of him. Seven times in the gospel of John the Lord Jesus affirms that He can only do His Father's will, yet Luke records His prayer, *"Father, if it is Your will, take this cup away from Me; nevertheless not My will, but Yours, be done"* (Luke 22:42). There was never a question of whether the Lord would do His Father's will, but the request highlights the anguish of His soul in doing what He knew would cost Him tremendous suffering and death. Likewise, Moses already knew the answer to his question for God's will had been revealed to him; there was no choice but to obey the Lord and go to Egypt. Moses would speak no more about his inabilities; he was going to Egypt with the staff of power in his hand, the name of I AM on his lips, a companion at his side, and Jehovah directing every step of the strenuous and unknown path ahead.

Thy way, not mine, O Lord, however dark may be!
Lead me by Thine own hand of love; choose out the path for me.
I dare not choose my lot; I would not if I might;
Choose Thou for me, O Lord my God; so shall I walk aright.

— Horatius Bonar

# Returning with Peace

## Exodus 4:18-20

After the dialogue with I AM was finished, the first order of business was for Moses to request leave from Jethro, his father-in-law (Ex. 2:21). He did not inform Jethro of his divine communication but, rather, asked him if he might go to Egypt to confirm the well-being of his family. Jethro was the leader of the clan of Midianites to which Moses belonged and it would have been disrespectful to depart without his approval. Jethro granted permission, saying, *"Go in peace."*

Because Moses demonstrated obedience, God rewarded him with more revelation, saying, *"Go, return to Egypt; for all the men who sought your life are dead"* (v. 19). After forty years of wondering whether or not Pharaoh still wanted him dead, the fact that everyone who had previously sought his life was deceased was welcomed news. This allowed Moses to clear his mind; he could now venture to Egypt without any anxiety relating to his past difficulties there.

Practically speaking, it is difficult to serve the Lord fully and faithfully if we are anxious over present situations or are harboring guilt over past mistakes. Worrying robs us of our peace and is not a good testimony of Christ to the world. An individual must know the peace of God to effectively share it with others. The Lord Jesus not only made *peace with God* on our behalf at Calvary (Rom. 5:1), but now offers us the *peace of God*: "*Be anxious for nothing, but in everything by prayer and supplication, with thanksgiving, let your requests be made known to God; and* ***the peace of God****, which surpasses all understanding, will guard your hearts and minds through Christ Jesus"* (Phil. 4:6-7). He not only offers salvation of the soul, but of the mind as well.

The Greek word translated "peace" is *eirene*. It is derived from a verb meaning "to bond together," it literally means "to be made at one again." The applied meaning of *eirene* in Romans 5:1 is that an individual is made "one again" with God in relationship when he or she trusts the gospel message; this is the saving of the soul. However, Philippians 4:7 refers to the saving of the mind – this is achieved when we are "one again" with Christ in thinking, affections, and attitudes.

The Lord Jesus understood the significance of being one with Him in salvation and in thinking. In fact, His first words to His disciples on the day of His resurrection conveyed this: "*Jesus came and stood in the midst, and said to them, 'Peace be with you.' When He had said this, He showed them His hands and His side. Then the disciples were glad when they saw the Lord. So Jesus said to them again, 'Peace to you! As the Father has sent Me, I also send you'*" (John 20:19-21).

Why did the Lord tell His disciples *"peace be unto you"* twice? Wouldn't once have been sufficient? At Christ's initial appearing, we find the disciples discouraged and fearful. The Lord knew that His apostles needed to have peace within before they could outwardly convey a message of peace. Once the disciples had been with the Lord, and were literally one with Him again, their hearts were made glad – there was peace within. Now the Lord could send them out to preach a message of peace to others. It is impossible to convey peace to others unless the believer has laid hold of the peace of God. Whenever a believer is not at peace, he or she should ponder the question: "In what area of my life am I not one with Christ?" Being one again with Christ brings peace to the soul.

The Lord had graciously cleared Moses' mind of past inhibitions so that he could fully concentrate on the matter at hand. After receiving permission from Jethro to depart, Moses put his wife Zipporah on a donkey with their two young sons, Gershom and Eliezer (Ex. 18:3-4), and began the journey to Egypt. Gershom means "a stranger is there," while Eliezer implies "my God is my help." Both names identify key features of Moses' life: he had been a stranger in Midian for forty years and Jehovah would assist him to live as a stranger and pilgrim in Egypt.

A stranger does not belong where he is, and a pilgrim belongs where he is going. Moses didn't belong in Midian, for his calling had removed him from that land. He didn't belong in Egypt either, but he would do the will of God there until deliverance was obtained. The hope of his pilgrimage was to possess the Promised Land. In the meantime, while enrolled in the Lord's school of training, he would be a stranger in Egypt and a pilgrim with the hope of Canaan. Resting on the hope before him, the Lord would use incredible challenges to shape and mold His servant Moses.

> Many men owe the grandeur of their lives to their tremendous difficulties.
>
> — Charles H. Spurgeon

This summarizes the Christian's experience; a believer is an ambassador of Christ representing the kingdom of God while on earth (2 Cor. 5:20). The world is not the believer's playground, but God's temporary classroom. Those answering the call of God have no ownership in the present perverse world nor have they yet inherited the eternal one to come. Though temporarily living between these two realms, each ambassador of Christ is called to maintain the blessed hope (Tit. 2:13), that is, to recognize the promise of Christ's return (John 14:1-4) as an imminent prospect (2 Tim. 4:8). Some, like Moses, will die before obtaining their inheritance, but in the resurrection all of God's people are assured of the same heavenly city that Abraham longed for by faith (Heb. 11:16).

> If, at the dawn of the early morning, He shall call us one by one,
> When to the Lord we restore our talents, will He answer thee – "Well done?"
> Blessed are those who the Lord finds watching, in His glory they shall share;
> If He shall come at the dawn or midnight, will He find us watching there?
>
> — Fanny J. Crosby

# Lessons on the Way

## Exodus 4:21-26

While Moses was en route to Egypt, God personally met with His servant; Moses would learn three important truths from this encounter. Previously, God had informed Moses that at first Pharaoh would not let the Hebrews go; only after He had worked mighty wonders would their release be obtained. The Lord now explained to Moses that there would be times that He would harden Pharaoh's heart in order to accomplish His sovereign plan in Egypt. In fact, there would be many times that God would harden Pharaoh's heart, but at other times, Pharaoh would harden his own heart against the Lord. Pharaoh had a free choice to bow to Jehovah or to continue revering the gods of Egypt, but in the matter of delivering the Jews, all of Pharaoh's decisions would ultimately be used to glorify God.

The second significant truth presented to Moses pertained to God's relationship with the nation of Israel. He had adopted them (Rom. 9:4) and they were as a firstborn son to Him. This adoption was not an adoption of individuals, as it is with believers in the Church Age (Rom. 8:15-16), but of a nation. Through His covenant with Abraham, Israel had been singled out from among the nations as a special object of God's favor: *"For I am a Father to Israel, and Ephraim is My firstborn"* (Jer. 31:9). Zechariah forewarned future nations of God's wrath if they should choose to invade Israel, for the nation of Israel is *"the apple of His eye"* (Zech. 2:8).

The firstborn son had a privileged position in the family, including the right of family leadership and the greatest share of inheritance. Israel, God's only covenant people on earth (until the Church Age), was extended an opportunity to testify to the world of the one true God, but, as Paul notes in the book of Romans, they failed miserably: *"You who make your boast in the law, do you dishonor God through breaking the law? For 'the name of God is blasphemed among the Gentiles because of you'"* (Rom. 2:23-24).

The Jews thought that they were a special people because God had given them His Law. Paul, however, clarifies that it was not merely having the Law that would mark them as a peculiar people in the world, but keeping it. Because they taught the tenets of the Law, but then broke the Law in practice, the testimony of God was blasphemed among the Gentiles. James summarizes the appropriate conduct of children of God: *"But be doers of the word, and not hearers only, deceiving yourselves"* (Jas. 1:22). To name Christ as Saviour and then to reject His call to holy living effectively blasphemes the name of Christ in the world. This problem seems to have been present even in the early Church, for Paul exhorts believers more than once to put away all evil speech and blasphemies (Eph. 4:31; Col. 3:8).

The third truth that Moses would learn was that delayed obedience was still disobedience. Abraham learned the same lesson while lingering in Haran instead of traveling to Canaan as commanded. In Moses' case the issue centered on his lack of obedience in circumcising his son, whom I believe to be his second son Eliezer.

As a continuing sign of God's covenant with Abraham, his descendants were to circumcise their males. Moses had apparently obeyed this command with Gershom, but not with Eliezer. Because Eliezer's name relates to Moses' newfound relationship with God, it is my opinion that Eliezer was a newborn at the time. While preparing to go to Egypt, Moses had become complacent about obeying God's command of circumcision, perhaps to avoid a family altercation with his wife Zipporah who opposed the rite. How serious a matter is obedience to the Lord? The Lord was ready to slay His chosen deliverer, if the act was not immediately carried out. As the head of the home, Moses was responsible to God for his family, and until things were right with God in his own house, there could be no God-honoring ministry outside the home. James Vernon McGee comments on this latter point:

> Moses obviously thought he could get away with this area of disobedience. He just let it slide like many Christian workers do who neglect their own families while trying to fix up other people's families. God intervened in Moses' life. He waylaid him on the way to Egypt and revealed to him the seriousness of the situation. There is a real danger

when husband and wife do not agree completely in spiritual matters. That is the reason Scripture warns against believers and non-believers getting married.[1]

In Moses' day, physical circumcision was the badge of the Jew for it marked them as God's covenant people. However, as Paul explains, circumcision had a deeper spiritual meaning which the Jews did not perceive: *"For he is not a Jew who is one outwardly, nor is circumcision that which is outward in the flesh; but he is a Jew who is one inwardly; and circumcision is that of the heart, in the Spirit, not in the letter; whose praise is not from men but from God"* (Rom. 2:28-29). Symbolically speaking, circumcision speaks of a life that has no confidence in the flesh (Phil. 3:3). To have no confidence in the flesh means to have no glory in it either. The circumcised life has an inner spiritual reality which is manifest in daily life. It is a quality of life that Law-keeping could never accomplish. Moses was about to enter the greatest contest of his life and his flesh must have no part in it. The victory would be God's and He alone would receive the glory. William Kelly summarizes God's handling of this situation and His rationale for it:

> God was going to put honour on Moses, but there was a dishonour to Him in the house of Moses already. God could not pass over that. How came it that Moses' son was not circumcised? How came it that there lacked that which typifies the mortifying the flesh in those who were nearest to Moses? How came it that God's glory was forgotten in that which ought to have been ever prominent to a father's heart? It appears that the wife had something to do with the matter. Accordingly mark how Jehovah deals in His own wisdom. There never is a hindrance but through flesh; there is no difficulty brought in to distract a faithful man of God from obedience, but God accomplishes the end, only in a far more painful way, and often by the very one who obstructed. What a safeguard then to be childlike and subject to the Lord![2]

The Lord had constrained Moses in some way, perhaps physically or more likely through sickness, such that Zipporah was the one who was forced to circumcise her son. She threw the bloody foreskin at Moses feet and called him "a bloody husband" twice. She had performed the act because her husband's life was at stake, but her own heart was not circumcised and submitted to the Lord. In fact, in type, she had recoiled from the cross of Christ, which demands daily mortification of the works of the flesh. Circumcision spoke of God's covenant plan for Israel and, as she was not a Hebrew, she did not recognize the symbolic significance of the act. However, the Lord was satisfied with her action and immediately released or healed Moses.

The lesson for Moses was that he must fully obey God to accomplish his mission in Egypt. The immensity of this realization and the fact that his wife lacked faith in the Lord caused him to send Zipporah and his sons back to Midian (Ex. 18:2-3). The work that Moses had to do in Egypt would require his full attention; he could not afford to have any family opposition to God's will. The Lord Jesus clearly stated that those who would receive Him would be brought into conflict with family members who would deny Him. The Lord does not mince words concerning who is to have devotional priority in such a contest:

> *Do not think that I came to bring peace on earth. I did not come to bring peace but a sword. For I have come to 'set a man against his father, a daughter against her mother, and a daughter-in-law against her mother-in-law'; and 'a man's enemies will be those of his own household.' He who loves father or mother more than Me is not worthy of Me. And he who loves son or daughter more than Me is not worthy of Me* (Matt. 10:34-37).

Depending on one's place within a particular family, there are obligations to care for and respect other family members, but in matters pertaining to allegiance, there is to be no competition for affection – Christ must be supreme in the believer's heart. This was the lesson Moses learned on the way to Egypt. He had previously yielded to his wife's pleading instead of obeying God's command on the matter of circumcision. But, after being made keenly aware of God's anger over this error, it would not be a mistake that he would repeat again.

> Teach me Thy Way, O Lord; teach me Thy Way!
> Thy gracious aid afford; teach me Thy Way!
> Help me to walk aright, more by faith less by sight,
> Lead me with heavenly light; teach me Thy Way!
>
> — B. Mansell Ramsey

# Who is the Lord?
## Exodus 4:27-5:12

God had previously directed Aaron to join Moses and the two brothers embraced for the first time in forty years on Mt. Sinai, the "Mount of God." Moses told Aaron all that God had commissioned him to do, including the signs he was to work before the people. The two companions ventured on to Egypt and gathered together the elders of Israel to inform them of God's plan. Moses performed all the signs before the elders and they indeed did believe that the Lord had observed their distress and had visited them to deliver them from affliction. The elders bowed their heads and worshipped the Lord.

The Jews did not know it at the time, but their treatment of Moses would be indicative of Israel's rejection and acceptance of their future Messiah. As Stephen explained to the Sanhedrin in Acts 7, the lives of the Patriarchs were given as prophetic pattern for the nation of Israel to learn from. He told them that neither Joseph nor Moses had been accepted the first time they were presented to their brethren as king and deliverer, respectively. But the second time, Joseph's brethren acknowledged their brother as king and confessed their wrong in selling him into slavery. Moses also, on his second presentation, was accepted as the deliverer (though he would be briefly ridiculed after the "bricks without straw" setback). The pattern is further strengthened by the fact that both Joseph and Moses married Gentile women after their Jewish rejections. Likewise, Christ received a Gentile bride, the Church, after the Jews had rejected and crucified Him. When Stephen drew the analogy of rejection to its climax, the Jewish leaders could not tolerate the truth any longer and murdered him.

Moses and Aaron appeared before Pharaoh and demanded in the name of the Lord God of Israel: *"Let my people go, that they may hold a feast unto me in the wilderness."* The progression of divine information to Moses as to what specifically was to be commanded of Pharaoh is significant. At the burning bush God told Moses that the Israelites were to travel three days journey into the wilderness to *"sacrifice to the Lord their God"* (Ex. 3:18). On the way to Egypt, God informed Moses that the Hebrews were to come out of Egypt that they *"may serve"* God (Ex. 4:23). Before Pharaoh, Moses commands the release of the Jews that *"they may hold a feast unto Me in the wilderness"* (Ex. 5:1). The latter statement stresses the fellowship of God's people with their God.

The order of sacrifice, service, and fellowship is important. *"For without the shedding of blood there is not remission of sins;"* that is, there is no other permissible way to righteously enter into God's presence. After reconciliation has occurred, the believer begins to have contact with the nature of God, which effectively constrains him or her to serve the Lord. As a believer serves the Lord in accordance with revealed truth, he or she then enjoys increasing degrees of fellowship with God. The path of spiritual progress is the same in the Old Testament and in the Church Age.

The reference to three days further develops the picture of redemption and restoration just explained. Why was it to be a three day journey into the wilderness and not four or five? It is because Genesis 22:4, the first mention of three days in the Bible, is connected with the journey to Moriah to sacrifice Isaac; the events occurring on Moriah would have their ultimate fulfillment in the death and the resurrection of Jesus Christ. It is also interesting that the first mention of the phrase "third day" is connected with the creation of life on the earth (Gen. 1:11-12) – the number three in Scripture is often associated with the creation of new life or more specifically, the act of resurrection. In Abraham's mind, Isaac was as good as dead those three days that he journeyed to Moriah. Though Isaac did not die that day, the entire scene typifies the then future event in which God the Father and God the Son would ascend the same mount and God's Son would be crucified. He would die, and be buried, but on the third day, He would be raised from the dead. The number three, then, when used metaphorically in Scripture, is often tied to resurrection. The three day journey into the wilderness for the Israelites would climax with a trip through the Red Sea, picturing death and resurrection. Brought out of Egypt by blood, they would experience a new life with God in the wilderness.

Moses and Aaron's declaration was a gallant confrontation, for in Egypt, Pharaoh was considered a god and his authority was not to be challenged. As God had already foretold, Pharaoh rejected their request – his response was one of ignorance and rebellion. Pharaoh denounced the authority of the Hebrew God, whom he did not know, and ignored the fact that there could be serious consequences to both the Jews and the Egyptians for not obeying Jehovah's command. How could Pharaoh understand the need of a wilderness experience to worship only one God, the one true God at that? He could not; for his life centered in conquering others, living sumptuously, enforcing burdens, cracking whips, and honoring his gods.

Pharaoh surmised that his slaves apparently had too much time on their hands if they were thinking about an extended holiday in the desert (v. 8). His remedy for this perceived inefficiency was to command the Jews to *"get to their burdens"* (v. 4) and he enlarged their workload *"the same day"* (v. 6). Not only would the Jews have to perform their existing duties, but they now had to scavenge for their own straw to produce bricks to build Pharaoh's cities (v. 12). Pharaoh's solution to Moses' and Aaron's request was to keep the Jews so busy they would have no time to think about getting alone with their God.

The same tactic is used today by Satan to divert the Lord's people from spending time alone with their Saviour. The world system that Satan controls devalues the things of God and exaggerates the value of what is temporary and sensual. Consequently, undiscerning believers have been deceived into forsaking the best for that which may be permissible, but which steals their available time. Satan's strategy: those Christians can have their religion, but I will not let them have any time to enjoy fellowship with their Saviour. This negatively affects not only the believer's devotional-life, but his or her home-life as well.

Many families have allowed the teen culture of our day and its associate busyness to rule the home. Some mothers have yielded to God's command to be "keepers of the home" (1 Tim. 5:14; Tit. 2:5), but in practice they are consumed with activities outside the home. Much time is expended transporting children to "fluff of life" activities while dads are beguiled into working more hours to financially support the extra entertainment and amusements of their children. Consequently, not only do many families have no time to be families, they have no time to wholeheartedly pursue the Lord.

The home thus loses its appeal as a safe haven and a place of significance and importance to the children. The lack of family devotions and family time together is devastating to family unity and promotes the isolation of its members. The way in which we use our time speaks frankly of our devotion to the Lord. This is why Paul exhorted the Ephesians: *"See then that you walk circumspectly, not as fools but as wise, redeeming the time, because the days are evil"* (Eph. 5:15-16). We cannot *buy back* time per se, but we can *buy up* opportunities to serve God, such that we will have no regrets later for how we spend our lives now.

> I wonder, have I done my best for Jesus,
> who died upon the cruel tree?
> To think of His great sacrifice at Calvary!
> I know my Lord expects the best from me.
> The hours that I have wasted are so many,
> the hours I've spent for Christ so few;
> Because of all my lack of love for Jesus,
> I wonder if His heart is breaking too.
>
> — Ensign Edwin Young

# Suffering in the Will of God
## Exodus 5:13-5:23

The two days following Moses' encounter with Pharaoh were oppressive ones for the Jews; they fell behind on their brick quotas and the Jewish foremen were beaten for the delinquency in production. When these men complained to Pharaoh about the logistics of making bricks without straw, Pharaoh repeated his earlier statement, accusing the Jews of just being lazy. If they had leisure to dream about venturing into the desert to have a feast and to worship their God, they obviously had too much time on their hands. No relief was granted and Israel was now suffering more at the hands of the Egyptians than before Moses had arrived to deliver them. Why would God allow the Hebrews to suffer greater hardship just prior to their deliverance? Edward Dennett provides this insight into the working of God:

> Already He [God] had accomplished two things; He had taught both Moses and the people the character of their oppressor, and the nature of their yoke. He had seemingly shut them up into Pharaoh's hand, and thereby produced in them a conviction of the hopelessness of their condition. This is uniformly His method. He never presents Himself as a Saviour until men know that they are guilty and undone. The Lord Jesus said, "I came not to call the righteous, but sinners to repentance." As soon as men are willing to acknowledge themselves lost, then the Saviour stands before their souls. It is so here.[1]

Besides bringing the Israelites to a fuller understanding of their hopelessness condition in Egypt, God would cause the Egyptians, and indeed the world, to know Jehovah's name and His great power (Ex. 9:16). The deliverance of the Israelites from the hand of the most powerful empire on earth would be an event the Jews would celebrate for generations to come (Ex. 10:2).

Returning from Pharaoh, the Jewish foremen confronted Moses and Aaron about their amplified misery: *"Let the Lord look on you and judge, because you have made us abhorrent in the sight of Pharaoh and in the sight of his servants, to put a sword in their hand to kill us"* (Ex. 5:21). Apparently, Moses gave no response to this statement for he knew the gist of their complaint was true – his actions had brought greater hardship to his people. In heaviness of heart, Moses petitioned the Lord on the matter: *"Lord, why have you treated your people badly?" "Why have you sent me?"* Moses informed the Lord, as if He needed more information, *"It has been worse for Your people since I have confronted Pharaoh in Your name and they have not been released."*

A prophet is a mouthpiece God uses to warn, to rebuke, and to proclaim judgment on individuals, groups, and nations. God's spokesmen often drank from their own ministries. Elijah suffered the cruelty of a three and a half year drought which he had pronounced upon wicked King Ahab. To demonstrate God's redeeming love to Israel, Hosea bought his own wife at an auction after she had deserted him and played the harlot. Ezekiel's wife (the apple of his eye) died in Babylonian captivity; he was told not to weep for her. God told Jeremiah that His judgment on Judah would be so severe that he should not marry a wife. Moses, too, suffered for doing the will of God and, like the prophets that would follow him, he suffered with his people in the will of God.

Should those who do the will of God expect suffering? The Lord Jesus told His disciples the night before He was crucified, *"If the world hates you, you know that it hated Me before it hated you. If you were of the world, the world would love its own. Yet because you are not of the world, but I chose you out of the world, therefore the world hates you"* (John 15:18-19). The disciples were warned that suffering would come to those who identified with Him because the world hates Christ. This profound truth is put by Paul in this simple way: *"Yes, and all who desire to live godly in Christ Jesus will suffer persecution"* (2 Tim. 3:12).

Over the course of his life, Peter learned much about living for and suffering for Christ. Napoleon Bonaparte once said, "It requires more courage to suffer than to die."[2] He also noted that, "It is the cause, and not the death, that makes the martyr."[3] After a heart-wrenching denial, Peter found the first statement to be true: he learned that it takes more courage to suffer daily for the Lord than it does to die once for Him. At the end of his days on earth, he demonstrated the latter statement to be true also. Though Peter was crucified upside down (because he did not consider himself worthy of being crucified the same way his Lord was), he understood that it was not the details of his death that were important, but rather, the cause which he had lived for and was ready to die for – the cause of Christ. In the latter years of his life, he was able to share this truth with other suffering Christians:

> *When you do good and suffer, if you take it patiently, this is commendable before God. For to this you were called, because Christ also suffered for us, leaving us an example, that you should follow His steps: "Who committed no sin, nor was deceit found in His mouth"* (1 Pet. 2:20-22).

> *For it is better, if it is the will of God, to suffer for doing good than for doing evil. For Christ also suffered once for sins, the just for the unjust, that He might bring us to God, being put to death in the flesh but made alive by the Spirit* (1 Pet. 3:17-18).

Peter understood that if a believer lives for Christ, he or she will suffer for it. But such suffering would be a sweet savor in the nostrils of God because it would remind Him of the way His Son suffered for doing His will. But there is yet another benefit of suffering with endurance in the will of God. Paul told both the saints at Philippi and Thessalonica that suffering patiently for the cause of Christ was a token of (a proof of) their salvation (Phil. 1:28; 2 Thess. 1:5). Naturally speaking, it is not possible to suffer patiently for doing what is right; however, it is possible for a Christian who draws on supernatural power from on high. Thus, suffering patiently in the will of God becomes a powerful witness to the lost; in fact this was the testimony that brought one thief, crucified with the Lord, to repentance.

As Peter learned, it is easier to die for the Lord than it is to live for Him daily by dying to self. There is no room for self-will, self-ambition, or self-exaltation in a life lived for Christ and all those who lose their lives for Christ's sake *"shall suffer persecution"* (2 Tim. 3:12). Suffering for righteousness is a promise of God, so we should not be surprised when it happens, but rather we should gird up our minds in preparation for its coming (1 Pet. 1:13). This promise is complimented by another: *"If we endure, we shall also reign with Him"* (2 Tim. 2:12). To suffer patiently for God takes real courage, but it is also rewarded by God! Nowhere in Scripture are both of these truths more evident than the example of our Lord Jesus Christ at Calvary and His exaltation to the throne of God.

Moses felt rejected by his brethren, so he took the matter directly to the only One who could remedy the dire situation. There is nothing wrong with a child of God asking the Lord, "Why?" when the events of the day become overwhelming. But, as Warren Wiersbe warns, even if God did choose to answer the "why" question, it still wouldn't alleviate the trial or provide hope for the aftermath:

> There is nothing wrong with asking why, as long as we don't get the idea that God *owes* us an answer. Even our Lord asked, "Why hast Thou forsaken Me?" (Matt. 27:46). But if the Lord did tell us why things happen as they do, would that ease our pain or heal our broken hearts? Does reading the X-ray take away the pain of a broken leg? We live on *promises,* not explanations; so we shouldn't spend too much time asking God why.[4]

God did not directly answer Moses' "why" questions, for such matters rest in divine sovereignty. However, the Lord did respond to Moses' petition by confirming who He was and is, what He had done, and what He was about to do (Ex. 6). Ultimately, all life's queries are answered by the character of God and His promises. Moses learned that he didn't have to know *why* particular events happen in life, but rather, *Who* it was that caused such things to happen.

> God holds the key of all unknown, and I am glad;
> If other hands should hold the key or if He trusted it to me,
>   I would be sad, I would be sad,
> What if tomorrow's cares were here, without its rest?
> I'd rather He unlocked the day, and as the hours swing open, say:
>   "My will is best, My will is best."
>
> — J. Parker

# An Outstretched Arm
## Exodus 6:1-9

It was difficult enough to challenge the most powerful man on earth, but to be disdained by his own people for doing something you did not want to do in the first place must have been heartbreaking for Moses. He was discouraged by the apparent setback after his first meeting with Pharaoh; he had done what I AM requested of him and had suffered for it. Moses asked the Lord why this had happened; God did not directly answer his inquiry – His sovereign design was working out the best outcome of the entire situation in Egypt – instead, the Lord cites several metaphors, the application of His name, and the affirmation of covenant promises to console Moses.

Speaking to Moses, God said, *"I appeared to Abraham, to Isaac, and to Jacob, as God Almighty, but by My name Lord I was not known to them"* (v. 3). What did Jehovah mean when He informed Moses, "by My name Lord (*Yahweh*) I was not known to them?" Had God previously revealed His personal name to the Jews? Abraham *"called on the name of the Lord [Yahweh]"* (Gen. 13:4). Of Isaac also, we read *"He built an altar there, and called upon the name of the Lord [Yahweh]"* (Gen. 26:25). While beseeching God for deliverance from Esau, Jacob refers to God by His personal name *Yahweh* (Gen. 32:9). Apparently, God had revealed His personal name to the patriarchs, but He was not intimately known to the Hebrews by it. Thus, in Genesis, God is normally referred to by titles of authority such as *Adonai, El Shaddai,* and *El Elyon* or by titles of association, such as *The God of Abraham.*

God was about to reveal Himself to His covenant people in a new and personal way. The patriarch's had known Him by titles of authority and power, but a fuller measure of the Self-Existing One would now be demonstrated to the Jewish nation. Commenting on this verse, J. N. Darby writes:

> Evidently this is the beginning of God's proper relationship with and taking up of Israel; He gives Himself a covenant name of relationship. What goes before is preparatory, and God gives Himself then (chap. 3) a personal name, *Eh'yeh,* which is not repeated here. Then He reveals Himself, though for Israel, here His name by which He was to be known by them.[1]

Not since Genesis 17, when God met with Abraham after thirteen years of silence in response to his lapse of faith (taking Hagar as a concubine and fathering Ishmael), has God issued so many "I will" statements. Abraham had slipped from the path of faith, but God graciously visited him and confirmed His covenant with Abraham thirteen times and announced ten "I will" decrees. By faith, Abraham believed God's promises and was fully restored to God. Abraham's faith permitted God to continue to reveal His plan of redemption.

Likewise, in Moses' situation, the disappointments of Exodus 5 are followed by eight "I will" declarations by God in Exodus 6. God promised twice to use *"a strong hand"* and once *"an outstretched arm"* once against Pharaoh to accomplish His will concerning His people. God again promised Moses that He would deliver the Jews from Egypt and from slavery, lead them to a new land (their heritage from God), and have personal communion with them. Moses had asked "Why?" while petitioning the Lord in prayer. God answered Moses' questions by affirming His awe-inspiring nature and resolve to bring about that which He had promised to do. As with Abraham, Moses was encouraged to keep plodding forward on the high road of faith.

God spoke of using His outstretched arm to redeem the Hebrews and to work judgments which would deliver them from bondage. The word "bondage" is found nine times in Exodus, but the highest saturation of the word in the entire book is found in Exodus 6:5-9. Three times the bondage of the Hebrews is spoken of, twice by the Lord and once by Moses. God said that He would deliver the Jews from their Egyptian captors. Yet, when Moses again informed the people of God's plan they did not believe him because of their anguish of spirit and cruel bondage (v. 9). Naturally speaking, the bondage of the world results in the bondage of the mind. God is the only One who can liberate man from both (Gal. 3:4; 2 Cor. 10:3-5). Perhaps their rejection of Moses' message is the reason God permitted them to suffer with the

Egyptians during the first three plagues, for God did not mark a difference between the Hebrews and the Egyptians in His judgments until the fourth plague (Ex. 8:22). Only God can chasten His people and punish the wicked by the same rod of power.

Exodus 6 is the last time that the Hebrew word *abodah*, which means "to do service of any kind," or its root *abad*, meaning "to work," is used to speak of Egyptian bondage in the book of Exodus. The transition of its usage is marked by the covenant promises of God in this chapter. In Exodus 7 through 12, *adab* is employed thirteen times in the dialogues between Moses and Pharaoh in reference to the release of the Jews from Egyptian rule to *adab* (serve) the Lord. For example, Exodus 7:16 reads, *"Let my people go, that they may serve Me."* The Hebrew word *abodah* is not used again until after the Jews are redeemed by the blood of the Passover lamb in Exodus 12, when they were told to *adodah* (serve) God by memorializing the Passover event. The word is used fourteen times in the remainder of Exodus to speak of the Hebrew's service unto God.

The Hebrew word used to speak of Egyptian bondage is the same one used to speak of worship and service to God. The Jews were being set free from the world to serve and worship God. It is the same for those in the Church Age today. Though Paul was once in the bondage of humanized religion and sin, he was liberated to become "a bondservant of Jesus Christ," an expression he often used to indicate his endearment and relationship to Christ (Rom. 1:1; Phil. 1:1).

The usage of these Hebrew words in Exodus indicates that God would deliver the Jews from their Egyptian bondage in order that they could freely serve (worship) Him. How was all this possible? God answered this question: *"I will redeem you with an outstretched arm"* (v. 6). John Hannah draws together the two keys aspects of "bondage" and "redemption" juxtaposed together in verse 6:

> It [Exodus] has two main parts. In the first part, the first eighteen chapters, we have the redemption of deliverance out of bondage itself. In the last part, from the 19th chapter onward, we have the other part, so to speak, of redemption – we are redeemed to God.
>
> In the first part, the tyrant who rules over us naturally is dispossessed; in the second part, we are brought under the yoke of our true

> Master. Each part is the complement of the other. It is absolutely necessary, in order that deliverance should be realized, that the Deliverer should become the Sovereign. His service is indeed the only perfect freedom.[2]

The Hebrew *gaal*, translated "redeem" in this verse is used elsewhere in Scripture to describe the act of a man who is next of kin redeeming or buying back a relative's property, which may include marrying his widow. This was allowed by law and viewed as a great act of kindness. The reference to *redeem* in verse 6 is only the second time in Scripture that the word *gaal* is found. Genesis 48:16 records its first usage: *"The Angel who has redeemed me from all evil."* Before Jacob pronounced blessings on his sons, he first spoke of one particular Angel (Messenger) that had redeemed him from all evil. We understand this Messenger to be the second person of the Godhead – the Son of God. He was both the Redemption Message and the Redeeming Messenger of God. God would redeem Israel by a Passover Lamb, which pictured the ultimate sacrifice of God's own Son, the Lamb of God who would be judicially punished for the sins of the world (John 1:29).

It would be through this redeeming Lamb that the power of God's outstretched arm would be demonstrated (v. 6). The prophet Isaiah uses the term "arm" a dozen times in his book to speak of God's strength to deliver and redeem His people: *"The Lord has sworn by His right hand and by the arm of His strength"* (Isa. 62:8).

Isaiah acknowledged Israel's moral deficiency and their need for God's arm of salvation, saying, *"But your iniquities have separated you from your God; and your sins have hidden His face from you so that He will not hear"* (Isa. 59:2). They were in the bondage of sin and thus separated from God without, naturally speaking, any hope of restoration.

But Isaiah continues: *"And He* [God] *saw that there was no man, and wondered that there was no intercessor; therefore, His arm brought salvation unto Him, and His righteousness it sustained Him"* (Isa. 59:16). When it ultimately came to finding someone to stand in the gap for the Jews, and for all humanity, there was no one found who could righteously plead man's case because all of humanity had fallen below God's minimum requirement to come into His presence – sinless perfection. Therefore, God sent His own Arm (His Son) to be the intercessor for us: *"The Lord has made bare His holy arm in the eyes of all the nations; and all the ends of the earth shall see the salvation of our God"* (Isa. 52:10). The intercessor had to be God Himself (His own Arm) to be the perfect sacrifice and to sustain the judgment of a Holy God for all man's sin. To properly demonstrate God's power, His Holy Arm was stripped bare for all to see.

The Hebrew word for "the salvation" in Isaiah 52:10 is *yeshuw` ah*, which is composed from the compounding of these two words. The name "Jesus" is derived from the Hebrew words *Yehovah* (Jehovah) and *Yasha* (salvation). Jesus literally means "Jehovah saves," a fact many Old Testament passages resound when the New Testament equivalent "Jesus" is substituted for the Hebrew word *Yeshuw` ah*: *"The Lord has made bare His holy arm in the eyes of all the nations; and all the ends of the earth shall see the* [Jesus] *of our God"* (Isa 52:10), *"Truly my soul silently waits for God; from Him comes my* [Jesus]. *He only is my rock and my* [Jesus]*; He is my defense; I shall not be greatly moved* (Ps. 62:1-2), *"That Your way may be known on earth, Your* [Jesus] *among all nations"* (Ps. 67:2). All Scripture declares the Lord Jesus as the divine Saviour – God's Salvation. The Lord Jesus Christ is the powerful redeeming Arm of God! He willingly stretched forth His own arms to receive the Roman nails and in doing so nailed our death sentence to His cross (Col. 2:14) – He is God's Salvation available for all humanity and for all time!

Moses spoke to the people of God's outstretched redeeming Arm, but they would not listen; misery had darkened their souls and closed their ears to the divine proclamation of their liberty. Their disbelief did not matter at this juncture, for Moses was commanded to take God's message and His rod before Pharaoh again. God's redeeming arm would secure Israel's deliverance.

O Christ, what burdens bowed Thy head! Our load was laid on Thee;
Thou stoodest in the sinner's stead – to bear all ill for me.
A victim led, Thy blood was shed, now there's no load for me.
Jehovah lifted up His rod – O Christ, it fell on Thee!
Thou wast sore stricken of Thy God; there's not one stroke for me.
Thy blood beneath that rod has flowed: Thy bruising healeth me.

— Ann Ross Cousin

# Go Again
## Exodus 6:10-30

The repercussion of God's "I will" declarations is an obvious one: the Lord instructed Moses to *"go in, speak unto Pharaoh"* again. It did not matter that the children of Israel, suffering under great affliction, could not bear that message; the message still must be delivered to Pharaoh. God's messenger had not changed – Moses was to go again to Pharaoh. Likewise, God's message to Pharaoh had not changed: *"Let the children of Israel go."* However, the method by which Moses was to convey this message would be quite dynamic in subsequent meetings with Pharaoh.

Likewise, the gospel message which the Church is to be proclaiming and the One in Whom that message centers have not changed since the beginning of the Church. Yet, the methods in which that message is conveyed to the world will be dynamic and diverse. The Lord Jesus commanded His disciples to make disciples while they were going to the nations, teaching them those things that He had taught them (Matt. 28:19-20). This command continues from generation to generation of disciples until the Lord's return for His Church, which will conclude the Church Age.

On the matter of making disciples, Paul exhorted his spiritual son Timothy: *"The things that you have heard from me among many witnesses, commit these to faithful men who will be able to teach others also"* (2 Tim. 2:2-3). Paul spoke of four generations of disciples in this verse: himself, Timothy, the faithful men Timothy was teaching, and those whom they would teach. The Lord would build His Church one disciple at a time about one central message, which centered in His death, burial, and resurrection (1 Cor. 15:3-4).

The Church is not to use flattering words and enticing gimmicks to persuade people into a profession or to trusting in a diluted message. What was Paul's example in gospel ministry? He said, *"My speech and my preaching was not with enticing words of man's wisdom, but in demonstration of the Spirit and of power"* (1 Cor. 2:4). Effective gospel ministry is centered in the truth and enabled by the power of God. The statement the Lord Jesus expressed to His disciples the night before His crucifixion is emphatically true: *"Jesus said to him, 'I am the way, the truth, and the life. No one comes to the Father except through Me'"* (John 14:6).

Paul obeyed the Great Commission by going town to town, preaching Christ publicly and from house to house (Acts 20:20). Why? Because Paul had a passion for Christ and for the lost, he labored fervently that others might know Him too. He explained, *"Him we preach, warning every man and teaching every man in all wisdom, that we may present every man perfect in Christ Jesus. To this end I also labor, striving according to His working which works in me mightily"* (Col. 1:28-29).

Like Moses, most of us have uncircumcised lips, meaning that we are not eloquent or powerful in speech; however, we still have a responsibility to preach the gospel to the lost. Twice in this passage Moses complains to God about his uncircumcised lips (vv. 12, 30). What was God's response? *"I am the Lord. Speak to Pharaoh king of Egypt all that I say to you"* (v. 29). Moses' speech deficiency was no excuse to remain silent; likewise, we must share that which Christ has commissioned us to preach regardless of our verbal inability to do so.

Pharaoh did not heed Moses' message at first and it is understood that the gospel message will be rejected by the masses and often by individuals several times before they believe it. Though Pharaoh would not yield to it, he would learn that the power of God was connected with Moses' message. Concerning the gospel, Paul writes, *"For the message of the cross is foolishness to those who are perishing, but to us who are being saved it is the power of God"* (1 Cor. 1:18). Beloved of the Lord, don't be still – share the gospel, so that the power of God connected with His message might be known to the lost.

Pharaoh wanted signs to believe that Jehovah really existed; it was God's plan to oblige him. In the future, each time that Moses would appear before Pharaoh some supernatural sign (most of which were devastating plagues) would be presented to Pharaoh as evidence that Jehovah was more powerful than the gods Egypt worshipped.

The ten Egyptian plagues, pronounced by Moses on God's behalf, were specifically designed for the purpose of proving I AM's superiority over the Egyptian gods. In fact, Numbers 33:4 informs us that the plagues were judgments upon the gods of Egypt. Through the onslaught of plagues, Jehovah would be glorified, the gods of Egypt and the Egyptians themselves would be punished, and the faith of the Jews would be strengthened. The table at the conclusion of this chapter shows the Egyptian gods or goddesses that each specific plague challenged.

These ten plagues can be categorized into four classifications of increasing intensity: loathsome – conversion of water to blood, frogs, and gnats; painful – biting flies, plagued cattle, and boils; appalling – hail, locust, and darkness, and finally overwhelming – death of the firstborn.[1] Jehovah steadily advanced the severity of these divine judgments upon the Egyptians. He progressed from removing their comforts, to liquidating their possessions, then to chastening them with pain and death. These plagues were of such a catastrophic nature that the fame of Jehovah spread among the nations like wildfire. Why were the inhabitants of Canaan terrified by the approaching Israelites forty years later (Josh. 2:8-9)? Why did the Philistines some four centuries later fear the approaching army of Israel (1 Sam. 4:8)? It is because they had heard of how powerfully God had crushed the Egyptians for opposing Him and His people.

According to the book of Revelation similar plagues will be unleashed upon the entire world with growing intensity during the Tribulation Period. For example, the fifth trump judgment releases from the bottomless pit armored locusts which sting like scorpions. The second and third bowl judgments turn all the sea water and all the fresh water into blood, respectively. The fifth bowl judgment causes darkness throughout the Antichrist's kingdom. The wrath of the Lamb will be worldwide, not merely restricted to Egypt. During Moses' day, the wrath that God poured out upon Egypt was for their abuse of the Jews and their defiance of His rule. God's judgment of Egypt is only a prelude to what the entire world will suffer during the Tribulation Period for the same reasons. "These plagues furnished a most striking prophetic forecast of God's future judgments upon the world," says Arthur Pink, and then he lists sixteen similarities between the scenario in

Egypt during Moses' day and to the future world events during the Tribulation Period:

(1) During the time of Jacob's Trouble Israel shall again be sorely oppressed and afflicted (Isa. 60:14; Jer. 30:5-8).
(2) They will cry unto God, and He will hear and answer (Jer. 31:18-20).
(3) God will command their oppressors to "Let them go" (Isa. 43:6).
(4) God will send two witnesses to work miracles before their enemies (Rev. 11:3-6).
(5) Their enemies will also perform miracles (Rev. 13:13-15).
(6) God will execute sore judgments upon the world (Jer. 25:15-16).
(7) God will protect His own people from them (Rev. 8:8, 16:4-5).
(8) Water will again be turned into blood (Rev. 8:8, 16:4-5).
(9) Satanic frogs will appear (Rev. 16:13).
(10) A plague of locusts shall be sent (Rev. 9:2-11).
(11) God will send boils (Rev. 16:2).
(12) Terrible hailstones shall descend from heaven (Rev. 8:7).
(13) There shall be awful darkness (Isa. 60:2; Rev. 16:10).
(14) Just as Pharaoh hardened his heart so will the wicked in the day to come (Rev. 9:20-21).
(15) Death will consume multitudes (Rev. 9:15).
(16) Israel will be delivered (Zech. 14:3-4; Rom. 11:26).[2]

Whether in Moses' day or in the Tribulation Period, God knows His people and will deliver them from oppression. God said, *"Let My people go,"* and having said it, He proceeded to name some of them in this chapter, as if to say, "These are all Mine and none shall be left in Egypt." The genealogies of three tribes are highlighted, with specific emphasis on Moses' and Aaron's tribe of Levi. The tribes of Reuben and Simeon, the first and second sons of Jacob, are briefly mentioned first, but this is only for the purpose of identifying Jacob's third son Levi. The title of the genealogy is *"These were the heads of their families."* The purpose for inserting this genealogy just prior to the plagues of Egypt is indicated in verses 26 and 27, where twice we read, *"It was the same Moses and Aaron"* (vv. 26-27), and then in verse 27: *"These are the ones who spoke to Pharaoh king of Egypt, to bring out the children of Israel from Egypt."* The Spirit of God sought fit to insert a formal record of Moses' and Aaron's prominent position in their associated clan, and their role as leaders of the nation of Israel.

Because Aaron was three years older, his name is mentioned before Moses' in verses 20 and 26. But since his younger brother Moses had been given the prominent role in leading the children of Israel out of Egypt, his name is listed first in verse 27 and elsewhere in Scripture where their names appear together.

At the Judgment Seat of Christ (2 Cor. 5:10; Rom 14:10-12), every believer will receive or lose rewards for those works done while on earth. Deeds which are done in Christ's strength and for His glory will be rewarded and that which is unprofitable for the kingdom of God will be burnt up (1 Cor. 3:11-15), and we, when in the presence of Christ, will be glad they were. Therefore, let us not be self-serving, but *"whatever you do, do it heartily, as to the Lord and not to men, knowing that from the Lord you will receive the reward of the inheritance; for you serve the Lord Christ"* (Col. 3:23-24).

As demonstrated in the genealogies of Exodus 6, God is faithful to recognize faithfulness and to reward it accordingly: *"By faith Moses ...* [esteemed] *the reproach of Christ greater riches than the treasures in Egypt; for he looked to the reward"* (Heb. 11:24-26). Moses had an obligation to suffer *reproach for Christ*, and he would be rewarded for valuing the *reproach of Christ* greater than anything Egypt had to offer. May all believers long to do the same.

Rescue the perishing, care for the dying,
snatch them in pity from sin and the grave.
Weep over the erring one, lift up the fallen;
tell them of Jesus the mighty to save.
Rescue the perishing, duty demands it;
strength for thy labor the grace the Lord will provide;
Back to the narrow way, patiently win them;
tell the poor wanderer a Saviour has died.

— Fanny J. Crosby

## The Ten Plagues of Egypt in Relationship with Egyptian Gods[3]

| Plague (Ex. ref.) | Warning | Plague Initiation | Pharaoh's Heart and Promise | Egyptian Deity Defeated |
|---|---|---|---|---|
| #1 Nile to blood (7:14-25) | Met with Pharaoh (morning) | Aaron stretched rod over the water. | His heart grew hard; did not heed Moses' warning. | *Hapi* (*Apis*): bull god of Nile, *Isis*: goddess of Nile, *Khnum*: ram god & guardian of the Nile. |
| #2 Frogs (8:1-15) | Met with Pharaoh | Aaron stretched rod over the water. | Agreed to let people go; hardened his own heart | *Heqet*: birth goddess with frog head, *Amon*: god with frog head. |
| #3 Gnats /Lice (8:16-19) | None | Aaron stretched rod over the land/smote it. | His heart grew hard; did not listen to his magicians. | *Set*: god of desert |
| #4 Flies (8:20-32) | Met with Pharaoh (morning) | None | Proposed the Jews offer in Egypt; hardened his heart | *Uatchit*: represented by the fly, *Bes*: god of destroying forces. |
| #5 Death of Livestock (9:11-7) | Met with Pharaoh | None | His heart grew hard; did not let the people go. | *Hathor*: goddess with cow head, *Apis*: bull god |
| #6 Boils (9:8-12) | None | Moses scattered ashes before Pharaoh. | God hardened Pharaoh's heart; did not let people go. | *Sekhmet*: goddess of disease, *Sunu*: the pestilence god |
| #7 Hail (9:13-35) | Met with Pharaoh (morning) | Moses stretched out his hand/rod to heaven. | Agreed to let people go; sin admitted, hardened his heart. | *Nut*: sky goddess, *Osiris*: god of crops & fertility, *Set*: god of storms |
| #8 Locusts (10:1-20) | Met with Pharaoh | Moses stretched out his hand/rod over the land. | Proposed that the men go; confessed sin, God hardened Pharaoh's heart. | *Nut*: sky goddess, *Osiris*: god of crops and fertility |
| #9 Darkness (10:21-29) | None | Moses stretched out his hand/rod toward heaven. | Proposed to let the people go, but not animals; God hardened Pharaoh's heart. | *Re*: sun god, *Horus*: sun god, *Nut*: sky goddess, *Hathor*: sky goddess, *Bastet*: goddess of sunlight. |
| #10 Death of firstborn (11:1-12:30) | Met with Pharaoh | None | Urged the people to go with their stuff. | *Min*: god of fertility, *Heqet*, *Isis*, & Pharaoh's firstborn son – considered to be a god. |

# "I AM the Lord"
## Exodus 7:1-7

As God magnified Himself in His dealings with Egypt He would also exalt Moses in the eyes of Pharaoh. In his darkened pagan mind, Pharaoh would even think of Moses as one of the gods (v. 1). God renews Moses' commission and affirms that Aaron was to be his spokesman before Pharaoh. God again prepares Moses for Pharaoh's initial rejection of His call to release the Hebrew slaves from his grip.

It was God's plan to harden Pharaoh's heart at times in order to ensure the most glory for His name and the greatest blessing possible for His people. If Pharaoh had just released them without a contest, the Egyptians would have never learned how great Jehovah the God of the Hebrews was, nor would they have been prompted to reward the Israelites with the spoil of Egypt. God's plan, as always, would accomplish the best outcome in righteousness.

Consequently, God would provide a righteous testimony of Himself throughout Egypt; this is why there are ten specific plagues and not eleven or nine. The number ten is repetitively used in Scripture to signify a divine testimony that results in human responsibility. For example, *ten* is used to reveal God's moral Law to the Israelites in Exodus 20 and their immediate accountability to it. The Ten Commandments represent God's standard of righteousness, the Jews would be blessed for obedience and judged for waywardness. Ten is the sum of four and six.

In the Bible, the number four represents *earthly order*: four directions, four seasons, and four realms in which life exists in the world (the sea, the air, above the ground, and below the ground) while the number six relates to man: Adam was created on the sixth day and was appointed six days to labor; also, just as six falls short of seven (the perfect number), man falls short of God's glory (Rom. 3:23). The combination of these numbers then represents man's accountability to

God's revealed order. The number ten is used extensively in the tabernacle's dimensions and features to again convey the idea of God's testimony among His people and their responsibility to obey His ordained system of worship. The ten plagues announced by Moses on God's behalf would provide an awesome testimony of God's power, and at the same time, put the Egyptians under personal accountability to Him.

The outcome of this plan would be to expose the Egyptians to the greatness of I AM as Lord (v. 5) and reveal their accountability to Him. The grace of God is thus witnessed in His dealings with the Egyptians. They deserved to be wiped out, yet, God personally revealed Himself to the mightiest nation in the world, that they might know His name, and, thus know Him. The Psalmist declares, *"O Lord, our Lord, how excellent is Your name in all the earth, Who have set Your glory above the heavens!"* (Ps. 8:1).

Centuries later, there would be another name of God that would be held up to the nations and propagated worldwide that men might know God. It is the name "Jesus," which is translated from the Greek word *Iesous*, and; as mentioned earlier, is derived from two Hebrew words: *Yehovah* and *yasha*` which when compounded mean "Jehovah's salvation." When we utter the name "Jesus," we are referring to the sacred covenant name of God in the English language. How important is the name of Jesus Christ? Peter said of Christ, *"Nor is there salvation in any other, for there is no other name under heaven given among men by which we must be saved"* (Acts 4:12).

In all, the name "Jesus" is found nearly one thousand times in the New Testament. In the Gospels, the Lord is normally referred to as "Jesus" for He was "the Son of man" who came to the earth to seek and save men. The Epistles, however, which were written after Christ's ascension and address those who knew Him as Saviour, contain a more exalted tone when referring to the "Lord Jesus." To the believer, He is more than just a man named Jesus; He is Lord and Saviour. The apostles, guided by the Holy Spirit, were very careful in declaring the Lord's name. Their example is a good one for all believers to follow – let us speak and write of the Lord Jesus in an honorable fashion.

Who addressed the Lord Jesus by His given name after understanding who He claimed to be? It was the Pharisees and the demons – namely, those who rejected Christ's rule over them. Why did Judas never call Christ "Lord?" It is because he did not recognize the Lord's rule over him. Paul precisely identifies the spiritual issue: *"Therefore I make known to you that no one speaking by the Spirit of God calls Jesus accursed, and no one can say that Jesus is Lord except by the Holy Spirit"* (1 Cor 12:3). Those who have not been born again will not freely declare Christ as Lord! But those who have life in Him are compelled to honor Him in their speech.

Yes, "Jesus" is a special name. It was by that name God declared His gift to the World, His Son, who was born of a peasant girl, swaddled in grave clothes, and laid in a feeding trough. Hopefully, every believer is well past God's introduction of His Son to the world and understands God's subsequent declaration after Christ's ascension to heaven: *"Your throne, O God, is forever and ever; a scepter of righteousness is the scepter of Your kingdom"* (Heb. 1:8). The Lord Jesus is "the King of Glory" and "The Lord of Hosts" (Ps. 24:7-10).

The writer of Hebrews declares, *"He* [Christ] *has by inheritance obtained a more excellent name than they* [the angels]*"* (Heb. 1:4). Our knowledge of His acquired positional glory demands our respect. For this reason, the apostles were careful in addressing Him after His ascension – when using His personal name they ascribed to Him titles of exaltation, such as "the Lord Jesus Christ" and "the Lord Jesus," or they associated His name directly with another member of the Godhead to proclaim His deity and to ensure reverence.

Seeing that Christ's exalted station in heaven is as great as His name, shall we ignore such monumental realities through careless speech? God forbid. Not only is God insulted, but diminished appreciation for Christ results in retarded spiritual growth (Heb. 5:12-6:1).

> All hail the power of Jesus' name! Let angels prostrate fall,
> Bring forth the royal diadem, and crown Him Lord of all.
> Let every kindred, every tribe, on this terrestrial ball,
> To Him all majesty ascribe and crown Him Lord of all.
>
> — Edward Perronet

# A Sign of Authority
## Exodus 7:8-10

It must have been quite exciting for Moses to know ahead of time what Pharaoh would do and say. Each day that the confrontation continued between the Lord and Pharaoh, Moses learned more of God's omniscience. David was overwhelmed by this attribute of God. He understood that he could not escape from "God's knowing." David's thoughts, speech, and doings were all foreknown by God; they were known "afar off."

> *O Lord, You have searched me and known me. You know my sitting down and my rising up; You understand my thought afar off. You comprehend my path and my lying down, and are acquainted with all my ways. For there is not a word on my tongue, but behold, O Lord, You know it altogether* (Ps. 139:1-4).

The writer of Hebrews summarizes the same truth: *"And there is no creature hidden from His sight, but all things are naked and open to the eyes of Him to whom we must give account"* (Heb. 4:13). Pharaoh's thoughts, speech, and actions were all open to God. Thus He instructed Moses, *"When Pharaoh speaks to you, saying, 'Show a miracle for yourselves,' then you shall say to Aaron, 'Take your rod and cast it before Pharaoh, and let it become a serpent'"* (Ex. 7:9).

Moses and Aaron followed the Lord's instructions and the shepherd's rod was cast upon the ground before Pharaoh during their next meeting. The rod, for the third time, turned into a serpent. Pharaoh summoned his sorcerers, who also cast down rods before Aaron and Moses. If the sorcerers were Jannes and Jambres, as identified by Paul in 2 Timothy 3:8, there may have only been two rods. In any case, the magician's rods by enchantments were transformed into serpents also. As Satan cannot create life, it is likely that the pagan rods were some sort of demonic illusion.

The actions of Pharaoh's sorcerers picture future supernatural feats to be accomplished by the Antichrist and False Prophet during the Tribulation Period. These also will be performed through demonic power (Rev. 16:14). The interaction between the magicians and Moses demonstrated not only Jehovah's superior authority and power, as worked through Moses, but also the fact that Jehovah was hostile to the Egyptian gods and to all who worshipped them.

The contest did not last long, for Moses' rod swallowed up the rods of the magicians. As mentioned previously, a rod speaks of "power." It is important to understand that there is no power in the rod itself; it is simply an instrument to which God has assigned meaning – symbolic truth. Satan was represented by a serpent in Genesis 3:1, thus, the serpent speaks of evil. Egyptian power was satanic in nature and God was going to reclaim that power to accomplish His purpose, as symbolized by Moses' rod/serpent swallowing the Egyptian rods/serpents. This was further confirmation to Moses that all the acquired wisdom and power of Egypt was no match for Jehovah's power.

On this particular meeting, Pharaoh had asked that a miracle be performed to prove Moses' claim that the Hebrew God had sent him to demand the release of the Hebrew slaves. Words of a God he did not know were unimpressive to Pharaoh, but if the God of the Hebrews visibly demonstrated Himself, that would be another matter. However, the time for release was not yet ripe, and God was working in Pharaoh's heart to accomplish His will. Accordingly, apathy, not fear, characterized Pharaoh's response to God's rod (the symbol of His authority).

There is another symbol of God's authority that often receives little acknowledgement among Christians today. Paul instructs that when believers are in God's presence for the spiritual exercise of prayer or prophecy (teaching) that there should be a visible salute to His authority. This salute, or sign of authority, is the covered head of the woman and the uncovered head of the man: *"For this cause ought the woman to have* [a sign of authority] *on her head"* (1 Cor. 11:10). The veil is a symbol of submission to God's authority; by wearing it, the woman shows visible agreement with divine order (1 Cor. 11:3).

The man is God's representative (God's glory) and is to remain uncovered; however, the woman, representing man's glory, is to be covered (1 Cor. 11:4-7). Long hair is a fitting covering for the woman, but this covering is also a glory in itself (1 Cor. 11:15), which must be covered so as not to compete with God's glory. When the brothers remain uncovered and the sisters covered during church meetings, all competing glories are thus concealed and only God's glory is seen. In this way, only God's glory, as represented by uncovered men, is seen by God and the angels overlooking the assembly – a visible salute to Christ's headship and God's order is thus affirmed for all to see. This pictures the scene in heaven as seraphim and cherubim cover their own glories with their wings in the presence of God, so God's glory is preeminent (Isa. 6:2; Ezek. 1:11). The angels are at present learning about submission to divine order from observing the Church's submission to it (1 Cor. 11:10; Eph. 3:10; 1 Pet. 1:12).

But in the case of the head covering, it is not a matter of God hardening the heart of a pagan king to accomplish His greater good, but of Satan beguiling believers to ignore divine revelation. Lucifer, a covering cherub (Ezek. 28:14), apparently no longer wanted to cover his glory in the presence of God, but rather desired the throne of God (Isa. 14:12-15). God cast the rebel off His holy mountain and foreordained him to spend an eternity in the Lake of Fire (Matt. 25:41).

Given this understanding, Watchman Nee, who was martyred for Christ in 1972 (after being in a Chinese labor camp for twenty years) explains why the head covering is an important sign of submission to God's authority:

> Today woman has a sign of authority on her head because of the angels, that is, as a testimony to the angels. Only the sisters in the church can testify to this, for the women of the world know nothing of it. Today when the sisters have the sign of authority on their heads, they bear the testimony that, "I have covered my head so that I do not have my own head, for I do not seek to be head. My head is veiled, and I have accepted man as head, and to accept man as head means that I have accepted Christ as head and God as head. But some of you angels have rebelled against God." This is what it meant "because of the angels."
>
> I have on my head a sign of authority. I am a woman with my head covered. This is a most excellent testimony to the angels, to the fallen and to the unfallen ones. No wonder Satan persistently opposes the

> matter of head covering. It really puts him to shame. We are doing what he has failed to do. What God did not receive from the angels, He now has from the church.[1]

Moses presented a "sign of authority" to Pharaoh who completely rejected it. May the Church not follow Pharaoh's example, but rather submit to every aspect of God's Word. We are a people that easily forget, so God uses symbolic truth to remind us of what He deems important in the Church: for example, the Lord's Supper causes us to regularly remember His Son, and the head covering to remember His authority in our lives.

> Some things are commanded because they are right; other things are right because they are commanded.
>
> — Harry S. Ironside

# The Sway of Imitation
## Exodus 7:11-13

A word concerning Pharaoh's sorcerers is needful. Paul warned his spiritual son Timothy of false professors who had a form of godliness, but lacked supernatural power to produce the real thing. Without spiritual fortitude, these religious charades excelled in leading people into folly. Paul provided a graphic character sketch of these false professors and how believers should react to their doings:

> *But know this, that in the last days perilous times will come: For men will be lovers of themselves, lovers of money, boasters, proud, blasphemers, disobedient to parents, unthankful, unholy, unloving, unforgiving, slanderers, without self-control, brutal, despisers of good, traitors, headstrong, haughty, lovers of pleasure rather than lovers of God, having a form of godliness but denying its power. And from such people turn away! For of this sort are those who creep into households and make captives of gullible women loaded down with sins, led away by various lusts, always learning and never able to come to the knowledge of the truth* (2 Tim. 3:1-7).

We would not know Pharaoh's magicians' names, Jannes and Jambres, if the Spirit of God had not moved Paul's pen further to record them: *"Now as Jannes and Jambres resisted Moses, so do these also resist the truth: men of corrupt minds, disapproved concerning the faith; but they will progress no further, for their folly will be manifest to all, as theirs also was"* (2 Tim. 3:8-9). Paul used Jannes and Jambres as an object lesson to illustrate how people having a form of godliness resist truth. Obviously, these sorcerers defied Moses, but in what way did they have a form of godliness in doing so? C. H. Mackintosh answers this question:

> The mode in which "Jannes and Jambres withstood Moses" was simply by imitating, as far as they were able, whatever he did. We do not find that they attributed his actions to a false or evil energy, but rather that they sought to neutralize their power upon the conscience [of those present], by doing the same things. What Moses did they could do, so that after all there was no great difference. One was as good as the other. A miracle is a miracle. If Moses wrought miracles to get the people out of Egypt, they could work miracles to keep them in; so where was the difference?
>
> From all this we learn the solemn truth that the most satanic resistance to God's testimony in the world is offered by those who, though they imitate the effects of the truth, have but "the form of godliness," and "deny the power thereof." Persons of this class can do the same things, adopt the same habits and forms, use the same phraseology, profess the same opinions as others. If the true Christian, constrained by the love of Christ, feeds the hungry, clothes the naked, visits the sick, circulates the Scriptures, distributes tracts, supports the gospel, engages in prayer, sings praise, preaches the gospel, the formalist can do every one of these things, and this, be it observed, is the special character of the resistance offered to the truth "in the last days" – this is the spirit of "Jannes and Jambres." How needful to understand this! How important to remember that, "as Jannes and Jambres withstood Moses, so do" those self-loving, world-seeking, pleasure-hunting professors "resist the truth." They would not be without "a form of godliness;" but, while adopting "the form," because it is customary, they hate "the power," because it involves self-denial. "The power" of godliness involves the recognition of God's claims, the implanting of His kingdom in the heart, and the consequent exhibition thereof in the whole life and character, but the formalist knows nothing of this.[1]

Those who have *a form of godliness but deny its power* are likened to slithering serpents *"who creep into households and make captives of gullible women loaded down with sins, led away by various lusts."* The threat to believers may be from other embedded false teachers in Christendom or canvassing cult members. Many modern cults, in pretense, identify with the name of Christ, but they deny His Word, degrade His attributes, and lessen His importance as Saviour by promoting a *good-works* message for salvation. Often these ambassadors of deception visit during the day when God's appointed protector of the home is absent, and the stress of caring for one's children and the home is at its highest. They slither in and secretly take the gullible captive. Edward Dennett states that these individuals are "one of Satan's most dangerous subtleties," and then explains why:

> If he [Satan] can succeed in open opposition to the truth, he will not conceal himself; but if this door of antagonism is closed, he will transform himself into an angel of light. It was so in Paul's days; and it is especially the case at the present moment. Professing Christians would scarcely be led away by the open exhibition of Satanic power; but how many are seduced by it because outwardly it is an imitation of the divine. ...There is not a single operation of the Spirit of God, nor a single form of His working, that Satan does not imitate. His counterfeits are around us on every hand, within and without.[2]

Thankfully, believers do not have to be deceived by the Jannes and Jambreses of the world. Besides His Word, God has provided a safeguard for believers so that they should not be deceived by the ensnaring arts of Satan's workers. John instructed the believers, *"Believe not every spirit* [teacher], *but test the spirits whether they are of God"* (1 Jn. 4:1-4). He also informed them of an anointing that they had received at spiritual rebirth. There is no need to pray for this anointing; every believer already has it. It is always spoken of in the past tense and has the purpose of giving spiritual discernment concerning what is true and what is false.

> *But you have an anointing from the Holy One, and you know all things* (1 Jn. 2:20-21).

> *These things I have written to you concerning those who try to deceive you. But the anointing which you have received from Him abides in you, and you do not need that anyone teach you; but as the same anointing teaches you concerning all things, and is true, and is not a lie, and just as it has taught you, you will abide in Him* (1 Jn. 2:26-27).

Deceit is often thoroughly mixed with something acceptable. Consequently, great discernment is required in one's daily conduct, or the believer will certainly fall prey to the enemy's trickery and craftiness. New Age propaganda has infiltrated into Corporate America, the medical profession, government-operated schools, and entertainment venues. Many self-promoting preachers today are using the gospel for profit. The cults are advertising strong pro-family and pro-morality themes; they often ensnare individuals into their ranks by promoting good intentions at the cost of sound doctrine. Contemporary children's movies often disguise pantheism, animism, reincarnation, and necromancy with carefully arranged humor, special effects, and exhilarating music to create a more palatable message for children to digest under the eye of undiscerning Christian parents.

Concerning the matter of discerning truth from evil deception, Luke endorsed the behavior of the Bereans as a good example to follow: *"These were more noble ... they received the Word with all readiness of mind, and* ***searched the Scriptures daily****, whether those things were so"* (Acts 17:11; KJV). When they were confronted with the gospel message, they sought to verify or disprove it by investigating Old Testament Scripture. Similarly, every child of God should be a Berean, proving what is true and identifying what is false by exploring the Word of God for answers (2 Tim. 2:15-16). There is no reason to be deceived by the Jannes and Jambreses of the world; the Lord guides those who desire to be led.

Saviour, I follow on, guided by Thee,
Seeing not yet the hand that leadeth me;
Hushed be my heart and still, fear I no future ill,
Only to do Thy will, my will shall be.

— Charles S. Robinson

# A River of Death

## Exodus 7:14-25

Without the Nile, Egypt would be a wasteland of sand and wilderness. Accordingly, the Egyptians believed the Nile was their source of life. The first plague that Moses was to levy on Egypt was to attack their perceived lifeline – the Nile and all the various gods and goddesses connected with it. Jehovah, the God of the Hebrews, would demonstrate that He was superior to *Hapi* the bull god of the Nile, *Isis* the goddess of the Nile, and *Khnum* the ram god and guardian of the Nile.

Blood is the life of the flesh (Lev. 17:11), and when it is shed, death results. The blood that filled Egypt's rivers, ponds, and streams would serve as a precursor of the greater judgments to come, judgments that would result in immense suffering and death. The Egyptians would soon learn that not even their illustrious gods and goddesses of the Nile would be able to save them from Jehovah's wrath.

The plague was to be executed early in the morning when Pharaoh went out to the Nile, perhaps for some pagan ritual to honor the river or to bathe in its sacred waters. Moses was to stand on the edge of the river and pronounce the judgment in front of Pharaoh while Aaron stretched Moses' rod over the water and smote the river. The miracle was done in the sight of Pharaoh's servants and the result was immediate: the Nile, its tributaries, and every pool connected with it turned to blood. The result was death to whatever lived within the Nile and could not escape (e.g. the fish). The stench of death from the river was intolerable. The plague lasted seven days, during which time the Egyptians probably dug wells around the river's edge to find drinking water.

Apparently, Pharaoh's sorcerers mimicked the plague, which is illogical on two counts. First, given the scarcity of drinking water, why would any Egyptian want to transform water fit for consumption into blood? Secondly, since the Nile fed the rivers, streams, and ponds throughout Egypt, and since these had already been turned into blood, the mimicked version of the plague was minute in comparison to the real thing. F. B. Hole offers this observation of the sorcerers' work: "But again the magicians proved that they could similarly produce death and stinking, so that Pharaoh's heart remained hard. That Satan could produce death, or that which is symbolic of death, is not at all surprising, since he is the author of sin, and by sin death has come to pass."[1]

What was Pharaoh's response to the plague? After Moses pronounced the judgment, Pharaoh turned away from him and departed to his house. Though the common people suffered greatly because of the plague, Pharaoh made light of it (v. 23). His opposition against releasing the Israelites had not changed.

The whole of Scripture contrasts the judgments of God upon the wicked in the Old Testament and the grace of God extended to the faithful through Christ in the New Testament. This is not to say that God did not show grace in days of old, or that He does not judge wickedness at present, but rather that what the Law could not accomplish (a pardon for sinners) was achieved by God in Christ. For example, at the Tower of Babel, God judged and dispersed the people by giving them different tongues. Ten days after Christ's ascension to heaven, at the feast of Pentecost, the Holy Spirit came to the earth as promised and gave believers the ability to communicate in different tongues (Acts 2). The first plague levied on Egypt in Moses' time was turning fresh water into blood, which brought death, but Christ's first miracle was performed at a wedding in Canaan (John 2) where He turned water into wine (which in the good sense is a symbol of joy). On the day that Moses brought the Law into the Israelite camp 3,000 souls were judged for worshipping the golden calf. But on the first day of the Church age, at Pentecost, Peter's preaching led to the saving of about 3,000 souls.

Scripture records two unmistakable facts: firstly, that human sin results in misery and ultimately the sting of death and secondly, that Christ brings blessing and offers eternal life to those who will trust Him by faith. Paul understood these great realities of life and penned these words:

> *O Death, where is your sting? O Hades, where is your victory? The sting of death is sin, and the strength of sin is the law. But thanks be to God, who gives us the victory through our Lord Jesus Christ* (1 Cor. 15:55-57).

No matter what ills life may present to the believer; his or her ultimate victory is secured in Christ. The Law showed sin, and by sin is death, but in Christ there is everlasting life. Paul therefore concludes: *"But thanks be to God, who gives us the victory through our Lord Jesus Christ. Therefore, my beloved brethren, be steadfast, immovable, always abounding in the work of the Lord, knowing that your labor is not in vain in the Lord"* (1 Cor. 15:57-58).

> Victory, victory, victory in Jesus! Sing His overcoming blood,
> sing the grace that frees us;
> Ring it out more boldly, song of faith and cheer, till the whole
> wide world shall hear.
>
> Over the powers of darkness, over the hosts of sin, victory in
> Jesus, victory!
> Trusting, watching, praying, we shall surely win, victory in Jesus evermore.
>
> — Eliza F. Hewitt

# Too Many Frogs
## Exodus 8:1-15

Moses was told again to *"Go unto Pharaoh,"* and he obeyed the Lord. The message he was to convey to Pharaoh had not changed: *"Let my people go, that they may serve Me."* The Lord's servant said no more, and no less, than the words God put in his mouth. This is a good example for all believers to follow, because augmenting God's Word is a serious offense against Him. Those expounding Scripture can go no further than the truth of Scripture and say no less than what it proclaims. In some instances, the book of Revelation for example, God has warned of divine plagues and condemnation to anyone who adds to or diminishes the truth of that book (Rev. 22:18-19).

Pharaoh had rejected God's sign of authority (i.e. when Moses' rod had turned into a serpent and swallowed the sorcerer's serpent-rods) and ignored the consequences of the first plague imposed on Egypt. The Lord told Moses to offer Pharaoh an ultimatum before smiting Egypt with the next plague:

> *If you refuse to let them go, behold, I will smite all your territory with frogs. So the river shall bring forth frogs abundantly, which shall go up and come into your house, into your bedroom, on your bed, into the houses of your servants, on your people, into your ovens, and into your kneading bowls. And the frogs shall come up on you, on your people, and on all your servants* (Ex. 8:2-4).

Apparently, Pharaoh did not respond to the warning, because God instructed Moses to proceed with the plague. As in the first plague, Aaron lifted Moses' rod above the Nile; however, he did not smite the water with the rod as he had done before. The frogs obeyed the authority of the rod and came out of the rivers, ponds, and streams and invaded the land. This would have been the same means by which the frogs had escaped death previously when the Nile was turned to blood.

The plague demonstrated Jehovah's superiority to the Egyptian goddess of birth, *Heqet*, whose image included the head of a frog. Besides punishing the Egyptians, the purpose of the plague was to prove to them that *"there is no one like the Lord our God"* (v. 10). This refrain echoed by the prophet Isaiah: *"I, even I, am the Lord, and besides Me there is no Saviour"* (Isa. 43:11). *"Thus says the Lord, the King of Israel, and His Redeemer, the Lord of Hosts: 'I am the First and I am the Last; besides Me there is no God'"* (Isa. 44:6). *"I am the Lord, and there is no other; there is no God besides Me"* (Isa. 45:5).

The frogs were so abundant that they infiltrated every aspect of Egyptian life. No home could escape their incursion. The frogs were in the cooking pans, the kneading troughs, and the beds of the Egyptians. The irony of the situation was the Egyptians regarded frogs as having the power of fertility, so in honor of *Heqet*, frogs were not to be killed! So loathsome was the plague that Pharaoh summoned Moses to take away the frogs. Pharaoh said, *"I will let the people go, that they may do sacrifice unto the Lord."*

The chaos of the rebel heart is demonstrated in three ways in this portion of Scripture. Firstly, the Egyptians mimicked the plague of the frogs through enchantments, which only added to their misery, especially since they could not kill their invaders to get rid of them. If they legitimately wanted to prove *Heqet* was superior to Jehovah, why not command the frogs back into the water by her power?

Secondly, when Moses inquired of Pharaoh about his preference for when to end the plague he responded, "tomorrow." Logically speaking, if you are suffering with some ill, and you have an opportunity to remove that affliction at any time, what sense does it make to wait another day? It has been my observation that those who suffer for their rebellion against God rarely act rationally, but rather go to great lengths to justify ludicrous behavior. The "father of lies" controls their minds, and he wants to inflict only pain and destruction on his prey. Moses honored Pharaoh's request to delay the removal of the frogs and, in doing so, made the miracle more impressive than at first.

Thirdly, Pharaoh lied. As soon as God killed all the Egyptian froggy-gods to end the plague, Pharaoh recanted on the release of the Hebrews. The frogs did die the next day and were piled in heaps and, as in the first plague, the stench of rotting flesh engulfed Egypt. No only did Pharaoh behave deceitfully, but the text states that *"he hardened his heart, and did not heed them."*

Though at times God hardened Pharaoh's heart to accomplish a particular purpose in time in accordance with His will, Pharaoh's heart was not entirely hardened by God for he hardened it himself afterwards. Pharaoh maintained free choice in his overall decision-making. James states, *"Let no one say when he is tempted, 'I am tempted by God;' for God cannot be tempted by evil, nor does He Himself tempt anyone. But each one is tempted when he is drawn away by his own desires and enticed"* (Jas. 1:13-14). James confirms that it would have been impossible for God to cause Pharaoh to lie, for a holy God does not tempt anyone to sin; such behavior would be an affront to His righteous character.

Pharaoh had free choice in whom he would choose to revere. God did not force Pharaoh to worship Egyptian gods, for a Holy God does not tempt humanity with evil or force anyone to do evil. Between Exodus 4 and 14, Pharaoh's heart is mentioned 20 times: on ten occasions it is the king's stubbornness at work (Ex. 7:13 {twice}, 13, 22, 8:11, 15, 28, 9:7, 34, 35, 13:5) and ten times it is God who hardens his heart to accomplish His will (Ex. 4:21, 7:3, 9:12, 10:1, 10, 27, 11:10, 14:4, 8, 17).

God would have been perfectly just to destroy a pagan like Pharaoh, but instead He designed ten specific plagues to prove to Pharaoh that He was superior to specific Egyptian gods. Pharaoh rejected this revelation and hardened his own heart against the Lord – he prepared himself to be a vessel of wrath fit for destruction (Rom. 9:17-22). God brought glory to His name by honoring Pharaoh's decision, one that God already foreknew. This example shows how human responsibility and sovereign design ensure that God will receive all the glory in every situation.

> Sovereign Ruler of the skies, ever gracious, ever wise;
> All my times are in Thy hand, all events at thy command.
> Plagues and deaths around me fly; till He bids I cannot die;
> Not a single shaft can hit, till the God of love sees fit.
>
> — Ryland

# Life from Dust
## Exodus 8:16-19

Because of Pharaoh's previous deceit, he was not extended an ultimatum before the advent of the third plague. The plagues would come in cycles of threes and the third in each cycle would be unannounced (i.e. the third, the sixth, and the ninth plagues). As in the first two plagues, Moses instructed Aaron to lift the rod of God to invoke judgment. He was told to smite the ground with the rod, which he did, and the inanimate matter that they had been standing upon became a living plague of *ken (kinnim)*. The Hebrew word *ken* is only found in Exodus 8 and once in Psalm 105, so the meaning of the word, which is "fasten," and the context of the passage are the best means for determining what type of insect or parasite is referred to. Reasonable conclusions are: gnats (The Darby Translation), lice (KJV), or mosquitoes (Septuagint).

If gnats or mosquitoes are in view, the irritation of insects flying into one's open eyes and mouth and crawling into one's ears or upon one's skin throughout the day would be unnerving. Female mosquitoes would be relentlessly drilling into the skin of both man and beast to obtain a blood supply. If the plague was lice, Edward Dennett notes:

> "Both ancient and modern historians testify to the scrupulous cleanliness of the Egyptians. Herodotus (2:37) says that so scrupulous were the priests on this point that they used to shave the hair of their heads and bodies every third day, for fear of harboring vermin [lice] while occupied in their sacred duties. In any case, this stroke would therefore humble their pride and stain their glory, rendering *themselves* objects of dislike and disgust."[1]

The plagues of the frogs, the flies, and the locust were concluded by Moses' authority, but there is no mention of this plague being terminated. It is quite possible that the gnats remained to further pester and frustrate the Egyptians throughout the remaining plagues. As before, Pharaoh's magicians attempted to reproduce the miracle in order to show that the God of the Hebrews had nothing over Egyptian gods. They had mimicked the sign of the rod turning into a serpent, had turned water into blood, and had summoned the frogs from their aquatic dwelling places, but they could not repeat this miracle. What was their limitation?

We read in Genesis 1:1, *"In the beginning God created the heavens and the earth."* The Hebrew word *bara* is translated *created* in this verse. Interestingly, this word is always used in connection with God's creative handiwork; it does not speak of human productivity. Only God can call into existence that which had no previous existence; only the Creator can create life. We understand from Genesis 2:7 how the first man was created: *"And the Lord God formed man of the dust of the ground, and breathed into his nostrils the breath of life; and man became a living being."* When God breathes upon something or someone, that which is breathed upon receives life, either physical (Gen. 2:7) or spiritual (John 20:22).

But Lucifer (Satan) is also a created being (Ezek. 28:12-15), which means there must be a superior Being to explain his existence. This explains Satan's limitation in mimicking the plague of the gnats which God brought upon Egypt through Moses. God caused gnats to materialize from the dust of the earth – life instantaneously came from what was not living. Satan cannot create life, for he is a created being.

Speaking of the Lord Jesus Christ, John writes:

> *In the beginning was the Word, and the Word was with God, and the Word was God. He was in the beginning with God. All things were made through Him, and without Him nothing was made that was made. In Him was life, and the life was the light of men* (John 1:1-4).

Relating the same truth concerning the Lord Jesus, Paul states:

> *For by Him all things were created that are in heaven and that are on earth, visible and invisible, whether thrones or dominions or principalities or powers. All things were created through Him and for Him. And He is before all things, and in Him all things consist. And He is the head of the body, the church, who is the beginning, the firstborn from the dead, that in all things He may have the preeminence* (Col. 1:16-18).

Scripture confirms that all things were created by the Lord Jesus in accordance to the will of His Father and through the power of the Holy Spirit. Consequently, the essence of all life is in God; apart from God there is no life. Thus, Pharaoh's baffled magicians rightly spoke, *"This is the finger of God."* They admitted to Pharaoh that a greater power than theirs was at work in Egypt. Satan can counterfeit the doings of God, but when it comes to creating life, he has no capacity for it – a fact the magicians voiced to Pharaoh.

But Pharaoh did not listen to his sorcerers, nor to Moses, nor to Aaron, for his heart was hardened against the Lord. Once a skeptic asked a gospel preacher, "Can God create a rock which is too heavy for Him to lift?" The preacher quickly responded, "Yes, if you harden your heart against God, He cannot lift you into heaven." The rebel heart will never experience the loving-kindnesses and tender-mercies of the Lord, beyond the fact that God permits it to beat one more time and, by abundant grace, one more day. *"The Lord is not slack concerning His promise, as some count slackness, but is longsuffering toward us, not willing that any should perish but that all should come to repentance"* (2 Pet. 3:9).

Immortal, invisible, God only wise,
In light inaccessible hid from our eyes,
Most blessed, most glorious, the Ancient of days,
Almighty, victorious, Thy great name we praise.
To all, life Thou givest to both great and small;
In all life Thou livest, the true life of all;
We blossom and flourish as leaves on the tree,
And wither and perish but naught changeth Thee.

— Walter Chalmers Smith

# Swarms of Flies
## Exodus 8:20-32

The fourth plague was to be initiated in the same manner as the first; Moses was to meet Pharaoh early in the morning when he came out to the Nile. What is the message Moses was to convey to Pharaoh? The same one he had already heard before, *"Let my people go, that they may serve Me."*

The second plague was preceded by an ultimatum and Pharaoh would be issued another prior to the fourth plague:

> *If you will not let My people go, behold, I will send swarms of flies on you and your servants, on your people and into your houses. The houses of the Egyptians shall be full of swarms of flies, and also the ground on which they stand. And in that day I will set apart the land of Goshen, in which My people dwell, that no swarms of flies shall be there, in order that you may know that I am the Lord in the midst of the land. I will make a difference between My people and your people. Tomorrow this sign shall be* (Ex. 8:21-23).

The Hebrew word *arob* is translated "swarm;" the translators supplied the phrase "of flies" seven times in this passage. Besides Exodus 8, *arob* is only found in Psalm 78:45 and 105:31, where it is also translated "swarms of flies." Obviously Pharaoh did not heed the warning and grievous swarms of flies (or perhaps a variety of different types of insects) invaded Egypt, but did not come to Goshen where the Hebrews lived. The word "grievous" would indicate that these were probably biting flies. Whereas the gnats would be an irritating nuisance in your face, the biting flies would inflict pain. There were so many flies that the Egyptians could not swat them fast enough to escape their biting assault.

The most unique aspect of the fourth plague is that the flies did not invade Goshen, the home of the Hebrews; the flies inflicted pain only upon the Egyptians. The Israelites had suffered hardship along with the Egyptians during the first three plagues, perhaps as divine chastening for rejecting Moses, their deliverer, after his first encounter with Pharaoh (Ex. 5:21). However, to further authenticate the supernatural origin of the Egyptian plagues, Jehovah maintained a strict distinction between the Egyptians and Israelites in all future judgments. This ethnic disparity would not only show the extent of Jehovah's power, but it would also provide a sign to the Egyptians of His personal identification with His covenant people and that He saw a difference between them and the Hebrews. Though God's people were suffering under Egyptian hardship they would be protected from further suffering; God's wrath would be poured out only on the Egyptians.

As in Pharaoh's day, there are only two groups of people in the world today: saints and ain'ts. Saints are those individuals who, by faith, have trusted God's revealed truth and received a standing of righteousness; ain'ts have not been justified through faith. The distinction during the plague would be a source of comfort for the Israelites. God knows who are His and marks a difference between His children and children of the devil who are appointed to wrath (Eph. 2:2-3). God continues to mark the same difference today; the children of the devil are destined to wrath, but the Church is not:

> *Much more then, having now been justified by His blood, we shall be saved from wrath through Him* (Rom. 5:9).

> *And to wait for His Son from heaven, whom He raised from the dead, even Jesus who delivers us from the wrath to come* (1 Thess. 1:10).

> *For God did not appoint us to wrath, but to obtain salvation through our Lord Jesus Christ* (1 Thess. 5:9).

There is a time of great trouble coming, called the Tribulation, which will affect the entire world (Matt. 24:21). But as John acknowledges to the believers in the Church at Philadelphia, the Church will be brought home prior to its initiation: *"Because you have kept My command to persevere, I also will keep you from the hour of trial which shall come upon the whole world, to test those who dwell on the earth"* (Rev. 3:10). The Greek preposition *ek* is rightly translated "keep – from" in this verse; if the Lord were to preserve the Church *through* the Tribulation the Greek preposition *dia* would be required. Although the Church will be taken to heaven before the Tribulation Period, there is no promise of God to preserve Gentiles who turn to Christ after that event, in fact many of those new believers will be slaughtered during the Tribulation Period (Rev. 7:9-14, 13:5). Only a remnant from the nation of Israel is promised safety from Antichrist during this time (Rev. 12:6-17).

The plague was announced a day in advance and was initiated as Moses and Aaron decreed. Pharaoh summoned Moses and Aaron in order to present a counter-offer to their demands – a compromise, if you will: *"Go, sacrifice to your God in the land"* (Ex. 8:25). When cornered by God, the rebel will offer a compromise to save face. Pharaoh was willing to allow the Hebrews to go and sacrifice, but within the borders of Egypt.

Paul states that bitterness (an unforgiving spirit) is a device that Satan uses to get an advantage over God's people. This ought not to be, *"for we are not ignorant of his devices"* (2 Cor. 2:11). Scripture records the various methods Satan employs to blind (2 Cor. 4:4), beguile (2 Cor. 11:3), and buffet (2 Cor. 12:7) humanity; therefore, we should not be ignorant of his devices, but rather, be wise to his ways. In the "no straw for bricks" scheme Pharaoh sought to keep the Hebrews so busy that they would have no time to think about their God. On this occasion, Pharaoh sought to keep them in the land. Pharaoh would later use three more devices in an attempt to ensnare the Hebrews.

Pharaoh agreed to allow the Hebrews to worship their God, but only if they remained in Egypt. Why did Moses decline the offer? There were several problems with this proposition. Firstly, it was not what God had commanded. It is not the dictates of a religious system or a secular movement which regulates the believer's worship and service, but the authority of God's Word. Moses would not compromise God's command on this matter and neither should the Church – the Bible is the Church's worship manual and the Holy Spirit its Leader.

Secondly, sacrificing animals in Egypt would create a problem for the Hebrews. The Egyptians thought many animals represented deities. For example, the Egyptians worshipped *Apis* – the sacred bull – as one of their premiere deities. If the Hebrews started offering bullocks as burnt sacrifices to Jehovah there would be a national riot, resulting in harm to the unarmed Hebrews.

Thirdly, and most importantly, if they remained in Egypt, they would have to sacrifice to Jehovah the very objects of abomination, the animals which the Egyptians worshipped as gods. Worship influenced by paganism would be an affront to the God of the Hebrews. Consequently, Pharaoh's attempt to hoodwink the Jews to worship their God in Egypt failed.

Satan uses this same tactic today to convince the saved that it is acceptable to worship God in a doctrinally corrupt church. As foretold in Scripture, in the latter days of the Church Age Satan will reside comfortably in various branches of Christendom (Matt. 13:32). Paul states that there will be great apostasy in the professing Church just prior to the appearing of the Antichrist (2 Thess. 2:3-4).

But just as a departure from truth characterizes the false church, Spirit-led worship founded upon revealed truth is a mark of the true Church (John 4:23-24). The Holy Spirit guides believers into truth (John 16:13-14). Satan exercises his delegated authority to promote the corruption of truth. The Lord Jesus plainly acknowledged this fact while speaking to the Pharisees, who were the leaders of religious corruption in Christ's day:

> *You are of your father the devil, and the desires of your father you want to do. He was a murderer from the beginning, and does not stand in the truth, because there is no truth in him. When he speaks a lie, he speaks from his own resources, for he is a liar and the father of it* (John 8:44).

It is the pagan, under Satan's control, who induces worship. However, it is the Holy Spirit, not any human, who is to be the "Worship Leader" in the local assembly; His role is to guide believers into a deeper understanding of truth concerning the Lord Jesus and the overall greatness and goodness of God. Only through Spirit-led worship, which will be completely founded in divine truth, can the believer offer any acceptable sacrifice of praise unto God. Egypt was under the curse of God; the children of Israel had to come out from that which was corrupt and under God's judgment to offer acceptable worship to Him. Christ, speaking to His disciples, acknowledged that the same truth would apply to the Church: *"If you were of the world, the world would love its own. Yet because you are not of the world, but I chose you out of the world, therefore the world hates you"* (John 15:19-20). The believer has been called out of Egypt, and the Lord hates to see what is of Egypt in the believer's life (Jas. 4:4).

The second tactic Pharaoh used to control the Hebrews is mentioned in verse 28: *"I will let you go, that you may sacrifice to the Lord your God in the wilderness; only you shall not go very far away."* When Satan cannot control the Lord's people from his stronghold in the world, he will settle for a "border position." Instead of blatant corruption, he is content to negatively influence believers and to dilute the certainty of truth in their minds. But the aftermath is still the same from God's perspective; following that which is not wholly true cannot please the Lord: *"For the wrath of God is revealed from heaven against all ungodliness and unrighteousness of men, who suppress the truth in unrighteousness"* (Rom. 1:18). Paul goes on to explain that all those who exchange God's revealed truth for a lie will be judged by God (Rom. 1:25).

Pharaoh would have allowed the Hebrews to leave Egypt to worship, but he wanted them close enough that he could still influence their relationship with Jehovah. He knew that if the people did "not go very far" it was not much different than for them to remain in Egypt. A week or two in a bland and arid wilderness and the fleshpots, garlic, leaks, and onions of Egypt would be calling the Hebrews back to Egypt. This satanic device highlights the critical need for a healthy separation from the world in the believer's life. The reason for resigning the world is to have Christ and Him alone – no border position is permissible. Spiritually speaking, God's people are not only to be out of Egypt, but as far as possible from its interfering tentacles. Arthur Pink says this is the calling of all believers:

> "Not very far away" is incompatible with the first law of the Christian life. ... The Son of God left heaven for earth that He might take a people from earth to heaven – bring them there first in spirit and heart, later in person. *"Set your affection upon things above"* (Col. 3:1) is God's call to His children. *"Holy* (separated) *brethren, partakers of the heavenly calling"* (Heb. 3:1) is one of our many titles, and heaven

> is "very far way" from the world! Separation from the world in our interests, our affections, our ways, is the first law of the Christian life. *"Love not the world, neither the things which are in the world. If any man love the world the love of the Father is not in him"* (1 Jn. 2:15).[1]

At Calvary, Christ died and passed out of this world. Three days later His body was raised from the grave. The Lord Jesus was then highly exalted by His Father to the right hand of majesty on high (Heb. 1:3). This is why God demanded that the Jews leave Egypt to worship Him. The world crucified His Son, and thus Christ is no longer in the world – to enjoy spiritual life with Him we must come along to where He is by faith. Believers are privileged to sit at His table and to receive from Him and commune with Him there (1 Cor. 10:16-21). How offensive it must be to the Lord Jesus to desert Him to party in the world with demons. Paul warns, *"You cannot drink the cup of the Lord and the cup of demons; you cannot partake of the Lord's table and of the table of demons. Or do we provoke the Lord to jealousy? Are we stronger than He?"* (1 Cor. 10:21-22). The Jews had been invited to Jehovah's table in the wilderness; it was a private affair, and no solicitations from Egypt would be allowed.

After agreeing to allow the Hebrews to venture into the wilderness to worship I AM, Pharaoh requested that Moses intercede with the Lord on his behalf. Before doing so, Moses warned Pharaoh about reneging on the agreement to let the Hebrews go. The Lord honored Moses' request and the flies were completely destroyed in Egypt; not one remained (v. 31). But Pharaoh again hardened his own heart and was determined not to let the Hebrews go.

> Far from my thoughts, vain world begone; let my worship hours alone;
> Fain would my eyes my Saviour see; I wait a visit Lord from thee.
> Haste, then but with a smiling face, and spread the table of thy grace;
>
> Bring down a taste of truth divine, and cheer my heart with sacred wine.
> Blessed Jesus! What delicious fare! How sweet Thy entertainments are!
> Never did angels taste above, redeeming grace and dying love.
>
> — Isaac Watts

# Livestock Smitten

## Exodus 9:1-7

Moses had forewarned Pharaoh against deceit, but despite the warning Pharaoh again reneged on his commitment to release the Hebrews after Moses had removed the flies from Egypt. Furthermore, Pharaoh hardened his heart against God's revealed truth. As Paul states in Romans 1:18, this always results in God's wrath: *"For the wrath of God is revealed from heaven against all ungodliness and unrighteousness of men, who suppress the truth in unrighteousness."* While the gods of Egypt may have condoned rash speech and a lying tongue, Pharaoh would learn that Jehovah did not.

God's punitive response to Pharaoh's lying tongue provides us with a reminder of how much God disdains lying; believers should convey to others only that which they believe to be true. Truth is that which perfectly conforms to reality. Unfortunately, most of what we perceive to be true by our senses and by our reason is only partially true; what is revealed in Scripture is wholly true and, thus, is our trustworthy foundation for speech. God desires His children to be truth-tellers! The Lord Jesus, who was full of both grace and truth (John 1:14), instructed His disciples, *"But let your 'Yes' be 'Yes,' and your 'No,' 'No.' For whatever is more than these is from the evil one"* (Matt. 5:37).

The Christian should not try to distort, change, or flavor the truth. That is what Satan, the father of lies, does because there is no truth in him (John 8:44). God desires us to speak only that which is true, can be expounded in love, and is determined to be necessary for the edification of others (Eph. 4:15). *"Let no corrupt word proceed out of your mouth, but what is good for necessary edification, that it may impart grace to the hearer"* (Eph. 4:29). On the whole, we talk way too much: *"In the multitude of words sin is not lacking, but he who restrains his lips is wise"* (Prov. 10:19). Not only does deceitful and ungracious speech have divine accountability, but the Lord Jesus also warned, *"But I say unto you, that every idle word that men shall speak, they shall give account thereof in the day of judgment"* (Matt. 12:36). Idle words are not evil in themselves; they just have no value to further the cause of Christ. May our communication be valuable to God and to others and may the rest not pass our lips.

Prior to the onset of the fifth plague, Moses presented Pharaoh with another divine ultimatum: he was to release God's people that they might serve Him or He would smite the livestock of Egypt. To demonstrate Jehovah's full control of disease, and time, the plague would affect all of Egypt except Goshen and would occur on the following day. The plague happened the next day exactly as announced. Though the herds of the Egyptians died, the livestock of the children of Israel was completely spared from the deadly epidemic (v. 6).

The plague proved Jehovah's rulership over the creatures He had made, both the visible animals and the microscopic organisms. Disease attacked only when and where He had commanded. The annihilation of Egypt's cattle, sheep, and goats would remove meat, milk, butter, wool, etc. from the market place. Without their horses, oxen, and donkeys, the Egyptian's agricultural work, commerce, and the transportation of available food across land would no longer be possible. But even a greater shock to the Egyptians was the fact that Jehovah had, in one stroke, sacrificed many of their gods before their eyes. For His own honor Jehovah had done what would have been sacrilege and dangerous for the Israelites to do – sacrificing to God what was an abomination to Him in Egypt.

Previous plagues had resulted in Egyptian discomfort and anxiety, but the fifth plague devastated their economy. Food would become scarce and the Nile would become the main method of transporting goods. Besides the staggering economic disaster and the crippling of Egyptian commerce, the nauseating stench of thousands, if not millions, of animals would linger over Egypt for weeks. These rotting carcasses would create even more health problems for the Egyptians.

Pharaoh sent out officials to verify that the plague had not harmed the livestock of the Israelites. How did Pharaoh respond after learning that every detail of the fifth plague had occurred as announced by Moses? *"The heart of Pharaoh was hardened, and he did not let the people go"* (Ex. 9:7). Suffering will either harden or soften the human heart towards God's working in our life – the same sun that melts the wax also hardens the clay. Suffering will either cause a believer to draw closer to the Lord or to flee His presence. The determining factor is the quality of his or her faith. Overwhelming circumstances may cause a child of God to lose hope and to lapse in his or her faith – it takes strong faith to trust the very hand that originates the waves and billows of adversity that crash upon our heads. Sometimes these storms of life are God's chastisement for sin (i.e. discipline to cause behavior correction), but at other times, our edification is the focus.

In the case of Job, for example, twice Satan told God that Job would curse God if he were allowed to assault him (Job. 1:11; 2:5). As Satan thoroughly enjoys dishonoring God's name, he did everything he could to cause Job to do just that. But even after the loss of all his wealth, his children, and his health, Job would not blaspheme God. Notice that it was God who began the conversation with Satan concerning His servant Job. In other words, God nominated Job for this perfecting storm! The next nominee could be you or me. The fact is that God loves us too much to permit us to remain the way we are. He knows that as we grow in faith we will also increase in holiness and fruitfulness. God obtained glory out of Job's situation, and at the same time further refined His servant whom Scripture declares *"was blameless and upright, and one that feared God, and shunned evil"* (Job 1:1).

During arduous circumstances, it is all too easy for the downcast and disheartened soul to think and speak evil of God's doings, but these are school days for the believer. Just as aggressive chiseling, chipping, sanding, and polishing are required to transform a chunk of granite into an attractive sculpture, God is ever laboring to mold and shape our hearts to beat for Him and Him alone. Our God is a God of promises, and we must simply trust Him in challenging times and not question His character – He does have a plan, and it is marvelous:

> *For I know the thoughts that I think toward you, says the Lord, thoughts of peace and not of evil, to give you a future and a hope* (Jer. 29:11).

> *And we know that all things work together for good to them that love God, to them who are the called according to His purpose* (Rom. 8:28).

> *No temptation has overtaken you except such as is common to man; but God is faithful, who will not allow you to be tempted beyond what you are able, but with the temptation will also make the way of escape, that you may be able to bear it* (1 Cor. 10:13).

If there were no God, our present sufferings would be overwhelming, for we would be a people without hope. But knowing that God is in all our distresses, and that He is personally working out each one for our good and His glory, affords joy in tribulations! In trials, let us maintain the uplook and not be guilty of looking down on God and hardening our hearts against Him. Pharaoh's heart had become harder than granite and as the battle of the wills raged on in Egypt, he only reinforced himself against the will of God.

> To him that overcomes God gives a crown,
> Through faith we shall conquer, though often cast down;
> He, who is our Saviour, our strength will renew,
> Look ever to the Lord Jesus, He will carry you through.
>
> — Horatio R. Palmer

# Boils and Ulcers
## Exodus 9:8-12

The sixth plague, like the third, was not announced, though Moses' actions in the sight of Pharaoh would have alerted the Egyptians to some forthcoming event. Moses and Aaron were instructed: *"And the Lord said unto Moses and unto Aaron, Take to you handfuls of ashes of **the furnace**, and let Moses sprinkle it toward the heaven in the sight of Pharaoh. And it shall become small dust in all the land of Egypt, and shall be a boil breaking forth with blains upon man, and upon beast, throughout all the land of Egypt"* (vv. 8-9; KJV). Was there a particular furnace that God had in mind? Arthur W. Pink provides this observation:

> The definite article implies that some particular "furnace" is meant, and that Pharaoh was near it, suggests it was no mere heating apparatus. The Companion Bible says of this furnace: "i.e., one of the altars on which human sacrifices were sometimes offered to propitiate their god Typhon (the evil Principle). These were doubtless being offered to avert the plagues, and Moses using the ashes in the same way produced another plague instead of averting it."[1]

Moses' actions would demonstrate the worthlessness of man's religious rituals and the failure of the Egyptian gods to thwart Jehovah's power. The Egyptians and their beasts that were not destroyed in the previous plague broke out with oozing bleeding ulcers. So grievous were the boils that Pharaoh's magicians could not enter Pharaoh's court to confront Moses and Aaron; perhaps these sorcerers received a double portion of the judgment. Though Pharaoh suffered along with them, his heart remained hardened such that he would not obey the Lord's command to let His people go.

The Egyptians engaged in pagan rituals and religious traditions to confront God's revealed truth and power – the same practice continues today. Men love to use religious symbols, figures, and traditions to improve their pious experience, but everything that is not biblically instituted will tend, with time, to detract from the work and person of Jesus Christ. There are only three symbolic practices commanded of the Church: the head covering to show visible agreement with God's creation order (1 Cor. 11:2-16); the Lord's Supper in which the bread and wine are to remind believers of the broken body and shed blood of Christ at Calvary (1 Cor. 11:17-33); and water baptism, which provides public identification with Christ (Matt. 28:19-20) and illustrates the identification truths of a believer dying with Christ and being made alive with Him (Rom. 6:3-6). There were no other symbols or metaphoric practices extended to the Church by Scripture, except perhaps in James 5, where church elders were to anoint a believer with oil to symbolize the healing that God provides, especially to those who had been suffering because of personal sin, but now were taking sides with God against themselves on the matter.

So how did the professing church ever incorporate crosses, denominational symbols, pictures of dead saints, and religious flags into its activities and gatherings? Satan, the great mimicker of God, often takes expression and symbols from the Bible and ascribes new meanings to them. For example: the rainbow, a symbol of God's promise to Noah, has been used to signify the New Age teaching of man's transition into the Aquarian age (his journey to deity), and the term "born again" is used by many to describe reincarnation or spiritual rededication. The devil will attempt to distort the true scriptural meaning of biblical symbols or to construct new symbols to distract Christians from scriptural teaching. The cross may be a good reminder of Christ, but how often the cross itself is sung about and worshipped. The cross was an instrument of shame and suffering; the Lord who hung upon it is to be the focus of our attention.

There is a proclivity of man to create visual stimuli to accentuate his religious experience. Many of the religious symbols that the Church has manufactured are simply Old Testament *figures* of what now is reality in Christ. Judaism was full of future-related imagery which appealed to the senses, whereas Christianity is spiritual and thus appreciated only by faith, not our natural senses. Christ has come and, therefore, has replaced all the types and shadows which were the prelude of the spiritual realities and good things to come (Heb. 8:13). So let us be careful not to allow refurbished Judaism or humanistic traditions to intrude into the gatherings of the Church.

The local assembly gathers in the name of the Lord Jesus Christ for teaching, for fellowship, for the Lord's Supper (breaking of the bread), and for prayer (Acts 2:42). The assembly is under Christ's authority, meets in His name, and gathers in His presence (Matt. 18:20) – He is Head of the Church and Lord of all its meetings. Thus, the New Testament assembly is recognized not so much by what you can see, but by what you cannot see – Christ. Keeping to Scriptural terminology, holding to infallible truths, and not misapplying terms will ensure that we do not displace Christ with counterfeit religious façades. The believer's allegiance is to Christ Himself; all that is humanly contrived for the sake of experience will dilute our commitment to Him in time.

> Occupied with Thee, Lord Jesus, in Thy grace;
> All Thy ways and thoughts about me only trace,
> Deeper stories of the glories, of Thy grace, of Thy grace.
> Taken up with Thee, Lord Jesus, I would be;
> Finding joy and satisfaction all in Thee,
> Thou the nearest and the dearest, unto me, unto me.
>
> — C. A. Wellesley

# Hail Fire
## Exodus 9:13-26

Moses had been instructed to meet Pharaoh early in the morning before initiating the first and fourth plagues; he was to do the same with the seventh. This would be a sign to Pharaoh that the three-plague pattern previously established was about to begin again.

The Lord explained to Moses the motive for and the goal of plaguing Egypt in verses 14-16. Firstly, that the Egyptians might know that there was none like Jehovah in all the earth. Secondly, the only reason God had exalted Pharaoh to be ruler of the world was to demonstrate His awesome power. Thirdly, that through the fall of Egypt all the earth would be furnished with a testimony of His great name (Rom. 9:17).

God's message to Pharaoh, *"Let My people go"* had remained unchanged. God informed Moses that as long as Pharaoh continued to exalt himself against Him, He would continue to plague Egypt. Moses went before Pharaoh and announced the forthcoming seventh plague of grievous hail mingled with fire. Moses had not used his rod to initiate the last three plagues, but after departing from Pharaoh's presence, Moses stretched forth his rod to heaven to execute the seventh plague. Though the plague of hail would be devastating, the grace of God to the Egyptians is demonstrated on three points: the plague was foretold, there was a way to escape its consequences, and there was time enough to do just that (vv. 18-20).

Though the plague would engulf all of Egypt, excluding Goshen, individual Egyptians were provided an opportunity to escape its consequences if they sheltered themselves, their servants, and their remaining animals. Those who heeded the warning lived, those who did not died in *hail fire*.

Several types of death are spoken of in Scripture, but there are three deaths, or literal "separations," that are most significant to all mankind. We are all born *spiritually dead*; we are spiritually separated from God.

Then, when *physical death* occurs, our soul separates from our body. If physical death occurs while a person is still spiritually dead, *eternal death* (judgment in hell) is assured. Hebrews 9:27 proclaims, *"It is appointed unto men once to die, but after this the judgment."* The only exception to the above is that, perhaps, God will demonstrate His grace by applying the blood of Christ to those wee souls who died in the womb or early in life, before they understood the moral law within them and God's solution to their sin problem. But as adults and older children, the unsaved are just one heartbeat, one breath away from sealing an eternal destiny of woe.

God does not enjoy punishing rebels, but His character demands it. He longs for all men to repent and to turn to Him by faith, as He has said, *"I have no pleasure in the death of the wicked, but that the wicked turn from his way and live"* (Ezek. 33:11). Everlasting *hell fire* was not originally prepared for mankind but rather for Satan and other rebellious angels (Matt. 25:41). However, God will use this place of torment to also punish those who would rebel against His only solution for sin – the substitutionary death of His Son. The Egyptians were offered only one means of escaping death the next day.

Peter, speaking of Jesus Christ said, *"Nor is there salvation in any other, for there is no other name under heaven given among men by which we must be saved"* (Acts 4:12). To alleviate any confusion about what the true gospel message actually is, the Lord Jesus Christ personally conveyed it to Paul: *"For I delivered to you first of all that which I also received: that Christ died for our sins according to the Scriptures, and that He was buried, and that He rose again the third day according to the Scriptures"* (1 Cor 15:3-4). So if by faith, one believes and receives Christ for the forgiveness of his or her sins, he or she is then born again (speaking of spiritual birth; see John 3:3; 1 Pet. 1:23). Believing any other gospel than this brings eternal damnation (Gal. 1:6-9).

The prophet Isaiah describes humanity as sheep which go their own way and become lost: *"All we like sheep have gone astray; we have turned, every one, to his own way"* (Isa. 53:6). Praise be to God that He comes seeking and calling to bring us back to Himself! What should be our response? Isaiah says, *"Seek the Lord while He may be found, call upon Him while He is near* (Isa. 55:6). But, to seek the Lord one must repent (turn from going his or her own way and agree with God about the matter of sin). Then, a seeking Saviour and a seeking sinner will find each other. Fortunately for us, God is seeking us out through the finished work of Christ and by the wooing ministry of the Holy Spirit. God's offer for salvation is to whomsoever will respond (Matt. 11:28-30, 22:17). As God demonstrated in the seventh plague on Egypt, He is *"not willing that any should perish but that all should come to repentance"* (2 Pet. 3:9).

Evidently, many of the Egyptians did heed the warning and saved their servants and their newly imported livestock alive. This conclusion is based on the fact that many horse-drawn chariots were involved in Pharaoh's last rebellion against God, as recorded in Exodus 14. The plague of hail arrived just as Moses had stated it would. The early crops of barley and wax were destroyed throughout Egypt, except for Goshen – there was no hail fire there.

Pharaoh was prompted by the plague's destructive outcome to offer a profession of faith, of a sort: *"I have sinned this time. The Lord is righteous, and my people and I are wicked. Entreat the Lord, that there may be no more mighty thundering and hail, for it is enough. I will let you go, and you shall stay no longer"* (Ex. 9:27-28). Everything that Pharaoh said about the spiritual condition of himself, his people, and God Himself was true, but truth alone cannot save. There will be many on the Day of Judgment who will learn that *knowing* about the Lord and *doing* works in His name are not the same as *trusting* Him for salvation (Matt. 7:7:21-23). Those who know Christ as Saviour do the will of the Father in works of righteousness (Matt. 7:21), while those who don't, brag about what they have done for Christ (Matt. 7:22).

Though the holiness of God is referred to several times in the book of Exodus, only once is God declared to be righteous (v. 27), and that pronouncement is offered by Pharaoh himself. The word "righteous" has the meaning "of purity, justness or correctness." "Righteous" is used to convey three separate ideas in Scripture. Firstly, it speaks of God's faultless character; He is without wrong or dishonor. Secondly, it speaks of God's method for justifying sinners. Lastly, it relates to the standing of those who believe on His Son – they become positionally justified in Christ forever. Even in his poor spiritual state, Pharaoh professed that God had a righteous character and was just in His dealings with him.

Did Pharaoh truly mean what he said? No. As soon as Moses went out of the city and spread his hands to end the plague, Pharaoh disavowed everything: *"When Pharaoh saw that the rain, the hail, and the thunder had ceased, he sinned yet more; and he hardened his heart, he and his servants. So the heart of Pharaoh was hard; neither would he let the children of Israel go"* (Ex. 9:34-35). God was not fooled by Pharaoh's false profession; He had previously informed Moses that Pharaoh would recant (v. 35) and Moses had also foretold this to Pharaoh (v. 30).

Though we may be fooled by a false profession or some outward show of spirituality, God peers into the depths of every human heart (1 Sam. 16:7) – He is never conned by a lying tongue. The Lord Jesus explained to His disciples that only those who continue to bear good fruit (to do righteous acts) can be identified as believers: *"Either make the tree good and its fruit good, or else make the tree bad and its fruit bad; for a tree is known by its fruit"* (Matt. 12:33-34). John echoes this truth, saying, *"Little children, let no one deceive you. He who practices righteousness is righteous, just as He is righteous"* (1 Jn. 3:7). James puts the matter this way, *"Faith by itself, if it does not have works, is dead"* (Jas. 2:17).

Pharaoh demonstrated what Christ would later teach, *"For out of the abundance of the heart the mouth speaks"* (Matt. 12:34-35). Or, poetically put, "The tongue is the tail of the heart that wags out of the mouth." Pharaoh's heart was dead, hardened towards God, and his tongue proved it.

> Come to the Saviour now! He gently calls thee;
> In true repentance bow, before Him bend the knee.
> He waits to bestow salvation, peace, and love,
> True joy on earth below, a home in heaven above.
>
> — John M. Wigner

# The Plague of Locusts
## Exodus 10:1-20

Whatever vegetation the hail did not destroy, the eighth judgment, the plague of locusts would consume (v. 5). As instructed by the Lord, Moses and Aaron appeared before Pharaoh, to demand that he humble himself before Jehovah by releasing the people and to warn him that Egypt would be invaded by locusts on the following day if he refused. The early crops of barley and flax had been destroyed by the hail, but the wheat and spelt remained for the locust to devour.

Moses and Aaron departed from Pharaoh's presence after issuing him the ultimatum. Pharaoh's servants pleaded with Pharaoh to let the Hebrews go since Egypt lay in ruins (v. 7). Pharaoh summoned Moses and Aaron to present his own terms for their departure – they could go, but their children (vv. 9, 24) must stay behind. Pharaoh seemed to know that if all the slaves received liberty to worship Jehovah in the wilderness they would not return to Egypt. He was right; Moses had never mentioned the possibility of returning to Egypt after worshipping the Lord in the wilderness.

Pharaoh thought to control the Israelites by holding their children (and likely the mothers of young children too) captive, thereby forcing the men to return to Egypt after their wilderness adventure. Moses already knew the will of God on the matter and immediately rejected Pharaoh's compromise. The Hebrews had no intention of seeking one thing for themselves, namely the promised land, and something different for their children; the entire Jewish nation would depart from Egypt with all their goods and livestock. Receiving no assurance that the Jews would return to Egypt, Pharaoh refused to free the Israelites, and Moses and Aaron were driven out of Pharaoh's presence.

Given the desperate nature of the situation, a compromise by Moses may have led to the slaughter of the Hebrew women and children after the men had departed. Because Moses did not say anything more or less than what God put in his mouth, God's glory and wisdom would be demonstrated again in Egypt without negative consequences for the Jews.

Pharaoh's proposed compromise demonstrates yet another technique of Satan to conquer God's people. The enemy first sought to keep the Hebrews so busy that they had no time to think about worshipping their God. Secondly, he proposed a compromise that would allow the Jews to worship, but only in Egypt. Thirdly, he would allow the Israelites to have communion with their God, but only in a *border position* so he could still entice and influence them. Overcome, the enemy concedes the older generation and is content to entangle, ensnare, and corrupt the next generation.

This same battle plan is still being used by the enemy today according to Edward Dennett:

> This was surely a cunning wile of Satan — professing willingness to let the men go if they would but leave their little ones behind in Egypt. Thereby he would have falsified the testimony of the Lord's redeemed ones, and retained a most powerful hold upon them through their natural affections. For how could they be done with Egypt as long as their children were there? Satan knew this, and hence the character of this temptation. And how many Christians there are who are entangled in the snare! Professing to be the Lord's, to have left Egypt, they allow their families to remain still behind. … If the children remained in Egypt, the parents could not possibly be said to have left it, inasmuch as their children were part of themselves. The most that could be said in such a case was, that in part they were serving Jehovah, and in part Pharaoh. But Jehovah could have no part with Pharaoh. He should either have all or nothing. This is a weighty principle for Christian parents. … It is our happy privilege to count on God for our children and to *"bring them up in the nurture and admonition of the Lord"* (Eph. 6:4). These admirable and weighty words should be deeply pondered in the presence of God. For nowhere does our testimony so manifestly break down as in our families. Godly parents, whose walk is blameless, are seduced into permitting their children practices which they would not for one moment allow for themselves, and thus to flood their houses with the sights and sounds of Egypt.[1]

Parents have a God-given responsibility to train up their children for the One who gave them, for *"He seeks godly offspring"* (Mal. 2:15). As C. H. Mackintosh explains, lackadaisical parenting produces unruly children:

> God has put into the parent's hand the reins of government and the rod of authority; but if parents through indolence [apathy] suffer the reins to drop from their hands, and if through false tenderness or moral weakness, the rod of authority is not applied, need we marvel if the children grow up in utter lawlessness? How could it be otherwise? Children are, as a rule, very much what we make them. If they are made to be obedient, they will be so; and if they are allowed to have their own way, the result will be accordingly.[2]

As children are permitted to dabble in a God-hating system of thinking, a proportionate lack of appetite for spiritual things will be observed. Just as it would be natural for a toddler to choose eating an ice cream cone instead of a serving of broccoli, it would be the propensity of the flesh to desire the onions, garlic, and leeks of Egypt rather than God's food for the spiritual man – bland manna. Just as the flesh cannot please God, no provision made for the flesh can please Him either, because such things strengthen the flesh and weaken the spiritual man (Rom. 6:11-12). How can Christian parents make an allowance for worldliness in the home and still proclaim they are raising their children for the Lord? C. H. Mackintosh states that such an ideology is delusional:

> But what shall my child say to me if I tell him that I am earnestly seeking Christ and Heaven for him, while at the same time I am educating him for the world? Which will he believe? Which will exert the more powerful practical influence on his heart and life – my words, or my acts? ... To say that I am counting upon God to bring my children to Canaan, and yet all the while educating them for Egypt, is a deadly delusion. My conduct proves my profession to be a lie, and I am not to wonder if, in the righteous dealings of God, I am allowed to be filled with the fruit of my own doings.[3]

Christian parents cannot enjoy communion with God while at the same time allowing their children to be drawn into secular philosophies and to be controlled by the world's pleasures. Satan, with striking subtlety, is carrying away many young people into the darkness of a "teen culture" while those stronger in the faith calmly watch and do nothing. Let us be mindful of Satan's devices before he devours the next generation!

God instructed Moses to stretch his rod out over the land to initiate the plague of the locust. A strong east wind brought hordes of locust into Egypt; so great was their number that the ground was darkened by their presence. The locust devoured all the vegetation in Egypt that the hail had not destroyed. Not only did they eat the green leaves of the plants and trees, but they consumed the fruit on the trees also. This plague demonstrated that Jehovah not only controlled the earth and the beasts upon it, but that He ruled over the atmosphere also. So swift and devastating was this plague that Pharaoh summoned Moses and Aaron in haste in an attempt to end it.

A seemingly remorseful Pharaoh declares, *"I have sinned against the Lord your God and against you. Now therefore, please forgive my sin only this once, and entreat the Lord your God, that He may take away from me this death only"* (Ex. 10:16-18). Moses does not warn Pharaoh about being deceitful, but rather departs from his presence and entreats the Lord on his behalf. The Lord responds to Moses' intercession by driving the locust out of Egypt and into the Red Sea with a strong west wind.

Moses did not warn Pharaoh about repeating his past dishonesty because Pharaoh acknowledged his sin against God and Moses and he asked to be forgiven. Whether or not Pharaoh was serious about his confession is doubtful, for he did not worship Jehovah after this and true repentance results in the adoration of God, the only One who can forgive sins. In any case, God chose to honor Pharaoh's request for mercy and the plague was stayed. God's example of extending forgiveness to those requesting it is a pattern we likewise are to follow (Matt. 18:21-27; Luke 17:3). To offend one another is natural, but to rightly handle our anger when offended is not.

First of all, when offended, believers are not to internalize their anger, which leads to resentment, or externalize it which leads to rage. Neither *clamming up* nor *blowing up* are godly responses to an offense, but rather we are to release offenses immediately: *"And be kind to one another, tenderhearted, forgiving one another, even as God in Christ forgave you"* (Eph. 4:32). If wronged, a believer must immediately release the offense into the Lord's care and wait until a righteous purpose can be engaged. Because anger is a powerful emotion meant to equip us to respond to unusual events, we cannot control our anger very well, and hanging on to it just leads us into sin. By immediately releasing offenses to the Lord, we usher these hurts from the foreground to the background of our thinking until God's timing allows for resolution. This response liberates the mind from being dominated by pain.

To bring closure to the matter, the offended party must decide whether or not to confront the offender. The focus of the confrontation is not personal hurt, as this has been released to the Lord, but rather what is best for the offending party, that is, what will benefit his or her character development. If the offense is trivial and there is no advantage to the offender in addressing the matter, it is best just to forget about it. If the offense is more serious and it is determined that a behavioral bent should be reproved or rebuked, then the offender should be confronted.

If the offending individual repents and confesses his or her sin to you, you must declare forgiveness to him or her, the Lord commands it: *"Take heed to yourselves. If your brother sins against you, rebuke him; and if he repents, forgive him and if he sins against you seven times in a day, and seven times in a day returns to you, saying, 'I repent,' you shall forgive him"* (Luke 17:3-4). This is the example God demonstrated in His interaction with Pharaoh. If the offender does not confess his or her sin, leave the matter open – do not offer him or her forgiveness without confession because this condones sin and is an unbiblical response. Rather, tell the offending party that your fellowship with them will be limited until there is repentance and restoration, and that you long for those events.

After forgiveness is conveyed, the matter should be forgotten from the standpoint that the offense has been resolved: *"Love keeps no record of wrongs"* (1 Cor. 13:5, NIV). With this said, forgiveness is not blind; it remembers the weakness in order to avoid undue injury in the future until trust is gained through continued well-doing by the offending party. Though forgiveness for a specific offense should be granted when asked, the offended party should recall the offense in order to wisely interact with the forgiven offender until he or she has overcome the offensive behavior. This recollection is for the purpose of assisting the offending parties in personal growth, not for reminding them of past failures that have already been forgiven.

We should not permit angry feelings to accumulate, but rather, we must assume responsibility for our behavior. Either let anger go or turn it into godly action. If your anger does not have a present righteous purpose, you must release it. Cain quickly learned that murder was an accessible door in his heart that anger effortlessly opened. Believers cannot afford to be angry people; it is a poor testimony of Christ, and as James says, *"The wrath of man does not produce the righteousness of God"* (Jas. 1:20).

Notice that verse 20 does not say that God hardened Pharaoh's heart so that he was unable to worship the Lord, but rather so that he would not let the Israelites go. Pharaoh had the free choice to bow before Jehovah or the Egyptian gods, but he had no choice in prematurely releasing the Israelites from Egypt. This event would be accomplished in God's way and in His timing. The end result would ensure the most benefit to His people, the greatest testimony of His power to the Egyptians, and the highest honor to His name.

O give us homes where Christ is Lord and Master,
The Bible read, the precious hymns still sung,
Where prayer comes first in peace or in disaster,
And praise is natural speech to every tongue;
Where mountains move before a faith that's vaster,
And Christ sufficient is for old and young.

— Barbara B. Hart

# Darkness in the Land

## Exodus 10:21-29

As with the third and sixth plagues, the ninth was not announced. God told Moses to stretch his hand towards heaven to begin the plague of darkness that could be felt throughout Egypt, but not in Goshen. Although the text does not specifically state the detail, it is assumed that Moses was holding his rod when this action was accomplished (compare with 9:22-23). Three days of "thick darkness" ensued.

The nature of the darkness is unknown. It could not have been an eclipse for that would have affected Goshen also and would have lasted less than an hour. Perhaps, without the vegetation to temper the wind and hold the soil in place, a fierce sandstorm occurred. This would have blotted out the light of the sun and would have held man and beast prisoner wherever they were lodged for its duration. The lack of sunlight for three days meant that Jehovah was stronger than one of Egypt's chief deities – *Re* (or *Ra*), the sun god.

Quoting from Wilkinson's *Ancient Egypt*, Arthur Pink notes, "In Egypt the sun was worshipped under the title of *Ra*: the name came conspicuously forward in the title of the kings, Pharaoh, or rather *Phra*, meaning 'the sun'."[1] The plague served as a prophetic calling-card to Pharaoh – like the sun, he too would be overcome by Jehovah.

Pharaoh again called Moses to him in order to present another compromise: *"Go, serve the Lord; only let your flocks and your herds be kept back. Let your little ones also go with you"* (Ex. 10:24). On their last meeting, Pharaoh had rejected the idea of allowing the Jewish children to depart from Egypt; he had hoped that, by keeping them in Egypt, he could force their parents to return to slavery after they worshipped their God in the wilderness. Moses again held his ground, for the will of God cannot be compromised on any detail: *"You must also give us sacrifices and burnt offerings, that we may sacrifice to the Lord our God. Our livestock also shall go with us; not a hoof shall be left behind. For we must take some of them to serve the Lord our God, and even we do not know with what we must serve the Lord until we arrive there"* (Ex. 10:25-26).

Pharaoh's proposed compromise demonstrates a fifth technique of Satan to conquer God's people. As previously summarized, the enemy sought to keep the Hebrews *busy in the land* so that they would have no time for their God. Secondly, he agreed to permit the Jews to worship Jehovah, but only *in the land*; thus, their sacrifices would be abominable. Thirdly, he would have allowed the Israelites to have communion with their God, but only *near the land* (a border position) so that he could still entice and influence them. Fourthly, the enemy conceded the older generation and was content to keep *part of them in the land*; he would then focus on entangling, ensnaring, and corrupting the next generation. In sheer desperation; Pharaoh offered a final compromise – all the Jews could leave Egypt, but *their flocks and herds must stay in the land.* If Pharaoh could not force the Israelites to sacrifice in Egypt, he would yet have a partial victory if he could send them out of the land with no sacrifices for Jehovah.

No doubt Pharaoh was thinking about replenishing the Egyptian livestock slaughtered by pestilence and hailstones. But beyond that, Satan desired to rob the Hebrews of their resources to worship God. If the animals stayed in Egypt, then there could be no sacrifices to Jehovah and a key provision to sustain the Israelites in the wilderness would be forfeited.

Not knowing in advance which animals would be needed to offer sacrifices to Jehovah, Moses told Pharaoh that all of their livestock must go with them. God's plan for delivering His people from Egypt included equipping them with abundant resources to adequately worship Him in the wilderness; consequently, the Jews would take with them not only their own livestock, but also the spoils of Egypt as they departed.

God likewise equips believers today with the resources to worship Him. First of all, the Christian is indwelt by the Holy Spirit (1 Cor. 6:19), Who leads and guides our worship. Secondly, in Christ we possess all spiritual blessings in heavenly places (Eph. 1:3), which enable us to manifest the character of Christ to the world. A believer can, by faith, lay hold of all the love, grace, and peace he or she desires to exhibit in his or her life. Thirdly, God supplies physical resources to those who want to willingly serve Him.

While acknowledging the giving spirit of the saints at Philippi, Paul noted that, not only would they receive a heavenly reward for their generosity, but that God would replenish their resources on earth to satisfy all their needs: *"My God shall supply all your need according to His riches in glory by Christ Jesus"* (Phil. 4:19). Those who are united with Christ are greatly blessed because of that union and will not lack resources to worship God. However, as Arthur Pink points out, it is not the lack of resources that hinders our ability to worship God, but rather, our devotion to serve the Lord instead of ourselves with what we receive from Him:

> Observe two things; "Not a hoof" must be left behind. The spiritual application of this is far reaching. We may place our money at the Lord's disposal but reserve our time for ourselves. We may be ready to pray but not to labor or labor and not pray. "Not a hoof" means, that all that I have and am is held at the disposal of the Lord. Finally, it is striking to observe that Israel would not know the full Divine claims upon their responsibility until they reached the wilderness. The mind of God could not be discerned so long as they remained in Egypt![2]

The Egyptians were shrouded in the darkness of paganism while the Israelites enjoyed the light of God's presence. This was a great encouragement to them and they did not depart from that light. We read in 1 John 1:5-7 that walking with God requires walking in the light of divine truth. A willingness to walk according to revealed truth brings happy fellowship with God and with other believers. We must have light to walk safely. When we choose to walk in the dark, we are inviting injury – the chastening hand of God.

Listen to Paul's medley of exhortations concerning the walk of the believer: do not walk as fools (Eph. 5:15), the way you formerly did (Eph. 5:8), or the way the Gentiles walk in the vanity of their minds (Eph. 4:17); walk as children of light (Eph. 5:8). In other words, don't be foolish, walk according to the truth, not in the darkness that you once did. The Lord Jesus promised that, if we obey His commandments, He will manifest Himself to us in deeper fellowship (John 14:21). In order to walk with the Lord, we must be in agreement with

Him on the matter of sin. For *"can two walk together except they be agreed?"* (Amos 3:3). Surely, light has no communion with darkness; thus, may each of us walk with God according to divine truth and in moral integrity.

This would be the last face-to-face meeting between Moses and Pharaoh, and Pharaoh threatened Moses with death if he ever saw his face again. The irony of Pharaoh's decree was that he had unknowingly declared the nature of the final plague. Pharaoh had threatened God's people with death; therefore, God would bring death to the Egyptians. Moses agreed with Pharaoh's statement, for there was to be only one more plague and the particulars of how to escape it were told only to the Hebrews, that they might exercise faith and be saved from its consequences.

> Holy, Holy, Holy! Though the darkness hide Thee,
> Though the eye of sinful man Thy glory may not see,
> Only Thou art holy; there is none beside Thee,
> Perfect in power, in love, and purity.
>
> — Reginald Heber

# A Great Cry
## Exodus 11

No words could have delighted the heart of Moses more than to hear God finally say, *"Afterwards he [Pharaoh] will let you go from here."* Since arriving in Egypt, Moses had hazarded his life by repeatedly intruding into Pharaoh's presence, but now he would not see Pharaoh's face again. There would be one more plague and then the Hebrews, with all their children, their belongings, and the spoil of land would depart from Egypt. Pharaoh would present no more counter-offers so as to maintain his labor force; in fact, after the holocaust of the final plague, he would "drive" the Hebrews out of Egypt.

Though Pharaoh's heart was hardened, the Lord had worked in the hearts of the Egyptian people to be favorable to the Hebrews and to admire Moses (v. 3). The Jews were to ask the Egyptians for their jewelry (v. 2) and God informed Moses that the Egyptians would liberally hand over their wealth to the Israelites.

The tenth and final plague would be the worst of all the judgments of God on Egypt: Moses announced that all the firstborn (human and beast) *"in the land of Egypt"* would die at midnight. Note that the judgment was pronounced against both the Egyptians and the Hebrews in the land, yet, the Hebrew's provision for adverting it would mark a stark *"difference between the Egyptians and Israel."* There was only one remedy to escape judgment; as explained in Exodus 12, the blood of a lamb had to be applied to the doorposts and lintel of each home. It was a simple choice; do nothing and die, or apply lamb's blood and live. Those who trusted God's Word and applied the blood would be safeguarded by the Lord Himself when the destroyer visited Egypt at midnight (Ex. 12:23). The judgment of death was against all of the inhabitants of Egypt, but a substitute (a lamb) could be used in the place of the firstborn of each family.

This historical scene clearly typifies God's judgment decreed towards all of humanity, for all of us were born into this world already condemned in Adam (Rom. 5:12-13). Yet, a willing Substitute took our place and shed His own blood to redeem our souls to God (John 10:17-18). As an individual trusts God's Word concerning salvation, Christ's blood is personally applied to his or her own soul; the outcome of which is that he or she escapes God's wrath for his or her sin. A holy God must judge sin: when the heavenly angels sinned He *"spared them not"* (2 Pet. 2:4), when His own Son was *"made sin for us"* (2 Cor. 5:21), God did not spare Him either. He was judged in our place. Without God's substitutional remedy for righteously dealing with sin, we, like those in Egypt during Moses' day, would have no hope of eluding God's judgment or of experiencing eternal life.

Since Moses was not to see Pharaoh's face again, it seems best to understand the pronouncement of the tenth plague in Exodus 11 as a continuation of the personal confrontation in Exodus 10:24-29. If this was the case, Pharaoh was told of the judgment, but was offered no remedy. Previously, Moses had presented Pharaoh with opportunities to repent as to either avoid or end the judgments, but the time of escape was past for Pharaoh – judgment was coming to his own house.

Pharaoh had deceitfully spoken to Jehovah's ambassador and had continued to embrace his gods; he had rejected Jehovah's awesome testimony and would be judged accordingly. The firstborn son of Pharaoh was heir to the throne of Egypt and God would demonstrate through this plague that He ruled Egypt from generation to generation. Additionally, the goddess *Isis*, the wife and sister of *Osiris*, supposedly protected the Egyptian children from harm, but this plague would demonstrate her power to be completely inadequate to avert Jehovah's wrath.[1]

The narrative records that Moses left Pharaoh's court in great anger (v. 8). It is not hard to guess who Moses was angry with, but why had he become angry with him now and not earlier? We can only speculate, as the text does not elaborate. Pharaoh had continued to provoke the Lord for some time, but now his provocation was full and God would vindicate His holy name with fierce wrath. Moses was Jehovah's servant and was keenly aware of God's swelling anger towards Pharaoh.

When God's righteousness is affronted it is a sin for the servant of God not to be angry. Stuart Briscoe puts it this way, "The wrath of God is as pure as the holiness of God. When God is angry He is perfectly angry. When He is displeased there is every reason He should be. We tend to think of anger as sin; but sometimes it is sinful not to be angry. It is unthinkable that God would not be purely and perfectly angry with sin."[2] Pharaoh witnessed the greatest display of supernatural power at work in the world since God laid its foundation, and he had pompously thumbed his nose at God. To willfully reject God's revelation of truth has the most serious of consequences – God's wrath (Rom. 1:18; John 3:36). "Sin is the dare of God's justice," John Bunyan writes, "the rape of his mercy, the jeer of his patience, the slight of his power, and the contempt of his love."[3] Pharaoh and Egypt's paganism deserved to be judged; God's wrath could be deferred no longer.

Pharaoh's great sin would result in a great cry throughout Egypt. Every Egyptian household would taste death and the agony of sorrow would permeate the land. It was certain that without the application of redeeming blood there would be no escape from death in Egypt. Likewise, man, left in his natural state, is dead in the world and destined for eternal judgment (Rom. 5:12). The only remedy is to apply the blood of the Lord Jesus Christ, God's Lamb, by faith to one's account.

There is no hope of eternal salvation for anyone dying without being first redeemed by Christ's blood (Heb. 9:23-28). It is only through the blood of Christ that a person may receive the forgiveness of sins and obtain a righteous standing before God. God has done everything He can to rescue man from eternal judgment, but He will not force anyone to go to heaven. The Bible provides the following vivid descriptions of hell, the ultimate fate of those who reject God's truth:

- *"Shame and everlasting contempt"* (Dan. 12:2)
- *"Everlasting punishment"* (Matt. 25:46)
- *"Weeping and gnashing of teeth"* (Matt. 24:51)
- *"Unquenchable fire"* (Luke 3:17)
- *"Indignation and wrath, tribulation and anguish"* (Rom. 2:8-9)
- *"Their worm does not die* [putrid endless agony]*"* (Mark 9:44)
- *"Everlasting destruction"* (2 Thess. 1:9)
- *"Eternal fire ... the blackness of darkness for ever"* (Jude 7, 13)
- *"Fire is not quenched"* (Mark 9:46)

Revelation 14:10-11 tells us the final, eternal destiny of the sinner: *"He shall be tormented with fire and brimstone ... the smoke of their torment ascended up for ever and ever: and they have no rest day or night."* The Bible's teaching of an eternal place of punishment for unforgiven sinners offends people; consequently, many are watering down the truth by teaching that hell is a state of non-existence or quick annihilation. Misrepresenting the truth in an attempt to avoid its consequences is never a good idea. Does affirming a picturesque sunny day in one's mind vanquish the colossal hurricane that is bearing down on the positive thinker? Truth enables man to face reality and realize that hiding from omniscient, omnipresent God is quite impossible.

The Lord Jesus spoke often of hell, addressing the subject of afterlife torment over seventy times. In accordance with God's foreordained plan of salvation, the Lord Jesus bore our hell at Calvary and appeased God's righteous anger for our sin so that we would not have to suffer judgment throughout eternity. He did not frighten people without reason. He lovingly warned them about their deadly disease (sin) and the fatal consequence of the disease (hell), and pleaded with them to internalize the cure (to exercise faith in Him for salvation).

As shown in His dealings with Pharaoh, God does not force anyone to receive the truth of salvation against his or her will. Heaven would be hell if you didn't want to be there, but hell will not be heaven for those who reject Christ, God's ultimate expression of truth (John 1:14). The Lord Jesus declared, *"I am the Way, the Truth, and the Life. No one comes to the Father except through Me."*

Moses and Aaron had no part in the tenth plague, other than announcing it and the way to avoid its consequences. Servants of the Lord are to be occupied with the same ministry today. The redemption of souls by blood and the judgment of the wicked is God's business and His alone, but warning the lost of His judgment and explaining His means of escaping it should be the believer's passion. The great cry heard throughout Egypt that Passover night is only a minute precursor to the ceaseless screaming that will ascend out of hell in a future day.

Art thou by sin a captive led? Is sin thy daily grief?
The Man who broke the serpent's head, Can bring thee sweet relief.
His name is Jesus, for He saves, And setteth captives free;
His office is to purchase slaves, And give them liberty.

— Berridge

# The Passover Lamb
## Exodus 12:1-5

Jehovah instituted the annual Passover Feast as a means of reminding the Israelites of their deliverance from Egypt and their restoration to Him through redemption. The Hebrew calendar was to align itself with this event marking "the beginning of months" (v. 2). The timing of the plagues is unknown, perhaps requiring several months, but after Israel was redeemed, the days, months, and years of their spiritual journey with God are measured out. Through the sacrifice of an innocent substitute (a lamb) and the application of its blood, the Jews obtained a new beginning and a new life with God.

Though a lamb would be sacrificed for each household during *Passover*, the language throughout Exodus 12 specifically states that God viewed this as one lamb that would be sacrificed by and for the entire nation: *"Then the whole assembly of the congregation of Israel shall* ***kill it*** *at twilight"* (Ex. 12:6). Though the Jews slaughtered thousands of lambs at twilight, the specific command was to kill the *Passover* –a single sacrifice was in view (vv. 6, 11, 21, 27). Clearly, Jehovah was preparing the nation of Israel for the coming of the Lamb of God, whom they collectively would nail to a cross.

In verses 3 through 5, the progression of personal identification with the selected lamb is significant: "a lamb" (v. 3), to "the lamb" (v. 4), to "your lamb" (v. 5). Many think of Jesus Christ as merely one of many ways to God – He is merely "a lamb." Others know particular things about Christ (e.g. He was born of a virgin, He was sinless, He died on a cross), but don't personally know Him as their Saviour – to them He is "the lamb." For those who have personally trusted Christ for salvation, the Lord Jesus is "their Lamb." These individuals understand that Christ personally took their place on a cross, was judged for their sin, and was raised up for their justification. Scripture declares to every individual that

Christ is his or her one and only Lamb, and true Christians are in full agreement.

Some four hundred years prior to the first Passover, another prelude to Christ's sacrifice took place. In obedience to God's command, Abraham went to the land of Moriah and upon the mount that God showed him Abraham built an altar to sacrifice his beloved son Isaac. God was testing and refining the quality of Abraham's faith through the ordeal. During this trial, Abraham uttered two prophetic statements which preface the events of Exodus 12 and have their ultimate fulfillment in the sacrifice of Christ at Calvary. First, *"God will provide Himself a Lamb for a burnt offering"* (Gen. 22:8). Second, *"In the mount of the Lord it shall be seen* [provided]*"* (Gen. 22:14). Both speak of the future sacrifice of Christ; the Lord Himself declared this to the Pharisees, saying, *"Abraham rejoiced to see My day: and he saw it, and was glad"* (John 8:56).

It took Abraham three days to reach Moriah, the appointed sacrificial site. Why did the journey require three days and not two or four? In Abraham's mind, God's will and His command could not be thwarted; thus, Isaac was as good as dead for those three days. After the Lord's crucifixion on Friday, His marred body, stiffened by the chill of death, was laid in a lonely tomb. His body lay lifeless in that dismal place until Sunday when He awoke from the slumber of death and was raised up in a glorified body just before dawn.

Abraham did rejoice that day, for God provided a substitute sacrifice in place of Isaac and, thus, delivered Abraham from the greatest trial of his life. Besides testing Abraham's faith, the entire situation had been divinely orchestrated to picture the future sacrifice of God's Lamb on that very mount almost two millennia later. His own Son would be offered there as a sin-sacrifice so that He might have a means of righteously extending forgiveness to humanity.

On the eve of the Exodus, God gave instructions to Moses concerning the Passover lamb. On the tenth day of the first month, the head of each Hebrew home was to choose a male lamb, a yearling without any blemishes. Once chosen, it was separated from the sheep and the goats and was watched closely for four days to ensure its fit condition. On the fourteenth day of the first month, the young, tested, unblemished lamb was to be killed in the evening. For the initial Passover, the lamb's blood was to be applied to the doorpost and lintel of the offerer's home in order to spare the life of the firstborn living there.

The sprinkling of blood was the visible expression of one's faith and thus adverted God's judgment. But this action occurred only because the sprinkler reckoned that Jehovah had spoken the truth and that He could not lie. Jehovah had promised not to judge the firstborn within the houses marked by lamb's blood, but rather to pass over them. *Security* of salvation would be obtained through the applied blood, but the *assurance* of that salvation would only be enjoyed by trusting in God's Word. A believer who has laid hold of both the security and assurance of salvation enjoys not only the peace with God, but also the peace of God in his or her life. This individual is obedient to God's Word and is characterized by a humble resolve to face each day with confidence, knowing that he or she is secure in Christ.

Some 1500 years later, John the Baptist declared that Jesus Christ was *"the Lamb of God which takes away the sin of the world"* (John 1:29). Paul taught that Christ was the literal fulfillment of the Passover lamb: *"For indeed Christ, our Passover, was sacrificed for us"* (1 Cor. 5:7). The millions of lambs previously slaughtered by the Jews served as a constant reminder of their sin, and a testimony that animal blood could never cleanse away the stain of sin. The Jewish animal sacrifices merely atoned for sin and pointed to God's once-for-all sacrifice – Christ!

As typified in the Paschal lamb, the Lord Jesus was perfect, unblemished, fully-tested, and in the prime of His life. But Christ exceeded the Old Testament type. Not only did He exhibit divine moral perfection, but He was a man and, therefore, could legitimately substitute for humanity and be punished in our stead. Through one man's disobedience (Adam's), death engulfed humanity, but through one Man's obedience (Christ's), humanity received the opportunity for eternal life (Rom. 5:12-21).

Unlike the Old Testament lambs that were unaware of their future fate, the Lord Jesus was fully cognizant of His mission and willingly gave Himself, as a sacrifice (John 10:17-18). Christ frequently foretold His suffering, death, burial, and resurrection to His disciples. The Lord spoke of these events as His approaching "hour" – a matter He mentioned seven specific times, as recorded in John's Gospel. The Lord Jesus Christ was God's Lamb to be sacrificed. God sent His beloved

Son to bear our sin (2 Cor. 5:21), to taste death for us (Heb. 2:9), and to redeem by His own blood those who would trust in Him alone for salvation (1 Pet. 1:18-19).

> Paschal Lamb, by God appointed, all our sins on Thee were laid,
> By our Father's love anointed, Thou has full propitiation made,
> All who trust Thee are forgiven through the virtue of Thy blood.
> Rent in Thee the veil of heaven, grace shines forth to man from God.
>
> — John Bakewell

# Worthy is the Lamb
## Exodus 12:6

Lambs are one of the most helpless creatures; they must receive proper care and protection to survive. A lamb is incapable of caring for itself. God created man as a dependent being and apart from God we are incapable of pleasing Him; we are like sheep, going our own way and doing what we think is best (Isa. 53:6). The Lord Jesus laid aside His glory and position in heaven to become a man in order to be our sin-substitute at Calvary (Phil. 2:6-8). The incredible meekness of the Lamb of God is observed in this action; He willingly stooped to humanity and was fashioned in the likeness of sinful flesh (Rom. 8:3). Through the incarnation, the Lamb of God completely identified with the wandering sheep He came to save.

The Lord was a spotless Lamb; He was thoroughly tested for some thirty-three years to prove His sinless perfection. The Lord Jesus lived His entire life without sin – He was without blemish, a fact that His enemies could not deny. We understand that Christ, as *holy humanity* (Luke 1:35), could not sin. There was nothing in Him that would respond to sin; He was and is *"sin apart"* (Heb. 4:15, Darby). The Lord's holy essence repulsed sin and loathed its working. Adam was created as *innocent humanity* (Eccl. 7:29) and had the free-moral agency to choose to honor God and, thus, demonstrate love for Him, or to rebel against Him. Adam and Christ were both born human, but they had different spiritual wherewithal. As God, Christ could not sin; there was nothing within Him to respond to the external solicitations by Satan to rebel against His Father (Jas. 1:13).

There are various erroneous teachings concerning the person of Christ. Some say Christ is not fully God, nor fully man. Others teach that Christ became some hybrid creature, a created being between God and man, but neither God nor man. This view, commonly held among many cults today, is one that Paul confronts in the book of Colossians.

Yet others see a schizophrenic Jesus, someone with a dual personality who vacillates in personality and nature. Christ is not diminished deity added to a human personality; God literally and personally became a human, without emptying Himself of any divine attributes (John 1:14).

Paul proclaims, *"Great is the mystery of godliness. God was manifest in the flesh"* (1 Tim. 3:16). It is difficult to understand how the Lord Jesus can be fully God and Man at the same time; humanly speaking we cannot comprehend it for *"No man knows the Son but the Father"* (Matt. 11:27). Yet, from Scripture we know Christ, the very Son of God, was also fully man, though He had a unique human nature, one which is different from ours. Because there is no definite article in the Greek before the word "flesh," this verse is better rendered as John Darby translates it, *"God has been manifested in flesh."*[1] God was manifest "in flesh," not "in the flesh." The Lord Jesus was veiled in flesh (Heb. 10:20), and He was made flesh (John 1:14), but He was never in the flesh – the nature of His flesh did not rule Him; it served Him. His flesh had not been invaded by the corruption of sin.

The New Testament further explains: *"What the law could not do in that it was weak through the flesh, God sending His own Son in the likeness of sinful flesh"* (Rom. 8:3). The Greek word *homoioma,* translated as "likeness" in this verse, is also applied in Philippians 2:7, which states that Christ *"was made in the likeness of men."* The word "likeness" in both verses means "resemblance" or "form." Humanly speaking, His form was that of a man, but He was more; He also possessed a divine nature. The Lord looked like everyone else, but He didn't act like everyone else. His life was unique for "*in Him is no sin"* (1 Jn. 3:5), He *"knew no sin"* (2 Cor. 5:21), and He *"did no sin"* (1 Pet. 2:22).

Speaking of Christ, the writer of Hebrews declares the matter frankly: "*who being the brightness of His* [God's] *glory, and the express image of His* [God's] *person, and upholding all things by the word of His power, when He had by Himself purged our sins, sat down on the right hand of the Majesty on high"* (Heb. 1:3). It was needful for Christ to be veiled in flesh, or mankind would have been consumed by the direct presence of Almighty God. The veil of flesh allowed Christ to uphold the moral glory of God to the World. J. B. Phillips wrote, "Christ is the aperture through which the immensity and magnificence of God can be seen."[2] When people looked upon the Lord Jesus, they saw the form of a man, with the character of God shining through. Mark the words of Christ to Philip:

> *Jesus said to him, "Have I been with you so long, and yet you have not known Me, Philip? He who has seen Me has seen the Father; so how can you say, 'Show us the Father'? Do you not believe that I am in the Father, and the Father in Me? The words that I speak to you I do not speak on My own authority; but the Father who dwells in Me does the works"* (John 14:9-10).

Some have suggested that the external solicitations of Satan upon the Lord Jesus caused some internal moral struggle within His person. This was not the case. How could the Father gaze down from heaven and declare, *"This is my beloved Son, in whom I am well pleased"* (Matt. 3:17) if the Lord were struggling internally with thoughts of sin? As John declared, the Lord Jesus *was*, not *might be, "the Lamb of God, which takes away the sin of the world"* (John 1:29). The Father never questioned the impeccability of Christ – only Satan and men do that. Christ was blameless and perfect, and thus, the only acceptable substitutional sacrifice for man's sin. He was God's only Lamb for sacrifice.

The Lord Jesus commonly referred to Himself by titles which referred to His mission to earth, such as "the Son of Man." However, other than His forerunner, John the Baptist, who spoke of Him as *"the Lamb of God who takes away the sin of the world,"* others did not speak of Christ in this way. It is appropriate to remember what the Lord has done, but on this side of Calvary, His people should not personally address Him by applying past expressions of His humiliation.

The only exception to this scriptural pattern is when the Bible affirms that a title of humiliation has become a title of exaltation; "Lamb" is an example of this. God's Lamb is prominent in Scripture, with one-fourth of all references to the word "lamb" being found in the book of Revelation: *"Worthy is the Lamb who was slain to receive power and riches and wisdom, and strength and honor and glory and blessing!"* (Rev. 5:12). May every child of God honor God's Lamb – our Lamb, our Saviour, and our Lord forever.

> Worthy, worthy is the Lamb; worthy, worthy is the Lamb,
> Worthy, worthy is the Lamb – that was slain!
>
> — William P. Mackay

# The Passover Feast
## Exodus 12:7-13

Before continuing through the Exodus 12 narrative, we must pause to consider a great truth that pertains to the lamb which is stated twice in this chapter: *"It is the Lord's Passover"* (v. 11), and *"It is the sacrifice of the Lord's Passover"* (v. 27). When related to the events of Calvary, which the Passover typifies, these statements emphasize an important aspect of the cross often neglected in today's preaching: the value of Christ's sacrifice to God. Arthur Pink explains:

> Gospellers have much to say about what Christ's death accomplished for those who believe in Him, but very little is said about what that Death accomplished Godwards. The fact is that the death of Christ glorified God if never a single sinner had been saved by virtue of it. … The more we study the teaching of the Scripture on this subject, and the more we lay hold by simple faith of what the Cross meant to God, the more stable will be our peace and the deeper our joy and praise.[1]

While exhorting the Corinthians to purity he reminds them: *"Christ, our Passover, was sacrificed for us"* (1 Cor. 5:7). While it is true that Christ, God's Lamb, is now our Passover, He was the Lord's Passover first. God was satisfied with the sacrifice of His Son long before we understood the value of that propitiation. Throughout Scripture, a sacrifice is identified as a bloody offering which appeases the righteous indignation of a sin-hating and sin-punishing God. God's anger was quelled and the righteous need to judge sin was satisfied once and for all by Christ's sacrifice (Rom. 3:25).

There is no polite way to describe the killing of a peaceable lamb – it simply had to be done; for God commanded it. The wee lamb was held tightly while its throat was slit. As the blood drained out of the fatal slash to pool on the door's threshold, the lamb gradually became limp and slipped into unconsciousness, and ultimately, lifelessness. The entire lamb was then roasted by fire with its inward parts. The lamb was to be totally consumed by the family members during the feast (any remnants were to be burned). Fire speaks of judgment, and the lamb was not only to die, but to come into full contact with the flames of judgment.

Without Christ, everyone would suffer God's judgment for sin after death (Heb. 9:27). Physical death and eternal death are two separate things; the first is an event that ends physical life and the second is an agonizing state of eternal existence apart from God. Thus, Christ God's Lamb had to suffer not only death on our behalf, but also God's full wrath for human sin (Heb. 2:9). God's Lamb was fully consumed in judgment.

Smaller Hebrew families could band together and share a lamb, but a lamb was to be slaughtered for every household gathering. This activity marked a clear distinction between the Egyptian and the Hebrew homes. Blood applied on the doorframe of the Hebrew homes saved the life of the firstborn within, but the absence of blood on Egyptian doorways meant that the night would not pass without deep sorrow. Previous obedience of the Hebrew household to the covenant rite of male circumcision would not prevent Jehovah's judgment – the life of a lamb had to be taken and its blood applied. This simple picture shows the utter futility of Law-keeping to somehow attain salvation, since God has already shown that substitution of an innocent sacrifice is His means of justifying the faithful. His Passover was killed to save others from the second death!

The blood-soaked doorways of the Hebrew homes would serve as a constant reminder to the Egyptians of how the Israelites had escaped Jehovah's judgment and why they themselves had not. Acknowledging the existence of a personal Saviour *provided* by God is not the same as personally receiv*ing* Him. The former viewpoint merely assents to historical credibility, but the latter position is one of vital consequence: a critical distinction that the Egyptians learned too late.

Not only was the lamb to be killed, but as mentioned previously, it was to be eaten (v. 8). Arthur Pink comments on the significance of eating the lamb:

> This was God's provision for those *inside* the house, as the blood secured protection from the judgment *outside*. A journey lay before Israel, and food was needed to strengthen them first. "Eating" signifies

> two things in Scripture: appropriation and fellowship. The "lamb" spoke of the person of Christ, and He is God's food for His people – "the Bread of Life." Christ is to be the object before our hearts. As we feed upon Him our souls are sustained and He is honored.[2]

Besides the lamb, the Passover meal included unleavened bread and bitter herbs. The unleavened bread spoke of the urgency of the forthcoming journey; there was no time to properly prepare leavened bread. In fact, the entire meal was to be eaten in haste (v. 11). The imminent expectation of deliverance flavored the entire feast; its participants were to have their loins girded, their shoes on, and their staffs in hand. Everyone was to be ready to go!

The bitter herbs represented the bitterness of Jewish bondage in Egypt. Bitterness on the earth resulted from the fall of humanity in the Garden of Eden. Because God's representative of Himself in the world sinned, God cursed the entire planet on which he lived – a corrupted crown of creation could not rule over a perfect world (Heb. 2:7-8). God informed Adam:

> *Cursed is the ground for your sake; in toil you shall eat of it all the days of your life. Both thorns and thistles it shall bring forth for you, and you shall eat the herb of the field. In the sweat of your face you shall eat bread till you return to the ground, for out of it you were taken; for dust you are, and to dust you shall return* (Gen. 3:17-19).

Because of sin, man would struggle to survive in a cursed world: Adam ate the herbs of the field instead of the fruit of the garden, and with sweat upon his brow he battled the thorns to till the ground. God's Lamb bore the judgments pronounced upon Adam: He wore a crown of thorns upon His head and tasted the bitter herbs (the gall). Moreover, in the garden of Gethsemane, *"being in an agony He prayed more earnestly: and His sweat was as it were great drops of blood falling down to the ground"* (Luke 22:44). Christ took man's place at Golgotha, as Paul writes, *"Christ has redeemed us from the curse of the law, having become a curse for us (for it is written, 'Cursed is everyone who hangs on a tree')"* (Gal. 3:13).

Some 900 years prior to the Exodus, God included in Scripture another important picture of God's judgment upon Christ. Those who were secured in Noah's ark were saved from the wrath of God which fell upon the ark and the wicked of the world. Yet, the symbolism of the ark reaches beyond the judgment of our Lord at Calvary to the blessings of the day of His resurrection. William Lincoln summarizes:

> There seems no reason to doubt that the day the ark rested on the mountain of Ararat is identical with the day on which the Lord rose from the dead. It rested "on the seventeenth day of the seventh month." But by the commandment of the Lord, given at the time of the institution of the feast of the Passover, the seventh month was changed into the first month. Then three days after the Passover, which was on the fourteenth day of the month, the Lord, having passed quite through the waters of judgment, stood in resurrection in the midst of His disciples, saying "Peace be unto you." They, as well as Himself, had reached the haven of everlasting rest.[3]

The Passover lamb was slaughtered and completely consumed, if its blood was applied each Jewish home would escape the 10$^{th}$ plague – if not the firstborn of that home died. The Passover meal year by year would serve as memorial feast of what God had accomplished through redemption in Egypt; however it has its culmination in the ultimate redemptive act of God at Calvary. The Lord Jesus instituted the Lord's Supper just hours before His death to commemorate in the hearts of believers for centuries to come what He had accomplished through the sacrifice of Himself (Luke 22:19-20).

The Passover feast was both a duty and a privilege, but merely eating the Passover meal did not provide safety for a Hebrew household. The lamb could be slain, roasted, and eaten with the unleavened bread and bitter herbs, but that would not stay Jehovah's hand from claiming the life of the firstborn in that household – the blood of the lamb had to be applied to the entrance of that home. Only if God saw the blood would He spare that family from death. In like manner, the Lord's Supper is a duty and a privilege of His people. Believers are to gather corporately to remember the Lord Jesus and to proclaim the value of His death (1 Cor. 11:17, 20). Eating the bread and drinking the wine does not convey salvation blessing, but it is rather to remind us of how our salvation was obtained – through Christ's broken body and shed blood. Knowing our tendency to forget Him and His work, the Lord Jesus inferred that believers should remember Him by keeping the Lord's Supper often. Yet, the command included no rules for how frequently Christians should gather to remember the Lord; our love for Him will determine this matter. It is noted that the early Church transitioned from breaking bread daily in Acts 2 to the established pattern of remembering the Lord once a week on Sunday (Acts 20:7).

During the Lord's Supper, as in all meetings of the Church, the audible ministry is to be accomplished by Spirit-led men (1 Cor. 14:26-35), as the man represents the glory of God (1 Cor. 11:7). The visual ministry of the coverings belongs to the sisters. In this manner, a divine distinction between the genders and their God-ordained roles is reinforced. God has appointed a specific way for the Church to uplift the name of His Son and to remember Him in the corporate setting; it is the Lord's Supper.

Not only does the Lord's Supper refresh the heart of God, but it is also a provision for the believer; it is difficult to be overcome by sin when consistently bringing the Lord Jesus into remembrance. It is hard to lust after an individual, to covet another's possessions, or to be given to substance abuse if our minds are stayed upon the Lord. Isaiah 26:3 reads, *"You will keep him in perfect peace, whose mind is stayed on You, because he trusts in You."* Perhaps this is why Jehovah instituted so many special days and feasts for the Jews to keep; He wanted their minds to be continually occupied with Him. This would make it more difficult for the Jews to forget their God. Likewise, the night before He died the Lord gave the Church a remembrance feast called the Lord's Supper in order to continually stir up our appreciation for His work at Calvary and to admire His moral beauty. The Lord's dying request was that His disciples would regularly remember Him through the keeping of the Lord's Supper.

Lord Jesus, we love Thee, and joyfully pour
    Our praise and our worship at Thy blessed feet;
Lord Jesus, we honor, exalt and adore
    The name that to God and to us is so sweet.
O, name of good savor, of peace and of rest –
    The name of the Victim, the Lamb that was slain!
O, name of God's loved One in Whom we are blest!
    Oh, name ever worthy all homage to gain!

— C. H. Von Poseck

# Sweep Your House Clean
## Exodus 12:14-20

In years to come, the Passover feast would be held on Friday, the feast of Unleavened Bread on Saturday, and the feast of First Fruits on Sunday. The feast of Unleavened Bread would last seven days, meaning that the total duration of the first three spring feasts would be eight days. These feasts were to be kept annually as a memorial to God's incredible feat of delivering the Jews from Egypt.

Only unleavened bread was eaten on the night of the Passover, but a further restriction was observed during the following seven days of the feast of Unleavened Bread; there was not to be any leaven in any of the Jewish homes (Ex. 12:15, 19). Leaven, in Scripture, speaks of sin, corruption, or evil doctrine (Matt. 13:33; 1 Cor. 5:8). Though the Israelites were immersed in a pagan culture, its filth and corruption should not be in their homes. Though they were in the world, they were not to be of the world. In a later tradition, Jewish parents actually hid leaven in their homes so that their children could search it out and sweep it out of the house before the feast of Unleavened Bread commenced.

Interestingly, the first mention of leaven in the Bible describes the simple meal Lot's wife prepared for the two visiting angels (Gen. 19:3). The unleavened bread stood in sharp contrast to Lot's "leavened" life (speaking of his failure to separate from worldliness). The next reference to leaven in the Bible relates to the unleavened bread which was to be a part of the Passover Feast (Ex. 12).

Did sweeping of the leaven out of the house merit salvation? No, the Israelites did not sweep out the leaven in order to be saved from the final plague, only applied lamb's blood would save them from that judgment. In years to come, they would put leaven out of their homes, not to be saved, but because they had been saved. If a Jew wanted to continue to enjoy fellowship with God's people (i.e. to remain a part of the general assembly), the leaven had to go (v. 19). Henry Morris explains: "Leaven, of course, being involved with the fermentation process, is a perfect symbol of decay and corruption, and it is important that spiritual fellowship not be contaminated with it."[1] Leaven in the home degrades our fellowship with God and with His people. So, dear Christian, if you have secret stashes of leaven lurking about in some dark secluded corner of your home, take immediate action and *get it out of your house*!

Something of the world can be ignorantly introduced into our homes and, by its very availability, ensure chaos the moment we walk in the flesh and not by faith. Often what lays dormant and harmless for a time will, in due season, solicit the flesh to manifest itself. These worldly influences are like spiritual land mines, which can lay hidden and dormant for a time, but with one missed step of faith the child of God becomes a casualty of his or her own carnal appetite. Just as the Jews symbolized spiritual sanctification by sweeping all the leaven from their homes during the feast of Unleavened Bread, believers should take great care to remove anything from their homes that might entice the flesh to sin. The Christian home should be a safe haven which encourages spiritual growth not a minefield of secular temptations. If the leaven is not there to begin with, it will never pull us under its power. It is much safer to never drive a car with poor brakes, than it is to stop it once it is in motion: *"All things are lawful for me, but all things are not helpful. All things are lawful for me, but I will not be brought under the power of any"* (1 Cor. 6:12-13).

The seven days of Unleavened Bread was to begin and end with a holy convocation; a day set apart to collectively honor Jehovah. To ensure that the Jews were available for these gatherings, no work other than meal preparation was allowed (v. 16). The feasts of Passover and Unleavened Bread would be annual events in which the Jews were to recall their miraculous deliverance from death in Egypt and to remove defilement from their homes; holy convocations can occur only when holy people gather together. The commandment concerning these feasts was a perpetual one; it was to be obeyed from generation to generation (v. 17). Even foreigners living among the Jews would need to obey this command. Those who ignored the feasts were to be cut off from the congregation of Israel.

Over time, the Jews instituted their own feasts to celebrate special events, or tragedies. While such traditions may be permissible (Rom. 14:5-6), these should never supplant what God has commanded. In the case of the Jews, their instituted feasts became of great importance. Meanwhile "the feasts of Jehovah" diminished in prominence until, by New Testament days, they had become "the feasts of the Jews" (John 5:1, 6:4). Jehovah was no longer in their feasts – He had been supplanted by the leaven of religious traditions.

The Lord Jesus did not command that the Church keep any special feasts other than the frequent observance of the Lord's Supper. He did not command an annual observance of His birth or death, yet these have developed over time through church tradition and, unfortunately, from pagan practices.

Long before the Easter bunny hopped into the homes of Christians, he was an integral part of the pagan festival of *Eastre* (please note the spelling), the Anglo-Saxon goddess of spring – a fertility god whose earthly symbol was that of a rabbit. In the Assyrian tongue, she is called *Astarte* or *Ishtar,* and is none other than *Beltis*, worshipped as "the queen of Heaven."[2]

The gestation period for humans is nine months, which, as A. Hislop explains, is why December 25th was chosen by the Roman Catholic Church in the fourth century as the day to commemorate Christ's birth:

> Long before the Christian era itself, a festival was celebrated among the heathen, at that precise time of the year, in honor of the birth of the son of the Babylonian queen of heaven; and it may fairly be presumed that, in order to conciliate the heathen, and to swell the number of the nominal adherents of Christianity, the same festival was adopted by the Roman Church, giving it only the name of Christ. … That Christmas was originally a Pagan festival is beyond all doubt. The time of the year, and the ceremonies with which it is still celebrated, prove its origin. In Egypt, the son of Isis, the Egyptian title for the queen of heaven, was born at this very time, "about the time of the winter solstice." The very name by which Christmas is popularly known among ourselves – Yule-day – proves at once its Pagan and Babylonian origin. "Yule" is the Chaldee name for an "infant" or "little child;" and as the 25th of December was called by our Pagan Anglo-Saxon ancestors, "Yule-day," or the "Child's day," and the night that preceded it, "Mother-night," long before they came in contact with Christianity."[3]

So the date which honored the sun-god *Mithras* became the celebrated birth date of the Son of God, Jesus. The son of Isis, Horus was claimed to have been born on December 25th, which is nine months after the vernal or spring equinox in late March – the time of the pagan fertility celebrations. The twelve day celebration was filled with pagan rituals, lascivious exploits, and with an animal or human sacrifice offered each day upon the ever-burning Yule log.[4] As Alexander Hislop noted, "Yule" is the Chaldean name for "infant" and is synonymous with Horus. The Christmas carol "The Twelve Days of Christmas" is derived from this pagan practice. A "Yule-tide" greeting acknowledges and honors the pagan god Yule. During the pagan twelve-day celebration in honor of Yule, oil lamps were placed in windows; this has evolved into the elaborate and costly strings of Christmas lights we see today.[5] The tie between paganism and the developed church traditions of Christmas and Easter is unmistakable.

The professing church has followed the example of the Jews, who created feasts of their own and ignored the significance of the ones Jehovah had decreed. Church traditions have caused many professing Christians to ignore Christ's command to remember Him often through the Lord's Supper or to transform the memorial feast into some unscriptural practice. Some, for example, associate the eating of the bread and the drinking of the wine in the Lord's Supper with receiving or maintaining their salvation. These false teachings undermine the gospel message of grace declared repeatedly in the New Testament (e.g. Gal. 1:6-9).

The leaven to be avoided in the believer's life comes in diverse varieties. The Lord Jesus warned His disciples against the influence of humanized traditions that oppose sound doctrine: *"Beware of the leaven of the Pharisees, which is hypocrisy"* (Luke 12:1). He also warned them concerning *"the leaven ... of the Sadducees"* (Matt. 16:6). The Sadducees were materialists who denied the existence of the supernatural, the spiritual nature of man, and the idea of a future resurrection. In our present day, the ideologies of the Sadducees live on in intellectualism, humanism, higher criticism, post-modernism, and naturalism. Lastly, the Lord Jesus warned His disciples not to be influenced by *"the leaven of Herod"* (Mark 8:15). Herod, a Jew, was in cahoots with the Roman Empire, and was, therefore, a friend of the world (Jas. 4:4). In the case of Herod and those like him, love for God and His Word has been supplanted by the love for materialism, fame, and political ambition. Little in one's life has value to God after he or she has become socially mesmerized by God-hating ideologies.

Moreover, Paul instructed the Church at Corinth to remove the leaven (those who continue in sin) out of their congregation (1 Cor. 5:6-7). Leaven within a single Christian household negatively influences the entire House of God (Gal. 5:9; 1 Tim. 3:15). Whether symbolizing vain philosophies of men, false doctrine, worldliness, or sin, leaven has no place in the believer's life. The Jews were to avoid all of these secular, enticing philosophies, as symbolized in the removal of the leaven from their homes (Ex. 12:19). F. B. Hole reminds us that this is to be a life-long endeavor for the believer:

> The Passover feast was a matter of a few hours at the most, whereas the feast of unleavened bread covered seven days. This had a typical bearing. The Passover was a prophecy, as well as a memorial commemorating a past event. The prophecy was fulfilled in the death of Christ which, though of eternal importance, took place within a few hours. But the seven days of the unleavened bread feast set forth a whole cycle of time, as signified in 1 Corinthians 5:8. For each believer today it covers the whole period of his life of responsibility. As long as we are in this world of sin, we are to keep clear of the "leaven," as those that are, "dead indeed unto sin, but alive unto God" (Rom. 6: 11).[4]

Dear reader, why not scan each room of your home for leaven, and don't hesitate to get out of your house and your life that which will only pull your heart from the Lord and from His people!

> Jesus Christ, God's only Son came at last our foe to smite,
> All our sins away hath done, done away death's power and right;
> Only the form of death is left; of his sting he is bereft.
>
> Now our Paschal Lamb is He, and by Him alone we live,
> Who to death upon the tree for our sake Himself did give.
> Faith His blood strikes on our door, death dares never harm us more.
>
> To the supper of the Lord gladly will we come today;
> The word of peace is now restored, the old leaven is put away;
> Christ will be our food alone, faith no life but His will own.
>
> — Martin Luther

# Redeemed by Blood
## Exodus 12:21-30

According to verse 21, Moses assembled the elders of Israel and conveyed to them all of the Passover instructions that he and Aaron had received from the Lord: Each family was to choose a Passover lamb and kill it. The blood of the lamb was to be collected *in the basin* and then applied to the doorposts and lintel with a bunch of hyssop. The Hebrew word *caph* is twice translated "in the basin" in verse 22.

Dr. Urquhart notes that this word was the ancient Egyptian word for the step before a door, or the threshold of a house.[1] In fact, *caph* is found thirty-two times in the Old Testament and is translated "door(s)," or "threshold(s)," or "doorposts" twenty-six of those occurrences. In the remaining six references, as in verse 22, *caph* is rendered "bowl," "cup," or "basin." The modern concept of *caph* (i.e. a basin) was not the historical meaning of the word. Consequently, the Jews did not kill their lambs elsewhere and then collect the blood in some sort of vessel to bring back to their homes; the lambs were slaughtered on the threshold of the front door. The basin (the entryway of the house) is where the lamb bled and where the lamb died.

A handful of hyssop was then used as a primitive paintbrush to smear the pooled blood on both sides and the top of the doorframe before it congealed on the threshold. Accordingly, the entrance to the Jewish home would be completely encased with lamb's blood. Hissop was a common bushy plant that grew on rocky surfaces and would be used later in the purification rite of the Law; however, it was never used directly in any offering which foreshadowed the Lord Jesus Christ Himself. In Jewish rites, the hyssop was always held in a human hand, and it was not a part of the sacrifice; it was rather used to perform ceremonial purification on behalf of those who desired restoration. Metaphorically, then, hyssop speaks of a sinner's humility before God in true repentance. By picking up the hyssop to apply the blood, the

Jews declared both its value of the blood for redemption and the fact that they wanted to appropriate this divine benefit to themselves.

The typology of collecting and applying the blood is clear: the blood of God's Lamb was to be shed and applied at the place where the Lamb died. For someone to escape God's wrath for sin he or she must come to the cross of Christ, the place where the Lord Jesus Christ bled and died: *"For the message of the cross is foolishness to those who are perishing, but to us who are being saved it is the power of God"* (1 Cor. 1:18). The warning Moses conveyed to the nation of Israel further foretells of God's ultimate redemptive plan:

> *None of you shall go out of the door of his house until morning. For the Lord will pass through to strike the Egyptians; and when He sees the blood on the lintel and on the two doorposts, the Lord will pass over the door and not allow the destroyer to come into your houses to strike you* (Ex. 12:22-23).

Not only did each family need to apply their lamb's blood to their homes in order to escape judgment, they had to remain under the blood until the judgment was past. Anyone leaving a home marked by blood had no assurance of life. When the Hebrews ventured out of their homes the next morning, they would have had to literally step over and through the lamb's blood. The entrance to the home was certainly not a pretty sight. A blood-stained "welcome mat" would not be too inviting to strangers, but to those who had survived the night, the blood-spattered door and threshold were symbols of their new life and a reminder of their redemption.

The believer is reminded that while nailed to the cross the Lord Jesus bled from His head, His feet, and His hands; the entire cross was stained with Christ's redeeming blood. He is the door (John 14:6) by which we must enter in order to escape God's wrath, and by that same door, we reenter a hostile world to serve Him as a redeemed people: *"I am the door. If anyone enters by Me, he will be saved, and will go in and out and find pasture"* (John 10:9). Those who have truly come in through the Door will be readily known as Christ-ones; their new life in Christ demands that they be strangers and pilgrims in the world. The cross of Christ was not a pretty sight, but the contemplation of it serves as a wonderful reminder to the redeemed of new life in Christ.

As individuals trust Christ for salvation, His redemptive work becomes effective for them. Because a profession of faith is based on hearing and understanding God's Word (Rom. 10:17), a true confession of Christ has lasting value: *"For godly sorrow produces repentance leading to salvation, not to be regretted; but the sorrow of the world produces death"* (2 Cor. 7:10).

Faith that brings salvation reacts according to revealed truth. Imagine for a moment that I am trapped on the fourth floor of a building engulfed in flames. Fortunately for me, rescue vehicles and several fire trucks arrive on the scene. After surveying the desperate situation, a fireman informs me through a bullhorn that my only chance to survive the fire is to jump from the window I am looking through into a fireman's net below. As there is no other way of escape, I am faced with two choices: remain and die, or jump and live. If I jump and indeed experience deliverance from death, would I ever regret jumping into the net or question my decision? No. In fact, I would be emboldened to encourage anyone else who was in that same situation to jump into the net also; I know experientially that jumping is the only means of escaping death.

The message of God's salvation is not exclusive; it is for anyone who will believe it (Rev. 22:17), but it is exclusive in nature, for trusting in any other message brings eternal judgment (Gal. 1:6-9). If an individual truly understands that all unsaved souls will spend an eternity in the lake of fire and that the only means of escaping hell is Christ, why would he or she ever turn back? This would be like walking back into a burning building! True faith based on God's truth lasts and for the Israelites there was no going back; they had been redeemed once and for all and their only recourse was to leave Egypt.

The Bible is full of pictures of redemption; the first example is found in Genesis 3. In the Garden of Eden, God exchanged Adam's and the woman's garments of fig leaves for those of animal skins. The fig leaves were their own attempt to fix their condition of nakedness. In general, the fig tree is a type of religion apart from God, and is most often applied to religious Israel (Luke 13:6-9). A fig tree was the only thing that the Lord directly cursed during His first advent – it withered up immediately. How God hates the traditions of men and the doctrines of demons! In Genesis 3, the fig leaves symbolized a bloodless religion that provided no atonement for sin. That is, the leaves were not an appropriate covering for sin because they did not reflect Christ's future propitiation for human sin through His own sacrifice. The fact that Adam and the woman still hid from God demonstrates that the fig leaves did not clear their consciences of the guilt resulting from their sin. In the mind of God, fig leaves would never do, so He killed innocent animals, removed their hides, and fashioned clothes for Adam and the woman.

Immediately after the fall of mankind, God's grace intervened. God labored to provide man an appropriate covering that would reflect His righteous solution to man's spiritual nakedness. Why were the skins of animals considered righteous attire? It was because they pictured the future work of God's Son. His Son, like the animals, would be innocent of wrongdoing and yet would be sacrificed to resolve man's spiritual nakedness before God. The skins would serve as a reminder to mankind of God's resolution concerning man's nakedness. Through Christ's efficacy, a gift of divine righteousness is accredited to all those who personally trust Christ as Saviour. This is called "justification." Although we are not righteous, we are declared righteous. This is why a repentant sinner can enter God's presence in heaven without fear. God sees the believer with a perfect standing because of our perfect union with His perfect Son.

Whether before Mount Sinai, after the Israelites had worshipped the golden calf, or outside Eden for Adam and Eve after they ate of the forbidden tree, God expediently seeks to restore lost fellowship with man through blood atonement. By shedding the blood of an innocent animal, atonement was accomplished. Atonement provided a temporary covering for sin; ultimately, all sin would be put away by Christ's shed blood. Jewish sacrifices and the sprinkling of the blood of bulls and goats could never take away sin (Heb. 10:4), or clear the conscience of guilt (Heb. 9:14). The Jewish sacrifices were commanded only to bring sin into remembrance and to picture the ultimate means (Christ's blood) in which sin would be put away and the conscience purged from guilt.

Apparently, even during the millennial reign of Christ on earth there is to be a remembrance of redemption. Jewish animal sacrifices will again be commanded during the millennial kingdom to ensure that the Jews never undervalue Christ's redemption for them (Ezek. 45:15-25; Zech. 14:16-21). The Church was created after Calvary and, thus, was not under the Jewish stewardship of the Law, but the Church presently remembers the value of Christ's redemptive work through the regular observance of the Lord's Supper until the Lord returns for the Church (Luke 22:19; 1 Cor. 11:26). In this matter of remembrance, there is a similarity to the millennial sacrifices of the Jews and the present practice of the Church in keeping the Lord's Supper.

After the Church has been caught up with Christ into heaven she will enjoy the Marriage Supper of the Lamb with her Beloved (Rev. 19:7-9). The Lord Jesus did not take part in Lord's Supper when He instituted it; for Him it was a time, not of joy, but of sacrifice. However, at His coming, the Church shall celebrate with Him.

At midnight, just as Moses had warned, the Lord smote the firstborn of Egypt, both man and beast. From Pharaoh's son in the palace to the prisoner in the most secluded dungeon, every household suffered death (v. 30). Perhaps one fourth of the Egyptians were judged that night; shrieks and wailing were heard throughout the land. Only those who took refuge under lamb's blood were spared death. The human mind is thrown into quandary: Why did God judge only the firstborn? Why did He judge the Egyptian children? Arthur Pink answers both questions:

> But why, it may be asked, should the "firstborn" be destroyed? At least a two-fold answer may be returned to this. It commonly happens that in the governmental dealings of God the sins of the fathers are visited upon the children. In the second place, Romans 9:22 teaches us that the "vessels of wrath" are made by God for the express purpose of showing His wrath and making known His power. The slaying of the children rather than their parents served to accomplish this the more manifestly. Again, the death of the firstborn was a representative judicial infliction. It spoke of the judgment of God coming upon all that is of the natural man; the firstborn like "the firstfruits" being a sample of all the rest. But why slay the firstborn of all the Egyptians, when Pharaoh only was rebellious and defiant? Answer: It is clear from Exodus 14:17 that the rank and file of the Egyptians were far from being guiltless.[2]

The destroyer may have been either an angel or the Angel of the Lord (preincarnate Christ). Based on verse 29 and other similar situations in Scripture (Num. 22:22; 1 Chron. 21:16), it seems more likely that the destroyer (v. 23), the one exacting justice, was the Angel of the Lord. On judgment day (i.e. at the Great White Throne Judgment) it will be Christ who executes justice on the wicked (John 5:22, 27). At the end of the Tribulation Period it will be Christ who is feared by the rebellious inhabitants of the earth:

> *Then the sky receded as a scroll when it is rolled up, and every mountain and island was moved out of its place. And the kings of the earth, the great men, the rich men, the commanders, the mighty men, every slave and every free man, hid themselves in the caves and in the rocks of the mountains, and said to the mountains and rocks, "Fall on us and hide us from the face of Him who sits on the throne and from the wrath of the Lamb! For the great day of His wrath has come, and who is able to stand?"* (Rev. 6:14-17).

In the future, the Lamb will execute justice upon the wicked. We do not know for sure who the destroyer in Egypt was, but we do know that Jehovah blocked the destroyer's way from entering every house marked by lamb's blood (v.23); ultimately, the power of life and of death culminate in the Lamb. The Lord Jesus is God's Lamb, His means of redeeming humanity and judging the rebel. Christ shed His own blood to save, but all those who reject His kind offer will suffer death. As the Egyptians learned, there is no escaping the power of the Lamb.

> Redeemed – how I love to proclaim it! Redeemed by the blood of the Lamb;
> Redeemed through His infinite mercy, His child, and forever, I am.
> I think of my blessed Redeemer, I think of Him all the day long;
> I sing, for I cannot be silent; His love is the theme of my song.
>
> — Fanny J. Crosby

# Egypt Despoiled
## Exodus 12:31-36

In the wee hours of the night, Pharaoh dispatched a courier to command Moses and Aaron to leave Egypt; they were to take all their children and livestock with them also. He said, *"Go, serve the Lord ... be gone, and bless me also."* It was an urgent matter, one that could not wait until morning, for the Egyptians knew that they were *"all dead men,"* as long as the Jews were in Egypt.

By requesting a "blessing" from Moses, Pharaoh circuitously acknowledged Jehovah's greatness, but by failing to admit his own wrong-doing, he also demonstrated his ignorance of Jehovah's holy character. Consequently, the request was ignored. God does not honor the prayer requests of the wicked (John 9:31), but His grace is freely bestowed on the brokenhearted and His mercy is lavished on the repentant:

> *The eyes of the Lord are on the righteous, and His ears are open to their cry. The face of the Lord is against those who do evil, to cut off the remembrance of them from the earth. The righteous cry out, and the Lord hears, and delivers them out of all their troubles. The Lord is near to those who have a broken heart, and saves such as have a contrite spirit* (Ps. 34:15-18).

It was at this juncture that God chose to come near to His people, to end their brutal saga, and to compensate them liberally for their previous suffering. Their countless tears and shattered dreams would be replaced with the joy of Jehovah's presence. He had worked in the heart of Pharaoh that he might crush Egypt and He now worked in the hearts of the Egyptians to lavish their remaining wealth upon the Jews. This too was another miraculous work of Jehovah, for He was the God of the Israelites, the One who had devastated the Egyptians' land, livelihood, and posterity; yet, they regarded His people favorably and handed over their clothing, jewels, gold, and silver to them. This fulfilled God's Word to Moses at the burning bush:

> *I will give this people favor in the sight of the Egyptians; and it shall be, when you go, that you shall not go empty-handed. But every woman shall ask of her neighbor, namely, of her who dwells near her house, articles of silver, articles of gold, and clothing; and you shall put them on your sons and on your daughters. So you shall plunder the Egyptians* (Ex. 3:21-22).

This was not the first time that Hebrews had left Egypt with an abundance of stuff. Some four centuries earlier, Abraham returned from Egypt with great wealth, much of which was acquired from the hand of Pharaoh as a goodwill gesture for the mistake of abducting his wife Sarah into his harem. However, their increased wealth posed a new difficulty for Abraham and Lot once back in Canaan: they could no longer dwell together for they were rich in cattle, silver, and gold (Gen. 13:2), and they had an abundance of stuff (Gen. 13:6). This is the first mention of "riches" in the Bible. Certainly, this first mention in Scripture has a lasting application concerning the "hoarding" of riches. What effect do too many possessions have on God's people? The result is strife among the brethren (Gen. 13:7). When brethren strive together, they cease to be a testimony for God.

How are brethren to consider their possessions? The early Church held the proper view of "equality" and thus maintained and enjoyed unity: *"And the multitude of those that believed were of one heart and of one soul; neither said any of them that any of the things which he possessed was his own; but they had all things common"* (Acts 4:32). The Apostle Paul teaches that there should be equality among the brethren: *"For I do not mean that others should be eased and you burdened; but by an equality, that now at this time your abundance may supply their lack, that their abundance also may supply your lack – that there may be equality"* (2 Cor. 8:13-14). If a brother is in need and another brother is able to meet that need, he should readily do so. Equality is not communism. Holding all things in equality is not the same as everyone having equal portions. When God's people properly value God, the things of God, and His people, they will enjoy unity; if their focus is shifted to temporal things, they will experience envy, dissatisfaction, and coveting. Consequently, Abraham and Lot had to separate before Abraham could again enjoy peace in the land. Carnal Lot journeyed towards that which reminded him of Egypt – Sodom, and Abraham continued his wilderness pilgrimage with his God.

For the children of Israel, who had been slaves with little personal property for decades, their sudden wealth could serve two possible purposes: it could be used to worship Jehovah or for idolatry. In the wilderness, there would be few opportunities to use the gold and silver of Egypt in trade. Besides that, there would be no need to buy clothing or food in the wilderness for Jehovah would sustain them. As all their basic necessities of life would be provided by God, their newly acquired wealth would serve as a test of their allegiance and loyalty to Jehovah. Unfortunately, before Moses could bring the commands of Jehovah down from Mount Sinai, the Jews had already used their provision to worship God to form an Egyptian god – the golden calf.

Joy in life is not achieved through things, but in knowing and living for Christ. Consequently, Paul instructed his spiritual son Timothy on how to maintain contentment in life:

> *Now godliness with contentment is great gain. For we brought nothing into this world, and it is certain we can carry nothing out. And having food and clothing, with these we shall be content. But those who desire to be rich fall into temptation and a snare, and into many foolish and harmful lusts which drown men in destruction and perdition. For the love of money is a root of all kinds of evil, for which some have strayed from the faith in their greediness, and pierced themselves through with many sorrows* (1 Tim. 6:6-10).

The Jews should have been content in the wilderness, for Jehovah had supplied all their basic needs. They were rich, but not content. They had the wherewithal to worship God by giving of their substance, but instead, they used their assets to honor *Apis*, the bull god of Egypt. Paul's instruction to Timothy on the subject of contentment concluded with a warning to the rich:

> *Command those who are rich in this present age not to be haughty, nor to trust in uncertain riches but in the living God, who gives us richly all things to enjoy. Let them do good, that they be rich in good*

> *works, ready to give, willing to share, storing up for themselves a good foundation for the time to come, that they may lay hold on eternal life* (1 Tim. 6:17-19).

It is not a sin to be rich, for such things are bestowed from God alone, but to trust in one's wealth to fix personal problems or to indulge in worldliness is sin. What we have is exactly what God wants us to have and is for the purpose of serving Him, helping others, and providing for our basic necessities. If our necessities are satisfied, Paul exhorts that we should keep working in order to have a provision to help those in need (Eph. 4:28). The Israelites would learn that wealth not consecrated to God soon leads to idolatry. As an idol is anything that draws our affection from God, the warning could never be more relevant than today. The western culture is immersed in "too much stuff" and it is strangling the life out of the Church.

> What is the world to me, with all its vaunted pleasure
> When Thou, and Thou alone, Lord Jesus, art my Treasure!
> Thou only, dearest Lord, my soul's Delight shalt be;
> Thou art my Peace, my Rest – What is the world to me?
>
> The world seeks after wealth and all that Mammon offers,
> Yet never is content though gold should fill its coffers.
> I have a higher good, content with it I'll be:
> My Jesus is my Wealth – What is the world to me?
>
> — Georg M. Pfefferkorn

# The Exodus Begins
## Exodus 12:37-42

The next morning, approximately six hundred thousand Hebrew men and many more women and children began the Exodus from Egypt. They set out on foot from Rameses and came to Succoth. Two expressions describe the group leaving Egypt; they were *"a mixed multitude"* (v. 38), and they were *"the hosts of the Lord"* (v. 41). The Jews did not leave as "the hosts of Israel," for they had been purchased by blood; they were the Lord's possession. Unfortunately, the Jews did not depart from Egypt alone, for they came out as *"a mixed multitude."*

Scripture represents Satan both as a threatening lion who is ready to devour God's people (1 Pet. 5:8) and as a cunning serpent who endeavors to deceive and trick them (Gen. 3:1). The strong and brutal lion had been defeated in Egypt by Jehovah. Defeated, the enemy now slithered along in the shadows of the departing nation; if he cannot keep God's people in Egypt, he would ensure Egypt kept to them. Through the "mixed multitude," Satan would corrupt the Israelites from within. C. I. Scofield identifies the following correlation with the Church today:

> This mixed multitude, similar to unconverted church members in the present age, was a source of weakness and division then as now (Num. 11:4-6). There had been a manifestation of divine power, and men were drawn to it without a change of heart (Luke 14:25-27).[1]

The supernatural feats of Jehovah had inspired many Egyptians to depart with the Jews. Why were these pagans leaving their homes, their people, and their way of life to venture into a desert with their now liberated slave population? Perhaps it was because Egypt had been decimated by plagues and there was nothing left to live for in Egypt. Verse 43 forbade any foreigner from eating the Passover, which means the Egyptians traveling with the Israelites had not been redeemed by lamb's blood. Perhaps there were some Egyptians who became Jewish proselytes, but that fact is not recorded in Scripture. Rather, this group of foreigners is referred to as "rabble" in Numbers 11:4. They complained against Jehovah, despite His goodness to them in the wilderness, and stirred up the Jews to voice dissatisfaction also. The carnal man longs to feed on the things of world and this mixed multitude lusted for the delicacies of Egypt; they were not humbled by Jehovah's magnificent presence nor satisfied with His simple provisions.

After coming up out of Egypt, Abraham separated himself from Lot: a carnal-thinking man and a wholly consecrated man cannot have fellowship with each other – there will always be contention between them. Lot had a taste of Egypt in his mouth that he could not get rid of; it led him to the Jordan plain, and on to Sodom, and on to Zoar; ultimately, it cost him everything, including his family and his dignity.

This is why the Apostle Paul directed the church at Corinth to cast out (excommunicate) the man who was boldly engaging in immorality (1 Cor. 5:1-5). The assembly did put him out; they were made aware that a little leaven (a little tolerated sin) leavens the whole lump (affects the whole assembly). Churches today must take the matter of holy living seriously. If there is sin in the camp, there must be exhortation and reproof, and if sin persists – the sinning individual must be formally swept out of assembly fellowship. This action appropriately acknowledges the choice of the erring individual to continue in sin rather than to be restored to God, for God's people cannot enjoy fellowship with anyone who is not first in fellowship with God. The children of Israel went into the desert "a mixed company" (Ex. 12:38), and it was this unholy faction that vexed their souls and brought God's judgment and wrath upon them again and again (Num. 11:4-6). As Abraham learned, sometimes it is better to have a *blessed reduction* than to suffer a reduction in blessing.

As stated earlier, worldliness is any sphere in which the Lord Jesus is excluded. The Lord Jesus told His disciples the night before He was crucified, *"If the world hates you, you know that it hated Me before it hated you. If you were of the world, the world would love its own. Yet because you are not of the world, but I chose you out of the world, therefore the world hates you"* (John 15:18-19). James likened worldliness to the sin of spiritual adultery. *"Adulterers and adulteresses! Do you not know that friendship with the world is enmity with God?*

*Whoever therefore wants to be a friend of the world makes himself an enemy of God"* (Jas. 4:4). Worldliness is the love of passing things, and things have no eternal value, except in how they are used to please God. Worldliness opposes God, and God hates it.

The story of Hosea and Gomer conveys a vivid picture to us of how offended God is by the worldly indulgence of His people. Hosea was an honorable man, but his wife Gomer was lascivious and actually conceived children that were not Hosea's. In time, Gomer abandoned Hosea to pursue a fast-life with her various lovers. It wasn't long before Gomer found herself in a poor and desperate situation. Hosea demonstrated sacrificial love for Gomer and sent supplies to her. From a distance Hosea watched his wife Gomer praise her lovers for the very provisions he had sent to assist her (Hosea 2:5-8). Later, Gomer was abandoned by her lovers and sold into slavery. The redeeming love of God is exemplified when Hosea buys back his own adulterous wife, who was shamefully sold during a public slave auction. After experiencing the magnitude of Hosea's love, she never departed from him again.

Paul reminds believers that they are the espoused bride of the Lord Jesus (Eph. 5:22-25; 2 Cor. 11:2; Rev. 19:9). If believers could understand in even a small degree Christ's redeeming love, they would not commit spiritual adultery by fraternizing with the world. Why? Because such behavior grieves the Saviour. The ideologies of the world oppose God and God opposes them. Gomer's lovers didn't care for Gomer or about the hurt they were inflicting on Hosea. They used and abused Gomer until the thrill of the moment was gone. This was what the prodigal son learned in Luke 15 – the world leaves a person nothing, but rather robs him or her of everything that has true value.

Paul told the believers at Corinth not to leave the Lord's Table to feast at the table of demons (1 Cor. 10:16-22). There is a spiritual table where the Lord communes with His people. At this table, believers enjoy full fellowship with God and receive all the necessary provisions to thrive spiritually. All believers are seated at this table after trusting the gospel message and being born again. Why would anyone ever want to leave this table to party with demons?

These vivid allegories convey to us the heartbreak God suffers when His people desert Him and venture into the world to indulge their flesh and to dance with the devil. Paul warns, *"Do we provoke the Lord to jealousy? Are we stronger than He?"* (1 Cor. 10:22). Believer, are you provoking the Lord to jealousy by flirting with the world? If so, tell the Lord you are sorry and repent – or are you stronger than God? The Lord has no desire to destroy a rebel child of His, but He has promised to chasten those He loves (Heb. 12:6). Whether we will be hurt by or helped by the Lord is our choice. Either by the painful rod or the comforting staff God will lead His people heavenward.

Worldliness is a system of thinking which is in direct opposition to the teachings of Christ. Erwin Lutzer puts the matter this way, "Worldliness is excluding God from our lives and, therefore, consciously or unconsciously accepting the values of a man-centered society." He goes on to explain the world's twisted value system, "Worldliness is not only doing what is forbidden but also wishing it were possible to do it. One of its distinctives is mental slavery to illegitimate pleasure. Worldliness twists values by rearranging their price tags."[2] Often our flesh will try to justify the price tag of sin, or something that is questionably permissible, while our inner man is sounding the Philippians 4:8 alarm to enjoin us to pursue the best, God-honoring course of action. The Israelites would learn the hard way the consequences of valuing the trifles of Egypt over the inexhaustible resources of God. But Jehovah was laboring to refine His covenant people, a matter that would require much time and even more patience.

Verses 40 and 41 indicate that the children of Israel sojourned in Egypt 430 years. The Genesis 15:13 prophecy states that Abraham's descendants *"shall be a sojourner in a land that is not theirs, and shall serve them; and they shall afflict them four hundred years"* (Gen. 15:13). As explained before, the 400 years is a round figure and the events themselves unfolded in accordance with the sequence revealed to Abraham – sojourning to serving to suffering. But the days of sojourning and suffering in Egypt were over; God had delivered His people from that troublesome place and had glorified His name throughout Egypt in the process. Now, the sanctifying work of removing Egypt from His people would begin; it was a task that would be aggravated by *the mixed multitude* in their company.

> To ransom His people from bondage great wonders and signs He displayed;
> He smote all the firstborn of Egypt, till Pharaoh made haste and obeyed.
> Great nations and kings that opposed Him were smitten by God's mighty hand;
> Their riches He gave to His people, and made them inherit the land.
>
> — Unknown

# A Circumcised People
## Exodus 12:43-51

Jehovah delivered more instructions to Moses and Aaron at Succoth concerning future Passover celebrations. These regulations were necessary because of the number of foreigners who left Egypt with the Israelites. Moses was commanded that, *"In one house it shall be eaten; you shall not carry any of the flesh outside the house, nor shall you break one of its bones. All the congregation of Israel shall keep it"* (Ex. 12:46-48). Not only was Israel's separation from the world to be strictly maintained, but the Passover feast itself would bolster national unity.

This unity was to be preserved at all costs: not one bone of the lamb was to be broken and the Passover had to be eaten in one house (it could not be shared with foreigners). If foreigners truly desired to identify with the God of the Hebrews and become part of the Jewish community they would first have to submit to male circumcision. Through the act of circumcision, they would identify with the covenant blessings made by God with Abraham.

As recorded in Genesis 17, Abraham received circumcision as a token of the covenant God had made with him. In obedience to God's command, ninety-nine year old Abraham and all the males of his house were circumcised that very day (Gen. 17:26-27). The descendants of Abraham continue to perform this symbolic ritual to honor God and to acknowledge His covenant with them. Paul tells us in Romans 4:11 that circumcision was *"a seal of the righteousness of the faith which he had yet being uncircumcised."* Circumcision was a "token" of Abraham's righteous standing that was gained by his faith in God's promise.

How is circumcision a sign? What is the organ of the body that best identifies an individual as a man? Right – that's it. So, by stripping away a piece of foreskin from this organ, God was symbolically stripping away Abram's old identity and showing him that receiving

His promises had nothing to do with the flesh (i.e. the very organ man used to produce seed, which was God's promise to Abraham, was to have flesh cut away from it). The act of circumcision in Genesis 17 beautifully complements the name changes given to Abram and Sarai in the same chapter. God was about to enact His covenant with them by giving them a son; it was fitting that they should comprehend their new identity as God's chosen people and human instruments to bless the entire world. Abraham was already declared righteous by God before circumcision was instituted (Rom. 4:11), but now he would learn to please God by living a *circumcised life.*

It is the same for the believer today. When individuals humble themselves as sinners before God and confess their need for a Saviour, God responds by justifying them (literally the act of imputing divine righteousness to their account; Rom. 4:4-5). *"If any man be in Christ, he is a new creature* [creation]*; old things are passed away; behold, all things are become new"* (2 Cor. 5:17, KJV). However, our new identity in Christ demands that we live the "circumcised life," which is the "cutting off" or "putting to death" of the desires and the will of our flesh. Paul concludes in Romans 2:29 that it is the circumcision of the heart that God wants in a believer's life, and not an outward show of contrived spirituality by the flesh.

In one sense, the act of *circumcision* for the Old Testament Jew is similar to the act of believer's baptism for the New Testament Christian. A circumcised life is one that reckons itself dead to selfish ambition and lusting in the flesh and rather lives in and for Christ. In this sense, physical circumcision and water baptism are alike. Yet, the similarities break down when examining the broader dispensational truth of Scripture. Under the Law, parents circumcised their baby boys without their consent; whereas believer's baptism in the Church Age was *always* done after individuals believed the gospel message (Acts 10:47, 16:31-34).

Regardless of the dispensational differences, we learn of Abraham's love for the Lord; he obeyed His command to be circumcised, though it caused him physical pain to do so. Abraham's obedience serves as an indictment against many who profess Christ as Saviour, but ignore His command to be baptized (Matt. 28:19). There will not be any lakes or baptismal tanks in heaven, so now is the time to honor the Lord and to obey His command to be baptized. Jehovah taught Moses that the circumcised life is marked by obedience to God. In the Church Age, believer's baptism should be one of the first expressions of one's love for the Lord Jesus Christ.

> Consecration is the narrow, lonely way to overflowing love. We are not called upon to live long on this planet, but we are called upon to be holy at any and every cost. If obedience costs you your life, then pay it.
>
> — Oswald Chambers

# The Firstborn is Sanctified

## Exodus 13:1-16

By the substitutional death of a lamb, the firstborn of man and beast among the Hebrews had been spared death in Egypt. The destroyer passed by each home that had lamb's blood on its doorway. Since God had purchased the lives of the firstborn, He now claimed special ownership of them. They were to be sanctified, or literally "dedicated," to Him. The Hebrew word *qadash* translated "sanctify" in verse 2 means "to dedicate." This is only the second time in Scripture that *qadash* has been employed; the first reference in Genesis 2:3 dedicated the Sabbath Day as holy. Later, this firstborn group would be exchanged for the tribe of Levi – soul for soul. Special substitutional sacrifices and redemption money would be required to account for the 273 more men in the tribe of Levi than the total number of firstborns in the nation (Num. 3:40-51). As a result of this exchange, the entire tribe of Levi would be consecrated to serve the Lord and to affect worship in the tabernacle/temple on behalf of the nation.

While the outcome of redemption was still fresh in the Hebrews' minds, Moses reiterated God's command concerning the keeping of the feasts of Passover and of Unleavened Bread. Moses added an additional instruction to the seven-day feast of Unleavened Bread: *"no leavened bread shall be seen among you"* (v. 7). Not only was leaven a symbol of sin and to be removed from their homes, the Jews were not to look upon it either. This illustrates a safeguard for avoiding sin in our own lives – don't watch or look at anything that would stimulate the flesh to sin.

There are a number of important teachings concerning sexual purity in the Bible, but space permits us to review only three at this time: (1) *"For this is the will of God, even your sanctification, that ye should abstain from fornication"* (1 Thess. 4:3, KJV). (2) *"To avoid fornication, let every man have his own wife, and let every woman have her own husband"* (1 Cor. 7:2). (3) God's judgment falls not only on fornicators, but also upon those who *"approve of those who practice"* it (Rom. 1:32).

Firstly, it is God's will that we abstain from fornication, which is any sexual relationship outside the bounds of marriage. Secondly, if married, a man is to have only his wife and the wife only her husband; there is to be no sexual lusting after or "touching" of another person (1 Cor. 7:1). Thirdly, to punctuate the prohibition of lusting after another, Paul states that those who look with approval on others committing fornication also deserve God's judgment. It is this *looking* upon sexual perversions to achieve pleasure that has become a scourge to our society and has led to many broken marriages and splintered families.

Having the same root word, pornography and *porneia* ("fornication") are closely association in meaning. *Porneia* is used in the New Testament to address all forms of sexual impurity and wanton behavior. The word initially meant "to act the harlot" but later evolved to mean "to indulge in unlawful lust." *Porneia* (and its root word) specifically describes various types of sins: pre-marital sex (1 Cor. 7:1-2), physical adultery (Matt.19:9), any form of unchaste conduct (1 Cor. 6:13, 18), prostitution or harlotry (Rev. 2:20-21), homosexuality (Jude 7), and spiritual adultery (Rev. 14:8, 17:4). Interestingly, when sins are listed in the New Testament, fornication normally tops the list (1 Cor. 5:11; Col. 3:5). Besides hurting others, fornication is a grievous sin which afflicts one's own body (1 Cor. 6:18).

In Proverbs 7, Solomon instructed his son to avoid the strange woman while journeying through the city streets, for death would result from her traps. With today's technology, a man no longer has to venture out of his home to meet the strange woman – techno-filth is readily available for private viewing anytime and anywhere. The word pornography is directly derived from the Greek word *pornographous* which meant "to write about prostitutes" (from the root words: *porne,* "harlot," and *graphos,* "writing"). Thus, pornography is a virtual form of fornication!

The ultimate goal of pornography is to promote fornication; the former stirs up unlawful lusting, the latter satisfies those lusts through immoral sexual acts. If we are to abstain from fornication, we must put up a mental-defense that will maintain a pure thought-life. We cannot lust in our members and expect to be holy in conduct. Indeed, the Lord

Jesus taught that if a man looks on a woman with lust he has already committed sexual immorality with her in his heart (Matt. 5:28).

Physically we are what we eat, but spiritually we are what we think: *"For as he thinks in his heart, so is he"* (Prov. 23:7). By properly controlling our thought-life we control our behavior! When we choose not to stimulate our flesh through suggestive media we will find it easier to maintain a Christ-honoring thought-life. Unchecked lusting leads to sin and separation from God (Jas. 1:14); He cannot have fellowship with us while we are in sin (1 Jn. 1:5-7).

An individual cannot change the reality of our current social situation, but, on a personal level, he or she can determine to remain pure and to pursue precautionary measures to maintain that commitment. During the feast of Unleavened Bread the Israelites were not only to remove the leaven from their homes, they were not to look at leaven either. This action would help preclude lusting for what they could not have.

Romans 6 is a premier portion of Scripture which speaks of God's desire for sanctification in the believer's life. In that chapter, Paul itemized several identification truths before addressing the practical side of sanctification: the believer was, positionally speaking, crucified with Christ (v.6), buried with Christ (v. 4), and made alive and raised up with Christ (vv. 4, 8). Paul wants the Christians to understand that their complete oneness with Christ is in itself motivation to refrain from sin:

> *How shall we who died to sin live any longer in it? Or do you not know that as many of us as were baptized into Christ Jesus were baptized into His death? Therefore we were buried with Him through baptism into death, that just as Christ was raised from the dead by the glory of the Father, even so we also should walk in newness of life* (Rom. 6:2-4).

Paul's main point in these verses is that our union with Christ should motivate us to not sin, for we, being one with Christ, should not want to make Him privy to our sin. In verse 11, the subject matter in Romans 6 transitions from identification truth (i.e. how God sees us "with Christ") to practical sanctification (i.e. our personal responsibility of holiness to God in light of our identification with Christ). Oswald Sander's outline of Romans 6 conveys progressive warnings for us to be mindful of, so that God's work of sanctification in our lives be not hindered:

Vv. 1-11: You cannot continue in sin.
Vv. 12-14: You need not continue in sin.
Vv. 15-19: You must not continue in sin.
Vv. 20-23: You had better not continue in sin.[1]

The divine work of sanctification begins in the believer's life immediately after he or she answers the call of salvation. God begins to fashion the new believer into a holy vessel and each believer is exhorted to cooperate in the working out of what God is working into his or her life (1 Thess. 5:23; Heb. 13:21). All believers will ultimately be conformed to the moral image of Christ (Rom. 8:29); there is no human choice of involvement in that aspect of sanctification – it is God's will and power that accomplishes this. Yet, there is an ongoing call to each believer to not resist God's working in his or her life, but instead to be yielded to Him. God promises to chasten those who choose not to submit to Him in order that they may be brought to a yielded position and experience sanctification (Heb. 12:6). Consequently, sanctification in a practical sense is happening to every believer, but some are more serious about it than others and, accordingly, will reap a greater blessing of further refinement here and now.

To convey the ongoing work of sanctification among the Israelites two ordinances were instituted: the yearly observance of the feast of Unleavened Bread and the perpetual redemption of the firstborn in Israel. Whoever opened the womb for the first time (man or beast) had to be redeemed by the life of a lamb. The firstborn was God's portion among the nation, and it had to be substitutionally purchased by a lamb. In this way, the firstborn were not put to death as a sacrifice to God, but rather were redeemed by a substitute sacrifice which then allowed them to live as God's purchased possession upon the earth. In other words, their consecration to God demanded that they "set apart" their first fruits to God. The Hebrew word *abar* translated "set apart" in verse 11 implies the act of "passing along." Because of their sanctification, the Jews were enabled to *pass along* acceptable service and worship to God.

In the same way today, the Lord desires a holy priesthood of believers who freely offer up living sacrifices in response to their redemption obtained by Christ's blood. The believer is "set apart" for this service and his or her eternal union with Christ demands consecrated living. Presently, the Church is Christ's portion upon the earth and *"to Him be glory in the Church"* (Eph. 3:21).

> I am Thine O Lord! I have heard Thy voice, and it told Thy love to me;
> But I long to rise in the arms of faith, and be closer drawn to Thee.
> Consecrate me now to Thy service Lord, but the power of grace divine;
> Let my soul look up with a steadfast hope, and my will be lost in Thine.
>
> — Fanny J. Crosby

# The Long Way Home
## Exodus 13:17-20

The Israelites had arrived safely at Succoth and now were continuing on to Etham, which was located on the edge of the wilderness. Verse 19 records the Israelites' faithfulness to complete their vow made to Joseph prior to his death: *"Joseph said to his brethren, 'I am dying; but God will surely visit you, and bring you out of this land to the land of which He swore to Abraham, to Isaac, and to Jacob.' Then Joseph took an oath from the children of Israel, saying, 'God will surely visit you, and you shall carry up my bones from here'"* (Gen. 50:24-26). By faith, Joseph foresaw the exodus and desired that his remains would depart with his people and be buried in the land of their inheritance.

One of the most awe-inspiring expressions in Scripture is found in verse 18: *"but God."* Found forty-two times in the Bible, "but God" normally identifies an incredible feat of God's grace in response to man's desperate need for it. Genesis contains five "but God" phrases and each announces an extraordinary work of God to resolve a human crisis. For example, God intervened after Abimelech took Sarah into his harem (Gen. 20:3), and also when Laban tried to take advantage of Jacob through devious business dealings (Gen. 31:7). Joseph uses the term twice to acknowledge that his difficulties in Egypt were not primarily because of his brother's deceitful actions, but rather because God was working to extend a great blessing to Israel specifically and to humanity in general (Gen. 45:8, 50:20).

The expression "but God" is used in the New Testament in the same way: *"But God demonstrates His own love toward us, in that while we were still sinners, Christ died for us"* (Rom. 5:8) and *"But God, who is rich in mercy, because of His great love with which He loved us, even when we were dead in trespasses, made us alive together with Christ (by grace you have been saved)"* (Eph. 2:4-5). Humanity was dead in trespasses and sins, *but God* found a way to resolve our hopeless spiritual condition by grace in Christ. Believer, be very thankful for this little phrase "but God" in Scripture; without it there would be no joy in this life and no hope for a future one.

The phrase *"but God"* appears only twice in Exodus (13:18, 21:13). In Exodus 13:18 the expression speaks of God's providential means of preparing the Israelites for Canaan. *"The way to the land of the Philistines"* was a quicker route to Canaan from Egypt, but God knew if He took His people by that way they would not be ready for battle when they arrived at Canaan. The Israelites had departed from Egypt in "military array" (v. 18; NASV), but they were neither trained nor conditioned for the rigors of warfare. The Jews were unprepared for this hardship and Jehovah knew the tendency of their flesh would be to circumvent the challenge and head back to Egypt. As C. H. Mackintosh explains, the Lord regarded the weaknesses and timidity of His people:

> The Lord, in His condescending grace, so orders things for His people that they do not, at their first setting out, encounter heavy trials, which might have the effect of discouraging their hearts and driving them back. "The way of the wilderness" was a much more protracted route; but God had deep and varied lessons to teach His people, which could only be learnt in the desert. [1]

The same is true today for the Christian. In matters that concern spiritual maturity and growing faith, there are no short-cuts in a believer's life. Wilderness experiences, tests, and trials are necessary to produce a battle-hardened soldier of the cross. Initially, a new Christian enjoys learning for the first time of God's love and grace towards them; yet, the hard road is still ahead. During the next several months, the excitement wanes as the new convert endures insults and demeaning statements from lost family members and friends. The natural tendency of the flesh when confronted with spiritual opposition is to retreat – there is nothing in the flesh that wants to engage in such a battle, nor does the flesh have any wherewithal to fight it. But the spiritual man presses forward, enters the fray, and is victorious in Christ: *"For whatever is born of God overcomes the world. And this is the victory that has overcome the world – our faith"* (1 Jn. 5:4).

At regeneration, a new convert typically knows little of the Word of God. In hand to hand combat a soldier will not fare well if his only weapon is dull, stubby knife. In spiritual warfare, the child of God will not be effective in defending and confirming the gospel without knowing how to properly apply Scripture (i.e. the Sword of Truth). God's dealings with the Israelites in the wilderness verifies that the reason He allows Satan to buffet Christians today is to better prepare them for battle tomorrow (Jas. 1:12-13; Job 1:6-12). God is holy; He cannot tempt believers to sin, but He does allow Satan to tempt and test believers for refinement purposes. With each successive trial, the believer better learns how to use his or her spiritual armor and weapons and to depend more and more on God's grace.

After Paul identifies the believer's enemy (Satan), and who the believer battles with (rulers of darkness), he itemizes the believer's spiritual armor and resources for confronting both (Eph. 6:11-18):

> **Loins girded with truth** (Eph. 6:14): A robe was pulled up and tied to allow a person to move more quickly – a must in battle. Application: Know what is true and what is false doctrine; quickly respond to uphold that which is true and flee what is not. Generally speaking, what the world runs after the Church should flee from.
>
> **Breastplate of righteousness** (Eph. 6:14): The breastplate covers a pure heart. Application: Keep short accounts with God concerning sin; having a pure walk will make you blameless, keep you from being accused, and thus limit the enemy's opportunities to attack you.
>
> **Feet shod with the gospel** (Eph. 6:15; 1 Pet. 3:15; 2 Tim. 4:2): The hobnails on Roman sandals provided a soldier with excellent footing in battle. Application: Stand firm in the gospel while in enemy territory (the world). Always be prepared to share the gospel – it brings the peace of God to others.
>
> **Shield of faith** (Eph. 6:16): The typical Roman shield was a 2 by 4 foot piece of wood covered with leather. The shield was capable of stopping darts, spears, and arrows. These shields could be connected together to form an impenetrable moving wall. The was no armor for the back of the soldier, meaning there was no provision for retreat; to use the shield effectively soldiers had to move forward to face the enemy. Application: Trust in the Lord for protection, move forward into battle, and don't withdraw from the enemy. A group of believers engaging the enemy provides encouragement and protection to the group as a whole.

**Helmet of Salvation** (Eph. 6:17): Hope propels the soldier of the Lord forward against adversity; he or she has assurance of ultimate victory. Application: The believer's destiny is secure in Christ.

**Sword of the Spirit** (Eph. 6:17): The sword can be used as an offensive or a defensive weapon. Application: The Word of God is able to cut to the heart and conscience of men (Heb. 4:12; Acts 2:37, 5:33). Christians need to know God's Word to effectively engage in spiritual warfare.

**Prayer for Empowerment** (Eph. 6:18): God's grace for each and every day is received through prayer. Application: A soldier of Christ relies on God's grace through prayer; the focus of the soldier's prayer is effectiveness for Christ rather than personal comfort. Diligent alertness and active prayer are marks of a believer who understands the tactics of the enemy and the greatness of his or her God.

The Christian's life begins when a sinner comes to Christ for salvation, but it does not end there – every believer becomes a soldier of the cross, just as every Jewish man coming out of Egypt was enlisted in the Lord's army. Initially there were no exceptions, though later the tribe of Levi would be consecrated to full-time service at the tabernacle and, therefore, be exempt from going to war. Likewise, every true Christian who has come to Christ's cross for salvation has enlisted; he or she is a soldier of the cross – there are no exceptions!

God was putting His people through boot-camp to ready them for conflict in Canaan. Without the wilderness training, they would not be able to seize their God-given possession in the Promised Land. Likewise, through properly using one's spiritual armor, personal victory over the enemy is not only possible, but is expected. With each new victory the believer becomes more aware of all their *"spiritual blessings in heavenly places in Christ"* (Eph. 1:3). So, beloved of the Lord, let us strap on the armor of God, train, pray, and be diligent to enter into the victory which Christ has already won.

Conquering now and still to conquer rides a King in His might,
Leading the host of all the faithful into the midst of the fight,
Not to the strong is the battle, not to the swift is the race,
Yet to the true and the faithful, victory is promised through grace.

— Sabine Baring Gould

## Guided by a Cloud of Fire
### Exodus 13:21-22

Escaping from brutal captivity, trekking through an unknown desert, and witnessing so many supernatural feats by Jehovah must have been an overwhelming experience for the Israelites. But God had a solution to soothe their apprehension: *"And the Lord went before them by day in a pillar of cloud to lead the way, and by night in a pillar of fire to give them light, so as to go by day and night. He did not take away the pillar of cloud by day or the pillar of fire by night from before the people"* (Ex. 13:21-22). Perhaps the ever-present cloud was not a vital provision to sustain the Israelites in the wilderness, but it was certainly a kind token of Jehovah's parental care; the cloud would reassure the Jews of God's abiding presence.

The Israelites were young in their faith and needed such displays of divine attendance to quiet their anxieties, much the same way a young child is calmed during the long nighttime hours by a familiar nightlight. Even during times of rebellion, the pillar of God's presence would never depart from the children of Israel. God would accompany His covenant people through the best of times and the worst of times to ensure that they entered into the Promised Land. Centuries later, David understanding the blessing of God's abiding presence in his life would write: *"Yea, though I walk through the valley of the shadow of death, I will fear no evil; for You are with me"* (Ps. 23:4).

While in the desert, the cloud would illuminate their camp at night and its shadow would protect them from excess solar radiation during the day. It is not likely that the cloud changed in appearance throughout the day; the upper portion appeared as a pillar of fire, while its base flattened out and spread over the entire camp (Ex. 14:24). The cloud would safely guide the Israelites through the wilderness; if the cloud moved the Israelites pulled up their tent pegs and followed it. If the cloud lingered in a particular location, the Israelites were to tarry under its shadow.

Approximately six months prior to His crucifixion, the Lord Jesus used this familiar icon from Hebrew history to teach of Himself. He was teaching at the temple during the Feast of Tabernacles when He declared the second of seven "I AM" statements recorded in John's Gospel: *"I am the light of the world. He who follows Me shall not walk in darkness, but have the light of life"* (John 8:12). Warren Wiersbe explains the significance of that event in association with the Jewish traditions of that day:

> Our Lord's I AM statement was also related to the Feast of Tabernacles, during which a huge candelabra was lighted in the temple at night to remind the people of the pillar of fire that had guided Israel in the wilderness journey.... To "follow" the Lord Jesus means to believe on Him, to trust Him; and the results are life and light for the believer.[1]

The wicks of the lamps in the candelabra were made from the priest's worn-out garments. Hanging the lamps over the women's court at the temple ensured that *all* would be able to see the spectacular illumination. Christ utilized this traditional ceremony in a spiritual sense to declare to the whole congregation, *"I AM the light of the world."* God's light, through Christ, was shining forth to all mankind; its illumination had no prejudice to gender, ethnic origin, or social status. Christ came into the world and He died for the whole world (1 Jn. 2:2; Heb. 2:9), that "whosoever will" may step into the light and have fellowship with God (1 Jn. 1:5-9).

At various times during the Israelites' journey through the wilderness we read of God, or more specifically, the Angel (Messenger) of the Lord, being present the midst of the cloud (Ex. 14:19, 24, 24:16). During the Feast of Tabernacles in Christ's day the same One who had spoken from within the pillar of cloud centuries earlier now declared, *"I AM the light of the world."* The Lord Jesus Himself was God's abiding presence in the world and through Him God would guide blind sinners into life-transforming truth. Earlier in His earthly ministry, He taught:

> *And this is the condemnation, that the light has come into the world, and men loved darkness rather than light, because their deeds were evil. For everyone practicing evil hates the light and does not come to the light, lest his deeds should be exposed. But he who does the truth comes to the light, that his deeds may be clearly seen, that they have been done in God* (John 3:19-21).

The ultimate test of whether someone has truly trusted Christ for salvation is whether or not they continue practicing evil. A true child of God does not persist in sin (1 Jn. 3:9); a child of light does not blatantly walk in darkness. Why? Because a true believer longs for God's abiding presence and fellowship. Not only are there deep longings to be with God, but profound remorse when under the conviction ministry of the Holy Spirit should lead a true child of God to repentance and restoration.

The evening before His death, the Lord explained to His disciples why the world hated Him and why it would hate them also; *"If I had not come and spoken to them, they would have no sin, but now they have no excuse for their sin"* (John 15:22). The Lord's sinless presence among sinners was a convicting testimony of the holiness of God and His words left no doubt in the sinner's mind as to their sinful state and their need for a righteous standing before God. They had been exposed to soul-penetrating light, and instead of walking into the light, they had scurried back into satanic darkness.

Light symbolizes divine truth, and believing is an action of faith not based on temporal sight; both are paramount topics throughout John's Gospel. The anti-type of each of these is strongly tied together in the behavior of the spiritually blind Pharisees. They were blind because they chose to ignore divine truth and continued in the darkness of self-righteousness. The Lord proclaimed this truth while speaking with the healed blind man of John 9 who had just gained spiritual sight also (i.e. he acknowledged Jesus Christ as the Son of God):

> *And Jesus said, "For judgment I have come into this world, that those who do not see may see, and that those who see may be made blind." Then some of the Pharisees who were with Him heard these words, and said to Him, "Are we blind also?" Jesus said to them, "If you were blind, you would have no sin; but now you say, 'We see.' Therefore your sin remains"* (John 9:39-41).

Spiritual blindness clouds human reasoning, perverts logic, and distorts our perception of reality. This is why, in spiritual matters, man must ignore sight-based faith and our mutable feelings, and simply trust God at His word; this is true faith and the only kind that pleases God (Heb. 11:6). God rewards true faith by opening our eyes to deeper spiritual truth; naturally speaking, we cannot understand the things of God without His help (1 Cor. 2:9-13). The Lord Jesus told His disciples, *"Know the truth, and the truth shall make you free"* (John 8:32). Mark the utter stupidity of the Pharisees' statements while speaking with the Lord Jesus:

> These strict, self-righteous, Law-keepers had to be reminded by Christ that their plans to murder Him would in fact, break the Mosaic Law (John 7:19, 8:59)
>
> Speaking to the Lord Jesus, the Pharisees said, *"Are you also from Galilee? Search and look, for no prophet has arisen out of Galilee"* (John 7:52). Perhaps they had forgotten that Jonah was of Galilee.
>
> The Pharisees brought a woman caught in the act of adultery before the Lord to be judged, but where was the man? The Law was no respecter of persons – adultery demanded the death of both parties (John 8:1-11, Lev. 20:10).
>
> The Pharisees proclaimed to Christ, *"We are Abraham's descendants, and have never been in bondage to anyone. How can You say, 'You will be made free'?"* (John 8:33). But, in fact, they had been ruled by four world empires and at that time had not been independent for over 600 years.

Oswald Chambers once said, "Darkness is my point of view, my right to myself; light is God's point of view."[2] God has offered mankind a choice – to hide in the calamity of darkness and experience eternal death, or to abide in divine light and experience life in and with God. There can be no fellowship with God in darkness!

Without the direction supplied by the cloud in the wilderness, the Israelites would not have known which way to venture in life, and similarly, without the revelation of Christ, man would not have known how to please God. John explains that to remain in fellowship with God a believer must continue to walk with God according to revealed truth:

> *This is the message which we have heard from Him and declare to you, that God is light and in Him is no darkness at all. If we say that we have fellowship with Him, and walk in darkness, we lie and do not practice the truth. But if we walk in the light as He is in the light, we have fellowship with one another, and the blood of Jesus Christ His Son cleanses us from all sin* (1 Jn. 1:5-7).

God is light, that is, His very character defines what is righteous. God will not, and indeed cannot, walk in darkness; that would offend His holy nature. Therefore, if we desire to have fellowship with Him, we must continue to live out revealed truth – this is synonymous with walking with Him. If we slip or trip from the lighted way, John explains that there is a provision for our restoration: *"If we confess our sins, He is faithful and just to forgive us our sins and to cleanse us from all unrighteousness"* (1 Jn. 1:9). As soon as broken fellowship is sensed the believer can immediately confess his or her wrong behavior or lustful thought as sin, and ask for His forgiveness. The blood of Christ is more than sufficient to cleanse the believer's conscience and again set his or her feet upon the straight and narrow road of holy living.

Christ, the Light of the world, challenges saint and sinner alike to step out from darkness and to walk in accordance with divine truth. In so doing, the unregenerate sinner will find salvation of his or her soul and the saint will learn more of the peace of God which surpasses all understanding. Accordingly, God's light without God's grace would be a miserable existence indeed, and thankfully God does not offer either exclusively from the other.

> Is the wilderness before Thee? Desert lands where drought abides?
> Heavenly springs shall there restore thee, fresh from God's exhaustless tides.
> Light divine surrounds thy going; God Himself shall mark thy way.
> Secret blessings, richly flowing, lead to everlasting day.
>
> — John N. Darby

# Fear Not, Stand Still

## Exodus 14:1-18

The exodus was proceeding without mishap. All of the Hebrews, their livestock, and the spoil of Egypt had moved from Rameses to Succoth, and then to Etham, which was on the edge of Red Sea wilderness. Yet, after leaving Etham, God commanded the Israelites to depart from the common route through the wilderness and to encamp before Pihahiroth, which was between Migdol and the sea (v. 1). God explained to Moses, who then told the people, that the detour would place them in such a vulnerable location that Pharaoh would be enticed to pursue after them. Arthur Pink notes that the names associated with the Israelite encampments are significant:

> Here, as everywhere in Scripture, these names are full of meaning. They are in striking accord with what follows. "Pi-hahiroth" is rendered by Ritchie "Place of Liberty." Such indeed it proved to be, for it was here that Israel was finally delivered from those who had long held them in cruel bondage. "Migdol" signifies "a tower" or "fortress." Such did Jehovah demonstrate Himself to be unto His helpless and attacked people. Newberry gives "Lord of the North" as the meaning of "Baal-zephon," and in Scripture the "north" is frequently associated with judgment (Josh. 8:11-13; Isa. 14:31; Jer. 1:14, 4:6, 6:1; Eze. 1:4). It was as the Lord of Judgment that Jehovah was here seen at the Red Sea.[1]

The cool sea breeze was a welcome benefit of their new encampment, but from a tactical standpoint, it was indeed a poor location to defend against an Egyptian attack. There was only one western entrance into the camp, with mountains to the North and South, and the sea directly to their East. If the Israelites were confronted by Pharaoh, there would be no means of escape and no natural means to fortify a defensive position. Naturally speaking, they were helpless, yet, this is where God wanted His people. Again, God worked His will in the heart of Pharaoh for this expressed purpose: *"that the Egyptians may know that I am the Lord"* (v. 4). Consequently, even Pharaoh's own servants who had earlier begged him to let the Israelites go were now bemoaning their release, saying, *"Why have we done this, that we have let Israel go from serving us?"* (v. 5). What was Pharaoh's response? *"He made ready his chariot and took his people with him. Also, he took six hundred choice chariots, and all the chariots of Egypt with captains over every one of them"* (Ex. 14:6-7). This was an all-out effort to recover the Israelites by military force. Pharaoh mustered all his choice soldiers and his best weapons of war to reclaim Egypt's lost possession.

Since all the horses of Egypt had been killed in the fifth plague, and since many of the horses bought after this plague would have again been slaughtered in the plagues of hail and of the death of the firstborn, it is likely that Pharaoh had to pull all his resources together for this final attempt to overcome Jehovah. All the horses that remained in Egypt would be used to pull his war-chariots. Besides the vast number of chariots involved in the engagement, there was also, apparently, a large contingent of foot-soldiers marching towards the Israelites (v. 10). Given the slow communication of intelligence information, and the time needed for Pharaoh's army to assemble and to journey to Pihahiroth, it is apparent that the Israelites must have been camped by the sea for days.

God had previously said that when the Israelites first saw warfare they would want to go back to Egypt and to slavery (Ex. 13:17) and that is exactly what happened when they learned of Pharaoh's approaching army. Had Jehovah gone to such extraordinary measures to deliver them from Egypt just to watch them be slaughtered by Pharaoh in the desert? The Israelites cried out to the Lord and they bitterly complained to Moses:

> *Because there were no graves in Egypt, have you taken us away to die in the wilderness? Why have you so dealt with us, to bring us up out of Egypt? Is this not the word that we told you in Egypt, saying, "Let us alone that we may serve the Egyptians?" For it would have been better for us to serve the Egyptians than that we should die in the wilderness* (Ex. 14:11-12).

Thankfully, the Lord loved the Israelites too much to leave them alone as they had requested. Likewise, He loves you and me too much to leave us the way we are. He was not going to allow His redeemed people to go back into bondage, no matter how much they screamed and hollered about their threatening predicament. He specializes in managing crisis situations; in fact, this entire predicament was completely of His design and would be used to refine His people and to manifest His glory to all of Egypt.

While enduring a distressing situation David wrote, *"I would hasten my escape from the windy storm and tempest"* (Ps. 55:8). If given a choice between enduring hardship with the Lord or having a life of ease, the flesh will also pick the latter. It is so easy to run from our difficulties, unless we understand that God has His way in the storms of life and that, if we flee prematurely, we are actually withdrawing from God's presence. John Darby puts it this way, "Although God in His faithfulness be with us, we are not always with Him."[2]

After feeding five thousand men (plus women and children), the Lord sought solitude in order to pray to His Father. He sent His disciples by boat to the other side of the Sea of Galilee. Those twelve men, obedient to their Lord, launched out into a sea that soon met them with life-threatening force. They toiled all night in a raging storm but did not prevail against it. The disciples believed death crouched within each wave that broke upon their battered vessel. Yet, they were safer in that boat than any other place on earth. Why? Because they had been obedient to the Lord's command and were in the center of His will.

The very thing that the disciples feared – the raging sea – was what the Lord used to bring Himself closer to them; He walked upon the sea to meet them. God's presence enables us to overcome what is feared. The result being we have a greater appreciation for His faithfulness and are more likely to confidently engage the next challenge in faith.

Pharaoh and his army was what the Israelites feared most. To strengthen their faith in Him, God would overcome their enemies as His people looked on. The situation was bleak, desperate in fact, but it is in such times that man becomes the most willing to recognize God's intervention. Although the Israelites were in military array they were not to fight; they had but two commands to obey: *"Fear not, stand still and see the salvation of the Lord"* (v.13), and *"Go forward"* (v. 15).

These two commands are not contradictory, as Edward Dennett explains:

> There is no inconsistency between the command of Moses, "Stand still," and that now given, "Go forward." They had truly to be reminded that they could do nothing; but faith should have perceived that the work was done, and marched boldly forward through the sea which seemed to bar their advance. Death, and the power of death, had been overcome, the salvation had been completed, and hence they were to go forward. The order and the teaching of the order are beautiful. The Lord completes the work, and by the finished work of salvation a way of escape from Satan's power through death has been opened. Being opened, it is for the believer to walk through it, to go boldly forward in confidence in Him who, having been their Judge, has now become their Saviour.[3]

They were not to fear, for this was God's battle (v. 14), not theirs; they had no strength to fight it anyway. The concise expression "fear not" that is used here appears sporadically throughout the Bible; it is God's rallying cry to prompt the faith of His people. When facing personal difficulties, Abraham (Gen. 15:1), Joshua (Josh. 8:1), Gideon (Judg. 16:23), Daniel (Dan. 10:12), and many others were instructed not to fear, but rather to have faith in God. In each instance, God answered faith with the fantastic and He still does so today.

> A perfect faith would lift us absolutely above fear.
>
> — George MacDonald

The Israelites were to *stand still.* Standing still in the midst of terrifying circumstances demonstrates faith, a quality of spirit which prompts God's consideration in every situation. Besides this, if the Israelites spent their time fortifying their weak position, they might miss seeing God's spectacular handiwork.

God did not use the Israelites to confront Pharaoh while they were in Egypt, neither would He have them fight Pharaoh as they were leaving Egypt. In Egypt, the Israelites had been sheltered from God's wrath by blood; now God would, by His power alone, bring them through the place of death (the Red Sea). These two monumental events relate in type to Christ's judgment on the cross leading to His death and the burial of His body in the grave. Positionally speaking, the believer died with Christ at Calvary and was buried with Him in His garden tomb. The souls redeemed by lamb's blood in Egypt would be brought through the place of death in the Red Sea to enjoy life with Jehovah on the other side. These events symbolize the total victory that Christ would gain over Satan through His death, burial, and resurrection in a then still future day.

The Lord Jesus Christ foretold of this victory a few days before He triumphed over Satan, his world system, and death itself: *"Now is the judgment of this world; now the ruler of this world will be cast out. And I, if I am lifted up from the earth, will draw all peoples to Myself"* (John 12:31-33). Believers will be oppressed by Satan's defeated system until it is put away once and for all, but the victory over it has already been achieved; therefore, the redeemed of God cannot be overcome by satanic authority for all those in Christ have been delivered from his domain (i.e. the world and death). Those in Christ are forever secure in Christ and those outside Christ are forever doomed; these identification truths are timeless, but the reality of one's destiny is proven out in time.

Because securing salvation is completely God's business, the Israelites could do nothing but *stand still and see the salvation of the Lord.* It is for this reason that we do not see the Israelites in battle until Exodus 17. In that chapter, Moses strikes the rock (a type of Christ) with the rod of God and an abundant flow of water gushes out from the rock to satisfy the thirst of the Israelites. The Lord clearly tied the water from this rock to the blessings of the Holy Spirit that resulted from His completed work at Calvary (John 7:37-39). After drinking from the rock, the Israelites, for the first time, would have the wherewithal to enter into battle and would be able to revel in the victory already secured by God over the world. But at that moment, the Israelites were completely helpless; they could do nothing but trust the Lord to save them.

When Satan, my foe, shall come in like a flood,
To drive my poor soul from the Fountain of good,
I'll pray to the Saviour who meekly did die;
Lead me to the Rock that is higher than I.

— John Price

# A Way of Escape
## Exodus 14:19-31

Pharaoh and his army neared the camp of the Israelites and, just as their intelligence report had indicated, the Jews were completely boxed in – there was no escape. It was the opportunity Pharaoh had longed for and he deployed his full army against what he thought were helpless slaves. About the time that Pharaoh was probably thinking that not even Jehovah could rescue His people out of this situation, the pillar of cloud that had been to the East of the Israelite camp moved to the far western side of the camp and blocked Pharaoh's approach.

The Angel of God was within the cloud and His glory illuminated the camp of the Israelites during the following nighttime hours, but the cloud provided no light to the Egyptians. This supernatural phenomenon explains how Satan is permitted to come into God's presence in heaven (e.g. Job 1), without being consumed by God's holiness. When permitted, Satan is allowed to come into God's veiled presence for communication purposes, but to him God appears as darkness, while to various holy creatures His glory is visible. It is the same God, but to the one there is darkness and to the other, glorious light: *"Clouds and darkness surround Him; righteousness and justice are the foundation of His throne"* (Ps. 97:2).

Pharaoh and his army were brought to a halt and had to wait for the cloud to lift before they could continue their assault. Meanwhile, at God's command, Moses stretched out his hand which held the rod of God over the sea (vv. 16, 21). This resulted in a strong East wind which not only parted the waters of the Red Sea, but which also provided a dry land bridge through it. The wind blew all night, which meant that the Israelites had a strong headwind against them as they crossed the sea (v. 21). Not only did the Lord provide an escape for His people through the midst of the sea, but the pillar of fire illuminated every step of the way.

C. H. Mackintosh believes that the sea gradually divided as the Israelites stepped forward in faith. While this is possible, it seems more likely that the sea parted from East to West throughout the course of the night since the strong wind was from the East. The wind also dried the sea floor to allow for travel upon it. Though the waters probably did not divide as the Israelites walked forward, it is likely that each step they took was one of faith and not of sight, for they crossed at night and could only venture as far as the pillar of fire illuminated the way. *"By faith they passed through the Red Sea as by dry land, whereas the Egyptians, attempting to do so, were drowned"* (Heb. 11:29). So whether the waters divided before the Israelites as they walked or the pillar of fire illuminated the open way before the Israelites as they ventured into the darkness, the practical lesson, as C. H. Mackintosh summarizes, for the child of God is the same:

> Here was the path of faith. The hand of God opens the way for us to take the first step, and this is all that faith ever asks. God never gives guidance for two steps at a time. I must take one step, and then I get light for the next. This keeps the heart in abiding dependence upon God. "By faith they passed through the Red Sea as by dry Land." … It does not require faith to begin a journey when I can see all the way through; but to begin when I can merely see the first step, this is faith. … Such was the path along which the redeemed of the Lord moved, under His own conducting hand. The Egyptians could not move in such a path as this. They moved on because they saw the way open before them: with them it was sight, and not faith — "Which the Egyptians assaying to do were drowned." When people *assay* to do what faith alone can accomplish, they only encounter defeat and confusion. The path along which God calls His people to walk is one which nature can never tread — "Flesh and blood cannot inherit the kingdom of God" (1 Cor. 15: 50). … It glorifies God exceedingly when we move on with Him, as it were, blindfolded. It proves that we have more confidence in His eyesight than in our own. If I know that God is looking out for me, I may well close my eyes, and move on in holy calmness and stability.[1]

At some point in the night, the pillar of fire moved and followed the Israelites through the midst of the sea to illuminate the path of faith. In utter darkness, and into a fierce wind, Pharaoh's army pursued the Israelites. During the morning watch (i.e. 3am to 6am) the Lord slowed their pursuit by a downpour of rain (Ps. 77:17). The impeding mud caused the Egyptian's chariots to pull heavily and forced many of their wheels to come off, thus stranding them in the midst of the sea (vv. 24-25). An intuitive fear gripped their souls as they clearly realized that it was futile to fight against Jehovah, the God of the Israelites. They fled for their lives, but it was too late. Moses again lifted the rod of God and the walls of water they were sandwiched between came crashing down upon them and they were swallowed up by the sea. The same water which had provided a wall of safety to the Israelites now formed the graves of their enemy. Their floating bodies testified to the Israelites that the Egyptian army had been utterly vanquished.

What was Israel's response to this great victory? *"The people feared the Lord and believed the Lord and His servant Moses"* (v. 31). The nation as a whole had been redeemed by blood (i.e. through substitutional death) and had also been baptized in the sea, which pictures the death and burial of the Lord Jesus Christ. Paul states that all the Israelites *"were baptized into* (or united with) *Moses in the cloud and in the sea"* (1 Cor. 10:2). They were a nation that, positionally speaking, was beyond Satan's power. In type, they had passed through death (the Red Sea) and were thus dead to Egypt; it was not possible to go back. J. N. Darby summarizes the typological scene:

> As a moral type, the Red Sea is evidently the death and resurrection of Jesus, ...and of His people as seen in Him; God acting in it, to bring them, through death, out of sin and the flesh, giving absolute deliverance from them by death, into which Christ had gone, and consequently from all the power of the enemy. As to our standing and acceptance we are brought to God: our actual place is thus in the world has become the wilderness on our way to glory. We are made partakers of it already through faith. Sheltered from the judgment of God by the blood, we are delivered, by His power which acts for us, from the power of Satan, the prince of this world. The blood keeping us from the judgment of God was the beginning. The power which has made us alive in Christ, who has gone down into death for us, has made us free from the whole power of Satan who followed us.[2]

The cloud and sea to the Israelites is what the cross and grave is to the Christian. The cloud had protected the Israelites from their enemies and the sea had separated them from Egypt. In the same way, the judgment of sin at Calvary and grave of Christ sufficiently answer any judicial claim the enemy may levy against a redeemed soul. Neither Satan, nor the world, have any claim on the Christian, for he or she, positionally speaking, died and was buried with Christ (Rom. 6:3-6). All our adversary's accusations against us are completely answered by our Advocate, Jesus Christ: His suffering and death was just payment for all of our offenses, and His grave is proof of full payment.

> *And if anyone sins, we have an Advocate with the Father, Jesus Christ the righteous. And He Himself is the propitiation for our sins, and not for ours only but also for the whole world* (1 Jn. 2:1-2).

Forty years later, under Joshua's leadership, the Israelites would pass through the Jordan River and enter the Promised Land to lay hold of their inheritance. Where the baptism of the Red Sea pictures separation from the world, the crossing of the Jordan typifies the outworking of resurrection life (i.e. the life of Christ). Both *Jesus* and *Joshua* mean "Jehovah's salvation." God's salvation for every Christian is more than just the forgiveness of sins and to be separated from the world; it also necessitates living out the very life of Christ.

> *I have been crucified with Christ; it is no longer I who live, but Christ lives in me; and the life which I now live in the flesh I live by faith in the Son of God, who loved me and gave Himself for me* (Gal. 2:20).

Positionally, all believers have been raised up with Christ and are presently seated with Him in heavenly places (Eph. 2:5-6). Christ's victory over the world is complete and we in Him are to continue delighting in and declaring that glorious fact day by day: *"These things I have spoken to you, that in Me you may have peace. In the world you will have tribulation; but be of good cheer, I have overcome the world"* (John 16:33). Each redeemed soul has the present opportunity to live out Christ's life by faith; this is *victorious Christian living*!

> Encamped along the hills of light ye Christian soldiers rise,
> And press the battle ere the night shall veil the glowing skies.
> Against the foe in vales below, let all our strength be hurled;
> Faith is the victory we know that overcomes the world.
>
> — John H. Yates

# The Redeemed Sing
## Exodus 15:1-21

Exodus 15 records the first occurrence of singing in the Bible as well as the lyrics of Scripture's first song. Euphoria swept through the Israelite ranks as they marched further into the wilderness under the shadow of Jehovah's cloud. They had escaped death twice in recent days, and by the most unlikely means: blood and water. Death in Egypt at the hands of the destroyer had been averted by lamb's blood, and death in the wilderness by Pharaoh's army had been circumvented by water. Jehovah had used unpretentious things to manifest His salvation to His people: a rod (a symbol of His authority), water (which represented death), and applied blood (the ransoming payment). Through these agents, Jehovah had delivered His people and toppled the mightiest power on earth.

God's redemption for His people was now complete; they had been purchased by blood in Egypt and had been powerfully delivered from Egypt through the sea. Arthur Pink explains that full redemption for sinners must include these two aspects:

> Now there are two great elements in redemption, two parts to it, we may say: redemption is by purchase and by power. Redemption therefore differs from ransoming, though they are frequently confounded. Ransoming is but a part of redemption. The two are clearly distinguished in Scripture. Thus in Hosea 13:14 the Lord Jesus by the Spirit of Prophecy declares, *"I will ransom them from the power of the grave; I will redeem them from death."* And again we read, *"For the Lord hath redeemed Jacob and ransomed him from the hand of him that was stronger than he"* (Jer. 31:11). So in Eph. 1:14 we read, *"which is the earnest of our inheritance until the redemption of the purchased possession."*[1]

Presently, the Church waits for the culmination of its redemption in Christ, that is, to be instantaneously caught up with Him into heaven in glorified bodies. The Church has already been ransomed by blood, but the fullness of that redemption will not be realized until the Church is raptured to heaven. In that event, the same phenomenal power which defeated the power of hell at Christ's resurrection will be exercised to resurrect believers from Satan's domain – the world. Paul wanted the Christians at Corinth to understand this important truth, saying, *"Who delivered us from so great a death, and does deliver us; in whom we trust that He will still deliver us"* (2 Cor. 1:10). Likewise, to the saints at Ephesus he wrote:

> *The eyes of your understanding being enlightened; that you may know what is the hope of His calling, what are the riches of the glory of His inheritance in the saints, and what is the exceeding greatness of His power toward us who believe, according to the working of His mighty power which He worked in Christ when He raised Him from the dead and seated Him at His right hand in the heavenly places* (Eph. 1:18-20).

Positionally speaking, the believer has already died with Christ, but, practically speaking, the believer will be delivered through death at the rapture to be with Christ forevermore. Just as the Israelites were brought through the place of death in the Red Sea, every child of God will ultimately experience the power of God and will be brought through death and will then receive an incorruptible and immortal body (1 Cor. 15:51-52). These two aspects of redemption are further illustrated by John's imagery of the Lord Jesus before the throngs of redeemed souls in heaven: the Lord is presented as both the Lamb that had been slain and the Lion of the tribe of Judah (Rev. 5-6). As the Lamb, Christ is the purchaser, and as the Lion, He is the powerful deliverer. The Israelites, understanding their great deliverance from death, were prompted to sing to God. This is a fitting response for all God's redeemed throughout every age!

It was a time for jubilation. Miriam, the sister of Moses and a prophetess, took a timbrel in her hand and began to dance before the Lord. The psalmist would later exhort God's people: *"Let them praise His name in the dance: let them sing praises unto Him with the timbrel and harp"* (Ps. 149:3). Other women followed Miriam's lead and joined the festive parade as Moses and the children of Israel sang this lyric, which contain over forty exaltations unto the Lord:

> *I will sing to the Lord, for He has triumphed gloriously! The horse and its rider He has thrown into the sea! The Lord is my strength and song, and He has become my salvation; He is my God, and I will praise Him; my father's God, and I will exalt Him. ...And in the greatness of Your excellence You have overthrown those who rose against You; You sent forth Your wrath; It consumed them like stubble. ...Who is like You, O Lord, among the gods? Who is like You, glorious in holiness, fearful in praises, doing wonders? ...You in Your mercy have led forth* ***the people whom You have redeemed****; You have guided them in Your strength to Your holy habitation. ...You will bring them in and plant them in the mountain of Your inheritance, in the place, O Lord, which You have made for Your own dwelling, the sanctuary, O Lord, which Your hands have established. The Lord shall reign forever and ever* (Ex. 15:1-18, selected portions).

Interestingly, the last mention of singing in the Bible is associated with this same song of redemption. In the book of Revelation, John describes the following heavenly scene: *"And I saw something like a sea of glass mingled with fire, and those who have the victory over the beast, over his image and over his mark and over the number of his name, standing on the sea of glass, having harps of God. They sing the song of Moses, the servant of God, and the song of the Lamb, saying:*

> *Great and marvelous are Your works,*
> *Lord God Almighty! Just and true are Your ways,*
> *O King of the saints!*
> *Who shall not fear You, O Lord, and glorify Your name?*
> *For You alone are holy.*
> *For all nations shall come and worship before You,*
> *For Your judgments have been manifested* (Rev. 15:2-4).

This song will not be sung by those just escaping death to begin a journey with Jehovah through the wilderness, but rather by those who will have suffered death at the end of their journey to escape the Antichrist on earth. These saints chose to die rather than to bow to the Antichrist and to take his identifying mark. The heavenly inheritance sung of by the Israelites long ago will now be also theirs to enjoy forever. Furthermore, God's own joy in His redeemed people is enthusiastically expressed in song directly after the tribulation period – God will sing over His people (Zeph. 3:17).

The book of Revelation records several groups of people that sing before the Lord, but they all have one thing in common – they were redeemed by the blood of the Lamb, the Lord Jesus Christ. Before the tribulation saints of Revelation 15 began to sing unto the Lord, the 144,000 Jewish evangelists (who had also been redeemed from the earth) were lifting up their voices in song to the Lamb: *"They sang as it were a new song before the throne, before the four living creatures, and the elders; and no one could learn that song except the hundred and forty-four thousand who were redeemed from the earth"* (Rev. 14:3). Prior to the 144,000 member choir of Revelation 14, an innumerable multitude of saints from the Church Age had been gathered up to heaven to sing their own new song before the Lamb:

> *You are worthy to take the scroll,*
> *And to open its seals;*
> *For You were slain,*
> *And have* ***redeemed us*** *to God* ***by Your blood***
> *Out of every tribe and tongue and people and nation,*
> *And have made us kings and priests to our God;*
> *And we shall reign on the earth* (Rev. 5:9-10).

Here is an inescapable conclusion: no matter where one reads in the Bible, only the redeemed sing to God. Nowhere in Scripture do we specifically read of spiritual creatures, such as angels, singing unto the Lord. Apparently, singing praises to God is reserved for those individuals who have experienced God's salvation, that is, those who have been redeemed by the blood of His dear Son. Consider Isaiah's enthusiasm for God: *"Behold, God is my salvation, I will trust and not be afraid; 'for YAH, the Lord, is my strength and* ***song****; He also has become my salvation.' Therefore with joy you will draw water from the wells of salvation"* (Isa. 12:2-3). David was so excited about the Ark of the Covenant and the blessing of the Lord's presence in Jerusalem that he *"danced before the Lord with all his might"* (2 Sam. 6:14).

Throughout the Bible, the redeemed of God break into spontaneous exclamations and into songs of praise to express their excitement at God's abiding presence that is achieved through redemption. Long before the Israelites danced and sang their songs of redemption, another of God's servants voiced his longing to be with his Redeemer. Suffering Job said:

> *For I know that my Redeemer lives, and He shall stand at last on the earth; and after my skin is destroyed, this I know, that in my flesh I shall see God, Whom I shall see for myself, and my eyes shall behold, and not another. How my heart yearns within me!* (Job 19:25-27).

Job's heart ached to be with the Lord. Do you long to be with your Redeemer? Thousands of years ago the Israelites sang and danced before the Lord and a billion years from now the redeemed of the Lord *"will have no less days to sing God's praise than when we first begun."* A mark of God's redeemed is their joyous singing. Unless you're presently some place where singing is prohibited (e.g. a public library) why not enter into a melodious song of joyful praise and thank your Redeemer for saving your soul!

> Redeemed how I love to proclaim it! Redeemed by the blood of the Lamb;
> Redeemed through His infinite mercy, His child and forever I am.
> I think of my blessed Redeemer, I think of Him all the day long;
> I sing, for I cannot be silent; His love is the theme of my song.
>
> — Fanny J. Crosby

# A Wilderness Experience
## Exodus 15:22-27

Moses led Israel from the Red Sea into the wilderness of Shur where for three days they did not find any water (v. 22). Before exploring the narrative further, let us examine what a wilderness experience is and what are its benefits to a believer. Arthur Pink offers this explanation:

> God's purpose in leading His people through the wilderness was (and is) not only that He might try and prove them (Deut. 8:2-5), but that in the trial He might exhibit what He was for them in bearing with their failures and in supplying their need. The "wilderness," then, gives us not only a revelation of ourselves, but it also makes manifest the ways of God.[1]

Such would be the outcome of God's dealings with Israel. Each time God's cloud guided the Israelites into adversity, His grace would overcome it. For example, when water was finally located at Marah, it was determined to be too bitter for human consumption; the situation was desperate. Did the Hebrews cast themselves upon the One who had already demonstrated that He could control an entire sea? No, instead they murmured to Moses, which in reality was a disguised complaint against God. The Israelites probably thought it was safer to vent their frustrations to Moses, but in the coming days they would learn how wrong they were.

Although this is the first mention of murmuring in the Bible, the Hebrew word *luwn*, translated "murmured" in verse 24, was first used in Lot's initial communication with the two angels at the gate of Sodom: *"And he* [Lot] *said, 'Here now, my Lords, please turn in to your servant's house and spend the night, and wash your feet; then you may rise early and go on your way.' And they said, 'No, but we will spend the night in the open square'"* (Gen. 19:2). The phrases *"spend the night,"* and *"we will spend the night"* are derived from *luwn*, the same word translated as *"murmured"* in Exodus 15:24.

The root meaning of *luwn* means "to stop," but by implication it means "to stay permanently" or, in a negative sense, "to be obstinate by continuing to complain." The meaning of the word and the context of the passage seem to indicate that Moses was not rebuked or threatened, but rather subject to relentless grumbling. Similarly, Solomon describes the ongoing complaining of a contentious wife to be like the steady dripping of water (Prov. 19:13). This word picture well expresses the meaning of *luwn.*

The steady complaining of the Israelites was more than Moses could bear, so he cried out to the Lord for a solution and the Lord provided one: *"the Lord showed him a tree. When he cast it into the waters, the waters were made sweet"* (v. 25). Once the tree was cast into Marah's water, its bitter taste was replaced with sweetness. Not only was the water made fit for human consumption, but it produced a sense of satisfaction and enjoyment in all those that drank from it. Consequently, the Lord is introduced in verse 26 has *Yahweh-Rapha,* "The Lord Who Heals."

In type, the tree that was cast into the water by faith represents the healing of the human soul made possible through the cross of Christ alone. Paul declares, *"Christ has redeemed us from the curse of the law, having become a curse for us (for it is written, 'Cursed is everyone who hangs on a tree')"* (Gal. 3:13-14). Consequently, *"the message of the cross is foolishness to those who are perishing, but to us who are being saved it is the power of God"* (1 Cor. 1:18). Christ's cross not only removed the bitterness from our pre-Christ life experiences, but it also transformed our lives into a satisfying and meaningful existence.

Many of our failures in life can be attributed to having the wrong view of what a wilderness experience is all about. If new converts would realize that they are destined for disappointments, hardships, and persecution because of their identification with Christ, then every provision of God's grace in the wilderness would be answered with joyful praise. But, if the new believer starts out on his or her wilderness journey expecting ease and rest in the world, the relentless hardships to follow will be overwhelming. The mental starting-point then, for all believers, is Marah, which means bitterness. By expecting bitterness in life, God's supplied grace to overcome each difficulty will just seem all the more *sweet.*

Every devoted Christian is destined for trouble, but not for despair: *"Yes, and all who desire to live godly in Christ Jesus will suffer persecution"* (2 Tim. 3:12). It is a promise of God that if you live to serve Christ, you will suffer for it. Dear believer, do not expect anything less and you will not be disappointed. Prepare your mind for the struggles ahead, and don't get bogged down in self-pity, grappling with despair when those forecasted storms of life arrive. If Christian in John Bunyan's *Pilgrims Progress* had girded his mind, he would have likely avoided the "slough of despond." Every Christian that righteously suffers for the cause of Christ will be rewarded: *"If we suffer, we shall also reign with Him"* (2 Tim. 2:12, KJV).

Just as the tree at Marah ended the murmuring of God's people, the cross of Christ should bring an end to dissatisfaction in life. Practically speaking, how can a believer be joyfully content in a life immersed with uncertainties, trials, and suffering? It is only possible by adopting a thankful mind frame.

Paul exhorted the believers at Thessalonica to *"in everything give thanks; for this is the will of God in Christ Jesus for you"* (1 Thess. 5:18). What was the reason for this exhortation? This question is answered in the Epistle of Romans: *"For we know that all things work together for good to those who love God, to those who are the called according to His purpose"* (Rom. 8:28). God has us right where He wants us in every situation to extend the most benefit to us and to affect His glory. Does a critical spirit strangle your mind from thinking positively? That is, do you see a glass of water that is half-empty or half-full? The reality is the same in both cases; it is your perception that makes the difference. Do the blooms of the rose bush or its thorns capture your attention? A thankful and critical mind frame cannot exist together.

There is always something to be thankful for if one is in the right frame of mind to look for it. When the antique vase accidentally slips from your hands and shatters into a thousand pieces upon impact with the floor, praise the Lord it did not hit your foot. If you are involved with a traffic accident in which your vehicle is ruled a total wreck, praise the Lord you were kept safe. After being robbed Matthew Henry penned his thankfulness to God, saying, "Let me be thankful, first, because he never robbed me before; second, because although he took my purse, he did not take my life; third, because although he took all I possessed, it was not much; and fourth, because it was I who was robbed, not I who robbed."[2] A thankful mind frame will always find something to praise God for, no matter how mentally stretching the exercise may be.

Thanksgiving and contentment are closely related. Paul informed the Christians at Philippi of what he had learned about these two virtues:

> *For I have learned in whatever state I am, to be content: I know how to be abased, and I know how to abound. Everywhere and in all things I have learned both to be full and to be hungry, both to abound and to suffer need. I can do all things through Christ who strengthens me* (Phil. 4:11-13).

Paul instructed Timothy, *"Now godliness with contentment is great gain ... having food and clothing, with these we shall be content"* (1 Tim. 6:6-8). Verse 10 of that chapter speaks of those who were neither content nor thankful for what God had provided. They coveted money and erred from the faith. If God wanted us to have more than what we have, He would have bestowed it upon us. Being thankful defeats dissatisfaction.

The most common cause of sin seems to be dissatisfaction, with selfishness and pride trailing close behind. When we are not content with what we have, we murmur against God. Murmuring is half-uttered complaints that God fully hears anyway. It results from looking backwards instead of Godward. The nation of Israel grumbled and complained the whole time they were in the Sinai Peninsula. Why? It was because they were always comparing what they presently had to that which they once had in Egypt – in slavery!

We complain and grumble today because our expectations are not met in comparison to what we had the previous month, whereas last month we complained because our expectations were not satisfied when compared to the preceding month. Looking backwards to that which once was and comparing it to our wanton desires leads to complaining. The spiritual response to life's difficulties should be to ponder potential God-honoring outcomes, to be thankful in all things, and to cease bemoaning our current predicament. We will find this mindset much easier to obtain if we do not peer back into history to compare where we once were to someone else's circumstances or our present ones to our present situation.

> *Every good gift and every perfect gift is from above, and comes down from the Father of lights, with whom there is no variation or shadow of turning* (Jas. 1:17).

The children of Israel were being led by God into consecutive wilderness experiences – this was for the purpose of testing and perfecting them. Verse 25 contains the second usage of the Hebrew word *nacah* in the Bible; it is translated "tested." *Nacah* means, "To test or to prove the dependability of something or someone." This meaning is conveyed in its first usage, *"God did **test** Abraham"* (Gen. 22:1). Genesis 22 records Abraham's ultimate test of love and faithfulness to Jehovah – he was asked by God to sacrifice his beloved son Isaac. God already knew what Abraham would do at Moriah, but Abraham did not know what he would do until faced with the situation. Through testing, Abraham learned that God was able to provide Himself a lamb. Testing is a necessary part of our spiritual growth; trials prove to us the quality of our faith and also that God is able to overcome every situation. Consequently, *nacah* is found four times (Ex. 15:25, 16:4, 17:2, 17:7) in the initial days of Israel's wilderness experiences. Jehovah would test them and they would quickly learn that the quality of their faith was deficient. Just as a child learns to walk more perfectly after falling, the Israelites would learn by successive trials and failures to increasingly trust Jehovah for their daily guidance and provisions.

If the Israelites set their minds on the uncertainties of the wilderness, anxiety and suffering would be the outcome; if they would trust and obey Jehovah, every need would be satisfied and every difficulty would be overcome by sovereign grace. Dear believer, do you believe that God is also leading you through successive wilderness experiences? Whatever situation you are presently in, He has led you into it. The lesson to learn from Marah is that every murmur against our circumstances is really a complaint directed at God, the One *"who works all things according to the counsel of His will"* (Eph. 1:11). So the next time your flesh prompts you to grumble about the weather, a flat tire, a financial crisis, an illness, etc. just remember to Whom your criticism is directed – the all-knowing, all-wise God of the universe.

After the trial at Marah was complete, the Lord led His people to an abundance of water, to the twelve wells at Elim where they could enjoy the comfort of seventy palm trees while drinking their fill. The numbers of twelve and seventy were not accidental. The number *twelve* represents governmental perfection; thus, the twelve princes of Ishmael (Gen. 17:20), the twelve tribes of Israel, the twelve apostles of the Church, the twelve officers over Israel (1 Kgs. 4:7), and twelve months in the year. *Seventy* is a number uniquely associated with the nation of Israel throughout Scripture. For example, just before the tragic events at Kadesh-barnea the Lord would sanctify seventy elders as the leadership of Israel (Num. 11:16) – this ruling body was still in existence during Christ's sojourn on earth. The twelve wells and seventy palm trees at Elim represented the *national* blessing that would be enjoyed by all, if the Jewish elders faithfully guided the people to follow the Lord.

At the conclusion of Exodus 15, God, for the first time, speaks of His statutes and commandments which were to be obeyed by His people. Obedience would be rewarded with His blessing, but disobedience would be met with severe judgment, even with plagues like those used to punish Egypt. The precise timing of this revelation, as Arthur Pink explains, is important to understand:

> Nothing had been said to Israel about Jehovah's "statutes and commandments" while they were in Egypt. But now that they were redeemed, now that they had been purchased for Himself, God's governmental claims are pressed upon them. The Lord was dealing with them in wondrous grace. But grace is not lawlessness. Grace only makes us the more indebted to God. Our obligations of obedience can never be liquidated so long as God is God. Grace only establishes on a higher basis what we most emphatically and fully OWE to Him as His redeemed creatures.[3]

The truth presented to the children of Israel was a simple one; it represents the same reality that parents must teach their children early in life: obedience brings blessing, but disobedience results in punishment. Accordingly, our children have a choice as to whether they will receive our warm embrace or the rod of reproof. Every child of God has the same choice: *"Be ye therefore followers of God, as dear children"* (Eph. 5:1); *"As obedient children, not fashioning yourselves according to the former lusts in your ignorance"* (1 Pet. 1:14); *"For whom the Lord loves He chastens"* (Heb. 12:6). There truly is only one way for a child of God to be happy in the Lord Jesus – to trust and obey!

Often to Marah's brink have I been brought;
Shrinking the cup to drink, help I have sought.
And with the prayer's ascent, Jesus the branch hath rent
Quickly relief hath sent, sweetening the draught.

— Charles S. Robinson

# More Lusting and Complaining
## Exodus 16:1-3

With Marah's lesson and Elim's blessing fresh in the minds of the Israelites, God led His people from the wilderness of Shur to the wilderness of Sin. There they would face a new wilderness experience to prompt new spiritual growth. Their destination was Mount Sinai, but there would be several stops along the way.

The Israelites had journeyed day by day with Jehovah for exactly one month when they arrived at Shur. It wasn't long before the murmuring began again. Elim had supplied the Israelites with plenty of water, but apparently the food supply they had brought out of Egypt was nearly exhausted. The Hebrews continued complaining against Moses and Aaron, saying, *"Oh, that we had died by the hand of the Lord in the land of Egypt, when we sat by the pots of meat and when we ate bread to the full!"* (v. 3). The Hebrew word *luwn*, which was rendered as "murmured" in Exodus 15:24, occurs twice in this chapter (vv. 2, 7). Another Hebrew word, *teluwnah*, is found six times in Exodus 16 (vv. 2, 7, 8 {twice}, 9, 12) and is translated "murmurings" or "murmur." The total usage of these two Hebrew words reveals that Exodus 16 has the highest concentration of the word *murmuring* of any chapter in the Bible.

What had started as dissatisfaction at Marah developed into widespread complaining against God and His leadership in the wilderness of Sin. The Hebrew words used to express the Israelites' complaining nature also become more intense with each passing chapter. By Exodus 17, full-blown strife is observed. This progression of complaining highlights two facts: first, that sin grows in the believer's life when lusting is left unchecked. Second, having one's needs completely satisfied, as the Israelites had, does not automatically alleviate murmuring. Complaining is a grievous behavior that stems from selfish attitudes, not life's circumstances. As this following story illustrates, complaining is a natural tendency of our flesh:

> When Daniel Webster wanted to give a person the impression that he remembered him, but could not recall his name or where they had met before, he would ask, "Well, how is the old complaint?" And nine times out of ten this worked. The person would begin to unfold some grievance that he had discussed with Mr. Webster on a former occasion, and thereby identify himself.[1]

The Israelites had been comparing their present wilderness situation to what they had in Egypt and their expectations were not met. This time, the urgent need was not water, but food. They became wanton because they compared their diminishing food supplies with the fresh oven-baked bread and plentiful flesh pots they had previously enjoyed in Egypt. Of course, one important detail had slipped their minds – they were ill-treated slaves in Egypt, not a liberated people enjoying the daily presence of Jehovah, their God. It is the tendency of our flesh to lay aside the incredible and eternal realities for the mundane facts of temporal existence. We rant and rave about things we have little or no control over and which usually don't continue very long anyway.

Even after all the miracles they had witnessed at the hands of Moses and Aaron, the Israelites accused God's servants of leading them into the desert to starve them to death. The logic of this statement is ludicrous, but this is where uncontrolled lusting leads God's people – into irrational thinking and rebellious behavior.

There are many things for which our flesh can lust: social status, fame, food, vices, sexual pleasures, money, beauty, etc. It is impossible to allow our flesh to lust for what it wants and not to expect our behavior to be adversely affected. Egypt was a moral wasteland; there was nothing within its borders that could enrich and strengthen the spiritual man – this is still true today. For what reason then would a Christian lust after what can only diminish his or her spiritual vitality?

Peter acknowledges that a believer cannot simultaneously live according to the flesh and be in the will of God (1 Pet. 4:2). Paul emphasizes the same truth when writing to the Christians at Rome:

> *For those who live according to the flesh set their minds on the things of the flesh, but those who live according to the Spirit, the things of the Spirit. For to be carnally minded is death, but to be spiritually minded is life and peace. Because the carnal mind is enmity against God; for it is not subject to the law of God, nor indeed can be. So then, those who are in the flesh cannot please God* (Rom. 8:5-8).

The battle zone for all conduct is the mind. Over time, the heart is shaped by what the mind repeatedly determines to do; moral decisions form a pure heart, while immoral choices strengthen its inherent depravity. A pure heart will freely exercise faith, demonstrate love, and rejoice in hope, but a depraved heart loves only sin. This is simply a demonstration of the sowing and reaping principles of the harvest. The three laws of the harvest are: (1) you reap what you sow, (2) you reap more than what you sow, and (3) you reap later than you sow. Paul explains that if *"a man sows, that he will also reap; for he who sows to his flesh will of the flesh reap corruption"* (Gal. 6:7-8). Others may not know of your secret sins, but God knows and you know and *"be sure your sin will find you out"* (Num. 32:23).

When a believer thinks upon what is corrupt, it must lead to a legitimate harvest of corruption. It will be realized long after the initial seeds were sown and the repercussions will be far more devastating than what could have ever been imagined. Consequently, believers must desire to be controlled by the Holy Spirit and not their lusting flesh – only then are the deeds of the flesh mortified and fellowship with God maintained: *"If by the Spirit you put to death the deeds of the body, you will live"* (Rom. 8:13). Positionally speaking co-crucifixion took place at the cross and became effectual for a believer at his or her conversion (Rom. 6:6). In Adam, we were *"made subject to vanity"* (Rom. 8:20). At the cross, the old man, the man in Adam, the man that we once were, the man who was dominated and controlled by the flesh died with Christ. Paul conveys the practical aspects of this positional truth to the Galatian believers: *"Those who are Christ's have crucified the flesh with its passions and desires"* (Gal. 5:24). The purpose of crucifixion was to end the life of someone, though death itself would occur sometime later. Practically speaking, the believer has been crucified with Christ so that his or her craving flesh will eventually die (i.e. there should be a diminishing influence of the old nature in the believer's life as he or she matures in Christ).

Furthermore, Paul commanded the saints at Colosse to *"Put to death your members which are on the earth: fornication, uncleanness, passion, evil desire, and covetousness, which is idolatry"* (Col. 3:5). In addition to the believer's lusting flesh eventually dying and the need to mortify its deeds whenever observed, Paul told the believers at Colosse not to feed (strengthen) the nature of the old man, but rather to put him off (Col. 3:9). The ungodly longings of the flesh (some of which are listed in Col. 3:5) should not be strengthened through sinful behavior or by wrong thinking, but rather these should be starved so that they lose their strength and can be "put off" from the believer's conduct completely. If not fed these ungodly longings lose their hold on the believer's life and die out more quickly – though ultimate freedom will not be achieved until glorification. Paul conveys this same fundamental truth to the believers at Rome:

> *Likewise you also, reckon yourselves to be dead indeed to sin, but alive to God in Christ Jesus our Lord. Therefore do not let sin reign in your mortal body, that you should obey it in its lusts* (Rom. 6:11-12).

> *But put on the Lord Jesus Christ, and make no provision for the flesh, to fulfill its lusts* (Rom. 13:14).

Mortification or gratification are the only two things the flesh understands, but if we choose to gratify the flesh, even a little, it will want more the next day because the flesh is never satisfied – *"The eye is not satisfied with seeing, nor the ear filled with hearing"* (Eccl. 1:8; KJV). The only spiritual recourse in dealing with the lusting of the flesh is to extend it a deadly blow and to keep on mortifying it day after day – this is God's will for every believer. Consistent mortification of the flesh ends murmuring and complaining.

So the next time you are tempted to complain against God's leadership over you, whether it be in the home, in the Church, in the workplace, etc., recall to mind the telltale signs of a false teacher as identified by Jude: they reject authority, speak evil of dignitaries (vv. 8-9), grumble, complain, and walk according to their own lusts (v. 16). Jude concludes by stating that these false teachers *"are sensual persons, who cause divisions, not having the Spirit"* (v. 19). God forbid that believers should mimic the evil ways of those who have not the Spirit of God.

The children of Israel would learn firsthand the consequences of lusting in the flesh and of complaining against God and His leadership; nearly all of them would die in the desert without inheriting the Promised Land. What blessing are you not receiving from God because of lusting and complaining?

> The Lord our portion is; what can we wish for more?
> As long as we are His, we never can be poor.
> In vain do earth and hell oppose, for God is stronger than His foes.
> The Lord our Shepherd is; He knows our every need.
> And since we now are His, His care our souls will feed.
> In vain do sin and death oppose, for God is stronger than His foes.
>
> — Samuel Barnard

# Bread from Heaven

## Exodus 16:4-13

An immense commissariat was needed to sustain two million people in an arid wilderness. The main food item was something never before seen by human eyes; the people called it manna, which literally means, "What is it?". Manna was small in size (similar to a hoar frost), white in color (like a coriander seed), round in shape, and tasted like a wafer made with honey (Ex. 16:14, 31). God's plan was to furnish a normal portion of manna five days each week, with a double portion on Friday to supply Saturday's needs.

The Israelites quickly learned that though the manna was God's provision for them, it had to be gathered in the morning (it spoiled by the afternoon), and only on the six days specified (none fell from heaven on Saturday morning). The pattern instituted by God during the creation week, as recorded in Genesis 1 would now be confirmed as the example God wanted His people to follow; one day in seven would be fully consecrated for rest and worship.

Skeptics have relentlessly either denied the biblical account of manna entirely or have tried to explain its existence through some unusual, but natural phenomena. Yet, the magnitude of manna provided and its peculiar delivery schedule confirm that its presence was a divine miracle. Logically speaking, some vast resource would be necessary to sustain a large population for forty years and, naturally speaking, the wilderness offered none. Just as God would airlift food to Elijah by ravens during a severe famine in his day, God daily rained down bread from heaven to the Israelites in the desert.

Four wilderness images are used in John's Gospel to show that the Lord Jesus was the only means of salvation: the serpent on a pole (John 3), the manna from heaven (John 6), the water from a rock (John 7), and the pillar of fire (John 8). In John 6, seven times the Lord Jesus declared Himself to be the *"bread of life"* that came from heaven; He also taught that if anyone ate of Him that person would receive eternal life.

Many of the Jews following the Lord Jesus were offended at His teaching because they interpreted His statements as pertaining to cannibalism instead of understanding their symbolic significance. Christ was not speaking of eating His literal body, but of giving His body at Calvary as a sacrifice, and that it would be the means of receiving life for those who chose to believe on Him: *"I am the living bread which came down from heaven. If anyone eats of this bread, he will live forever; and the bread that I shall give is My flesh, which I shall give for the life of the world"* (John 6:51). The Greek verb *didomi*, translated twice in this verse as "will give," is in the future tense, meaning that Christ at a future date would give His life for the world, but His hearers had the opportunity to believe on Him even then for salvation. Thus, to eat of the Bread of Life is the same as to trust Christ for salvation (John 6:35, 50-57). His redemptive work at Calvary would then be appropriated by all those who would personally exercise faith in Him.

Many today are still confused and misled by literally interpreting certain metaphorical names applied to Christ. The *Lamb of God* was not a fluffy four-legged creature, nor did the *Good Shepherd* hold a crook in His hand, nor was the *True Vine* full of sap, nor was the *Stumbling Stone* of Israel a conglomeration of solidified minerals. These titles do not describe literal offices of the Lord Jesus, but they represent different facets of His *spiritual* ministry through allegorical depiction.

When He spoke of Himself as the Bread of Life, the Lord Jesus implied another sense of what it meant to feed upon Him. He likened the Israelites who fed daily upon the manna in the wilderness for physical survival to a believer who feeds daily upon Him in order to have the spiritual strength to live for Him.

> *Then Jesus said to them, "Most assuredly, I say to you, Moses did not give you the bread from heaven, but My Father gives you the true bread from heaven. For the bread of God is He who comes down from heaven and gives life to the world." Then they said to Him, "Lord, give us this bread always." And Jesus said to them, "I am the bread of life. He who comes to Me shall never hunger, and he who believes in Me shall never thirst"* (John 6:32-35).

Believers who continually feed on the Lord Jesus, that is, those who read and mentally digest His Word will find help and guidance for each day. Those who spend time with the Lord learn of Him and of His will; Christ speaks to believers in the quietness of His presence. The main reason the Church is spiritually weak and frail today is not because it lacks spiritual food and drink, but because many of her members refuse to be strengthened by that which Christ has provided for them.

Instead of feeding on Christ, many Christians are feasting on the *"Turkish Delights"* of the world. Physically, we are what we eat; spiritually speaking, we are what we think upon: *"For as he thinks in his heart, so is he"* (Ps. 23:7). What we spend our time thinking upon will ultimately determine if our inner man (Eph. 3:16) or our flesh is being strengthened. On this point, C. H. Mackintosh is painfully forthright:

> It is truly deplorable to find Christians seeking after the things of this world. It proves, very distinctly, that they are "loathing" the heavenly manna, and esteeming it "light food." They are ministering to that which they ought to mortify. ... As in nature, the more we exercise, the better the appetite, so in grace, the more our renewed faculties are called into play, the more we feel the need of feeding, each day, upon Christ. It is one thing to know that we have life in Christ, together with full forgiveness and acceptance before God, and it is quite another to be in habitual communion with Him – feeding upon Him by faith – making Him the exclusive food of our souls. Very many profess to have found pardon and peace in Jesus, who, in reality are feeding upon a variety of things which have no connection with Him. They feed their minds with the newspapers and the varied frivolous and vapid literature of the day. Will they find Christ there? Is it by such instrumentality that the Holy Ghost ministers Christ to the soul? Are these the pure dew-drops on which the heavenly manna descends for the sustenance of God's redeemed in the desert? Alas! No; they are the gross materials in which the carnal mind delights.

How then can a true Christian live upon such? We know, by the teaching of God's word, that he carries about with him two natures; and it may be asked which of the two is it that feeds upon the world's news and the world's literature? Is it the old or the new? There can be but the one reply. Well, then, which of the two am I desirous of cherishing? Assuredly my conduct will afford the truest answer to this en-

> quiry. If I sincerely desire to grow in the divine Life – if my one grand object is to be assimilated and devoted to Christ – if I am earnestly breathing after an extension of God's kingdom within, I shall, without doubt, seek continually that character of nourishment which is designed of God to promote my spiritual growth. This is plain. A man's acts are always the truest index of his desires and purposes. Hence, if I find a professing Christian neglecting his Bible, yet finding abundance of time – yea, some of his choicest hours – for the newspaper, I can be at no loss to decide as to the true condition of his soul. I am sure he cannot be spiritual – cannot be feeding upon, living for, or witnessing to, Christ.[1]

Eating of the Bread of Life confers eternal salvation, and continuing to feed on Him is the only spiritual food which satisfies the human soul and strengthens the inner man for spiritual conflict (these two truths are symbolized later in Exodus by the Table of Showbread in the Tabernacle). Just as the Israelites had to eat manna in the wilderness to live, the believer will be destitute of spiritual vigor unless he or she consistently feeds on the Bread of Life. The manna of Exodus and the Bread of Life of John 6 have a number of specific typological correlations. Both the manna to the Israelites and Christ to the world:

(1) Were a supernatural gift from God (rained down from heaven vs. directly from heaven's throne).
(2) Were supplied where the people were (in the wilderness vs. in the world).
(3) Were to be eaten (to sustain physical life vs. to gain spiritual life).
(4) Were to be gathered daily (each morning vs. throughout each day).
(5) Were obtained by labor (going out to gather vs. meditation on God's Word).
(6) Were not to be neglected (turned to worms vs. lost opportunities to know and serve).
(7) Were incomprehensible to the natural man (not natural vs. obviously supernatural).
(8) Were despised by the mixed multitude (hated by the Egyptians vs. despised by the world).
(9) Were preserved for future generations (placed in the ark vs. the eternal Word).
(10) Were supplied until the destination was reached (ceased at Canaan vs. grace received by faith no longer needed in heaven).[2]

Personally appropriating the finished work of Christ by faith is the only means of gaining Christ's life, and obeying His Word the only means of living it out for Him. His Word is our spiritual food for each and every day! No believer can gather another's manna; each one must personally meditate on the Word of God to obtain his or her provision of grace for the day.

The Israelites gathered their manna individually each morning (other than on the Sabbath day). Believers would be wise to dedicate to God the first part of each day for reading His Word and spending time before Him in prayer. This assures that the day's stress and fatigue does not spoil the opportunity to glean your spiritual sustenance for that day. If this is not your habit, why not start tomorrow morning? As you read through Exodus, jot down in a journal items of personal application (i.e. what you think the Lord would have you change in your life) and what you have learned about the character and attributes of God. Use this journal to keep track of your prayer requests and God's answers to them. After you finish Exodus, why not turn to the New Testament and keep the same routine going. It is surprising how much God speaks to us through His Word, if we only take the time to listen.

Daily feeding on the Bread of Life is crucial to building robust faith and rejuvenating the inner man; the believer's spiritual vitality depends on it. What the believer feeds on will ultimately determine whether the flesh or the inner man wins life's battles; thus, *make no provision for the flesh, to fulfill its lusts* (Rom. 13:14).

> Riven the rock for me, thirst to relieve,
> Manna from heaven falls fresh every eve;
> Never a pang severe causes my eye a tear,
> But thou dost whisper near, "Only believe."
>
> — Charles S. Robinson

# No Lack and No Hoarding
## Exodus 16:14-22

Their safe passage by night through the Red Sea had shown the Israelites the importance of walking by faith and not by sight. Each successive wilderness experience would the more deeply impress this infallible truth in their minds, for every child of God must learn that *"without faith it is impossible to please Him"* (Heb. 11:6).

Whether one gathered little or much on a particular day, the outcome was still an omer for each person. An omer is approximately six English pints. Assuming a population of two million people, the daily amount of manna supplied by God would be 12 million pints or about 9 million pounds.[1] Over the course of forty years, Jehovah would provide approximately 66 million tons of manna to preserve His people in the wilderness! If there was not a supernatural supply of manna, how would it be possible to explain Israel's survival during those forty years of wandering in a barren wilderness. God's daily provision of manna would teach the Israelites to rely on Jehovah each and every day for their nutritional needs. In application, F. W. Grant explains what it means for Christians to gather their daily manna:

> The manna was a daily provision for daily need. It could not be hoarded; if attempted, it bred worms and stank. So also we cannot live upon yesterday's enjoyment of Christ. We must enjoy Him today. Our past experiences will otherwise only turn into corruption; they will feed pride; they will be a knowledge that puffs up. And how much we see of this! Constant dependence upon God, constant drawing from Him, is what He ordains as the way of blessing for us. He would thus keep us with Himself. We must realize the divine hand that ministers to us, and gives us no stock to live upon in any measure of independence of Him.[2]

Manna was a daily provision which could not be hoarded; it was always collected fresh. Similarly, each day the believer must draw a fresh portion from God's Word for that day. Some will labor longer and harder for their portion, just as some of the Israelite men labored more than others to collect manna for their families, but yet none lacked any provision from God. But why do some work harder than others for their daily portion? F. W. Grant again provides some helpful insight:

> You cannot have too much of Christ. Of the mere outside of the Word, one may. You can have a breadth of truth out of proportion to depth; but where Christ it is that you seek, it will ensure depth as well as breadth. We can never have too much of Christ. On the other hand, the amount that we shall possess does not depend upon the mere measure of time of effort spent in the gathering. Not the amount of time, but the amount of heart counts with God, and in which fruit is found. ... He knows well our need as well as our hearts, knows how to minister to the needs as He sees our hearts in reality occupied with Himself. Much study may be but a weariness to the flesh; but negligence of His Word God will not own nor countenance [tolerate].[3]

If our hearts are right with the Lord, gathering new manna each morning will be a refreshing experience; it will be an activity that is longed for and then appreciated throughout the day. A believer should so relish his or her time with the Lord that he or she would never think of facing the toils of the day without first strengthening the inner man with the joy of the Lord: *"Do not sorrow, for the joy of the Lord is your strength"* (Neh. 8:10).

While teaching His own disciples how to pray, the Lord Jesus emphasized the need for divine dependency with the words *"Give us this day our daily bread"* (Matt. 6:11). He then informed them that there was no need to worry about daily staples; these would be provided by God if they first sought to do His will in their lives:

> *Therefore I say to you, do not worry about your life, what you will eat or what you will drink; nor about your body, what you will put on. Is not life more than food and the body more than clothing? Look at the birds of the air, for they neither sow nor reap nor gather into barns; yet your heavenly Father feeds them. Are you not of more value than they? Which of you by worrying can add one cubit to his stature? So*

> *why do you worry about clothing? Consider the lilies of the field, how they grow: they neither toil nor spin; and yet I say to you that even Solomon in all his glory was not arrayed like one of these. Now if God so clothes the grass of the field, which today is, and tomorrow is thrown into the oven, will He not much more clothe you, O you of little faith? Therefore do not worry, saying, 'What shall we eat?' or 'What shall we drink?' or 'What shall we wear?' For after all these things the Gentiles seek. For your heavenly Father knows that you need all these things. But seek first the kingdom of God and His righteousness, and all these things shall be added to you. Therefore do not worry about tomorrow, for tomorrow will worry about its own things. Sufficient for the day is its own trouble* (Matt. 6:25-34).

For those of us who live within the affluent western culture the idea of trusting the Lord for our daily bread is a mostly an untested theoretical concept. Little of our abundance is needed to supply our actually daily necessities and even less of it is used to feed and clothe the poor. Rather, our vast wealth is used to insulate ourselves against any conceivable mishap, to collect stuff we really don't need, and to indulge or pamper our flesh with thrills and creature comforts that last only a moment and waste valuable time.

Ponder for a minute all the resources we use to protect ourselves against potential calamities: we carry car insurance in case we have an automobile accident, home insurance for possible floods or fires, life insurance in case we die prematurely, medical insurance for when we might become ill. We cram piles of money into retirement accounts so that we can relax in our autumn years (if we live that long), and into educational accounts to insure our children and grandchildren get good educations (if they pursue one that is). With religious smugness and callused hearts we close our selfish eyes to the needy while we empty our pocketbooks for trinkets, high-tech gismos, and tons of other dust collectors that count for nothing in the light of eternity. There is certainly nothing wrong with planning ahead, the point is this: few Christians in our post-modern society actually rely on God for anything, let alone everything. No wonder the western world has become a God-denying, self-centered culture; the cosmopolitan man has no need that he cannot provide for himself – he therefore surmises that he has no need for God.

The normal avenues of God's grace in human lives are blocked by our self-reliant measures, meaning that God must become increasingly more innovative to get our attention. He must work through some means in which we have not put up a financial defense and, thus, have no self-sufficiency. Such means might include: incurable diseases, catastrophic disasters, a financial crisis, lingering wars, etc. The Church must awaken from its religious slumber. For believers to superficially ask the Lord for their *daily bread* and then to willfully hoard their wealth is an unscriptural paradox. A *needy-stockpiler* is an oxymoron that identifies an egocentric person who is both faithless and selfish. How does God get the attention of someone who pretends to be disadvantaged before the throne of grace, but hoards their wealth in real life? May we never know!

While explaining the application of the *Parable of the Unjust Steward*, the Lord Jesus commanded His disciples (i.e. the Greek verb *poieo* is in the imperative mood) to use their money wisely to further the cause of Christ in the world before their money inevitably lost its value. He then tells them that if they did not do this, they were mastered by money and not by God:

> *And I say to you, make friends for yourselves by unrighteous mammon* [money], *that when you fail, they may receive you into an everlasting home. He who is faithful in what is least is faithful also in much; and he who is unjust in what is least is unjust also in much. Therefore if you have not been faithful in the unrighteous mammon, who will commit to your trust the true riches? And if you have not been faithful in what is another man's, who will give you what is your own? "No servant can serve two masters; for either he will hate the one and love the other, or else he will be loyal to the one and despise the other. You cannot serve God and mammon"* (Luke 16:9-13).

William MacDonald concisely sums up what the believer's attitude should be towards temporal things: "Use it up, wear it out, make it do, do without."[4] Moses understood the proper value of things in relationship to doing the will of God. He turned his back on the riches and fame that Egypt offered in order to suffer the reproach of Christ. Forty years later, after sending his family back to the Midianites to be cared for, he proceeded towards Egypt with nothing but the rod of God – God was his full sufficiency. What motivated this dangerous pilgrimage to do God's will? Moses wanted to see the glory of God and wanted his children to know of God's majestic power also. Moses prays:

> *So teach us to number our days,*
> *That we may gain a heart of wisdom.*
> *Return, O Lord!*
> *How long?*
> *And have compassion on Your servants.*
> *Oh, satisfy us early with Your mercy,*
> *That we may rejoice and be glad all our days!*
> *Make us glad according to the days in which You have afflicted us,*
> *The years in which we have seen evil.*
> ***Let Your work appear to Your servants,***
> ***And Your glory to their children.***
> *And let the beauty of the Lord our God be upon us,*
> *And establish the work of our hands for us;*
> *Yes, establish the work of our hands* (Ps. 90:12-17).

Why do we collect things? So that we can glory in them before others. Why do we spend money for things we don't need? So that our flesh can glory in what weakens the inner man. Why do we hoard our wealth? To secretly glory in our independence from God. Such a materialistic lifestyle strengthens the flesh and robs the child of God from seeing the spectacular in his or her life. Do you want to see the hand of God move in your life? Then surrender to Him what you have and trust Him for what you don't; then you will be able to gather your manna joyfully and be able to sincerely pray: O God, *let Your work appear to Your servants, and Your glory to their children.*

> I need Thee, precious Saviour! For I am very poor;
> A stranger and a pilgrim, I have no earthly store.
> I need Thy love, Lord Jesus! To cheer me on my way,
> To guide my doubting footsteps, to be my strength and stay.
>
> — Frederick Whitfield

# Remember the Sabbath
## Exodus 16:23-36

The word "rest" is first mentioned in the Bible in Genesis 2. The key words in Genesis 2:1-3 are "seven" and "sanctified." The number seven is God's number and a fundamental building-block throughout Scripture. God uses this number to speak of completeness or perfection. The word "sanctified" means "set apart" or "holy." The week of creation ended with a day of rest for the Lord. This was a divine response not to weariness, but to satisfaction (Isa. 40:28).

We never read in Scripture of God resting again until a final and eternal rest is achieved in Revelation 21 and 22. Between Genesis 2 and Revelation 21 is the biblical record of God laboring for the redemption and restoration of man. The Lord Jesus said, *"My Father has been working until now, and I have been working"* (John 5:17). There are only two Sabbaths that God could truly call a day of rest – the seventh day of creation and the eternal rest after the new creation (i.e. the eternal state, Rev. 21:1-2). Only then may He finally cease from laboring. The Son finished His labor on earth at Calvary, but in heaven He continues, even now, to make intercession for His Church. A Greek scholar, Dudley Sherwood, paraphrased John 5:17 in this manner, *"My Father has been working up till now and I am continuing His work to bring it to completion."* This is a tremendous claim, asserting His oneness with the Father. Likewise, the Holy Spirit is laboring to convict the world of sin and to woo a bride for the Son. God is still working today!

Although God did not command mankind to keep the Sabbath holy in Genesis 2, He taught, through example, the principle of resting one day in seven. In Exodus 16, God practically identified the Sabbath as a special day by providing manna six days, but not on the Sabbath. The setting apart of the seventh day of the week became law at Mount Sinai

(Ex. 20:8-11). Unfortunately, it would be a command that was to be consistently broken by Israel for centuries to come.

The question may arise as to whether a Christian should observe the seventh day of the week as a day of rest. William MacDonald summarizes the significance of the Sabbath for the believer:

> It is a picture of the rest which believers now enjoy in Christ and which a redeemed creation will enjoy in the Millennium. The Sabbath is the seventh day of the week, from sundown on Friday to sundown on Saturday. Nowhere in the NT are Christians commanded to keep the Sabbath.[1]

God has displayed a pattern in which we should rest one day in seven (Gen. 2:1-3), yet this is not commanded. It seems logical that periodic rest would help remedy physical fatigue and emotional strain. The Law commanded the Jews to keep the Sabbath, which they miserably failed to do. The Lord issued no such command to the Church, as individual believers can worship God any time and anywhere as believer priests (John 4:23-24). In the dispensation of grace, men must *"go forth, therefore, to Him outside the camp, bearing His reproach"* to be saved (Heb. 13:13). The writer of Hebrews informed the Jews that they were no longer under the Law but under a new covenant of grace that was established by Christ. The pattern of the early Church was to gather corporately, not on Saturday, but on Sunday – the first day of the week, which was Christ's resurrection day (1 Cor. 16:2; Acts 20:7). These believers gathered to worship their Saviour, not to keep the Law. This is why John refers to Sunday as "the Lord's day" (Rev. 1:10).

Paul strictly forbade Christians from legislating special days, feast days, or Sabbaths and from forcing their personal convictions on others (Col. 2:16). Rather Paul says, *"Let every man be fully persuaded in his own mind"* (Rom. 14:5) about such things. In practice, it seems wise to rest the body one day out of seven and to follow the pattern of the early Church, which dedicated the first day of the week for corporate worship and service. We continue doing this on earth until the Church enters God's final rest in heaven.

This final and eternal Sabbath has been secured by the Bread of Life who came down from heaven, so it is not accidental that the remembrance of the Sabbath day is tied with the provision of manna in

Exodus 16. The Lord commanded Moses to "*take a pot and put an omer of manna in it, and lay it up before the Lord, to be kept for your generations*" (Ex. 16:33). Hidden away in the Ark of the Covenant that pot of manna was ever before Jehovah; similarly, the Lord Jesus is ever present at God's right hand in heaven and by His Spirit He ever lives in our hearts as the Hidden Manna.

The Lord Jesus promises believers that, *"To him who overcomes I will give some of the hidden manna to eat"* (Rev. 2:17). The Lord Jesus Christ is the Hidden Manna; He Himself is the reward of heaven for every believer who finishes well. Manna speaks of Christ in His humiliation; may we never forget what the Bread of Life suffered when He came down from heaven.

Safely through another week
God has brought us on our way;
Let us now a blessing seek,
Waiting in His courts today.
Day of all the week the best.
Emblem of eternal rest.

— John Newton

# Water from "the Rock"

## Exodus 17:1-7

Guided by Jehovah, the children of Israel had traveled through the wilderness of the Red Sea, the wilderness of Shur, and the wilderness of Sin to arrive at Rephidim. They soon discovered that there was no water at Rephidim, although it was the very place that God had put them. The complement to the Exodus 16 question "What shall we eat?" is found in Exodus 17, "What shall we drink?" God's life-sustaining provision would amply answer both questions.

By God's provision, the children of Israel had already overcome the challenge at Marah, so why were they now vehemently complaining to Moses about their thirst? The trial at Marah lasted only three days, but nothing has been said in the narrative about water since the children of Israel left Elim, perhaps two weeks earlier. In the same way that a runner builds endurance by slowly increasing his or her running distance each day, God was bringing them through a harder repeat-trial. Just about the time we feel we can relax after the last difficulty is overcome, God allows a new trial to intrude into our lives in order to increase our faith in Him. Being stretched is not comfortable, but it is necessary to increase our capacity for service.

Not only were the Israelites being tried at Rephidim, but God was maturing His servant Moses also. The Israelites' complaining developed into full-fledged strife against Moses. Moses warned them, *"Why do you contend with me? Why do you tempt* [test] *the Lord?"* (v. 2). But the people would not listen and they accused Moses of leading them into the wilderness to kill them. As their hostility grew more intense, Moses began to fear for his own life. His only recourse was to cry out to the Lord for help, which he did.

God's answer to Moses' plea was a most unusual one; he was to take the elders of Israel to the rock of Horeb and strike the rock once with the rod of God. Moses did so, and an abundant flow of water came gushing out of the rock. Moses called the place *Massah* and *Meribah* because the children of Israel strove with God and tested Him there (v. 6). Though the Israelites strove with God at Rephidim they were not chastened at that time, for God's full judgment fell upon the Rock in one stroke. The Rock, of course, pictures Christ, who was crucified and suffered divine wrath for our sin (1 Cor. 10:4). As a result of God's completed work at Calvary, the blessings of God can freely flow out to humanity through Christ. C. H. Mackintosh expounds on this point:

> This is the true foundation of the Church's peace, blessedness, and glory, forever. Until the rock was smitten, the stream was pent up, and man could do nothing. What human hand could bring forth water from a flinty rock? And so, we may ask, what human righteousness could afford a warrant for opening the flood-gates of divine love? This is the true way in which to test man's competency. He could not, by his doings, his sayings, or his feelings, furnish a ground for the mission of the Holy Ghost. Let him be or do what he may, he could not do this. But thank God, it is done; Christ has finished the work; the true Rock has been smitten, and the refreshing stream has issued forth, so that thirsty souls may drink. *"The water that I shall give him,"* says Christ, *"shall be in him a well of water, springing up into everlasting life"* (John 4: 14).[1]

From the opening pages of Genesis, the Bible presents a uniform lesson concerning the association of God's rest and His work. After God rested from His work of creation, a river flowed out of Eden to provide the whole land with the blessing and refreshment. Symbolically speaking, a river is often connected with God's rest and blessing (Gen. 2:10; Rev. 22:1) – He being the fountainhead of both. As the Israelites drank from the water flowing from the rock they would be refreshed and sustained. The Lord identified Himself as the Rock struck by the rod of God, from which sprang forth an abundant flow of living water; those who would drink of Him would receive everlasting life and the peace of God.

Centuries later, the Lord would meet a runaway bondservant named Hagar in the wilderness by *"a fountain of water"* (Gen. 16:7), commonly referred to as *"a well"* (Gen. 16:14). This is the first mention of a well in Scripture. How fitting for the all-sustaining Lord to meet a distressed woman in a life-threatening situation by a well in a desert place! Interestingly, the first occurrence of a well in the New Testament is when the Lord met a Samaritan woman with a sin-devastated life at Jacob's well (John 4:6). He offered her "living water" (Himself) to satisfy her spiritually-parched life. Like Hagar, she believed and obeyed the Lord and received a great blessing from Him.

The prophet Isaiah writes, *"Therefore with joy you will draw water from the wells of salvation"* (Isa. 12:3). A fountain of lasting joy springs up from the believer's spirit when Christ dwells within. For Hagar, this refreshment was not found in Egypt (the world); it was received on the way to Shur (Gen. 16:7). How often the Lord has protected His children from the world's entangling circumstances which lead to despair, through direct communion with Himself in the wilderness experience of Shur!

Peter mentions a well, for the final time in Scripture, when he warns against false teachers: *"These are wells without water, clouds carried by a tempest, for whom is reserved the blackness of darkness forever"* (2 Pet. 2:17). False teachers offer falsehoods, which culminate in false hopes. The "lie" is more than happy to escort those parched souls willing to follow it to the closest open grave. No bubbling fountain of refreshment is there; only a deep dry hole waiting for its next victim to fall into it. In contrast, the Lord Jesus is God's messenger of truth, and offers an abundant life of joy despite circumstances (John 10:10). When one embraces the Saviour, a jubilant fountain of refreshing spiritual drink is enjoyed, blessings are obtained and the abundant life is found. Dear believer, like Israel in the midst of the wilderness, we too can sing to the fountain of life, *"Spring up, O well"* (Num. 21:17). Drink, yes, drink abundantly from the everlasting springs of God; for from out of such are the sheep watered (Gen. 29:2), and God refreshes His sheep through Christ.

Moses smote a rock to provide much needed water for the children of Israel in the desert – it saved their lives (v. 6). Forty years after this, Moses received the rebuke of God for striking another rock in the same manner when he had been instructed by God to simply speak to the rock in order to receive the necessary water (Num. 20:7-13). Israel desperately needed water, so what did it matter if Moses struck the rock or spoke to it? It mattered to God, because it broke the "type" of Christ that He wanted to be conveyed to the nation of Israel. Christ was to suffer for sin only once, then the blessing of His work would be received through personally asking Him (Heb. 10:10-18). Both the work and the blessing of Christ are pictured in the rock.

In the New Testament, the Lord Jesus often used Jewish traditions as a platform to teach of certain spiritual realities which centered in Him. In addition to asserting Himself as *"the Light of the world"* during the candelabra lighting ritual at the Feasts of Tabernacles, He used a second tradition to teach of Himself as being God's source of supernatural blessing (John 7:37-39). Edwin Blum and John Walvoord explain:

> The Feast of Tabernacles was celebrated with certain festival rituals. One was a solemn procession each day from the temple to the Gihon Spring. A priest filled a gold pitcher with water while the choir sang Isaiah 12:3. Then they returned to the altar and poured out the water. This ritual reminded them of the water from the rock during the wilderness wanderings (Num. 20:8-11; Ps. 78:15-16). It also spoke prophetically of the coming days of Messiah (Zech. 14:8, 16-19). The Feast's seventh and last day was its greatest (Lev. 23:36). Jesus stood, in contrast with the Rabbis' usual position of being seated while teaching. Said in a loud voice (John 1:15, 7:28; 12:44) was a way of introducing a solemn announcement. His offer, *Come to Me and drink*, was an offer of salvation (John 4:13, 6:53-56).[2]

The Lord likened the blessings of the Holy Spirit in the Christian's life to a river of abundant flowing water. As a believer yields to God's will for his or her life, the full joy, peace, and blessing of God is experienced. But God must labor on the behalf of the believer to get him or her to this blessed state – it is not natural to us to seek after or trust God. This is why, as George Rodgers explains, God allowed the Israelites to experience hunger, thirst, and weariness in the wilderness:

> He feeds souls with the bread of life, but He suffers them to hunger first. It is a blessed thing to hunger, because if God has made us to hunger, it is that He may feed us. He suffers men to thirst, and then He gives them the water of life. He suffers men to get very weary, and then He gives them rest. He suffers them to get very sick, and to feel the plague of their own heart, and to spend all they have on physicians, and then to feel that they are nothing bettered, but rather worse for the things they have suffered and then He heals them in a moment. He lets

> men first feel themselves lost, entirely lost, and then He shows them that He has found them.[3]

God's ministry to the human soul then is more effectual after we have become more fully aware of our need and hopeless situation (i.e. our appreciation for His mercy is greater after we have keenly felt desperation). The water from the rock allegory is the final of three wilderness illustrations in Exodus 14-17 that point to Christ. Paul uses Israel's wrong reaction to God's goodness and the consequences of their lusting and lack of faith as an object lesson to warn the believers at Corinth:

> *Moreover, brethren, I do not want you to be unaware that all our fathers were under the cloud, all passed through the sea, all were baptized into Moses in the cloud and in the sea, all ate the same spiritual food, and all drank the same spiritual drink. For they drank of that spiritual Rock that followed them, and that Rock was Christ. But with most of them God was not well pleased, for their bodies were scattered in the wilderness. Now these things became our examples, to the intent that we should not lust after evil things as they also lusted* (1 Cor. 10:1-6).

Because Israel lacked faith, they fell into lusting and they complained against God; consequently, the older generation never entered the Promised Land – they died in the desert. Nationally speaking, Israel had common privileges that they all enjoyed: God guided them by day and illuminated the camp at night; His abiding presence was visible at all times. Though their enemies perished in the sea, they had all been brought safely through and from that place of death. They all enjoyed manna, God's daily provision to sustain them. Without water from the rock they would have perished, but instead they all satisfied their thirst by drinking from the same rock (picturing Christ). Israel enjoyed all these common benefits, yet they still craved carnal things, murmured against God, and committed idolatry.

Paul's application is straightforward: learn from the mistakes of others; don't leave the Lord's Table and provoke Him to jealousy, anger, and disciplinary action (1 Cor. 10:22). The Lord's Table is a place of common blessing and communion for all believers in Christ. Anyone who leaves this privileged place of communion will ultimately repeat the mistake of the Israelites. Grumbling, idolatry, and fornication are the natural outcomes of lusting flesh, and historical precedence shows that God must and will judge such behavior. The offer of a seat at His table of fellowship and blessing cost God greatly; His Son (the Rock) was struck by His own rod. The choice for every Christian is simple: enjoy communion and the blessing of God, or experience His chastening hand!

> Jehovah lifted up His rod – O Christ, it fell on Thee;
> Thou was't sore stricken of Thy God; There's not one stroke for me.
> Thy blood beneath that rod has flowed; Thy bruising healeth me.
>
> — Ann Ross Cousin

# Heavy Hands
## Exodus 17:8-16

The children of Israel had hardly quenched their thirst from the water flowing out from the rock at Horeb when they were threatened by the Amalekites. Amalek means "war-like" and Amalekites were living up to their patriarch's name. The attack of the Amalekites occurred about two months after the Exodus and, as F. C. Cook explains, the timing has historical relevance:

> The attack occurred… towards the end of May or early in June, when the Bedouins leave the lower plains in order to find pasture for their flocks on the cooler heights. The approach of the Israelites to Sinai would of course attract notice, and no cause of warfare is more common than a dispute for the right of pastureage. The Amalekites were at that time the most powerful race in the Peninsula; here they took their position as the chief of the heathens. They were also the first among the heathens who attacked God's people, and as such are marked out for punishement.[1]

The spiritual significance of the conflict with Amalek is best understood by a close examination of verses 7-8: *"So he called the name of the place Massah and Meribah, because of the contention of the children of Israel, and because they tempted the Lord, saying, 'Is the Lord among us or not?' Now Amalek came and fought with Israel in Rephidim."* From this text and from the following verses please note that, first, Amalek's attack is morally linked with the unbelief of the people. Second, the water from the Rock was provided before the Israelites fought the Amalekites. Third, Amalek came against the Israelites unprovoked. Fourth, the Amalekites threatened the Israelites when they were tired and weary; in fact, he attacked the feeble who strangled behind (Duet. 25:17-18). Fifth, the Israelites initiated a full scale attack on the Amalekites before they were fully ready to engage the Israelites.

Sixth, previously the Lord had fought Pharaoh for the Israelites, but now He would fight Amalek with them. Pharaoh had hindered their departure from Egypt and Amalek threatened to impede their walk with God through the wilderness.

Symbolically speaking, the Israelites had died and were raised up with Christ as symbolized by their passage through the Rea Sea. Now that the Rock had been smitten and living water, picturing the ministry of the Holy Spirit, was freely available to them, the Israelites as a nation, would face an old, well-known enemy in a new way. Amalek was the grandson of profane Esau, *"who for one morsel of food sold his birthright"* (Heb 12:16). Consequently, both Esau and Amalek are used in Scripture to picture lusting flesh which continues to war against God's people.

Likewise, the new nature of the believer received at regeneration cannot sin (1 Jn. 3:9) and therefore also continually wars against the flesh nature: *"For the flesh lusts against the Spirit, and the Spirit against the flesh; and these are contrary to one another, so that you do not do the things that you wish"* (Gal. 5:17). There is nothing in the old nature that can please God (Rom. 8:8) – only when our vessels are under God's control do we have the capacity to please Him.

What initiated the Amalekite attack? The Israelite's failure of faith. A failure to look to the Lord by faith strengthens the flesh – a losing proposition for any believer. Consequently, when Peter wrote to a distressed group of Christians, he exhorted, *"Beloved, I beg you as sojourners and pilgrims, abstain from fleshly lusts which war against the soul"* (1 Pet. 2:11-12). When it comes to battling the desires of our flesh, we are our own worst enemies; we ensnare ourselves by lapsing faith. The only means of being liberated from our own fleshly entanglements is to yield to God's Word and be controlled by His Spirit. God will enable us, but only if we are willing to help ourselves. This is the main application of Exodus 17.

When answering Pilate's question about His kingship, the Lord Jesus showed the validity of using spiritual weapons versus relying on flesh and blood to do God's will by saying, *"My kingdom is not of this world. If My kingdom were of this world, My servants would fight, so that I should not be delivered to the Jews; but now My kingdom is not from here"* (John 18:36). All believers are positionally identified with Christ in His death and resurrection, but practically speaking, one must exercise faith in Him and make no provision for the flesh in order to live out the resurrected life. A corpse is incapable of lusting; it has been freed from such things. As believers hold fast to the fact that they have died with Christ, the right motivation to mortify the deeds of the flesh will be sustained. Confrontation with my Amalek (i.e. my flesh) results when my faith loses its grip on who Christ is and who I am in Him.

Amalek came down to pick a fight, but to his surprise, the Israelites attacked him before he could organize his forces for a full offensive (he had only attacked the Israelite stragglers previously). The scene is glorious: Moses was upon the mount holding up the rod of God over the raging battle below. As long as Moses held the rod of God over the battlefield, the Israelites trounced the Amalekites, but if the rod of God dropped, the Amalekites overcame the children of Israel. To ensure victory, Moses is seated on a rock and Aaron and Hur steadied Moses' hands holding the rod. But on the battlefield, among his people and in the fray of the conflict, is a new figure, a new leader – it is Joshua the son of Nun. F. W. Grant explains the application of the typology:

> Joshua is Jesus. The names, as we know, are the same, and Christ in us is our Leader now. Christ acting by the Spirit is distinctively what Joshua represents to us, the Captain of our salvation, who leads us into the practical apprehension of our portion in the heavenly places into which He is gone. ... Joshua, then is our leader; but even Joshua's success is dependent, as we see directly, upon Moses being on the hilltop before God, and the holding up of the rod of power – God's rod.
>
> Moses is here also a type of Christ, as he is almost everywhere. And his position on the mount, holding up the rod of power, speaks plainly enough of Christ [having gone before] God, presenting before Him the value of that work in which divine power has acted in behalf of His people. All spiritual actings in us depend upon the position Christ has taken for us. And these supporters of Moses' hands figure, as it seems, [represent] Him in the place He has taken for us. On the one hand Aaron represents the priestly character of One *"touched with the feeling of our infirmities,"* gracious and compassionate; on the other, Hur, "white," [or purity] speaks to us as the manna did, of one who fully reflects the light which God is. Here, then, is mercy towards man, with righteousness Godward: an *"Advocate with the Father,"* and also *"Jesus Christ the righteous."*[2]

Moses, on the mount, held up the rod of God and thus pictured Christ's intercessory power for His people from the throne of grace in heaven. While Moses interceded above, Joshua was in conflict below. Joshua, whose spirit has been refreshed by the divine spring at Horeb, wields the sword victoriously on the battlefield. This sight portrays Christ's unrestrained power in the believer's life as he or she uses the Word of God (the sword of Truth, Heb. 4:12) and relies on the strength of the Holy Spirit in full measure.

Moses' uplifted hands are emblematic of petitioning God in prayer. Paul knew that real spiritual power was supplied through answered prayers; consequently, he instructed the saints at Thessalonica to *"pray without ceasing"* (1 Thess. 5:17) and the believers at Ephesus to pray always *"with all prayer and supplication in the Spirit, being watchful to this end with all perseverance and supplication for all the saints"* (Eph. 6:18). To his spiritual son Timothy, he exhorted that *"men pray everywhere, lifting up holy hands, without wrath and doubting"* (1 Tim. 2:8). God's people have the opportunity to lift their hands to God in prayer anytime and anywhere to ask for wisdom and grace for anybody in any situation. But our lifted hands must be holy (i.e. reflecting a pure heart), and we must pray without doubting and without wrath (no works of the flesh can be present). It is evident from the weak condition of the Church that much of our praying does not comply with these criteria. Unconfessed sin, wrong motives, or carnal intentions (Jas. 4:1-3) stagnate the flow of God's blessings into our lives.

Under Joshua's leadership and Moses' intercession Amalek was beaten that day, but not destroyed; indeed, the war against the Amalekites would rage on from generation to generation (v. 16). Likewise, the believer's flesh lives on and must be defeated again and again for the Christian to be a witness for Christ in the world for the deeds of the flesh oppose God. Paul understood what would happen if he did not keep his flesh under control – he would suffer a shipwrecked testimony for Christ.

> *And everyone who competes for the prize is temperate in all things. Now they do it to obtain a perishable crown, but we for an imperishable crown. Therefore I run thus: not with uncertainty. Thus I fight: not as one who beats the air. But I discipline my body and bring it into*

> *subjection, lest, when I have preached to others, I myself should become disqualified* (1 Cor. 9:25-27).

Victory over one's flesh requires the removal of that which entices the flesh to dissatisfaction and, as Paul says, a willingness to land blows against one's own carnal appetites. To keep the flesh in subjection requires constant discipline, no matter how mature one is in Christ. Such is the believer's conflict until glorification; then, every soldier of the cross will have the final victory. At the Judgment Seat of Christ, those who took this challenge seriously will be rewarded with an imperishable crown. In the eternal state, the fulfillment of verse 14 will be realized: *"I will utterly blot out the remembrance of Amalek from under heaven."* At the Great White Throne Judgment, God will completely do away with any wicked thing throughout all His new creation; sinful flesh will no longer exist in God's kingdom and all believers will be eternally thankful for its eradication!

There was no spoil taken from the Amalekites, for the flesh has nothing of value to God (Rom. 8:8). If spoil was not the motivation, then why did Joshua lead a preemptive attack against the Amalekites? The victory was not to be substantiated by the number of enemy causalities or by the value of captured goods, but by the fact that the Israelites chose to fight in God's strength to gain an unhindered path through the wilderness to the Promised Land. The writer of Hebrews puts it this way: *"Let us lay aside every weight, and the sin which so easily ensnares us, and let us run with endurance the race that is set before us, looking unto Jesus, the author and finisher of our faith"* (Heb. 12:1-2). While sojourning on earth, the victor's prize for overcoming his or her own flesh is to enjoy unbroken fellowship with God and to be unhindered in service for Him.

To lay hold of our spiritual possessions in heavenly places believers must travel along the unencumbered path of righteousness, but our flesh will always be blocking the way of such a journey; it must therefore be fought, beaten, and driven out of the way again and again. There are no other paths leading to spiritual blessings in Christ – the enemy must be engaged and defeated in His strength. The Israelites would learn this lesson the hard way at Kadesh-barnea the following year. The Amalekites would again block their way into the Promised Land (Num. 14:25), but this time the flesh was victorious for the Israelites believed the evil report of the ten spies who said they were not able to take the land, instead of the favorable report by Caleb and Joshua. Despite all God's demonstrated goodness and power, the Israelites doubted God's ability to keep His promises to them – just the threat of the Amalekites and giants in the land was enough to detour them off the path to blessing. The flesh magnifies the believer's opposition, whereas the Holy Spirit enables us to overcome it and to seize our spiritual blessings in Christ.

In celebration of the victory, Moses built an altar and called it *Jehovah-Nissi* meaning, *"The Lord is my Banner"* (Ex. 17:15). Today, the same expression of honor and loyalty are conveyed by saluting a national flag or by reciting the words, "I pledge allegiance to the flag …." May the Lord Jesus Christ be our high banner in life; He deserves our full allegiance and devotion as we walk through His way to blessing.

> A rock that stands forever is Christ my righteousness,
> And there I stand unfearing in everlasting bliss;
> No earthly thing is needful to this my life from heaven,
> And nothing of love is worthy save that which Christ has given.
>
> — Paul Gerhardt

# Reunion at the Mount
## Exodus 18:1-12

According to verse 5, the Israelites left Rephidim and arrived *"at the mount of God,"* that is, Mount Sinai. It had been several months since Moses had seen his family; the work of the Lord in Egypt was such that they could not accompany him there. Now that the children of Israel had arrived at Sinai, Moses was visited by his father-law Jethro, who brought Moses' wife Zipporah and their sons, Gershom and Eliezer. This was the mount in which God had first spoken to Moses while he attended Jethro's sheep, so the trip for Jethro was not a long one.

After Moses informed Jethro of all that God had done in Egypt to deliver His people and to defeat Pharaoh, and of how God had repeatedly helped and delivered them in the wilderness, Jethro rejoiced (v. 9) and praised the Lord (v. 10). He acknowledged that *"Jehovah is greater than all the gods"* (v. 11) and then proceeded to offer burnt offerings to the Lord. The serenity and felicity of the occasion was enjoyed by both Jews and Gentiles (v. 12). With the Mount of God as a backdrop, both Jew and Gentile gathered to worship the one true God, Jehovah.

Symbolically speaking, mountains refer to *kingdoms* in Scripture. Daniel invokes this imagery to speak of the Lord Jesus coming into His kingdom after all the Gentile powers have been judged (Dan. 2:44-45). John applies the metaphor in Revelation 17, where seven mountains are described as seven kingdoms. Matthew, upholding the nobility of Christ, references mountains to signify His forthcoming earthly kingdom. The prophet Micah uses the mountain allegory to foretell the same futuristic scene presented before us in Exodus 18:

> Now it shall come to pass in the latter days that **the mountain of the Lord's house shall be established** on the top of the mountains, and

> shall be exalted above the hills; and peoples shall flow to it. Many nations shall come and say, "Come, and let us go up to the mountain of the Lord, to the house of the God of Jacob; He will teach us His ways, and we shall walk in His paths." For out of Zion the law shall go forth, and the word of the Lord from Jerusalem. He shall judge between many peoples, and rebuke strong nations afar off; they shall beat their swords into plowshares, and their spears into pruning hooks; nation shall not lift up sword against nation, neither shall they learn war anymore (Mic. 4:1-3).

The exact timing of Exodus 18 is difficult to determine; Moses had already received the Law of God (v. 16), though the record of this event is contained within following chapters. Perhaps, it is best to view Exodus 18 as a parenthetical narrative to the many events which occurred at Mount Sinai during the time the Israelites sojourn there. Prophetically speaking, this chapter foretells the millennial reign of Christ, as both Gentile and Jew are gathered at the base of God's mountain in complete agreement, *"The Lord is greater than all gods"* (v. 11). It is significant that God's kingdom is mentioned for the first time in Scripture at this time (Ex. 19:6). It is at this moment and this place that God first chose to convey His Law to His people; however, during the millennial reign of Christ the entire world will know the righteousness and glory of God.

In time, Jethro (Ex. 18:27) and his son Hobab who came with him to visit Moses would leave the mount and return to their own land and people (Num. 10:29-30). They heard the Law of God and were invited to go on with the Israelites to Canaan, yet they declined the offer. This may picture the sad event that will occur at the conclusion of Christ's millennial kingdom when Satan, after being sequestered for one thousand years in the bottomless pit, will be released and will proceed to deceive the nations to rebel against Christ (Rev. 20). Christ will respond by casting Satan, his demons, and all that is wicked into the Lake of Fire, which burns forever and ever.

In most of the books of the Old Testament we find either prophecy that foretells, or narrative that depicts the future millennial kingdom of the Lord Jesus Christ. In Genesis, for example, the typology sequence initiated in Genesis 21 pictures the incarnation of Christ, to Genesis 22 which displays the glory of Christ at Calvary, to Genesis 23 which foretells Israel's spiritual blindness, to Genesis 24 where a Gentile bride is brought to God's Son, to Genesis 25 where the Son inherits all that the Father has. This passage is a wonderful pronouncement of Christ's future reign on earth, when He will rule and reign over all that His Father has. Abraham took a second wife after the death of Sarah, but before Isaac received his inheritance in Genesis 25. The new wife's name was Keturah, and Abraham's marriage to her likely foreshadows the restoration of Israel to Jehovah and the resulting blessings to the Gentile nations during the Kingdom Age that will follow Israel's restoration. Note the specific prophetic sequence in Genesis 24-25: Isaac (picturing Christ) receives His bride (a type of the Church), at the place He had prepared for her (Gen. 24:61-67), which was prior to Abraham's marriage to Keturah (picturing the restoration of the Jews during the Tribulation Period, Gen. 25:1); afterwards, Isaac inherits all that the Abraham has (depicting the Lord Jesus returning to the earth to establish His kingdom, Gen. 25:5).

The death of Sarah, from whom Isaac came, pictures the spiritual separation between the nation of Israel (from whom Christ came) and Jehovah. Israel had played the harlot by embracing other gods, so the one true God wrote the nation of Israel a *"bill of divorce"* (Jer. 2:26-29, 3:8; Isa. 50:1). Yet, the prophets foretold that the repentant wife (Israel) would be restored unto her husband (God) in a future day (Hos. 2:14, 19-20; Ezek. 16). This restoration, as depicted in Abraham's marriage to Keturah, will occur during the latter part of the Great Tribulation (Zech. 12:10, 14:4-21).

In Exodus, we have a similar typological sequence that reaches its climax in Exodus 18: Writers from yester-years well explain the pattern of future events that is portrayed in this portion of Exodus:

> Arthur Pink:
> The dispensational scene which is here foreshadowed is very beautiful, and the place which this one has in the series of typical pictures, in which the book of Exodus abounds, evidences once more the hand of God, not only in their production but also in arranging their order. In Exodus 16 the manna speaks of the incarnate Son, coming down from heaven to earth. In the first part of Exodus 17, the smiting of the rock views the Lord Jesus stricken of God. In the issuing of the water, we get a lovely emblem of the Holy Spirit ministering to the people of

God. In the second half of Exodus 17, where we find Amalek attacking Israel, and the defeat of the former through the supplications of Moses – upheld by Aaron and Hur – we have adumbrated the believer's conflict with the flesh, and him sustained in that conflict by the joint intercession of Christ and the Holy Spirit. This goes on to the close of the Church age. Here in Exodus 18 we are carried forward to the next dispensation and are furnished with the blessed foreshadowment of the millennial conditions.[1]

William Kelly:
The Gentile will unfeignedly rejoice for all the goodness Jehovah will have done to Israel, delivering them from the hand of all enemies from first to last. The inhabitants of the world will learn righteousness when His judgments are in the earth, and will then know with Jethro that Jehovah is greater than all gods, for in the thing wherein they dealt proudly [judgment came] upon them. And He shall be King over all the earth: in that day shall there be one Jehovah, and His name one.[2]

C. H. Machkintosh
This is a deeply interesting scene. The whole congregation assembled, in triumph before the Lord — the Gentile presenting sacrifice — and in addition, to complete the picture, the bride of the deliverer, together with the children whom God had given him, are all introduced. It is, in short, a singularly striking foreshadowing of the coming kingdom. ... "The Jew, the Gentile, and the Church of God" are scriptural distinctions which can never be overlooked without marring that perfect range of truth which God has revealed in His holy Word. They have existed ever since the mystery of the Church was fully developed by the ministry of the Apostle Paul, and they shall exist throughout the millennial age. Hence, every spiritual student of Scripture will give them their due place in his mind.[3]

In the first half of Exodus 18, we have pictured the millennial scene in which the Jews (as a restored nation), various Old Testament saints, and saved Gentiles (the Church and tribulation saints), and Gentile tribulation survivors will all agree – Jehovah is the one true God. At that time, the glory of God will fill the earth. *"It shall be that I will gather all nations and tongues; and they shall come and see My glory"* (Isa. 66:18).

The Jews particularly stand forth as *"a light to the nations"* (Isa. 49:6), that is, a great witness to the entire world of God's faithfulness, mercy, and longsuffering nature. As the Jews look back over ruined centuries stained with blood and tarnished by rebellion and idolatry, they will gladly and forever declare, *"The Lord shall be King over all the earth. In that day it shall be – 'The Lord is one,' and His name one"* (Zech. 14:9).

> Face to face with Christ my Saviour, face to face – what will it be,
> When with rapture I behold Him, Jesus Christ, who died for me?
> What rejoicing in His presence, when are banished grief and pain,
> When the crooked ways are straightened, and the dark things shall be plain.
> Face to face! O blissful moment! Face to face – to see and know;
> Face to face with my Redeemer, Jesus Christ, who loves me so.
>
> — Carrie E. Breck

# Working too Hard?
## Exodus 18:13-27

Moses had been divinely appointed to lead the Israelites and to be God's mouthpiece to His people. As Jethro witnessed the arduous nature of his son-in-law's workday, he felt that Moses was undertaking too much. In his estimation, there were too many people for one man to effectively teach, advise, and judge; anyone trying to do so would *"wear away"* (v. 18; KJV). Jethro genuinely feared for Moses' health and suggested that his son-in-law appoint some assistants.

Arthur Pink supplies this commentary on Moses' response:

> In listening to Jethro, Moses did wrong. From a natural standpoint Jethro's counsel was kindly and well-meant. It was the amiability of the flesh. It presented a subtle temptation, no doubt. But the man of God is not to be guided by natural principles; only that which is spiritual should have any weight with him. Nor should he heed any human counsel when he is engaged in the service of the Lord; he is to take his orders only from the One who appointed him. ... Subtle as was the temptation presented to Moses, if he had remembered the Source of his strength, as well as his office, he would not have yielded to it. "Hearken now unto my counsel" said Jethro (v. 19). But that was the very thing which Moses had no business to do. "So shall it be easier for thyself" (v. 22) pleaded the tempter. But was not God's grace sufficient! It is sad to see the effect which this specious suggestion had upon Moses.[1]

After listening to Jethro's counsel, Moses appointed various helpers among the people without consulting the Lord (vv. 25-26). Shortly after this, he complained to God about his overwhelming leadership responsibilities: *"I am not able to bear all these people alone, because the burden is too heavy for me. If You treat me like this, please kill me here and now – if I have found favor in Your sight – and do not let me see my wretchedness!"* (Num. 11:14-15). In the same conversation, Moses also expressed his doubts that God could supply meat for the entire nation in a wilderness. The Lord's response to Moses' complaints was twofold: to remove some of his so-called "burden" (and its associated honor) and to rebuke him:

> *So the Lord said to Moses: "Gather to Me seventy men of the elders of Israel, whom you know to be the elders of the people and officers over them; bring them to the tabernacle of meeting, that they may stand there with you. Then I will come down and talk with you there. I will take of the Spirit that is upon you and will put the same upon them; and they shall bear the burden of the people with you, that you may not bear it yourself alone"* (Num. 11:16-17).

> *And the Lord said to Moses, "Has the Lord's arm been shortened? Now you shall see whether what I say will happen to you or not"* (Num. 11:23).

The spiritual correlation between doubting the goodness of God and having a diminished capacity to serve Him is thus apparent. God had chosen Moses to be Israel's deliverer and given him the Holy Spirit to enable Moses to prosper in his calling. Moses' service was a testimony of God's abundant power, which was a tremendous privilege extended to Moses. As long as Moses trusted in the Lord instead of his own abilities, every difficulty he would face would be amply met with divine grace. Moses had given ear to a different one, an earthly and familiar voice; Jethro's well-meaning advice prompted Moses' flesh to respond in an earthly way, one that was not under the Spirit's control.

Edward Dennett notes that there are two distinct matters which must distinguish in Moses' actions in Exodus 18: the failure of Moses, and the thing symbolized by the appointment of the rulers over the people.

Addressing the first point Dennett suggests that the biblical narrative recorded the details of Moses' failure for our benefit – that is, that we might learn from his mistake:

> The first mistake he made was in listening to Jethro on such a matter. The Lord had given him his office; and it was to Him he should have had recourse on every subject that concerned His people. The pleas Jethro advanced were indeed specious and subtle. They were grounded

upon his anxiety for the welfare of his son-in-law. ...If Moses would but do as he advised, then he said, "So shall it be easier for thyself," etc.; and again, "Then thou shalt be able to endure, and all this people shall go to their place in peace." It was not therefore concern for God, but for Moses, that actuated Jethro. But the arguments he advanced were those most calculated to influence the natural man. Who is there, even among the Lord's servants, that does not at times feel the weight of his responsibility, and who would not rejoice at the prospect of its being lessened? There is indeed no more seductive temptation presented at such a moment than that of the need of a little care for one's self and one's comfort. But, dangerous as it is, and as it was in the case of Moses, if he had remembered the source of his office, as well as his strength, he would not have yielded to it. For if his work in judging the people were of the Lord, and for the Lord, His grace would be all-sufficient for His servant.

According to man, the counsel of Jethro was wise and prudent, evincing much sagacity in human affairs; but according to God, its acceptance was characterized by doubt and unbelief. In reality it left God out of the calculation, and made the health of Moses its chief aim, losing sight altogether of the fact that it was not Moses, but the Lord through Moses, who bore the burden of the people; and hence that it was not a question of the strength of Moses, but of his resources in God. How apt are all to lose sight of this important truth — that in any service, if occupied in it for the Lord, the difficulties in it should be measured, not by what we are, but what He is. [2]

Concerning the latter point, Dennett argues that Moses decision to appoint judges diminishes the accuracy of the prophetic picture of the Millennial Kingdom of Christ portrayed in Exodus 18. In the Kingdom Age, Christ alone will reign supreme over the world; Dennett writes:

It is evident that this arrangement of [Moses] judging the people emblematically portrays the order in government which the Messiah will set up when He assumes His kingdom. As the Psalmist speaks, "He shall judge Thy people with righteousness, and Thy poor with judgment. The mountains shall bring peace to the people, and the little hills, by righteousness." (Ps. 72: 2, 3.) Hence it is that this section closes with this account.[3]

Instead of following God's Word and His Spirit, new thoughts and ideas infiltrated Moses' thinking. Unexpectedly and abruptly, he was awakened to the overwhelming nature of his calling. The work had not changed and he still had God's Spirit upon him; nothing had changed but Moses' attitude. He had a new perspective, an earthly vantage point of his ministry that he had not comprehended before. Such are the contemplations of God's servants when they allow earthly suggestions to creep in and rule their minds. C. H. Mackintosh surveys this situation and offers a warning to all believers:

> There was no fresh power introduced. It was the same Spirit, whether in one or in seventy. There was no more value or virtue in the flesh of seventy men than in the flesh of one man. *"It is the Spirit that quickeneth; the flesh profiteth nothing"* (John 6:63). There was nothing, in the way of power, gained; but a great deal, in the way of dignity, lost by this movement on the part of Moses. ... The man who shrinks from responsibility, on the ground of his own feebleness, is in great danger of calling in question the fullness and sufficiency of God's resources. ... If God honour a man by giving him a great deal of work to do, let him rejoice therein and not murmur; for if he murmur, he can very speedily lose his honour. God is at no loss for instruments.[4]

Any of us can fall prey to the subtle suggestion of a sincere and well-meaning person, especially when he or she is a loved-one. Adam listened to Eve and ate of the forbidden fruit when he knew it was wrong to do so. Abraham, against God's promise, yielded to Sarah's forlorn nagging and took Hagar as a concubine and fathered Ishmael. Our emotions can easily sway our thinking and misguide what should have been a sound judgment. The right thing to do is to humbly wait at our assigned posts and fully rely upon the Lord in the execution of our duties until new marching orders arrive and the Captain of the Hosts relocates us to other strategic positions.

The Lord Jesus provides a good example to follow. After revealing to His disciples that He must go to Jerusalem to suffer and die, He disregarded Peter's sincere reprimand, *"Far be it from You, Lord; this shall not happen to You!" But He turned and said to Peter, "Get behind Me, Satan! You are an offense to Me, for you are not mindful of the things of God, but the things of men"* (Matt. 16:22-23). Peter meant well, but he spoke for Satan and not for God; thus, he was rightly rebuked by the Lord.

Beloved of the Lord, beware of heartfelt suggestions, especially by those closest to you, who want to promote your ease and comfort but neglect to consider God's plan for your life: "You need to slow down and take it easy." "You need to get away for a while and relax." "You need a hobby." I have heard all of these and more. Please remember this: *"As is the earthy, such are they also that are earthy: and as is the heavenly, such are they also that are heavenly"* (1 Cor. 15:48; KJV). Don't expect earthy counsel to reflect heaven's interests and don't expect heaven's approval if you lend your ear to human wisdom.

> When doubts and fears arise, teach me Thy way;
> When storms overspread the skies, teach me Thy way.
> Shine through the cloud and rain, through sorrow, toil and pain;
> Make Thou my pathway plain, teach me Thy way.
>
> — B. Mansell Ramsey

# A New Age Dawns
## Exodus 19:1-2

Two full months after departing from Egypt, the Israelites arrived in the wilderness of Sinai and camped before the Mount of God (Ex. 18:5, 19:1-2). God had kept His promise to Moses, fulfilling the sign presented to him during their first meeting: *"This shall be a sign to you that I have sent you: When you have brought the people out of Egypt, you shall serve God on this mountain"* (Ex. 3:12).

The Israelites would remain at this location for the next eleven months (until the twentieth day of the second month in the following year, Num. 10:11). During this time, Moses received the Law and many other instructions which would govern the nation's worship and conduct. A large portion of the Pentateuch (from Exodus 19 to Numbers 10) record God's dealings with Israel during this time.

Although the events recorded in Exodus 18 occurred at the Mount of God, it is Exodus 19 that forms the most significant division in Exodus. There are a variety of vantage points from which to view various themes within Exodus. Focusing on geography, Exodus 1-12 relates to the Israelites in Egypt, Exodus 13-18 refers to their journey to Sinai, and the remainder of Exodus records their stay at Sinai. Looking at the doctrine of sanctification, Exodus 1-12 covers the progression of events leading up to positional sanctification, which was made possible by redemption, while the remainder of Exodus relates to practical sanctification. Reviewing the dispensational content of Exodus, one clear division, the giving of the Law to Moses at Sinai in Exodus 19 marks not only a significant division in Exodus, also but in the entire Bible.

As there is often confusion regarding what the word "dispensation" actually means, clarification is warranted. Dispensations describe God's differing administrations among mankind, which are often initiated with divine covenants. God reveals certain truths – spiritual economies, if you will – for man to abide by. A dispensation is not a period of time, though dispensations advance within time. A dispensation works in time, but is not constrained by time. In fact, time simply proves or disproves man to be a faithful steward of the divine revelation he was entrusted with; in this sense, each dispensation is a divine classroom in which man will learn of God's righteousness and of his failure. When humanity falters, a holy God is just in rendering judgment.

Throughout biblical history, God has revealed distinct administrations of order (dispensations) to meticulously demonstrate that, when given divine rules to live by, man will eventually go his own way and rebel against God. The purpose of these revealed economies is to show man his depraved heart (Rom. 3:20) and to prompt man to trust God for salvation alone (Gal. 3:24). L. Laurenson observes that the construction of Scripture relates directly to dispensations:

> The Bible is a book in two parts. The Old Testament has to do with the earth. It is the mind of Heaven revealed to man upon the earth to fit him for the earth. But man closed his ears to the voice of God, disobeyed the divine will, and made himself unfit for the earth in which God had placed him. Eden and innocence were lost by Adam. Canaan and liberty were lost by Israel. Happiness and holiness have been lost by all because of sin and disobedience. Hence the New Testament has to do with heaven. It reveals the mind of God as to how men, who had made themselves unfit for the earth, might be made fit for heaven itself through the Gospel.[1]

A dispensation, then, is an economy of truth that God reveals to man, holds him accountable to, and then punishes him for failing to obey it (1 Cor. 9:17; Eph. 3:2; Col. 1:25). A dispensation is not a period of time, for often God's economies of truth overlap, but as stated earlier, each dispensation does have its working in time.

The new stewardship of truth revealed at Sinai related to the Jews only; it was not given to the Gentiles, a fact that the apostles confirmed at the Jerusalem Council (Acts 15:10). In the dispensation of the Church, Paul would use this fact to exhort the Gentile believers in Galatia not to give ear to the Judaizers: *"For in Christ Jesus neither circumcision nor uncircumcision avails anything, but a new creation, and as many as walk according to this rule, peace and mercy be upon them"* (Gal. 6:15-16). These legalists were teaching that salvation was by grace through Christ, but that a believer had to continue to keep the Law to maintain his or her salvation. As the Galatians had never been under the Law in the first place, it would be irrational to want to be put under its bondage now by the Judaizers, especially since the Law only condemned man and could not save anyone.

Hebrews contains the Jewish complement of this message: they were no longer under the Law; the entire system had been replaced by what it anticipated in Christ. The Law was not dead, for it still declares the righteousness of God, but the Jews were dead to it in that they had been liberated by Christ from its condemning outcome (Rom. 7:4-6). Thus, the Church Age marks the end to the dispensation of the Law. The purpose of the Law was, and still is, to show sin (Rom. 3:20) and to point the sinner to the solution – God's grace through Christ: *"For the law was given through Moses, but grace and truth came through Jesus Christ"* (John 1:17). As C. H. Mackintosh convincingly explains, a single system cannot mingle Law and grace; each has its distinct purpose, the former to show sin and the latter to be God's means of extending salvation to those who desire it:

> It is of the utmost importance to understand the true character and object of the moral law.... There is a tendency in the mind to confound the principles of law and grace, so that neither the one nor the other can be rightly understood. Law is shorn of its stern and unbending majesty; and grace is robbed of all its divine attractions. God's holy claims remain unanswered, and the sinner's deep and manifold necessities remain unreached by the anomalous system framed by those who attempt to mingle law and grace. In point of fact, they can never be made to coalesce, for they are as distinct as any two things can be. Law sets forth what man ought to be; grace exhibits what God is. How can these ever be wrought up into one system? How can the sinner ever be saved by a system made up of half law, half grace? Impossible. It must be either the one or the other.[2]

The Law was a conditional covenant between God and the Jews. God revealed a special set of commandments for the Jews to follow in order to please Him; if they obeyed it, they would be justified in His sight and be blessed by Him. The Israelites had been redeemed by the blood of the Passover Lamb because they exercised faith and obeyed God's Word while in Egypt. God would continue to teach them through the Law that no one could earn a righteous standing before Him by human efforts, for no one could keep the Law:

> *For as many as are of the works of the law are under the curse; for it is written, "Cursed is everyone who does not continue in all things which are written in the book of the law, to do them." But that no one is justified by the law in the sight of God is evident, for "the just shall live by faith." Yet the law is not of faith, but "the man who does them shall live by them." Christ has redeemed us from the curse of the law, having become a curse for us (for it is written, "Cursed is everyone who hangs on a tree")* (Gal. 3:10-13).

Undoubtedly, the Jews sincerely wanted to obey all that God would command them, but time would show their utter failure to do so. Failure to keep the Law brought the penalty of the Law – death. In the following centuries, Jewish religious leaders added their *Oral Laws* to God's Law, creating an even more cumbersome system of "doings" in an attempt to cleanse their guilty consciences through doing good works. Consequently, all such efforts to justify oneself eventually lead to one outcome – some form of idolatry (i.e. esteeming something or someone more reliable than God for salvation). Jehovah could not tolerate this grievous sin and therefore punished His covenant people by scattering them among the nations, where they are to this day.

Today, the Jewish nation is still held in the bondage of legalism. In general, Jewish rabbis no longer teach that blood sacrifices are necessary to atone for sin. Now repentance, good deeds, or prayer have atoning value and thus replace the animal sacrifices demanded by Scripture. But these sacrifices were pictures of the future once-for-all blood sacrifice of Christ, which would provide complete propitiation for man's sin. Judaism teaches that individuals can make atonement for their own personal sins against God without shedding blood (quotes are from *Everyman's Talmud* by Abraham Cohen):

> What can be a substitute for the bulls which we used to offer before thee? Our lips, with the prayer which we pray unto thee (Pesikta 165*b*; p. 158).

> Whence is it derived that if one repents, it is imputed to him as if he had gone up to Jerusalem, built the Temple, erected an altar and of-

> fered upon it all the sacrifices enumerated in the Torah. (Lev. R. VII. 2; p. 105).

This idea of alternative atonement (doing good works to atone for one's sins) is utterly contrary to Scripture: *"For the life of the flesh is in the blood, and I have given it to you upon the altar to make atonement for your souls; for it is the blood that makes atonement for the soul"* (Lev 17:11). God's justice concerning a guilty sinner is satisfied through the judgment of an innocent substitute – in time, God's own Son would pay the price.

Judaism today has become like every other world religion, in that it is a system of humanly devised doings to earn reward and paradise; it denies the need to be saved – Judaism is another "do-it-yourself" religion that excludes Christ. Consequently, Judaism smacks of the same humanism that is found in paganism and blatant idolatry, the only difference being that man worships himself instead of carved images, ancestral spirits, or some roaming creature.

In contrast, biblical Christianity is unique; it emphatically declares that without repentance and forgiveness through Christ, there is no heaven. For the Christian, it is being in the presence of Christ that makes heaven, heaven. What is prized is not the street of gold, pearly gates, precious gems, eternal bliss nor (as the world's religions seek) the fulfillment of fleshly lusts. A true Christian longs for heaven because he or she longs to be in intimate fellowship with God.

It was not the majestic nature of the mountain that Moses prized or the spectacular postcard view from its summit; Moses climbed its slopes for only one reason – to be with Jehovah, his God. The Lord, not things, is the believer's eternal inheritance (Ps. 16:5; Jer. 3:24). For the Christian, being with the Lord Jesus Christ forever is what ensures that heaven will be paradise!

> I'm a pilgrim and a stranger, rough and thorny is the road,
> Often in the midst of danger, but it leads to God.
> O how sweet is this assurance midst the conflict and the strife!
> Although sorrows past endurance follow me through life.
> Home in prospect still can cheer me; yes, and give me sweet repose,
> While I feel His presence near me: for my Father knows.

— Mary S. B. Dana

# Ascending the Holy Mount
## Exodus 19:3-4

Evidently, God summoned Moses to meet with Him on Mount Sinai; it would be the first of seven encounters Moses would have with the Lord on the mount. An inquisitive Moses had ascended this same mount several months earlier to investigate what appeared to be a burning bush. Now he scaled its heights again, but this time with the expectation of speaking directly with Jehovah.

As was appropriate, God initiated that conversation: *"Thus you shall say to the house of Jacob, and tell the children of Israel: 'You have seen what I did to the Egyptians, and how I bore you on eagles' wings and brought you to Myself"* (Ex. 19:3-4). The only way for a young eagle to experience flight is to trade the security of its nest for the uncertainty of air. The mother eagle knows when to commence such training and will actually push her offspring out of her nest to teach them how to fly. She is both the instructor and the safety net, and when necessary she will fly underneath her young with her wings spread out in order to catch a tumbling juvenile. God had brought His people, the young nation of Israel, out of Egypt into a dangerous world; just as the mother eagle cares for its young, He would continue to both guide and protect His people.

God used this historical synopsis to show that the entire matter of Israel's existence, deliverance, and protection had been founded in His grace. From this vantage point, God's stewardship of truth to the nation of Israel initiated with redemption in Exodus 12, and every aspect up until Exodus 19 had been secured and sustained by His grace. Actually, grace generally characterized God's dealings with mankind up until this point in history. Now God would teach His children what was necessary on their part to maintain fellowship with Him; they would learn that the privileges secured in grace merit personal responsibility. Commenting on this fact, F. W. Grant writes:

> Thus the whole of this period, from Adam to Moses, was what the apostle Paul calls "the time before the law." A law to bring into relationship to Himself by obedience to it, God never proposed. Relationship to Him, for sinners, must be of His grace. Outside of this there can be only wrath and judgment; and from this, as our natural portion, there must be deliverance, wrought by God Himself, before there can be any proper relationship to Him. This the sacrifices always recognized, and in the most solemn way we have seen the Passover enforcing it. Brought into relationship, God gives them a law upon the express basis of the wonderful deliverance He had vouchsafed to them: "I am the Lord thy God that brought thee out of the land of Egypt, out of the house of bondage: thou shalt have no other gods before Me.[1]

Why then was the Law given to the Jews? God, here as in every dispensation, has always maintained a testimony of man's need for divine grace and mercy to be saved, yet, man in his lost state is ignorant of this need. Man knows the heartache of his existence, but does not understand that his sufferings are a result of spiritual failure. The Law would cause man to more deeply search out such matters, and to gain an awareness of his spiritual state before a holy God and of his inadequacy to please God though personal efforts.

As God's emissary, Moses ventured up and down the mountain three times in Exodus 19. The first trip was to receive God's covenant offer, which he then presented to the people (vv. 3-7). In the second trip, Moses personally conveyed to the Lord the people's willingness to obey His commandments; he then returned down the mount to inform the Israelites that God would visit them in three days and that they would hear His voice (vv. 8-9). The third trip occurred three days later after God descended upon Mount Sinai and summoned the people by a long blast on a trumpet (perhaps a ram's horn) to come to the mountain. Moses led them out to its base and then ascended its slopes again to speak with God. He was only in the Lord's presence briefly before being ordered down to ensure that the people did not trespass upon the mount, lest they die (vv. 20-25). Aaron was to accompany Moses on the next trip up (v. 25), at least part of the way (Ex. 24:1-2). At this time, only Moses and Aaron were allowed on the mount; even the priests, perhaps the firstborn representatives of the people, were prohibited from venturing upon it.

Moses was an eighty-year-old man and, naturally speaking, such trips up and down the mountain's slopes would be quite tiring, but Moses had the Spirit of God and His power enabled Moses to do God's bidding no matter how strenuous, humanly speaking, the task was. The people would expect him to be exhausted, but Moses did not waver; he was under God's authority and received His infusing power. Moses' supernatural tenacity to carry out Jehovah's errands would serve only to accentuate the importance of Jehovah's message to His people: He had brought them out of Egypt with a mighty hand for a particular reason – so that He could dwell among them.

Jehovah wanted the Israelites to personally understand that He wanted to enter into a covenant with them and continue to commune with them. The Psalmist expresses this joyful awareness this way: *"Know that the Lord, He is God; it is He who has made us, and not we ourselves; we are His people and the sheep of His pasture"* (Ps. 100:3). Not only did God want the Jews to understand that they *were* His people, He also wanted them to know that He *wanted* them for His people. It was not just the reality of the relationship that was to be understood, but that God's love had instigated it (see also Ezek. 16:1-14).

But such a relationship could only be maintained in holiness, for Jehovah is holy. Thus, the Israelites had to agree to keep God's Law as a condition of maintaining fellowship within the relationship that God had secured by grace. The main stipulation of fellowship stated clearly by God in verse 5, *"If you will indeed obey My voice and keep My covenant, then you shall be a special treasure to Me."* The promise of God's communion for obedience is in essence what God confirmed with Adam in the Garden of Eden: *"Of every tree of the garden you may freely eat; but of the tree of the knowledge of good and evil you shall not eat, for in the day that you eat of it you shall surely die"* (Gen. 2:16-17). As long as Adam obeyed the Lord there would be open fellowship with Him, but Adam's disobedience would sever communion with God.

If the Jews obeyed God's commandments they would be a holy nation – a kingdom of priests unto God. If not, they would disgrace Jehovah and be punished, which as Paul explains is ultimately what happened: *"You who make your boast in the law, do you dishonor God through breaking the law? For 'the name of God is blasphemed among the Gentiles because of you,' as it is written"* (Rom. 2:23-24). The

Jews thought that they were a special people because they possessed the Law, but Paul states that the mere possession of the Law counts for nothing; rather, those who obey the Law would display God's holiness to the nations – this indeed would have insured that the Jews were a peculiar people. Peter announces that the Christian has the same obligation to be a holy people so that the nations might know a Holy God:

> *Therefore gird up the loins of your mind, be sober, and rest your hope fully upon the grace that is to be brought to you at the revelation of Jesus Christ; as obedient children, not conforming yourselves to the former lusts, as in your ignorance; but as He who called you is holy, you also be holy in all your conduct, because it is written, "Be holy, for I am holy."* (1 Pet. 1:13-16).

Although the Christian is not under the Law, it would be good to remember that the Lord Jesus affirmed each of the Ten Commandments as being valid for the Jews during His earthly ministry (i.e. just prior to the Church Age). So while we do not see the Church commanded to keep the Sabbath presently, we do see the assembling of believers on the first day of the week to corporately remember the Lord Jesus Christ through the breaking of the bread (Acts 20:7). The divine pattern of setting aside one day in seven for the Lord (Gen. 2:1-3) is still to be followed. During the dispensation of the Law that day was Saturday (according to the fourth of the Ten Commandments), but during the Church Age, Sunday (resurrection day) is designated as the Lord's Day. In time, the Jews brought reproach upon the name of Jehovah because they neglected the Law of God and ceased to honor Him and the Sabbath day; consequently, they were severely punished. May the Church not repeat this same offense, but rather live as a holy people before the nations and consecrate to God what is His.

> Take time to be holy, speak oft with the Lord;
> Abide in Him always, and feed on His Word.
> Take time to be holy, be calm in thy soul,
> Each thought and each motive beneath His control;
> Thus, led by His Spirit to fountains of love,
> Thou soon shall be fitted for service above.
>
> — William D. Longstaff

# A Peculiar Treasure
## Exodus 19:5-8

The conditional aspects of God's covenant with His people are stated in verse 5: *"Now therefore, if you will indeed obey My voice and keep My covenant, then you shall be a special treasure to Me above all people; for all the earth is Mine.*" If the Jews obeyed the Word of God and kept His Law then they would be blessed by God and be His highly esteemed people. Jehovah considered them to be a peculiar treasure upon the earth and they were to act accordingly. God is the Creator of all and He chose to reveal Himself and offer His communion and blessing to a specific people group, the descendants of Abraham through Jacob. However, as William Kelly points out, the conditional nature of this covenant also highlighted the limitations of how God would be able to relate to the Jews:

> God was dealing with Israel in their responsibility as witnesses of Jehovah, the one true self-existing God, the almighty God of Abraham, Isaac, and Jacob. His relationship was with them as they then were, redeemed from Egypt by His power and brought to Himself indeed, but only after an outward sort, neither born of God, nor justified. They were a people in the flesh. They had been wholly insensible to His ways of grace in leading them out of Egypt to Sinai. They lost sight of His promises to the fathers. They stood in their own strength to obey the law of God, as ignorant of their impotence as of His holy majesty. Accordingly we may regard the law as a whole, consisting not only of moral claims but of national institutes, ordinances, statutes, and judgment under which Israel were put.[1]

Jehovah had redeemed His people through grace and He had delivered them from Egypt by His power, but His future blessing and fellowship would depend upon national obedience to His Law. Moses, at the end of his life, would emphasize this fact again while addressing the

Israelites: *"You shall remember that you were a slave in the land of Egypt, and the Lord your God redeemed you; therefore I command you this thing today"* (Deut. 15:15-16).

As long as the Jews yielded to God's Law they would be *"a kingdom of priests and a holy nation"* on the earth to testify of Jehovah's greatness (v. 6). Prior to this, Scripture refers to two Gentile kingdoms: Nimrod's (Gen. 10:10), and Abimelech's (Gen. 20:9), but verse 6 is the first reference in the Bible to God's kingdom. This spiritual domain is to be composed of a holy people who both desire to worship God and continue to do so.

This kingdom was foretold in the Old Testament, announced by John the Baptist and Jesus Christ, but then rejected by the Jews (i.e. its spiritual aspects and its King). The seven Kingdom Parables of Matthew 13 bridge the gap between the first advent of the Lord to earth to become a man to suffer for our sin and His second advent in which His kingdom will be established and all that is wicked will be removed. After the Jews rejected Christ's offer of a literal, earthly, political kingdom with Him as King, the kingdom, in its spiritual sense, was then offered to the Gentiles. God's rule presently encompasses the hearts of believers, the Church. This spiritual interim of God's kingdom will conclude at the end of the Church Age, and then the same kingdom offered to the Jews long ago will be physically established on earth at Christ's Second Advent. God's kingdom in its final phase will be the establishment of a new heaven and a new earth; this will be the eternal state of righteousness – *"that God may be all and all"* (1 Cor. 15:28).

Through the Kingdom Parables, the Lord Jesus foretold that the Jews, who had already been scattered and lost among the nations for 600 years for committing spiritual adultery (Ezek. 36:16-25), would be found again by Messiah for the purpose of offering Himself to them as their King. However, they would reject Him and, thus, continue to be lost among the nations until their repentance during the last days of the Tribulation Period. In order to retrieve them in the future from the nations and to restore them as His people, the Lord first had to pay the debt of their sin at Calvary. In the fifth of the Kingdom Parables, Christ alludes to this: *"Again, the kingdom of heaven is like treasure hidden in a field, which a man found and hid; and for joy over it he goes and sells all that he has and buys that field"* (Matt. 13:44).

God considers Israel *a treasure* unto Himself (Ex. 19:5; Ps. 135:4). It seems then, that what is pictured in the fifth parable is the spiritual blindness of the nation of Israel; they were cut off from God for rejecting Christ who then turned to woo a Gentile bride for Himself. This "treasure" was thus hidden again in a field (among the nations of the world) a second time. However, at the Lord's Second Coming, He will be accepted by the Jewish nation (Zech. 12:10), and they will then receive the Holy Spirit and be restored unto God as His people. God will regather the Jews to the land of Israel; He will not leave one of them among the nations (Ezekiel 39:28-29). In that day, God's *peculiar treasure* spoken of in verse 5 will be found again and recovered.

Moses descended the Mount of God and informed the people of God's covenant-offer. They responded, by saying: *"All that the Lord has spoken we will do"* (Ex. 19:8), and Moses again ascended the mountain to personally convey their response to God. This may have been the aspiration of their hearts at the time, but their promise to obey Jehovah was self-confident and short-lived, for in just a few days they would construct and worship a golden calf and be judged accordingly. In fact, their history would be marred with rebellion and scarred by divine judgment. Almost a millennium later, after King Josiah heard God's Law for the first time, he sent five priests to inquire of the Lord to see what should be done, *"for great is the wrath of the Lord that is aroused against us, because our fathers have not obeyed the words of this book, to do according to all that is written concerning us"* (2 Kgs. 22:13). For much of their history, the Jew's behavior was worse than the pagans (2 Chron. 33:9). Not only did they commit blatant idolatry, but they knew God and His commandments and chose to ignore them. Edward Dennett summarizes why the Jewish nation ultimately failed to obtain God's blessing:

> Instead of clinging with tenacity, because of their own felt impotence, to what *God was for them, which is grace,* they foolishly offered to make everything depend upon what *they could be for God, which is the principle of law.* It is ever the same. Man in his folly and blindness ever seeks to obtain blessing upon the ground of his own works, and rejects a salvation which is offered to him in pure grace; for he is unwilling to be nothing, and grace makes everything of God, and nothing of man.[2]

Jewish failure, however, would not prohibit God from establishing His kingdom of holy worshippers (Rom. 3:3-4). During the Church Age, all Christians become the Holy Spirit-indwelt temple of God. These believer-priests are able to lift up worship unto God and offer themselves as living sacrifices wherever and whenever they desire (Rom. 12:1). These redeemed saints are a part of God's holy and royal priesthood (1 Pet. 2:5, 9).

Speaking of Christ and what He had accomplished for all those who believe on Him, John writes, *"To Him who loved us and washed us from our sins in His own blood, and has made us kings and priests to His God and Father, to Him be glory and dominion forever and ever. Amen"* (Rev. 1:5-6). As believer-priests, let us endeavor today to offer up to God what Israel failed to do – lives that are yielded to His revealed will; let us not neglect this wonderful opportunity to please the Lord.

> Though our nature's fall in Adam shut us wholly out from God,
> Thine eternal counsel brought us nearer still, through Jesus' blood.
> For in Him we found redemption, grace and glory in Thy Son;
> Oh, the height and depth of mercy! Christ and His redeemed are one.
>
> — Robert Hawker

# God Speaks from the Darkness

## Exodus 19:9-25

The events on Mount Sinai, as recorded in this chapter, mark a new era in divine revelation. Until this time, God had on rare occasions revealed His will to individuals in the form of a charge or a call; now, He spelled out His code of ethics in intricate detail. In this respect, the Jews had an advantage over all other nations. Yet, privilege and responsibility are yoked together, meaning that the Jews had greater accountability to God for their actions than the other nations did. Obedience would be rewarded, but disobedience against God's Law would be reckoned as transgression against God: *"The law brings about wrath; for where there is no law there is no transgression"* (Rom 4:15), and *"For until the law sin was in the world, but sin is not imputed when there is no law"* (Rom. 5:13).

All of mankind was condemned in Adam and through Adam all humanity received a fallen nature, which opposes God (Rom. 5:12). Sin, therefore, has continued in the world, but from the time of Adam until the time of the Law it was not imputed as transgression. This does not mean that human sin during this time did not offend God – all sin offends God – but rather that sin was not explicitly regarded as transgression against God. During this interim (and at the present time), the human conscience experientially proved to one's own soul that he or she had an imbedded code of ethics which could not be perfectly obeyed no matter how hard one tried (Rom. 2:15). Internal feelings of guilt meant only one thing – sin had been committed. Now that the Law of God had been specifically revealed, ignorance would no longer be an excuse; sin would be accounted as transgression against God.

To illustrate this point, consider the following example. Until a particular highway has a posted speed limit, a highway patrol officer has no authority to pull you over and write you a citation for speeding – you have broken no law. However, this does not mean that you have not been driving excessively fast, for one's conscience bears witness of what appropriate conduct is. But once the law is decreed (posted, in this case), a legal responsibility to obey it is realized. If an individual drives responsibly he or she is able to maintain the privilege of driving, but if he or she doesn't, fines and loss of privilege normally result. The Jews now had no excuse for continuing in sin; they knew exactly what was expected of them and the consequences for not obeying God's moral demands upon them. The Israelites enjoyed special privileges that no other people on the planet had, but that rich blessing also made them more accountable to God for their actions. What were these privileges specifically? To answer this, Paul poses another question to the believers at Rome: *"Who are the Israelites?"* He then lists a number of unique privileges that the Jews had received, that is, special revelation from God that the Gentiles were not given (Rom. 9:4-5):

They were an adopted nation, a special people for God (Ex. 4:22; Deut. 7:6).

They witnessed God's glory as connected with the tabernacle and later with the temple (Ex. 40:35).

God made certain covenants with Israel which He will honor.

God gave the Jews the Mosaic Law (Ex. 19:5, 31:13).

They were given a special service towards God: to worship Him at the tabernacle/temple (Ex. 19:6).

God made specific promises to Jewish individuals and the Jewish nation (Josh. 1:2).

They had patriarchs: Abraham, Isaac, Jacob, etc.

They were given Christ as their Messiah (2 Cor. 5:16).

God chose the Jewish nation to be a testimony for Him among the nations (Ps. 67:1-7), but they failed miserably (Rom. 2:24). Paul continues in Romans 9 to show that the basis of being a true Israelite is related to spiritual, not physical, birth (Rom. 9:6-7). True Israelites are the spiritual offspring of Abraham, those who follow his example of exercising faith in

God's word alone. Thus, anyone following Abraham's example of trusting God's word by faith will be imputed a righteous standing in the same way that Abraham was declared righteous for trusting in God's word (Gen. 15:6). In the spiritual sense, these individuals become children of Abraham and of God.

After Moses had personally conveyed to God the Israelites' pledge to fully obey all that God would command of them (v. 8), the Lord told His servant to sanctify the people, for in three days He would descend upon the mount and would speak to him again in the hearing of the people. The Israelites were about to personally meet Jehovah and hear His voice, though He Himself would be engulfed by a dark cloud on the mount. The Lord instructed Moses to impose a strict boundary about the mountain's base; any person or beast that trespassed upon the mount should be put to death. This was a precautionary measure to keep the people from casually approaching God and, thus, being consumed by His presence.

In preparation for this meeting with God the Jews were to clean up. They were to wash their clothes (v. 10), and husbands and wives were to abstain from sexual relationships during this preparation time (v. 15). This unique restriction punctuated the solemn nature of the upcoming event and the necessity for complete devotion while preparing to meet Jehovah (1 Cor. 7:5, 32-33). The three days were used to awaken the Israelites' understanding of their sinful condition in contrast to God's righteousness. Though they saw manifestations of Jehovah's presence each day, such familiarity should never lead to a lackadaisical attitude about approaching Him, for God is a holy God, *"a consuming fire"* (Heb. 12:29).

When the day came for the nation of Israel to meet the Lord, a long blast of a trumpet, or perhaps a ram's horn, signaled Moses to lead the people to the base of the mount. The mount quaked exceedingly, it burned like an overheated furnace, and thick billows of smoke ascended up from it into heaven. From the thick darkness, a deafening voice which increased in volume uttered words as if blasted from a trumpet. So overwhelmed were the people by what they heard, felt, and saw that they *"begged that the word should not be spoken to them anymore"* (Heb. 12:19) and *"they moved and stood afar off"* from the mountain (Ex. 20:18). So mighty was the scene that day that even God's deliverer, Moses, said, *"I am exceedingly afraid and trembling"* (Heb. 12:21). This day would never be forgotten in Israel, some 1,500 years later the writer of Hebrews referred to this event to epitomize the holy nature of God (Heb. 12:18-21).

Though the Israelites had cleansed themselves the best they could by washing and scrubbing, they immediately felt unclean in Jehovah's presence. The prophet Jeremiah explains why, *"'For though you wash yourself with lye, and use much soap, yet your iniquity is marked before Me,' says the Lord God"* (Jer. 2:22). This was the purpose of the Mount Sinai experience; the manifestation of Jehovah's holiness made the Israelites keenly aware of their own sinful state before Him. They understood the message and fearfully retreated from the foot of the mount and *"stood afar off"* (v. 18).

An awesome expression of God's nature was witnessed at Mount Sinai that day; who of us, if we had been there, would have behaved any differently than those fearful Jews? Seeing the majesty of God so prominently displayed would cause anyone great trepidation. Yet, there would be a future day when an even greater display of God's holy character would take place. That day, now past, also took place on a quaking mount covered with thick darkness. God demonstrated His holy character in that when His own Son was made sin for us, God did not spare Him from judgment; sin had to be judged and the Lord Jesus Christ, engulfed by darkness, bore the wrath of God for our sins. The Law at Sinai and then the Law's righteous judgment at Calvary emphatically proved God to be a holy God!

God has not changed (Mal. 3:6), and He still demands of His people today: *"Be holy, for I am holy"* (1 Pet. 1:16). Christians would do well to remember the events that transpired on Mount Sinai in Exodus 19; God is a sin-hating God and we dare not test His merciful patience by endorsing sin with compromising conduct. Like Moses, Paul strictly warns believers to sanctify themselves before coming together as a congregation into the Lord's presence to worship. God has appointed a specific way for the Church to uplift the name of His Son and to remember Him corporately – the Lord's Supper. Believers must not use the Lord's Supper as a means to satisfy their own desires and needs; this is to partake of the Lord's Supper in an unworthy manner and invites God's chastening (1 Cor. 11:23-32). When believers assemble for the Lord's Supper, they must do so in the beauty of holiness (with sins humbly confessed) and with a spiritual offering ready to present to the Lord: *"Give to the Lord the glory due His name; bring an offering, and come before Him. Oh, worship the Lord in the beauty of holiness!"* (1 Chron. 16:29).

Just as 1 Corinthians 11 repeatedly warns believers to sanctify themselves before taking part in the Lord's Supper, God repeatedly warned the Israelites to sanctify themselves before coming to Mount Sinai long ago. God's supplementary command to Moses to return back down the mountain in order to warn the people shows His deep concern for them. Moses obeyed God's command and descended the mountain again to warn the people and to instruct them concerning God's Law (Ex. 20). His holiness was unapproachable. He could be observed from a distance, but if the people did not heed His "no trespassing" warning, offenders would die. When Moses returned to the mountain, he was to bring Aaron with Him, but only Moses was permitted to speak with the Lord and then only through a thick cloud of darkness (Ex. 20:22). Thankfully for the Christian, the veil is rent, and each believer has the great privilege to walk beyond the thick cloud of darkness into the light, for God is light, and in so doing he or she can enjoy full fellowship with God (1 Jn. 1:6-8).

The writer of Hebrews refers to this as *"the new and living way"* of approaching God; a way that is now available to all who have trusted Christ as Saviour:

> *Therefore, brethren, having boldness to enter the Holiest by the blood of Jesus, by a new and living way which He consecrated for us, through the veil, that is, His flesh, and having a High Priest over the house of God, let us draw near with a true heart in full assurance of faith, having our hearts sprinkled from an evil conscience and our bodies washed with pure water* (Heb. 10:19-22).

Moses' entrance before God at Sinai was so threatening that he said, *"I am exceedingly afraid and trembling"* (Heb. 12:21). Yet, believers in the Church Age can boldly approach the same awesome God that Moses stood before in terror with great confidence and assurance. How is this possible? Because Christ is the Mediator of the New Covenant and through the sprinkling of His own blood He has opened the way for us to approach Almighty God and call upon Him as Abba Father (Rom. 8:15; Heb. 12:24). In light of this fact, what exhortation does the writer of Hebrews offer to believers: "*Let us hold fast the confession of our hope without wavering, for He who promised is faithful* (Heb. 10:23). Dear believer, be holy for God is a consuming fire (Heb. 12:29), and hold fast to Christ – He is the means and the assurance of all good things to come!

> Without a cloud between, to see Him face to face;
> Not struck with dire amazement dumb, but triumphing in grace.
> Without a cloud between, to see Him as He is;
> O, who can tell the height of joy, the full transporting bliss!
>
> — Albert Midlane

# The Ten Commandments
# Exodus 20:1-17

The verbal transfer of the Law of God to the Jews began after Moses returned from the Mount of God the third time. The preamble of the Law was brief; it identified Jehovah as the one true God and the Deliverer of Israelites from Egypt and from bondage (v. 2). The foundation of the Law was then decreed in ten distinct moral commandments. God would provide Moses with specific details of the Law's implementation afterwards.

Probably no other incident in all human history so specifically identified behavior that offends God as what was communicated to Moses on Mount Sinai. Sin has always been an unpopular word and still is today. It describes lawlessness, rebellion, failure to do what we know is right, and falling short of God's standard of righteousness (Rom. 3:23; Jas. 4:17). Though the dispensation of the Law has been replaced with the stewardship of grace, the Law still declares God's moral standard for right and wrong today; the Ten Commandments show us our sin (Rom. 3:20) and affirm that we need a Saviour: *"Therefore the law was our tutor to bring us to Christ, that we might be justified by faith. But after faith has come, we are no longer under a tutor"* (Gal. 3:24-25).

The first two of the Ten Commandments relate to the subject of recognizing God as Creator and not worshipping creation. The first commandment is: *"You shall have no other gods before Me"* (Ex. 20:3). Moses explained how one obeys this commandment – it is by believing in the one true God and giving Him first place in your life: *"The Lord our God, the Lord is one! You shall love the Lord your God with all your heart, with all your soul, and with all your strength"* (Deut. 6:4-5). The Lord Jesus reiterated this teaching, *"'You shall love the Lord your God with all your heart, with all your soul, and with all your mind.' This is the first and great commandment"* (Matt. 22:37-38).

On another occasion, the Lord explained the commandment's meaning, *"He who loves father or mother more than Me is not worthy of Me. And he who loves son or daughter more than Me is not worthy of Me. And he who does not take his cross and follow after Me is not worthy of Me"* (Matt. 10:37-38). When it comes to having no other god besides the Creator, it means that He has first place in your life, your thinking, your allegiance, and your affection – and there are to be no close seconds concerning our love for God. Do you love the Lord God above all else – including yourself?

The second commandment is: *"You shall not make for yourself a carved image – any likeness of anything that is in heaven above, or that is in the Earth beneath, or that is in the water under the Earth; you shall not bow down to them nor serve them. For I, the Lord your God, am a jealous God"* (Ex. 20:4-5). Have you ever heard someone say, "God to me is …." The individual is revealing to you his or her self-concocted god, an imaginary image of a god which fits his or her liking and, therefore, will readily condone that person's moral standard of doings. In this way, holiness becomes relative; a self-manufactured god will not judge sin. This idol may not be a golden calf, but neither is it the Lord revealed in the Bible.

God does not have varying degrees of holiness and righteousness; His very character defines moral integrity, and all that does not measure up to it will be judged. When an individual replaces the true God of Scripture with a created image (whether visible or imaginary), he or she has violated the second of the Ten Commandments. To reject God as Creator is to violate both the first and the second commandments. Evolutionary teaching exalts man and demotes or denies God – it is an intellectual religion which is high on self and applauds nature's ability to do what only God can do – create life!

The first two commandments alone are sufficient to prove that each and every one of us has offended God. Yet, if there is any doubt about this fact, the remaining commandments prove the point:

Do not blaspheme God or use His name disrespectfully.

Put aside one day in seven to honor the Lord (e.g. the Sabbath day).

Honor your parents.

Do not murder.

Do not commit adultery.

Do not steal.

Do not lie.

Do not covet (lust after what is not yours).

If you ask people on the street if they are a good person, most will say "Yes, I am a pretty good person." Their moral standard of reckoning, however, is all wrong, and they don't even know it. They have fabricated a self-righteous system in which they weigh their good deeds against their bad ones (sin), thinking that their good deeds will somehow offset their sins. God's standard of judgment is quite different – absolute perfection!

Coveting, for example, is a sin generally perceived to be less of an offense to God than committing adultery or murder, but in God's mind coveting is a form of idolatry (Col. 3:5). To adore anything more than Him, whether by one's actions or in one's thoughts, is the same to Him as committing idolatry. In such cases, the Lord loses significance and prominence in an individual's life; this greatly grieves Him. Consequently, by His standard, coveting is a sin and is sufficient to keep anyone out of heaven (Gal. 3:10-12).

Someday, each of us will be judged by God's standard of perfection (Eccl. 12:14; Rom. 14:10-12; Rev. 20:11-15). None of us measures up to this. No matter how hard we try, we cannot undo wrong-doing by doing good. We are all born spiritually dead (i.e. separated from God) and we prove it by our ungodly conduct. The bottom line is that we desperately need forgiveness of our sins and spiritual life and both are received through the Lord Jesus Christ; the former through His death and the latter through His life.

> *"O Death, where is your sting? O Hades, where is your victory?" The sting of death is sin, and the strength of sin is the law. But thanks be to God, who gives us the victory through our Lord Jesus Christ* (1 Cor. 15:55-57).

The Law displayed a holy standard for man to follow (Rom. 7:12), but it did not reveal God's full character, for the Law conveyed nearly no divine grace and mercy towards man: *"Anyone who has rejected Moses' law dies without mercy*" (Heb. 10:28). As C. H. Mackintosh summarizes, the purpose of the frightful scene at Mount Sinai that day was to declare God's holiness and righteousness, not His grace and mercy:

> Indeed, Mount Sinai was not the place to look for any such thing. There Jehovah revealed Himself in awful majesty, amid blackness, darkness, tempest, thunderings, and lightnings. These were not the attendant circumstances of an economy of grace and mercy; but they were well suited to one of truth and righteousness; and the law was that and nothing else.[1]

Consequently, to earn heaven through Law-keeping was, and still is, an impossibility, but the offer of grace and mercy has *come near* to all, and those who will trust the Lord Jesus Christ alone for salvation receive both grace and mercy. As Paul explains, an individual does not need to search the far ends of the earth, or venture into heaven or explore Hades to learn how to be saved; God has brought the message of salvation to us:

> *For Moses writes about the righteousness which is of the law, "The man who does those things shall live by them." But the righteousness of faith speaks in this way, "Do not say in your heart, 'Who will ascend into heaven?'" (that is, to bring Christ down from above) or, "'Who will descend into the abyss?'" (that is, to bring Christ up from the dead). But what does it say? "The word is near you, in your mouth and in your heart" (that is, the word of faith which we preach): that if you confess with your mouth the Lord Jesus and believe in your heart that God has raised Him from the dead, you will be saved. For with the heart one believes unto righteousness, and with the mouth confession is made unto salvation* (Rom. 10:5-10).

Like the Law, Christ descended from heaven, but He accomplished what the Law could not: *"Moreover the law entered that the offense might abound. But where sin abounded, grace abounded much more, so that as sin reigned in death, even so grace might reign through righteousness to eternal life through Jesus Christ our Lord"* (Rom. 5:20-21). The Law revealed the exceeding sinfulness of man's heart and decreed death upon the sinner (Rom. 7:13), but through Christ alone, the believer receives the forgiveness of sins and eternal life. "Because I am weak," wrote C. H. Mackintosh, "the law gives me no strength and shows me no mercy. The law *demands* strength from one that has none, and *curses* him if he cannot display it. The gospel *gives* strength to one that has none, and *blesses* him in the exhibition of it. The law proposes life as the *end* of obedience. The gospel gives life as the only proper *ground* of obedience."[2] Again, we must acclaim the utter truthfulness of this statement: The gospel of Jesus Christ accomplished what the Law could not. Consequently, there is *"now no condemnation to those who are in Christ Jesus"* (Rom. 8:1). The love, mercy, and grace of God are fully declared and offered in Christ alone!

> Is, then, the Law of God untrue, which He by Moses gave?
> No! But to take in view, that it has power to save.
> The Law was never meant to give new strength to man's lost race,
> We cannot act before we live, and life proceeds from grace.
> By Christ we enter into rest, and triumph over the fall.
> Whoever would be completely blest must trust to Christ for all.
>
> — Gadsby's Hymns

# Worshipping a Holy God
## Exodus 20:18-26

Although the people, because of fear, had moved away from the mountain and stood afar off, Moses (and likely Aaron) ventured into the thick darkness which enveloped Sinai to speak with Jehovah; this was Moses' fourth trip up the mount. Jehovah reminded Moses that He had descended from heaven to engulf the mount with fire and smoke in the sight of the people and had spoken in their hearing. In recounting this, God was drawing a clear distinction between Himself and the supposed earth-dwelling gods. He was superior, the one true God of heaven and, thus, the only One to be worshipped. Accordingly, the Israelites were to be warned again of engaging in the Egyptian practice of forging idols of silver and gold. Jehovah alone was to be worshipped.

Exodus 20 concludes with instructions concerning how the Israelites were to properly worship Jehovah. How wonderful this announcement must have been to the Israelites, who had fled the base of the mountain in fear. If comprehending God's holiness only resulted in the sinner's awareness of his or her separation from God, why would Jehovah have displayed His glory upon the mount in the first place? Thankfully, frightening His covenant people into exclusion was not His final objective; rather, God wanted the Israelites to understand His holy nature so that they would yield to His revealed means of coming near to Him. On this important matter of God's objective, C. H. Mackintosh writes:

> Here we find man not in the position of *a doer*, but of *a worshipper*; and this, too, at the close of Exodus 20. How plainly this teaches us that the atmosphere of Mount Sinai is not that which God would have the sinner breathing; that it is not the proper meeting place between God and man. "In all places where I record *my name, I will come unto thee, and I will bless thee.*" How unlike the terrors of the fiery mount

is that spot where Jehovah records *His name,* whither He "comes" to "bless" His worshipping people![1]

Now that the Law had established a new covenant relationship between Jehovah and His people, the opportunity to worship Jehovah could be extended. Although a much more involved system of worship would later be revealed in the book of Leviticus, for the time being, the Israelites were encouraged to offer sweet-savor (free-will) offerings to the Lord. Edward Dennett notes three distinct regulations that would govern Israelite worship at this time:

> First, that God could not be approached except through sacrifices. Secondly, He could come and bless them in all places where He would record His name — notwithstanding what they were, on the ground of the sweet savor of their offerings. Thirdly, the character of the altar is specified. It might be an altar of earth. If of stone, it must not be of hewn stone, "for if thou lift up thy tool upon it, thou hast polluted it. Neither shalt thou go up by steps unto Mine altar, that thy nakedness be not discovered thereon." (vv. 24-26.)[2]

Concerning the character of the altar, J. N. Darby notes that human work and design in worship were completely prohibited: "Two things are pointed out as to worship – the work of man, and his order, in which his nakedness will certainly be made manifest; and they are equally and together prohibited by God."[3] Thus, man may worship God only according to His revealed order and may offer to Him only that which He says is acceptable. The Jews had been forewarned; if, in time, they developed elaborate ceremonies and religious rituals to offer God their self-approved sacrifices, both their self-righteous doings and their polluted sacrifices would be rejected.

Fallen humanity has a natural propensity for religious pride (i.e. making religious choices that neither show faith in God nor turn us from a path of sin). Nadab and Abihu, two sons of Aaron the high priest of Israel, offered strange incense to God in worship just after God had given specific instructions as to the proper way for priests to offer sacrifices to Him. God struck them both dead for their arrogance, and their father was not permitted to mourn their deaths since they had offended God (Lev. 10:1-6). More religious doings do not impress God, nor do they have any eternal value.

On this point, the rebuke of the Lord Jesus to the Church at Laodicea is most pertinent: *"You are wretched, miserable, poor, blind, and naked – I counsel you to buy from Me gold refined in the fire, that you may be rich; and white garments, that you may be clothed, that the shame of your nakedness may not be revealed; and anoint your eyes with eye salve, that you may see"* (Rev. 3:17-18). Those in the Church at Laodicea were not living for Christ; consequently, God's righteousness was not displayed in their lives. Though all believers in the Church have been positionally declared righteous in Christ, each believer has the opportunity to labor in righteousness for Christ. Those things which are done in accordance with revealed truth and in power of the Spirit have eternal value; these righteous acts are what the believer is adorned with throughout eternity. In heaven, the bride of Christ must have righteous attire; she is *"arrayed in fine linen, clean and bright, for the fine linen is the righteous acts of the saints"* (Rev. 19:8).

Paul explains in 1 Corinthians 15:40-42 that after the resurrection, some saints will shine forth the glory of God more brightly than others, just as some stars in the nighttime sky are brighter than other stars. This acquired glory directly reflects the righteous acts (good works) that are done for Christ by His strength in this present life. Eternal glory, evidently, has a weight to it; in other words, its quality is measurable (2 Cor. 4:17) and can be earned by believers through selfless service for Christ now. Thus, to be appropriately dressed for eternity, believers should secure for themselves a covering of eternal glory, which consists of righteous acts. Though saved, a believer may still appear to be spiritually naked in heaven (i.e. personal acts of righteousness on earth provide believers with varying reflections of God's glory in heaven: Rev. 3:18; 1 Cor. 15:41-42; 2 Cor. 4:17). Endeavoring to worship God through any means or method other than what His Word authorizes does not contribute to one's eternal attire.

How utterly putrid to God, then, are all the ceremonies, the holidays, and the rituals which the Church has created to obtain some religious experience or to try impress Him. In the Church Age, believers are commanded to regularly observe the Lord's Supper in remembrance of Christ, they are to be living sacrifices by mortifying their fleshly desires and yielding to God's will, and they are to fulfill their work of ministry within the Body of Christ. Whatever is beyond this is humanized religion and an offense to God.

God had sought out the Israelites, and if the Israelites were going to respond to His invitation to worship there had to be an altar upon which blood flowed and fire consumed. Blood was necessary for atonement, and fire signified God's acceptance of the offering (i.e. the sacrifice would be consumed off the altar and disappear). The Israelites were permitted to build two types of altars to place burnt offerings and peace offerings upon (v. 24); one of earth and one of uncut stones. No human tools, which picture man's works, were allowed to be used in the altars' construction – what God had provided in creation would suffice. Also, there were to be no steps on the altar. The pagan altars often had steps, for it was thought to be advantageous to drawn near to one's god by ascending steps. The Jews were not to have steps because they could not approach God by their own efforts; this would also prevent onlookers from peering upwards and seeing the nakedness of the priests.

Spiritually speaking, any effort to approach God other than His prescribed means shows off one's spiritual nakedness. This was a lesson that our first parents soon learned after that dreadful day in the Garden of Eden. After eating from the forbidden tree, Adam and his wife immediately sought to hide their nakedness from each other by sewing fig leaves together as clothes. Yet, this "cover up" did not resolve the feelings of guilt their consciences were inflicting upon them for the first time. So many new thoughts and feelings swarmed their minds. So what did Adam and his wife do when their Creator called for them? In their darkened state they sought seclusion and hid themselves in the shadows of trees. Their response to God's call essentially demonstrated that the "fig clothes" which they had made were insufficient to deal with their guilt before God. How did God respond? God did what He continues to do today; He came looking and seeking that which was lost.

Psalm 104:2 (KJV) speaks of God's attire, saying, *"Thou coverest Thyself with light as with a garment...."* Man could not hide from God. His presence penetrates, both the vastness of creation and the deepest slumber of the human conscience. David understood the difficulty of hiding from God when he wrote, *"Where shall I go from Your Spirit? Or where shall I flee from Your presence?"* (Ps. 139:7). Yet to this very day, men, encompassed by the darkness of sin, still scurry into the shadows of self-misery when the Creator comes seeking that which is lost. He beckons them to face the shame of their condition by venturing out into the light of divine truth and grace. Unfortunately, many today are like Adam and Eve, who tried to hide from God when He called to them, or are like the Israelites who stood afar off after hearing God's voice. God is patient and persistent, and continues to seek out and to call sinners to repentance and that they might be saved:

> *For this is good and acceptable in the sight of God our Saviour, who desires all men to be saved and to come to the knowledge of the truth. For there is one God and one Mediator between God and men, the Man Christ Jesus, who gave Himself a ransom for all, to be testified in due time* (1 Tim. 2:3-6).

> *The Lord is not slack concerning His promise, as some count slackness, but is longsuffering toward us, not willing that any should perish but that all should come to repentance* (2 Peter 3:9).

As demonstrated in the Garden of Eden, man cannot approach God; God must approach man to offer salvation – not even one step towards God is possible though human effort, for salvation is the work of God's grace alone (Eph. 2:8-9; Tit. 2:5). God the Father sent His Son from heaven to the earth so that man could have the opportunity to be adopted into His family with full privileges of sonship forever: *"But when the fullness of the time had come, God sent forth His Son, born of a woman, born under the law, to redeem those who were under the law, that we might receive the adoption as sons"* (Gal. 4:4-5). This is God's work, which we can enter into only by faith. Having done so, what joy could possibly surpass knowing God as Father, being in His family forever, being clothed in righteous, and being co-inheritor of all things with His Son (Rom. 8:14-17)? Adam had none of this in Eden; despite human rebellion, God found a way through Christ to richly bless all believers in Him beyond anything imaginable through human devices!

> Walk in the light, so shalt thou know that fellowship of love,
> His Spirit only can bestow, who reigns in light above.
> Walk in the light, and thou shalt find thy heart made truly His,
> Who dwells in cloudless light enshrined, in whom no darkness is.
>
> — Bernard Barton

# Social Regulations
## Exodus 21:1

After conveying the fundamental statutes of the Law, Jehovah instructed Moses on the finer points of personal rights and social practices. Reason would dictate that a new nation composed of liberated slaves would strongly disdain the practice of slavery; hence, it was doubtful that Jewish slaves were among the Israelites at this time. So why did God after announcing the Ten Commandments to Moses immediately speak of slavery regulations? Why not first convey ordinances relating to the resolution of personal disputes, or the penalties of and the restitutions of particular crimes? There are many reasons for addressing the matter of slavery initially; here are three to consider.

First, the bondservant is a strong type of the Lord Jesus Christ. Therefore, it would be appropriate for God to remind the Jews that the covenant of the Law could be offered to them only because grace first found a way to redeem them in Egypt. Christ is typified by the loyal bondservant who willingly allowed himself to be marked for life to express his undying love for his master. Thus, Christ's love for His Father, a love to be indelibly declared for all time by Calvary's wounds, is brought before our minds prior to the specifics of man's responsibility in the Law.

The writer of Hebrews quotes Psalm 40:6 to ensure that we do not miss the link between the willing bondservant of Exodus 21 and the willing, suffering Son of God (Heb. 10:5-10). A comparison of the two texts reveals that the One who had His ear opened in Psalm 40:6 is the same One who offered His body to God in sacrifice:

> Sacrifice and offering You did not desire; **My ears You have opened**. Burnt offering and sin offering You did not require. Then I said, "Behold, I come; in the scroll of the book it is written of me. I delight to do Your will, O my God, and Your law is within my heart" (Ps. 40:6-8).

> Therefore, when He came into the world, He said: "Sacrifice and offering You did not desire, **but a body You have prepared for Me**. In burnt offerings and sacrifices for sin You had no pleasure. Then I said, 'Behold, I have come – In the volume of the book it is written of Me – To do Your will, O God.'" Previously saying, "Sacrifice and offering, burnt offerings, and offerings for sin You did not desire, nor had pleasure in them"(which are offered according to the law), then He said, "Behold, I have come to do Your will, O God." He takes away the first that He may establish the second. By that will we have been sanctified through the offering of the body of Jesus Christ once for all (Heb. 10:5-10).

C. H. Mackintosh, commenting on the faithful bondservant being a wonderful type of Christ, writes:

> The application of this to the Lord Jesus Christ will be obvious to the intelligent reader. In Him we behold the One who dwelt in the bosom of the Father before all worlds — the object of His eternal delight — who might have occupied, throughout eternity, this His personal and entirely peculiar place, inasmuch as there lay upon Him no obligation (save that which ineffable love created and ineffable love incurred) to abandon that place. Such, however, was His love to the Father whose counsels were involved, and for the Church collectively, and each individual member thereof, whose salvation was involved, that He, voluntarily, came down to earth, emptied Himself, and made Himself of no reputation, took upon Him the form of a servant and the marks of perpetual service. ...Thus we have, in the Hebrew servant, a type of Christ in His pure devotedness to the Father.[1]

Besides putting His Son in remembrance as the ultimate Bondservant, a second reason the matter of slavery was addressed initially was to show the Israelites the depravity of the human heart. Indeed, not only slavery, but many of the hideous crimes mentioned in Exodus did not exist among the children of Israel at the time the Law was given. But the fact that God was imposing severe penalties for gross and putrid behavior, yet unfamiliar to them, showed the Jews that God knew more about the depravity of their hearts than they did. In time, they would violate every dictate of the Law, despite being forewarned of God and despite, in many cases, the threat of the death penalty.

The Bible does not promote slavery, but it does acknowledge its existence, and provides regulations to govern it. Similarly, divorce was never God's plan for marriage – He hates it (Mal. 2:16) – but the Law allowed for it and issued rules to govern it. Divorce resulted from the hardness of the human heart (Matt. 19:8), and slavery sprang from the same fountainhead.

The fallen nature of man enslaves him to sin (Rom. 6:19), and thus he will naturally endeavor to pull others under its influence and to enslave them too. As a result, natural man yearns to control and to use others for his advantage, rather than serving and assisting them. Even when natural man does assist others, it is still unacceptable to God because his motivation to do so is impure; he either desires to gain something from his initial effort, to earn spiritual promotion, or to merit some reward. This is all humanized religion, but the fact remains that outside of Christ man can do nothing to please God: *"But to those who are defiled and unbelieving* ***nothing is pure;*** *but even their mind and conscience are defiled. They profess to know God, but in works they deny Him, being abominable, disobedient, and* ***disqualified for every good work"*** (Tit. 1:15-16). Consequently, the sum total of all the good works a sinner does in his or her entire lifetime is still counted as filthy rags to God (Isa. 64:6). From this perspective, the Law showed the depravity of man before man understood that he was depraved.

The third reason for beginning with slavery regulations was that the Lord knew that man must be properly motivated to serve Him before he would want to avoid the conduct that offends Him. If one loves the Lord, submitting to the precepts of the Law will be a delight. Love for the Lord is a stronger motive for obedience than is the fear of consequences: *"There is no fear in love; but perfect love casts out fear, because fear involves torment. But he who fears has not been made perfect in love"* (1 Jn. 4:18).

This is a principle that parents must understand, if they are to ever enjoy a happy home. If the only way parents are able to control their children is by the constant threat of chastening, there will be problems in the home during their children's adolescent years. Children (older than toddlers) who truly love their parents will require little discipline. God teaches us through His dealings with His own children that child-rearing must focus on changing the heart: win the heart, mold the heart, train the child to keep his or her heart pure, and then assist him or her to pledge his or her heart to another for life – and to God be all the glory.

As an illustration of this love versus fear principle as the primary means to motivate obedience, let us consider the marriage relationship. Most husbands are bigger and stronger than their wives. Naturally speaking, then, is a husband's motivation to remain faithful to his own wife centered in the fear that his wife will severely hurt him for his infidelity, or that he would deeply hurt his wife by his unfaithfulness? Though the former is a distinct possibility, the latter is the better motivation for faithfulness! Likewise, the preeminent motive for not continuing in sin is not that we will be punished by God (which He promises to do, Heb. 12:6), but rather that we do not want to hurt the heart of God by such conduct. Why cause pain to the One who has done so much for us? Love for the Lord is the best motivation to obey and serve Him, a principle that is shown to us in the character sketch of the faithful bondservant.

> Slain for a sinful world, and me, our Surety hung upon the tree;
> Thy body bore our guilty load: my Lamb for sin an offering made,
> The debt of all mankind hath paid, and bought, and sprinkled us with blood.
> That blood applied by faith I feel, and come its healing power to tell,
> Through which I know my sins forgiven, a witness I, that all may find,
> The peace deserved for all mankind, and walk with God, my God, to heaven.
>
> — Charles Wesley

# I Will Not Go Out Free!
## Exodus 21:2-11

Hebrew history shows that there were two main reasons Jews would become slaves to other Jews: they could sell themselves into slavery in order to pay off a debt (such as a bride's dowry or an economic hardship) or they could be forced into slavery as a result of a punitive judgment (e.g. recompense for a crime committed). In any case, God did not desire His people to be forced to serve others as slaves, but rather, to be a liberated people who would freely serve Him. Consequently, no Jew was to be held in slavery against his or her will for more than six years, no matter what circumstances caused the servitude. Female slaves, as John Hannah explains, had special regulations to protect them from abuse:

> Female slaves were treated differently. Many times female slaves were concubines or secondary wives (cf. Gen. 16:3, 22:24, 30:3, 9; 36:12; Judg. 8:3; 9:18). Some Hebrew fathers thought it more advantageous for their daughters to become concubines of well-to-do neighbors than to become the wives of men in their own social class. If a daughter who became a servant was not pleasing to her master she was to be redeemed by a near kinsman (cf. Lev. 25:47-54) but never sold to foreigners (Ex. 21:8); she could also redeem herself. If she married her master's son she was to be given family status (v. 9). If the master married someone else he was required to provide his servant with three essentials: food, clothing, and shelter (marital rights probably means living quarters, not sexual privilege).[1]

For the Christian, both the legislation on slavery and the ill-treatment of women is loathsome, but, as F. B. Hole reminds us, the Law was not God's best for man, the best was yet to come:

> As the weaker party she might become the victim of wrongful treatment, so her rights are clearly defined. We may remark that under the law things were permitted that should not be tolerated by Christians today. That this was so is shown by the Lord's own words recorded in Matthew 19: 7, 8. We must ever bear in mind that, "the law made nothing perfect" (Heb. 7: 19), since it set forth the **minimum of God's demands**, so that all, who **in any way** or **at any time** fell short of it, came under the sentence of death. The maximum of all God's thoughts and desires are realized and set forth **in Christ.**[2]

God instituted slavery regulations to protect His people from abusing each other in future generations; however, His desire for them was that they assist one another in economic hardships, not take advantage of each other: *"If one of your brethren becomes poor, and falls into poverty among you, then you shall help him, like a stranger or a sojourner, that he may live with you. Take no usury or interest from him; but fear your God, that your brother may live with you"* (Lev. 25:35-37). Though Christians are not under the Law, this regulation highlights what God deems appropriate conduct for His people throughout all ages, that is, to rally around and help each other during times of distress: *"Bear one another's burdens, and so fulfill the law of Christ"* (Gal. 6:2). Indeed, this was the practice of the early Church (Acts 4:32-35, 6:1; 1 Tim. 5:3-5).

After six years of service, or at the fifty-year Jubilee if it occurred prior to the six year tenure (Lev. 25:39-42), a Hebrew slave was to be released, unless the slave desired to remain with his master for life. If this was the slave's choice he was taken to a doorpost, his ear was placed next to the wood, and the master pushed or pounded an awl through the slave's ear. The resulting hole marked him as a bondservant for life. In the Epistles, Paul often applied this phrase to express his own love for the Lord Jesus Christ. The only reason a man would become a perpetual bondservant would be to express love for his master, or perhaps, if had been given a wife while in slavery, love for his family (for his family would not be released if he chose to go free). Though not addressed in this passage, a female slave was given the same choice after six years of service (Deut. 15:17).

As love for the master is mentioned first, it seems to be the primary reason a slave would be willing to enter into a life-long commitment to his master. Certainly, the exceptional care of the master for his slave had already been experienced, otherwise the slave would not enter into a lifetime commitment; brutality would never cause a slave to make such a pledge. However, if the slave determined that he could never be happier than in serving his master, this action becomes understandable. In type, the slave's love for his master pictures the love and pure devotion of the Lord Jesus for His Father, but "there is more than this," says C. H. Macintosh:

> "I love my wife and my children." "Christ loved the church and gave himself for it, that he might sanctify and cleanse it with the washing of water by the word, that he might present it to himself a glorious church, not having spot, or wrinkle, or any such thing; but that it should be holy and without blemish" (Eph. 5: 25-27). There are various other passages of Scripture presenting Christ as the antitype of the Hebrew servant, both in His love for the Church, as a body, and for all believers personally. ...The apprehension of this love of the heart of Jesus cannot fail to produce a spirit of fervent devotedness to the One who could exhibit such pure, such perfect, such disinterested love. How could the wife and children of the Hebrew servant fail to love one who had voluntarily surrendered his liberty in order that he and they might be together? And what is the love presented in the type, when compared with that which shines in the antitype? It is as nothing. "The love of Christ passeth knowledge." It led Him to think of us before all worlds — to visit us in the fullness of time — to walk deliberately to the door post — to suffer for us on the cross, in order that He might raise us to companionship with himself, in His everlasting kingdom and glory.[3]

The slave had two options at the conclusion of his time of binding service: he could *"go out free and pay nothing"* (v. 2), or he could tell his master, *"I will not go out free"* (v. 5). If he chose the first option he was to be set free; he was at liberty to live his life however he chose to do so, but he departed empty-handed. Likewise, since his association with his master was severed, there would be no future assistance or benefits received from him either. If the slave chose the latter option, he would be committing himself for the remainder of his life to serve his master and he would also enjoy all the blessings of that association.

Commitment entails being given over to a cause without reservation, such was the pledge of a slave to his master, and such should be the pledge of every child of God to his or her Master. Only after a believer has consciously made such a determination will he or she have the unwavering obedience and devotion of a true disciple of Christ. The Lord does not force us to pledge our lives to Him, but He does warn us:

> *If anyone desires to come after Me, let him deny himself, and take up his cross daily, and follow Me. For whoever desires to save his life will lose it, but whoever loses his life for My sake will save it. For what profit is it to a man if he gains the whole world, and is himself destroyed or lost?* (Luke 9:23-25).

Like the slave when the day of freedom arrived, those who have received a new life in Christ have only two ways to live while sojourning on the earth: to completely yield one's life to Christ thus gaining a life worth living and fellowship with God, or to live one's life the way one wants. The latter decision results in a spiritually desolate life that knows neither the peace, nor the joy of God and counts for nothing in eternity.

The Lord Jesus warned of two hindrances that would keep believers from committing to live their lives for Him. The first is having more than one master: *"No one can serve two masters; for either he will hate the one and love the other, or else he will be loyal to the one and despise the other. You cannot serve God and mammon"* (Matt. 6:24). Divided allegiance is not possible, for ultimately a slave can be devoted to only one master. The Lord states that there can be no middle ground, He is either the believer's first love or He is not the Master of the believer's life.

Christ's second warning to believers relates to enthroning one's self and rejecting Him as Master: *"But why do you call Me 'Lord, Lord,' and not do the things which I say?"* (Luke 6:46), or to put in the modern vernacular, "Don't call me Lord if you are not going to do what I say." Normally, when Scripture speaks of the will of God, it explicitly states what it is. There is no mystery about it; God has declared to us His general will for our lives. Consequently, the more pertinent question becomes, not what the will of God is for my life, but will I obey the revealed will of God for my life? The Lord Jesus says, *"If you love*

*Me, keep My commandments"* (John 14:15). Obedience to the Lord Jesus practically proves our love for Him. A lack of love for the Lord will be shown through an unyielded spirit and through disobedience. There is such an intimate tie between genuine love for the Lord and obedience to the Lord that Paul bluntly states, *"If any man love not the Lord Jesus Christ, let him be Anathema* [eternally condemned]" (1 Cor. 16:22).

Do you want to prove that you love the Lord Jesus Christ? If so, make a fresh commitment that He be the only Master of your life; only then will you gain a life worth living! Dear believer, life is short, a fleeting vapor in time, don't waste it for nothing! What you do for eternity the world cannot destroy, nor can anyone steal (Matt. 6:19-20). What is desperately needed in the Church today is for believers to look heavenward and tell the Master: "I will not go out free for nothing!"

My glorious Victor, Prince divine, clasp these surrendered hands in Thine,
At length my will is all Thine own, glad vassal of a Saviour's throne.
My Master, lead me to Thy door, pierce this now willing ear once more.
Thy bonds are freedom; let me stay with Thee to toil, endure, obey.
Tread them still down, and then, I know, these hands shall with Thy gifts over flow,
And pierced ears shall hear the tone which tells me Thou and I are one.

— Handley C. G. Moule

# An Eye for an Eye
## Exodus 21:12-36

God had commanded Noah, *"Whoever sheds man's blood, by man his blood shall be shed; for in the image of God He made man"* (Gen. 9:6). The sixth commandment of the Law, *"You shall not murder"* (Ex. 20:13) affirmed this decree. In this chapter, more specifics regarding the implementation of this commandment are relayed to the people. *"Murder,"* the premeditated act of ending another person's life, is a better translation of the Hebrew word *rasah* than is the word *"kill."* One may kill a sheep without breaking the commandment, but sheep cannot be murdered; thus, the Law prohibited the unwarranted ending of human life by another human. The Law also protected the life of the accused until proven guilty. To insure that this protocol was adhered to, Jehovah would later assign six cities of refuge as temporary sanctuaries where the accused could reside safely until his or her case was tried. If the accused was found innocent, he or she could dwell within the confines of these cities without the threat of retaliation by the relatives of the deceased. If the slayer was found guilty of premeditated murder he or she was put to death; a lesser penalty was required for accidental deaths or those caused by a non-premeditated act of violence. Under this section of the Law, six types of crimes were to carry the death penalty:

1. Premeditated murder.
2. Slaying one's parents.
3. Kidnapping.
4. Cursing or rebelling against one's father or mother.
5. Injuring a pregnant woman and causing her unborn child to die.
6. Allowing a bull, known for "pushing," to kill someone (both the bull and the master were to die).

The offense of killing the unborn child clearly shows that God considers the life of the fetus to be of equal value to that of an adult man. Although an offender could be spared the death penalty if he slew without premeditation, there was no mercy given to one who caused the death of an unborn child, even if it were not premeditated. This Law specifically highlights the great concern God has for protecting unborn children, and also His anger against those who destroy what He has wondrously created. David reminds us that all the names of the unborn boys and girls are recorded in God's *Book of the Living* and that each one's life has been planned out by the Lord before his or her conception occurred:

> *I will praise You, for I am fearfully and wonderfully made; marvelous are Your works, and that my soul knows very well. My frame was not hidden from You, when I was made in secret, and skillfully wrought in the lowest parts of the earth* [speaking of the womb]. *Your eyes saw my substance, being yet unformed. And in Your book they all were written, the days fashioned for me, when as yet there were none of them* (Ps. 139:14-16). Note: The *Book of the Living* is also spoken of in Ps. 69:28 and Ex. 32:31-33.

Enthusiasm for life and felicity in life are the believer's when he or she understands that God has foreordained wonderful plans for his or her life: *"For we are His workmanship, created in Christ Jesus for good works, which God prepared beforehand that we should walk in them"* (Eph 2:10). Before creation, God previewed the corridors of time, considered all the possible permutations of natural cause and effect as well as the future choices of cognitive beings, and made sovereign choices to bless humanity, glorify His name throughout time and eternity, and use each one of us in the elaborate process. As only a triune God existed when the plan of redemption was devised, the plan is solely His – it originated in His mind and He deserves all the glory for it. God's choices ensure that humanity will receive the greatest possible blessing and that He will obtain the most glory as a result. Why we are the recipients of such extraordinary grace is a question that will require all of eternity to answer (Eph. 2:7).

As Moses affirmed the various statutes of the Law to the children of Israel, it became obvious that under the Law the deterrent for wrong-doing was just and equal retaliation for the offense. God was enacting strict, even-handed justice, which afforded no mercy to guilty offenders and set forth specific *equitable* punishments to right the wrong; yet, the Law prohibited brutality. Thus, if an individual caused someone else to lose an eye, the offender then forfeited one of his or her eyes in retaliation for the offense: *"Eye for eye, tooth for tooth, hand for hand, foot for foot, burn for burn, wound for wound, stripe for stripe"* (Ex. 21:24-25).

Properly identifying all the nuances of this retaliator legislation would be difficult, but here are a few examples: If a slave were maimed by harsh treatment he or she was to be set free. If one man's slave were gored by another man's bull there was to be financial restitution. If an individual or his bull caused the loss of another man's livestock there was to be restitution according to the value of the animal. If the matter involved two bulls, and there was no neglect found in pen upkeep, the living bull was to be sold and the money split between the owner of the dead bull and the owner of the living one. If someone caused, intentionally or unintentionally, a pregnant woman to prematurely deliver a surviving baby there was restitution to be paid for the inconvenience. Edward Dennett observes two divine themes demonstrated in the giving of these statutes and how the latter aspect causes man to long for God's grace:

> The first is that all these enactments reveal the tenderness of God in protecting the bodies of His people – and especially of those occupying a subject position. The second is that we find here the true character of law. Grace is absent. It is eye for an eye, and tooth for a tooth, etc. Our blessed Lord especially cites these provisions to point out their contrast with grace. He says, "Ye have heard that it hath been said, An eye for an eye, and a tooth for a tooth: but I say unto you, that ye resist not evil: but whosoever shall smite thee on thy right cheek, turn to him the other also" (Matt. 5:38, 39). On the ground of law an exact equivalent is demanded – no more, and no less; but grace can remit every claim; for dealt with in grace ourselves, our whole debt remitted, we must act on the same principle in our relationships with one another. Be it, however, never forgotten, that the foundation of grace itself is laid deep in righteousness, and hence it reigns through righteousness (Rom. 5: 21), having thus been established upon an everlasting and immutable basis.[1]

The Law taught stringent justice for crimes and offenses, even if they were unintentionally committed. Its tit-for-tat restitution would satisfy the injured party's desire for vengeance, but it did not teach man how the divine qualities of love, grace, and mercy should govern one's behavior. Certainly, the lack of these in resolving life's offenses would cause man to be more appreciative of God's ultimate means of making restitution for our intentional and unintentional offenses against Him – the giving and judging of His Son in our place. The Lord Jesus Christ would be, and indeed was, the sin-sacrifice for all humanity. Through Christ we don't get what we do deserve (all the horrors of hell) and we do receive what we don't deserve (all the blessings of heaven); the former is God's mercy to us and the latter is His grace. Consequently, every aspect of our salvation is permeated by the sweet aroma of Christ's love. May we never get over the love of Christ and may we long for others to know it too!

> We will love with tender care, know the love of Christ,
> Brethren who His image bear, for "the love of Christ."
> Jesus only shall we know, and our love to all shall flow,
> In His blood-bought Church below, for "the love of Christ."
>
> — William Reid

# Righting Wrongs
## Exodus 22:1-31

The Law affirmed man's right to both life and property. Exodus 22 can be divided into two main sections: Instructions concerning property rights (vv.1-15) and the judgment of specific crimes against humanity (vv. 16-31). Moses began by imposing stiff penalties for the theft of livestock. If the stolen animal were sold or killed, the thief would have to pay five head of cattle in restitution for a stolen ox, or four sheep in retribution for a stolen sheep. A repentant Zachaeus referred to this provision of the Law when he told the Lord Jesus, *"If I have taken anything from anyone by false accusation, I restore fourfold"* (Luke 19:8). If the stolen animal were returned to its rightful owner, the thief would only have to pay double. Damage to vineyards, destruction of crops, and loss of personal property were to be justly recompensed; it did not matter if the loss was the result of an accidental or intentional act. The retribution for theft was particularly steep and would be a deterrent against stealing another's possessions.

King David would learn firsthand of the Law's punishment for theft. God sent the prophet Nathan to confront David concerning his sin of adultery with Bathsheba and the instigated murder of her husband Uriah to conceal his sin from others. As Nathan told David a story about a rich man seizing a poor man's only ewe lamb in order to serve it to a visitor, David became enraged: *"And David's anger was greatly kindled against the man; and he said to Nathan, 'As the Lord liveth, the man that hath done this thing shall surely die'"* (2 Sam. 12:5, KJV). Nathan used this story to express God's anger over David's sin. David had abused the power of the throne which God had given him; thus, judgment would be forthcoming.

David's anger invoked by Nathan's story was just, but hypocritical (i.e. the Law demanded four-fold restitution for stealing, not death to the guilty party; yet, under the Law, the consequences for David's more grievous sin was the death penalty). David was enraged at the injustice done to the poor man, yet he had committed a much worse offense and had remained unrepentant for more than a year. It demonstrates how easy it is for anger to cloud rational thinking and logical conclusions. When we are not in communion with God, our anger has the greatest opportunity to be provoked and to cause ungodly behavior. It is also good to remember that though others may not know your secret sins, both God and you know all about them and *"Be sure your sin will find you out"* (Num. 32:23). David's sins had made his life miserable, but after repenting of his offenses, his fellowship with God was fully restored.

The Law demanded that four lambs be given in restitution for a stolen lamb that had been killed. David had stolen what was not his and had then killed Uriah, and God would exact from him the life of four of his own sons for the crime: his newborn son conceived in adultery with Bathsheba, Amnon (who raped his own half-sister), Absalom (who led a national rebellion against his father), and Adonijah (who unsuccessfully conspired to be king). Though David, as he acknowledged in Psalm 51, did receive unmerited mercy from God (crimes of adultery and murder were punishable by death), the Law was upheld in that David experienced the loss of four sons. God spared David's life, but God's justice cost David dearly and his household never knew peace after this. No doubt as David looked back over his life, he greatly regretted that moment of uncontrolled lust. The message of the Law is that that *"the wages of sin is death"* (Rom. 6:23) and that God will judge all that offends His holy character.

The latter portion of Exodus 22 speaks to crimes against humanity. Some of the Law's regulations related to the Jewish betrothal and marriage customs and would serve to protect women from being abused. For example, if an unmarried woman (meaning she was not betrothed) were seduced by an unmarried man into committing fornication, the man was to pay the woman's father the virgin's dowry price. Unless her father forbade it, the two were to be married. If he were not allowed to marry her, he still had to pay the virgin's dowry as she could no longer be presented by her father as a virgin to any other suitor.

It is understood that there are various social customs presented in Scripture concerning marriage, and that the Law brought order and fairness to the Jewish marital process. Generally speaking, most marriages were arranged and children were *"given in marriage"* (Matt. 22:2, 30, 24:38; Mark 12:25; Luke 17:27, 20:34-35). Abraham initiated finding a wife for Isaac, Judah took a wife for Er, and Jehoiada took wives for King Joash. Sons would leave the home to establish themselves as new family heads, and daughters were then given by their fathers in marriage (Ps. 78:63; 1 Cor. 7:38). In this way, the woman experiences a transfer of authority (from her father's to her husband's). This transition of authority is clearly inferred in Numbers 30:2-16 in that a father could nullify his daughter's vow to God (if she was living under his authority), or a husband could nullify his wife's vow to God.

The biblical pattern for family life is that children remained with their parents at home and under their authority until they married – this pattern is especially true of daughters (Gen. 24; Acts 21:8-9). However, our western culture has brought about numerous difficulties in following this example because of the mobility that is often necessary to pursue education and vocations. Each family situation will be unique, but to the extent that it is possible, a provision of authority and protection should be in place to watch over, guide, and train older children. Where parents cannot directly oversee their children, the oversight of church elders, other family members, or a godly older couple (e.g. a missionary couple) should be used to ensure watchful oversight. This is a topic of scriptural principle, not command. Protective authority will be hard to implement at times, yet Scripture widely demonstrates the principle (e.g. Ruth 3:1, 4:13; John 11:1; Luke 8:2-3, 23:49; Rom. 16:1-2).

Single Christians should remain in happy fellowship with their parents (hopefully believers) and heed their counsel in the matters of marriage and ministry. In the case of marriage, it is the bride and groom who ultimately consent to marry, but if it is the mind of the Lord, all those who are spiritually-minded will be of one accord.

The laws imposed in this chapter also protected foreigners, widows, and orphans from being abused (vv. 21-22). In fact, the Lord warned of His personal wrath against anyone committing crimes against the latter two; He threatened to make the wives and children of the offenders, widows and orphans themselves (vv. 23-24)! Also, the Law demanded that witches, people committing bestiality, and idolaters be put to death – there were no second chances for such crimes, for each is a deliberate act of rebellion against God's revealed order and His sovereignty over all creation. As this is the first mention of a "witch" in the Bible (though the Hebrew word *kashaph* was employed earlier to describe Pharaoh's sorcerers in Ex. 7), a word of explanation is needed. Concerning witches and sorcerers, Edward Dennett writes:

> The essential idea of a witch was commerce with spirits, which finds its counterpart in the spiritualism of the present day. Hence in Leviticus she is described as "a woman that hath a familiar spirit." (Lev. 20: 27.) The witch of Endor is the exemplification of her kind; for we read that Saul went to her and said, "I pray thee, divine unto me by the familiar spirit, and bring him up whom I shall name unto thee." (1 Sam. 28: 8.) This is the very thing that spiritualists profess to do — to bring the inquirer into communion with departed spirits. Like Saul, unable to obtain communications from God, they seek information concerning things unknown and unseen through the agency of spirits. It is in fact a turning from God to Satan. The whole system, whether in Israel or our own day, is Satanic. A witch therefore was to be destroyed.[1]

Furthermore, the Jews were not to exact interest from the poor (v. 25), nor were they to speak evil of their God-appointed rulers (v. 28; Rom. 13:1-2). Finally, in addition to their obedience of God's commandments, their love and devotion to God would be affirmed by consecrating to Him the first fruits of the field, the vineyard, and the womb. The Law affirmed that it was both appropriate and expected that the Jews offer their best back to God in adoration. How about you, are you giving back to God the best you have? The prophet Malachi warned the Jews that offering anything less than their best to God was an insult to Him, not an act of worship (Mal. 16:14)! God gave us His best, His only Son the Lord Jesus Christ; may we endeavor to give Him our best too!

> Jesus, Thou art all compassion; pure, unbounded love Thou art,
> Visit us with Thine affection, enter every longing heart.
> Firstfruits of Thy new creation, faithful, holy, may we be,
> Joyful in thy great salvation, daily more conformed to Thee:
> Changed from glory into glory, till in heaven we take our place,
> Then to worship and adore Thee, lost in wonder, love and praise.
>
> — Charles Wesley

# Riots, Bribes, Lies, and Rest
## Exodus 23:1-13

God's people were not to circumvent justice by distorting the truth; to do so would bring disdain on the Law and God's authority. Absolute truth stands the test of time – it is immutable. There are no shades to divine righteousness nor degrees of God's holiness; therefore, man is commanded not to color, flavor, change, or dilute truth; to do so is in direct opposition to God's authority and Word. The Israelites were to be truth-tellers and they were to ensure that the accused were justly tried by God's Law; those found guilty were to be punished. Where justice was concerned, the Jews were to be no respecters of persons. All men were to be treated equally; those of the lowliest social class and even the foreigner were to be treated fairly.

The prohibition against distorting justice by sins of the tongue also included a ban against issuing and accepting bribes, and being privy to a riot in order to pressure magistrates or governmental authority to pervert justice. These statutes were clearly violated at the civil trial of the Lord Jesus Christ. Not only did the Pharisees bribe false witnesses (Matt. 26:60), and then later the Roman soldiers (Matt. 28:12), but they also organized a public riot to demand that Pilate put Christ to death because He had claimed to be the Son of God. However, after Pilate examined the Lord Jesus, he publicly stated to the Jews that Christ was innocent of any wrongdoing according to Roman law. Yet Pilate caved in to the demands of the vicious mob and ordered his soldiers to crucify Jesus Christ:

> *Pilate then went out again, and said to them, "Behold, I am bringing Him out to you, that you may know that I find no fault in Him." Then Jesus came out, wearing the crown of thorns and the purple robe. And Pilate said to them, "Behold the Man!" Therefore, when the chief priests and officers saw Him, they cried out, saying, "Crucify Him,*

*crucify Him!" Pilate said to them, "You take Him and crucify Him, for I find no fault in Him"* (John 19:4-6).

Public riots were not to influence Jewish authorities from executing righteous justice. This commandment was clearly ignored when an angry Jewish mob gathered at Christ's Roman trial to demand that Pilate put Jesus to death. Jewish hatred for Christ's message and His person was so intense that the Greek text does not include the pronoun "Him" in association with the word "crucified;" the people cried out, "Crucify, crucify." Those hard-hearted Jews not only wanted an innocent man to be put to death, but they also demanded that Jesus be nailed to a tree so that God would have to curse Him, for the Law states, *"If a man has committed a sin deserving of death, and he is put to death, and you hang him on a tree ... he who is hanged is accursed of God"* (Deut. 21:22-23).

Unbeknown to the Jews, that was exactly what God planned to do – to make His Son accursed. After He was whipped, stripped, and nailed to a cross, God cursed His own Son on humanity's behalf (Gal. 3:13), and in so doing, nailed the death sentence that we each deserved to His cross (Col. 2:14). The Jewish riot perverted Jewish and Roman justice that day, but God used man's injustice to work His righteous judgment of sin. As a result, God can righteously and justly offer forgiveness of sins and eternal life to those who will trust Christ for salvation!

This section of text also affirms that the Sabbath Day was set aside to rest and to honor God. The Jews, their slaves, and their beasts of burden were all to rest on the Sabbath Day. Likewise, the Israelites were to honor a Sabbath year also. Certainly, the Sabbatical Year would remind the Jews that God owned the land they dwelled upon and that they were merely stewards of it (Lev. 25:23). Every seventh year the fields, the olive groves, and the vineyards were to receive a full year's rest. Whatever grew naturally during the Sabbath year was to be freely gleaned by the poor, and anything left would be God's provision for the beasts of the field.

This was God's Law for the land; unfortunately, the Jews often ignored the Sabbath year and ultimately God would severely judge them for it and extend seventy years of rest to the land (i.e. one-seventh of the 490 years the Jews did not honor the Sabbath year). This judgment occurred during the Jewish exile to Babylon. Exodus 23 teaches us that there are no loop-holes in God's judicial system. Those who reject God's Word and authority will be punished. The Lord Jesus said that His Father had committed the judgment of all men into His hands (John 5:22). At the Great White Throne judgment, justice will be administered in accordance with His Word: *"He who rejects Me, and does not receive My words, has that which judges him – the word that I have spoken will judge him in the last day"* (John 12:48). God will righteously judge all things according to His decrees; therefore, it behooves man to behave righteously now and to uphold the justice God demands against those who do not.

> And must I be to judgment brought, and answer in that day,
> For every vain and idle thought, and every word I say?
> Yes, every secret of my heart, shall shortly be made known,
> And I receive my just desert for all that I have done.
>
> How careful, then ought I to live, with what religious fear!
> Who such a strict account must give for my behavior here.
> Thou awful Judge of quick and dead, the watchful power bestow;
> So shall I to my ways take heed, to all I speak or do.
>
> — Charles Wesley

# Feasts and Conquest
## Exodus 23:14-33

The Jews were to gather at the tabernacle initially, and then later at the temple in Jerusalem for three national feasts. Each feast was tied to the Jewish agricultural calendar. The Feast of Unleavened Bread occurred in the March and April time frame and related to the barley harvest. The Feast of Harvest (also called the Feast of First Fruits or the Feast of Weeks) occurred during the wheat harvest; this feast was to occur seven weeks (50 days) after the Feast of Unleavened Bread and was later referred to as Pentecost. The Feast of Ingathering, also known as the Feast of Tabernacles, occurred at the end of the agricultural year in September or October. All adult males had to attend these three feasts each year, which meant that their associated families likely attended the festivals as well.

These feasts were celebrations of the Lord's goodness, and each provided the Jews with the opportunity to offer back to God an offering of what He had provided. By keeping the feasts the Jews would acknowledge both their dependence upon God and that He was their source of blessing. Thus, they would reaffirm year by year, feast by feast, that they belonged to the Lord. Not only would the feasts of Jehovah continually remind the Jews of God's faithfulness to bless them, but from an eschatological standpoint these feasts and the remaining four mentioned in Leviticus 23, provide a prophetic outline of God's future dealings with the nation of Israel. These seven feasts picture both of Christ's advents to the earth and major events in between.

**Spring Feasts**

**Passover** pictures Christ on the cross; the Lamb of God slain (1 Cor. 5:7).
**Unleavened bread** typifies a sinless Christ who died in the place of sinners and was placed in a tomb (unleavened bread has no life in it).
**First fruits** refers to Christ's resurrection (1 Cor. 15:20).

**Pentecost** pictures the forming of the Church (Acts 2); the loaves from the wave sheaf were offered to the Lord but were not burned – the Church will not experience the wrath of God.

**Church Age** is the gap between the spring and fall feasts (this is also the interval between Daniel's 69th and 70th week revealed in Dan. 9:24-27).

**Fall Feasts**

**Trumpets** speak of God's gathering of the Jews back to Israel before and during the Tribulation Period (Ezek. 39:28-29; Matt. 24:29-31).
**Day of Atonement** pictures the Jewish repentance and reception of Christ at the end of the Tribulation Period (Heb. 9:28; Zech. 12:10).
**Tabernacles** refer to the release of the Jews from the Antichrist's authority and the blessings of the Millennial Kingdom under Christ's rule (Zech. 14).

Though it is in veiled form, perhaps the Spirit of God presented this outline as a preface to the foretelling of Jewish victory over their enemies in the Promised Land under the leadership of God's messenger and guardian (vv. 20-23). It is possible that the angel mentioned in verses 20 and 23 is Gabriel or one of the many other heavenly angels, but given the personalized language of divine protection, guidance, deliverance, and forgiveness, it is more likely that the messenger spoken of is a theophany – a preincarnate visit of the Second Person of the Godhead to earth (notice that the translators of the NKJV of the Bible capitalize the word Angel and all of the pronouns referring to Him):

> *Behold, I send an Angel before you to keep you in the way and to bring you into the place which I have prepared. Beware of Him and obey His voice; do not provoke Him, for He will not pardon your transgressions; for My name is in Him* (Ex. 23:20-21).

This divine Messenger would lead the Children of Israel to victorious conquest once they arrived at the Promised Land. He would lead them into battle and either vanquish or drive the inhabitants out of the land through supernatural wonders such as fear and panic (v. 27) and swarms of hornets (v. 28). He also promised to remove sickness from the Israelites so that they would prosper in battle. The Lord would drive out the inhabitants little by little each year until the conquest of the entire land was complete; this would prevent the farmland from becoming overgrown through neglect. If all the men were busy conquering the land, there would not be any to maintain agricultural prosperity; thus, God would give the Israelites the land slowly. According to the time intervals recorded in Joshua 14, the conquest of Canaan took seven years.

The boundaries of the land that Jehovah had set aside for the Jews are recorded in verse 31. The southeastern boundary would be the Red Sea (this probably refers to the Sea of Aqaba). To the southwest, the border would be the river of Egypt, which would be on the far side of Sinai desert. The Mediterranean Sea would be the northwestern border and the Euphrates River would be the northeast one. The conquest of Canaan would be the initial phase of receiving this inheritance, which God initially promised Abraham in Genesis 15 (the borders spoken of in Exodus 23 agree with God's specific promise to Abraham in Genesis 15).

The land promised to Abram and his descendants has never been fully realized by the Jews. Even during the glorious reigns of King David and King Solomon, Israel never occupied more than about a tenth (approx. 30,000 square miles) of the land that God gave Abram according to Genesis 15:18-21. So, although the nation of Israel is partially back in the Promised Land through conquest (as prophesied in Ezek. 38:8), they do not inhabit the full portion God issued Abram. We understand the "literal" fulfillment of this to be future, after the Jews receive Jesus Christ whom they crucified as their Messiah (Zech. 12:10; Rom. 11:26-32).

Interestingly, each encounter Moses had with Jehovah on the mount seems to correlate to a particular dispensational economy. As discussed previously, the first dispensation of innocence is pictured in the *"If you will obey"* clause spoken by God to Moses during his initial visit to the mount (Ex. 19:5). As long as Adam and Eve obeyed God's prohibition of eating from the tree of good and evil they would enjoy blissful life with God in Eden.

The dispensation of conscience began after our first parents sinned and their consciences became active; likewise the children of Israel were awakened to their own unworthiness in the presence of a holy God after Moses' second visit to the Sinai. The Jews feared God's voice and chose to stand afar off from Him – when God called to Adam (after he and Eve had eaten of the forbidden tree) they initially hid from Him in the shadows of trees.

After pronouncing judgments, God cast our first parents from Eden; they were sinners separated from a holy God. As instructed by God, Moses put boundaries about the mount after his third encounter with God to protect and care for the people. This may picture God's third dispensation of working with humanity, in which He invoked human government to teach human submission and to serve the people (Gen. 9:6).

Similarly, the fourth dialogue Jehovah had with Moses on Sinai ended with a promise of land for the descendants of Abraham and the instructions of an altar and sacrifices to allow the Jews to worship God. This connects with the fourth dispensation of promise in which God entered into an unconditional covenant to bless Abraham's descendants and that Abraham was known as a worshipper, as testified by his many erected altars. These observations are nothing to be dogmatic about, but Moses' visits with Jehovah on the mount seem to correlate well with the classrooms of stewardship He has historically placed man under. In other words, the pattern of what God taught the Israelites at Sinai pictures the complete lesson plan of God for all humanity.

God's Messenger would lead the Israelites to victory and the conquest of Canaan, but it was imperative that the Jews completely avoid idolatry (v. 33) and destroy the idols and sacred stones of the Canaanites as they conquered the land (Ex. 23:24, 34:13; Duet 7:5, 12:3). Jehovah is a holy God and His people must not tolerate paganism – it was to be thoroughly wiped out in Canaan. Consequently, there could be no compromising with or surrendering to the enemy; they were idolaters and must be driven from the land. This ultimatum against paganism likely gave rise to the statute that the Jews were not to boil the kid of a goat in its mother's milk (v. 19); the Canaanites did this as part of a pagan fertility ritual. This is not a prohibition against consuming milk or milk products while eating meat as some unfortunately teach!

If the Jews honored God, He would, by His Guardian, conquer the land for them. Some forty years later, on the eve of the battle for Jericho, Joshua met this divine Emissary:

> *And it came to pass, when Joshua was by Jericho, that he lifted his eyes and looked, and behold, a Man stood opposite him with His*

> *sword drawn in His hand. And Joshua went to Him and said to Him, "Are You for us or for our adversaries?" So He said, "No, but as Commander of the army of the Lord I have now come." And Joshua fell on his face to the earth and worshiped, and said to Him, "What does my Lord say to His servant?" Then the Commander of the Lord's army said to Joshua, "Take your sandal off your foot, for the place where you stand is holy." And Joshua did so.* (Josh. 5:13-15).

This text confirms that the divine Messenger of Exodus 23 is the Lord Himself. Ultimately, it is through the Lord Jesus Christ alone that victory over the enemy is realized and the believer is able to lay hold of his or her spiritual possessions: *"Blessed be the God and Father of our Lord Jesus Christ, who has blessed us with every spiritual blessing in the heavenly places in Christ"* (Eph. 1:3). The temporary trinkets we often clutch now are not even comparable with what we have spiritually in Christ.

For the believer, every character deficiency and every temporal shortcoming can be amply compensated by an appropriation of God's provision for us from the treasures of heaven. By faith, the vast riches of God's love, grace, and peace can be apprehended and enjoyed now: *"But my God shall supply all your need according to His riches in glory by Christ Jesus"* (Phil. 4:19, KJV). Those who are united with Christ are blessed because of that union, but victorious living will only be realized by those who abide in Christ: *"I am the vine, you are the branches. He who abides in Me, and I in him, bears much fruit; for without Me you can do nothing"* (John 15:5), and *"For whatever is born of God overcomes the world. And this is the victory that has overcome the world – our faith. Who is he who overcomes the world, but he who believes that Jesus is the Son of God?"* (1 Jn. 5:4-5). In time, the Israelites would learn to depend on the Lord for victory; may we do the same today.

> Simply trusting every day, trusting through a stormy way,
> Even when my faith is small, trusting Jesus, that is all.
> Trusting Him while life shall last, trusting Him till earth is past,
> Till within the jasper wall, trusting Jesus, that is all.

— Edgar Page Stites

# Thrones and Altars
## Exodus 24

Rather than addressing seemingly unconnected or even contrasting subjects separately, Scripture often presents them in tandem to draw out their deeper spiritual meaning. For example, God called upon *prophets* to represent Himself to the people but used *priests* to represent the people to Himself. Moreover, it may seem that Paul and James disagree regarding how salvation is received, yet their teachings are merely two bookends for the whole truth: man is saved by grace through faith, but faith never stands alone; it will be evidenced by good works. Similarly, many have been confused concerning the two advents of Christ, but both are absolutely necessary. The purpose of Christ's first advent was to be a sacrifice for sin and to offer grace to whosoever will accept it, but His second advent to the earth will be to judge the wicked, to comfort the oppressed, and to rule the world in righteousness.

Another topical pairing that proclaims a broader truth than if the items had been depicted individually is that of the *throne* and the *altar*. To better understand God's tie between the throne and the altar, let us consider three examples, the latter being from this passage in Exodus. First, Adonijah, who had aspired to be king, feared Solomon after their father David had put Solomon on the throne. Adonijah fled to the Bronze Altar in the temple. As he embraced the horns of the altar, Solomon granted him mercy; however, Solomon's mercy was contingent upon Adonijah's continuance in well-doing. His warning was not heeded, and Adonijah was judged (I Kgs. 1:48–52). In this story, we first read of the throne (a symbol of authority); after an awareness of this authority was understood, the altar was sought to obtain mercy.

In a second example, Isaiah beheld the majestic glory of God's throne (Isa. 6:1-7). His response to the revealed holiness of God was *"Woe is to me, for I am undone."* At that moment, he was not mindful of what he had or had not done, nor of what he should have done, but of his spiritual position before Almighty God. When man stands before the throne of God, there is no excuse, nowhere to shift blame; outside of Christ, we all stand condemned as sinners. But as soon as Isaiah acknowledged his condition before God, God's response was immediate and effectual. A seraph hovering about the throne of God swooped down and snatched a hot coal from off the altar and pressed it to Isaiah's lips to show God's ability to purify sinners. Through the altar, he received grace and found a holy standing before God. This spiritual throne/altar connection and order is noticed throughout Scripture, and it is also presented in Exodus.

In Exodus 21 and 24 Mount Sinai is God's majestic throne, His glorious habitation before His people, though not intimately among them. Gazing upon God's throne-mountain, the Israelites witnessed His awesome nature and received His righteous Law (Ex. 21). Their immediate response to God's holiness was to fear and to stand afar off – this is the proper response of sinful man to God's throne. The chapter then closes with God's provision for His people to worship Him – an altar upon which to present burnt offering and peace offerings (Ex. 21:24). The altar did not allow the people to come intimately near Jehovah, but it did allow them to worship Him from a safe distance. On this matter, C. H. Mackintosh writes:

> We may search from end to end of the legal ritual, and not find those two precious words, "*draw nigh.*" Ah! no; such words could never be heard from the top of Sinai, nor from amid the shadows of the law. They could only be uttered at heaven's side of the empty tomb of Jesus, where the blood of the cross has opened a perfectly cloudless prospect to the vision of faith. The words, "afar off," are as characteristic of the law, as "draw nigh" are of the gospel. Under the law, the work was never done, which could entitle a sinner to draw nigh. Man had not fulfilled his promised obedience; and the "blood of calves and goats" could not atone for the failure, or give his guilty conscience peace. Hence, therefore, he had to stand "afar off." Man's vows were broken and his sin unpurged; how, then, could he draw nigh. The blood of ten thousand bullocks could not wipe away one stain from the conscience, or give the peaceful sense of nearness to God.[1]

Moses had verbally reviewed God's Law with the people and had also communicated their verbal acceptance of it in Exodus 21; now God would formally ratify the covenant with them and document the matter in writing in order to have a permanent record. In Exodus 24, Moses built an altar at the foot of Mount Sinai according to the instruction provided in Exodus 21; this altar was for all the people since it had twelve pillars (stones), one for each tribe. Young men, who were perhaps the firstborn, acted as the priests, for as yet Aaron and his sons had not been formally appointed to the priesthood.

Apparently, after returning down the mount in Exodus 21, Moses wrote God's Law in a book so he would not forget any of its details; this he reviewed again with the people (v. 7). Oxen were prepared and offered upon this altar as burnt offerings. Half of the blood of the oxen was sprinkled on the altar to sanctify it and the remainder was sprinkled upon the people to sanctify them. By sprinkling the people with blood, Moses was acknowledging the basis of the covenant – shed blood: *"This is the blood of the covenant which the Lord has made with you according to all these words"* (v. 8).

The writer of Hebrews informs us that it was *"not possible that the blood of bulls and goats could take away sins"* (Heb. 10:4), for the Law was *"a shadow of the good things to come"* (Heb. 10:1); the applied blood of animals merely sanctified and ceremonially purified the flesh (Heb. 9:13). Hebrews also furnishes a few details that were not recorded in Exodus; Moses *"took the blood of calves and goats, with water, scarlet wool, hyssop, and sprinkled both the book itself and all the people"* (Heb 9:19). Not only the altar and the people, but also the book of the Law he had written was purified by blood – blood was the basis for the covenant of the Law.

After the people were sprinkled with blood, Moses, Aaron, Nadab and Abihu (who were the oldest sons of Aaron), and the seventy elders of Israel (the elders represented all the people) ascended part way up the mountain to see God; only Moses was permitted upon the summit. The description of what the leaders of Israel saw and did is astounding:

> *Then Moses went up, also Aaron, Nadab, and Abihu, and seventy of the elders of Israel, and they saw the God of Israel. And there was under His feet as it were a paved work of sapphire stone, and it was like the very heavens in its clarity. But on the nobles of the children of*

> *Israel He did not lay His hand. So they saw God, and they ate and drank* (Ex. 24:9-11).

Originally, the people fled from God's presence when they witnessed His grandeur in a smoking and quaking mountain, but now they were permitted to come part way up the mount to view the base of His throne. What affected this change? The answer is found in God's altar, which allowed the people to be sanctified by blood – the Law was a covenant of blood and only through the death and sacrifice of a substitute could man come near to God in worship. The throne of God which represents His holiness causes man to comprehend his sinful state and isolation from God, but God's altar allows man to come into His presence and enjoy His fellowship. Interestingly, this was Moses' fifth trip to the summit and the revelation of the tabernacle, the sacrifices and the priesthood which would allow Jehovah's covenant people to come near to God in worship clearly typifies the fifth dispensation of human reckoning with God – the dispensation of the Law. Though the Jews could not come intimately in God's presence they were permitted to come near to God through blood atonement, as offered by His appointed priests.

Note that the leaders of Israel did not actually see God's person or they would have died (Ex. 33:20), yet God did visually manifest His light, purity, and majesty to them in a way that was not lethal to sinful flesh. Similarly, Ezekiel did not personally see the Lord, but described *"the likeness of the glory of the Lord"* which he saw in a vision (Ezek. 1:28). The reason Moses did not describe the glory of the Lord was that the Hebrews saw only the base of God's throne; they did not view His direct presence.

The mutual acceptance of the covenant was signified by the eating of a meal before God, though the Lord did not eat with them. The eating of a meal was a customary way for two parties to show their agreement to a covenant (Gen. 26:30, 31:54). This circumstance is similar to the upper room scene in which the Lord's disciples, the future leaders of the Church, ate the Lord's Supper in Christ's presence, though He Himself did not partake of it (Luke 22:18).

The upper room meal occurred on the eve of the ratification of the New Covenant, which would be sealed by Christ's own blood: *"This cup is the new covenant in My blood, which is shed for you"* (Luke

22:20). The New Covenant, which was made with the house of Judah and Israel (Heb. 8:8), would end the dispensation of the Law and usher in the age of grace – the Church Age. Thankfully, the Gentiles would be a second benefactor of this covenant (Eph. 2:11-3:6). The events on Mount Sinai in Moses' day all pointed to a future incredible event on Mount Calvary in Christ's day. There, God's supreme Altar and Sacrifice would once and for all satisfy the righteous claims of God's throne in relationship to human wickedness.

Matthew's Gospel was written to the Jews and presents the Lord Jesus as the rightful heir to the throne of David. In comparison with the other Gospel accounts, Matthew often refers to a throne and to an altar. The word "throne" is found five times in the four Gospels; four occurrences are in Matthew. Likewise, the word "altar" is translated eight times altogether in the Gospels, with six of these references being in Matthew. His message to the Jewish nation involves two things – the throne of Christ and the altar of Christ. The Law was God's righteousness in writing; Christ was God's righteousness in person. Anyone acknowledging His divine righteousness will also be compelled to repent and embrace God's altar, the finished work of Christ at Calvary. This is why righteousness and repentance are so appropriately stressed in Matthew. The throne must be understood first, or the altar will have no meaning nor benefit. Only when man understands his lost state before God can he be found and saved by God. This, states C. H. Mackintosh, is the message of the Exodus scene before us:

> Looking at this entire scene as a mere illustration, there is much to interest the heart. There is the defiled camp *below* and the sapphire pavement *above*; but the altar, at the foot of the hill, tells us of that way by which the sinner can make his escape from the defilement of his own condition, and mount up to the presence of God, there to feast and worship in perfect peace. The blood which flowed around the altar furnished man's only title to stand in the presence of that glory which "was like a devouring fire on the top of the mount in the eyes of the children of Israel."[2]

For those awakened to their depraved and destitute state, God's finger quickly points the way to restoration – the cross of Christ. As the writer of Hebrews proclaims, *"We have an Altar,"* but it is completely outside of Judaism or any humanized merit system, and it requires an individual to identify with Christ and, thus, to bear His reproach (Heb. 13:10-13). Those who reject God's offer in Christ will be judged. Because the Jews rejected His throne and altar, Christ, from the Mount of Olives, wept over them and then foretold the devastating judgment that would come upon them.

Shortly after Israel's leadership descended from the lower portion of the mountain, God summoned Moses back up its slopes to receive the stone tables on which God had already recorded His Law. The tablets would supply Moses with a permanent record and a means of teaching God's Law to the Israelites (v. 12). It would also serve as a written testimony of God's Law for generations to come. Moses must have known that he would be gone for a while, because he put Aaron and Hur in charge of resolving problems among the people in his absence. Joshua accompanied Moses part of the way up the mount and there they both waited until Moses was called to go further up and into the glorious cloud that had engulfed the upper part of the mount seven days earlier:

> *Now the glory of the Lord rested on Mount Sinai, and the cloud covered it six days. And on the seventh day He called to Moses out of the midst of the cloud. The sight of the glory of the Lord was like a consuming fire on the top of the mountain in the eyes of the children of Israel. So Moses went into the midst of the cloud and went up into the mountain. And Moses was on the mountain forty days and forty nights* (Ex. 24:16-18).

From the text it seems that Moses was apart from the people for forty-seven days, forty of which were spent in the presence of Jehovah to receive the pattern of heavenly things. Moses was completely shut in with God, and it was while isolated from all earthly distractions that Moses learned of the deep mysteries pertaining to the work and person of Christ. Though not upon a burning and quaking mount, it is still true today that God speaks to us in the quietness of His presence – that is where we learn of Christ and of our calling in Him. The more each of us learns from this privileged communion puts us under deeper responsibility and permits us to be more useful to God. On this point, F. B.

Hole identifies an important application for the believer to learn from the Exodus 24 mountain experience:

> It is noticeable that of the sons of Aaron only Nadab and Abihu are mentioned. The two who died under judgment, almost as soon as they were consecrated as priests, had no excuse for their sin. They fell in spite of this great privilege; whereas Eleazar and Ithamar, who carried on as priests, did not apparently have this unique experience. It is often the way that failure is most pronounced in those who are most highly privileged.[3]

Another interesting parallel between the events of Sinai and of Calvary is that after Christ's resurrection He spent forty days on the earth to enjoy a season of sweet fellowship with His disciples before permanently departing to heaven to sit at the right hand of Majesty on high – His Father's throne (Heb. 8:1, 10:12; Rev. 3:21). There He waits, until that glorious day when He will return to the earth to conquer wickedness and to establish His throne and to rule in righteousness forever.

All hail to Thee, Immanuel, the ransomed hosts surround Thee;
And earthly monarchs clamor forth their sovereign King to crown Thee.
While those redeemed in ages gone, assembled round the great white throne,
Break forth into immortal song: All hail! All hail! All hail Immanuel!

All hail to Thee, Immanuel, our risen King and Saviour!
Thy foes are vanquished, and Thou art omnipotent forever.
Death, sin and hell no longer reign, and Satan's power is burst in twain;
Eternal glory to Thy Name: All hail! All hail! All hail Immanuel!

— D. R. Van Sickle

# Materials for the Tabernacle
## Exodus 25:1-7

Exodus 25 introduces to us a new subject, that of the tabernacle, and accordingly commences the final section of Exodus. Other than the various genealogies of the Bible, this section of text is perhaps the most neglected in personal study. Yet, the space given to the subject of the tabernacle reveals it to be one of the paramount teachings of Scripture. The Spirit of God expressed the events of creation in only two chapters, the record of the deluge in three chapters, but then required sixteen chapters to convey all the explicit details pertaining to the tabernacle (Ex. 25-40). Why is more detail provided for the tabernacle? Because the tabernacle, its furnishings, and the priestly attire to be worn while within the tabernacle are some of the most instructive types of Christ in all of Scripture. On this point, Arthur Pink writes:

> The key to the Tabernacle, then, is Christ. In the volume of the book it is written of Him. As a whole and in each of its parts the Tabernacle foreshadowed the person and the work of the Lord Jesus. Each detail in it typified some aspect of his ministry or some excellency in His person. Proof of this is furnished in John 1:14: "And the Word became flesh and tabernacled among us" (R.V. margin). The reference here is to the Divine incarnation and first advent of God's Son to this earth, and its language takes us back to the book of Exodus.[1]

Most commonly, the tabernacle was called the "tabernacle of the congregation," or the "tent of meeting" because it was the appointed site for God to personally reveal His will to Moses (Ex. 29:44; Num. 11:16; Deut. 31:14). God would commune with His people, but He would directly speak only with Moses from above the Ark of the Covenant. Scripture also refers to God's dwelling place among men as the tabernacle of the Lord (Num. 16:9), and the tabernacle of the testimony

(Ex. 38:21; Num. 9:15). The latter term pertains to the location of the stone tables upon which the Law was written; these were stored in the Ark of the Covenant in the Most Holy section of the tabernacle. The tent of testimony acknowledged God's holiness and served as a reminder for man to honor His order for worship; man dare not intrude in His presence contrary to His will.

God had not delivered the Israelites out of Egypt empty-handed, and the reason for this was now evident – the spoil would be used to build His tabernacle. The Israelites were presented with an opportunity to examine the quality of their own love for Jehovah. Would they willingly contribute to the building of the tabernacle or would they hoard the spoil that God had given them for this purpose? Had they grown attached to the Egyptian trinkets of gold and silver or were they yearning for an opportunity to give back to the One who had given them so much? Moses announced that a free-will offering would be received for constructing and furnishing the tabernacle.

The offering was not actually announced until Exodus 35 (this was after the unfortunate events surrounding the golden calf). The people must have been delighted with the idea that God wanted to dwell among them in a tent, instead of before them on the mount, for Exodus 35:29 records their generous response to the invitation: *"The children of Israel brought a freewill offering to the Lord, all the men and women whose hearts were willing to bring material for all kinds of work which the Lord, by the hand of Moses, had commanded to be done."* So open were their hearts for Jehovah that a proclamation to stop the offering had to be decreed:

> *So Moses gave a commandment, and they caused it to be proclaimed throughout the camp, saying, "Let neither man nor woman do any more work for the offering of the sanctuary." And the people were restrained from bringing, for the material they had was sufficient for all the work to be done – indeed too much* (Ex. 36:6-7).

This is a logistical problem that few local churches experience today, that is, having more resources than what is necessary to accomplish the ministries desired. The Jews demonstrated their love for Jehovah by generously responding to His invitation to donate to His work. This should be a common reality in the Church today – God provides ample resources to accomplish His will, the problem is that too few are obeying His calling for their lives. Hudson Taylor, a pioneer missionary into China in the mid-nineteenth century, had two important sayings on this matter. First, "God always gives His very best to those who leave the choice with Him."[2] Second, quoting the missionary Anthony Norris Groves, Taylor would say, "When God's work is done in God's way for God's glory, it will not lack for God's supply."[3]

Unfortunately, the Jews' love for Jehovah grew cold over time. For centuries the Jews nonchalantly engaged in religious charades void of love; they practiced tradition and form without even knowing that they were angering the Lord (Rom. 10:1-3). Many continue this practice today by identifying with Christ through religious rote without knowing Him personally as Saviour (Matt. 7:21-23). Worship that pleases God must emerge from a willing heart that is illuminated by the Holy Spirit in accordance with revealed truth: *"God is Spirit, and those who worship Him must worship in spirit and truth"* (John 4:24); *"When He, the Spirit of truth, has come, He will guide you into all truth; for He will not speak on His own authority, but whatever He hears He will speak; and He will tell you things to come. He will glorify Me, for He will take of what is Mine and declare it to you. God is Spirit, and those who worship Him must worship in spirit and truth"* (John 16:13-14). If what we say or do is neither true nor Spirit-led, it does not honor God; it is mere form, religious fanfare, and has no eternal value.

God was long-suffering with His people; He sent prophet after prophet to call them to repentance. The prophet Malachi was sent to issue the House of Judah a final warning. After Malachi's message was delivered God did not speak to the nation of Israel again until He sent His own Son to plead with them some 400 years later:

> *"And now, O priests, this commandment is for you. If you will not hear, and if you will not take it to heart, to give glory to My name," says the Lord of hosts, "I will send a curse upon you, and I will curse your blessings. Yes, I have cursed them already, because you do not take it to heart"* (Mal. 2:1-2).

> *"Will a man rob God? Yet you have robbed Me! But you say, 'In what way have we robbed You?' In tithes and offerings. You are cursed with a curse, for you have robbed Me, even this whole nation. Bring all the*

> *tithes into the storehouse, that there may be food in My house, and try Me now in this," Says the Lord of hosts, "If I will not open for you the windows of heaven and pour out for you such blessing that there will not be room enough to receive it"* (Mal. 3:8-10).

Malachi's warning to the Jews reminds us that stinginess towards the Lord is a spiritual problem, not a financial one. The Lord provides resources for His children to worship Him – that is, if they have willing hearts to honor Him with what He has graciously bestowed on them.

At Sinai, God's people were both willing and abundantly able to worship the Lord through giving. Through their generosity, all the resources needed to build the tabernacle of the Lord were secured. Jehovah would indeed dwell on earth and among men for the first time ever. What a blessing for redeemed Israel – God was going to dwell among them, care for them, and protect them. No other people on the planet were extended that special privilege or that momentous responsibility. Consequently, the tabernacle would serve as both a pledge and a proof that Jehovah, through redemption, had established a relationship with His covenant people and would dwell among them.

> O Lord of hosts, how lovely the place where Thou dost dwell!
> Thy tabernacles holy in pleasantness excel.
> My soul is longing, fainting, Jehovah's courts to see;
> My heart and flesh are crying, O living God for Thee.
>
> One day excels a thousand, if spent Thy courts within;
> I'll choose Thy threshold rather than dwell in tents of sin.
> Our Sun and Shield Jehovah, will grace and glory give;
> No good will He deny them that uprightly do live.

— From Psalm 84
(author unknown)

# The Pattern
## Exodus 25:8-9

Proper order in worship and, indeed, in the affairs of life is exceedingly important to God, *"for God is not the author of confusion but of peace"* (1 Cor. 14:33) and He desires that *"all things be done decently and in order"* (1 Cor. 14:40). Satan is the author of deception and confusion (John 8:44), but God sets in place standards of proper order to confound his attempts to pervert divine truth. The tabernacle is such a standard; it is meticulously designed to present to man the timeless realities of God's holiness and righteousness, as well as His means to reconcile sinners to Himself.

The theme of this final section of Exodus is defined by God's words to Moses: *"And let them make Me a sanctuary, that I may dwell among them. According to all that I show you, that is,* ***the pattern of the tabernacle*** *and* ***the pattern of all its furnishings****, just so you shall make it"* (Ex. 25:8-9). Accordingly, the next six chapters can be summarized as follows: the construction and furnishing of the tabernacle (Ex. 25:1-27:19); the priest's attire, provision, and consecration (Ex. 28:1-29:46); and lastly, a description of who may worship in the tabernacle and of how they should worship God (Ex. 30).

In Exodus 25 through 30, two contrasting themes are presented: first, how God approached the sinner through Christ, and second, how the blood-atoned sinner is permitted to approach God through Christ; C. H. Mackintosh explains:

> This section is divided into two parts, the first terminating at Exodus 27:19, and the second as the close of Exodus 30. The former begins with the Ark of the Covenant, inside the veil, and ends with the brazen altar and the court in which that altar stood. That is, it gives us, in the first place, Jehovah's throne of judgment, whereon He sat as Lord of all the earth; and it conducts us to that place where He met the sinner,

> in the credit and virtue of accomplished atonement. Then, in the latter, we have the mode of man's approach to God — the privileges, dignities, and responsibilities of those who, as priests, were permitted to draw nigh to the Divine Presence and enjoy worship and communion there. Thus the arrangement is perfect and beautiful.[1]

The pattern of the tabernacle shown to Moses went well beyond mere ceremonial function; its deeper intent was to reveal the character of God and of man, and to picture the means of man's reconciliation with God. As a result, the order in which the various features of the tabernacle are presented is a crucial part of the overall pattern and God's message to man.

The first furnishing mentioned was the Ark of the Covenant (Ex. 25:10-16) and its covering – the Mercy Seat (Ex. 25:17-22), above which Jehovah would dwell in the midst of Israel. Next, the Table of Showbread is described (Ex. 25:23-30), and then the Golden Lampstand (Ex. 25:31-40), the curtains (Ex. 26:1-14), the boards which composed the walls of the tabernacle (Ex. 26:15-30), and its separating veils (Ex. 26:31-37). Lastly, the Bronze Altar (Ex. 27:1-8) and the hangings about the courtyard and its entrance (Ex. 27:9-19) are described. Thus, God explains the tabernacle furnishings from the inside out. This is the order of sovereign grace; God venturing from His heavenly throne as the Light of the World and the Bread of Life to the outer door to find the sinner where the sinner resides! This wonderfully speaks of the incarnation of Christ – God became flesh and sojourned with hell-bound sinners in order to offer them His grace.

Only after the sinner has been purified by blood does the privilege of serving and worshipping God become possible. The next tabernacle items mentioned relate to worship. Jehovah commences by describing the most precious of these: the breastplate of the high priest which was worn over his heart at all times (Ex. 28:4). He then explains the consecration of a priesthood (Ex. 29:4-9), the animal sacrifices (Ex. 29), then the holy incense to be offered (Ex. 30:1-10), and the Bronze Laver in which Aaron and his sons were to wash their hands and feet any time they entered the tabernacle (Ex. 30:18-21). This is the order followed by a sinner who responds to sovereign grace – man ventures from his earthly abode into God's glorious habitation (though under the Law this access was limited). Arthur Pink concisely summarizes the spiritual significance of the tabernacle order:

> Marvelous is the progressive order of teaching in connection with the various objects in the tabernacle. At the brazen altar sin was judged, and by blood-shedding put away. At the laver purification was effected. In the holy place provision was made for prayer, food and illumination; while in the holy of holies the glory of the enthroned King was displayed. The same principle of progress is also to be seen in the increasing value of the sacred vessels. Those in the outer count were of wood and brass whereas those in the inner compartments were of wood and gold. So too the various curtains grew richer in design and embellishment, the inner veil bearing the costliest and most elaborate. Again, the outer court, being open, was illumined by natural light; the holy place was lit up by the light of the golden candlestick; but the holy of holes was radiated by the Shekinah glory of Jehovah. Thus the journey from the outer court into the holy of holies was from sin to purification, and from grace to glory. How blessedly did this illustrate the truth that *"the path of the just is as the shining light, that shineth more and more unto the perfect day"* (Prov. 4:18).[2]

It is notable that the first thing Jehovah revealed to Moses was that He desired to have a habitation, a holy dwelling place, among His people. God had never personally dwelt among men before, but now that the Israelites had been redeemed and knew of His Law, He could do what He had always longed to do, to dwell among them. This desired communion would occur in the tabernacle's sanctuary, the pattern of which He revealed to Moses. Though some of the craftsmen received guidance from the Holy Spirit, the blueprint for the tabernacle and its furnishings was revealed only to Moses (Acts 7:44; Heb. 8:5). Seven times God commanded Moses to follow this pattern; it was from these directions that Jehovah's home among His people would be erected. Besides a sanctuary where God could dwell among His people Edward Dennett notes two additional purposes of the tabernacle:

> The first is their object – which is making a sanctuary. "Let them make Me a sanctuary, that I may dwell among them." The primary idea of the tabernacle therefore is, that it was the dwelling-place of God. The tabernacle may, however, be viewed in another way. The house in which God dwelt must be of necessity the scene of the revelation of

> His glory. Hence, as will be seen when considering it in detail, every single part of it is fraught with some manifestation of Himself. There is yet a third aspect of the tabernacle. It is a figure of the heavens themselves. There were the court, the holy place, and the holy of holies. The priest thus passed through the first and second into the third heavens — the scene of the special presence of God.[3]

The Israelites were ready to make God a habitation on earth. God had walked with Adam in Eden, He had eaten with and spoken with the patriarchs, but only now was it possible that He would dwell among men. By blood the Jews had been redeemed and by the Law they knew how they could safely approach the holy and eternal God of the universe. The tabernacle would be erected in the center of the camp and stand as a continual testimony of their redemption, as proof that God had both redeemed and established a relationship with the Israelites. The tabernacle with all of its coverings would be a sign of God's presence among His people. Similarly, the head covering serves as a reminder to the Church that God is present during times of prayer and teaching (1 Cor. 11:4-5).

However, God's habitation on earth had to be constructed, in every detail, according to the intricate blueprint He issued to Moses; not just any kind of erected structure would do. Likewise, the Church, God's dwelling place on earth during the dispensation of grace, is to reflect the glory of God. Paul instructed the believers at Colosse to maintain good order as a testimony of Christ: *"For though I am absent in the flesh, yet I am with you in spirit, rejoicing to see your good order and the steadfastness of your faith in Christ"* (Col. 2:5). God's home on earth must be an accurate extension of His own character and attributes – a testimony for all to see and ponder.

Great God of wonders! All Thy ways are matchless, God-like, and divine,
But the bright glories of Thy grace above Thine other wonders shine.
Such deep transgressions to forgive! Such guilty sinners thus to spare!
This is Thy grand prerogative, and in this honor none shall share.
In wonder lost, with trembling joy, we take the pardon of our God.
Pardon for crimes of deepest dye, a pardon bought with Jesus' blood.
Who is a pardoning God like Thee? Or who has grace so rich and free?

— Samuel Davies

# The Ark of the Covenant
## Exodus 25:9-22

The tabernacle would have two inner compartments created by three outer walls of gold-covered boards and an inner woven veil. A tri-layered ceiling composed of goat hair, ram skins, and badger skins above a linen tapestry would cover both compartments. The actual tent itself would be surrounded by a spacious courtyard bordered by a 7.5 foot curtain wall. God would speak to Moses from above the Mercy Seat upon the Ark of the Covenant in the Most Holy Place (v. 22). The dimensions of this room would be fifteen by fifteen feet. The Holy Place, where the priests would enter twice a day to conduct worship, would be twice as spacious (thirty by fifteen feet). The only furnishing within the Most Holy Place would be the Ark of the Covenant:

> *And they shall make an ark of acacia wood; two and a half cubits shall be its length, a cubit and a half its width, and a cubit and a half its height. And you shall overlay it with pure gold, inside and out you shall overlay it, and shall make on it a molding of gold all around* (Ex. 25:10-12).

A cubit (the length of a man's forearm with his fingers extended) is approximately 18 inches, meaning the Ark of the Covenant was a chest that was three feet-nine inches long, two feet-three inches wide, and high. It was to be constructed of acacia wood and overlaid with gold. Four gold rings on each of its upper corners would allow it to be carried by gold-covered poles of acacia wood (vv. 13-16). A Mercy Seat of pure gold was to be crafted and placed on top of the Ark of the Covenant. It was to be the same length as the Ark. We refer to a "county seat" as the place where the authority of a particular governing body resides; similarly, the Mercy Seat was the location where blood atonement for sin would be accepted and from which divine mercy to Israel would be extended. The Mercy Seat was to be adorned with two gold cherubim, one on either end:

> *And you shall make two cherubim of gold; of hammered work you shall make them at the two ends of the mercy seat. Make one cherub at one end, and the other cherub at the other end; you shall make the cherubim at the two ends of it of one piece with the mercy seat. And the cherubim shall stretch out their wings above, covering the mercy seat with their wings, and they shall face one another; the faces of the cherubim shall be toward the mercy seat* (Ex. 25:18-20).

As the work of the two craftsmen who sculpted the Mercy Seat was guided by the Holy Spirit, the depictions of the cherubim must have been quite beautiful and fascinating (Ex. 31:1-6). Cherubim have four wings, but only use two of them for flying; the other two are used to cover their intrinsic glories in God's presence (Ezek. 1). The prophet Ezekiel informs us that Lucifer, before his fall, was a beautiful cherub, sheathed with precious stones and inherently equipped with musical ability (Ezek. 28:11-16). Apparently, cherubim are protectors of God's holiness; this is not to say that God needs protection, but they keep that which is sinful from coming into His presence and being consumed by His glory. For example, cherubim guarded Eden after the fall of man to ensure that every return route would be met with judgment (Gen. 3:24).

All creation, visible or invisible, provides a wonderful testimony of God's greatness. Included in this chorus of praise are the spiritual beings in heavenly realms who continually declare the glory of God and praise His name (Ps. 103:20). The Bible informs us that classes of spiritual beings do indeed exist in heaven for this very purpose. Besides Michael the archangel, there are cherubim, seraphim, the four living creatures, and a host of innumerable angels with various functions and roles. Furthermore, God describes to us what many of these spiritual beings do and how they appear before God's throne in heaven. All things recorded in Scripture have a divine purpose, so why did God go to the effort of documenting all these details? What is it that He wants us to learn from these angelic descriptions?

God the Father calls our attention to His Son through the appearance of these created beings. When the cherubim and seraphim cover themselves, it is for the purpose of concealing potential competing glories in God's presence – only God's glory will shine forth, for He alone is to be adored and worshipped in heaven. However, when the faces, eyes, or feet of these creatures are described, it is because they are not covered and, in fact, should not be, for some emulated glory of Christ is being proclaimed through them. This exercise of revealing and concealing glories is something that the Church is to remember and practice now; in so doing, we pattern the holy scene in heaven (1 Cor. 11:2-16).

The scriptural accounts of the cherubim who bear up God's mobile throne in Ezekiel 1 and 10, of the seraphim who praise God in Isaiah 6, and of the four living creatures who do the same in Revelation 4 all disclose that these beings have the same faces – four kinds of faces, to be more exact. Apparently, each cherub has all four: the face of a lion, the face of an ox, the face of a man, and the face of an eagle. The faces of these beings reflect the various glorious themes of the Lord Jesus presented in the four Gospel accounts. The *lion* is the king of the beasts, which reflects Matthew's perspective of Christ being the King of the Jews. The *ox*, as a beast of burden, is harnessed for the rigors of serving, and pictures Mark's presentation of Christ as the lowly Servant of Jehovah. The face of the *man* clearly agrees with Luke's prevalent theme of the Lord's humanity. Lastly, the *eagle* flies high above all the other creatures – in view is the divine essence of the Saviour declared in John's Gospel. So in heaven presently and upon the Mercy Seat in Moses' day the various glories of Christ as revealed in the Gospels are declared. God uses illustrations from creation to teach humanity about the wonders of His Son. We wholeheartedly agree with the words of the Psalmist, *"Bless the Lord, all His works in all places of His dominion: bless the Lord, O my soul"* (Ps. 103:22).

In the Ark of the Covenant and the Mercy Seat, we see a striking figure of Christ's person and work. The fact that the blood-sprinkled Mercy Seat rested upon the Ark which contained the tables of stone on which the Law was written is significant; both Christ and His redemptive work were wholly perfect, and thus satisfied the righteous demands of His Law. On this point, C. H. Mackintosh writes:

> He [Christ] having, in His life, magnified the law and made it honorable, became, through death, a propitiation or mercy-seat for every one that believeth. God's mercy could only repose on a pedestal of perfect righteousness. *"Grace reigns through righteousness unto eternal life*

> *by Jesus Christ our Lord"* (Rom. 5:21). The only proper meeting place between God and man is the point where grace and righteousness meet and perfectly harmonize. Nothing but perfect righteousness could suit God; and nothing but perfect grace could suit the sinner. But where could these attributes meet in one point? Only in the cross. There it is that *"mercy and truth are met together; righteousness and peace have kissed each other"* (Ps. 85:10). Thus it is that the soul of the believing sinner finds peace. He sees that God's righteousness and his justification rest upon precisely the same basis, namely, Christ's accomplished work. When man, under the powerful action of the truth of God, takes his place as a sinner, God can, in the exercise of grace, take His place as a Saviour, and then every question is settled, for the cross having answered all the claims of divine justice, mercy's copious streams can flow unhindered. When a righteous God and a ruined sinner meet, on a blood-sprinkled platform, all is settled for ever — settled in such a way as perfectly glorifies God, and eternally saves the sinner.[1]

Besides the Mercy Seat's presentation of Christ, the Ark of the Covenant also foretells of His attributes. The Mercy Seat was constructed of pure gold, speaking of Christ's purity and holiness. However, the Ark of the Covenant itself was made of wood and covered with gold. The humanity of Christ is symbolized by wood in the ark and other tabernacle furnishings. God commanded, as recorded in Exodus 25-27, that the Ark of the Covenant, the Golden Altar of Incense, the Table of Showbread, and the boards and the rods that formed the walls of the tabernacle all be made of wood overlaid with gold. Yet, the gold boards required a base-plate of silver sockets to stand erect (Ex. 26:15-28). Silver speaks of blood atonement under the Law (Ex. 30:16) and, more fully, of redemption in general. Thus, in the tabernacle, the gold and the wood combine to express the full deity and full humanity of Christ, while the silver speaks of Christ's redeeming blood.

> Come, let us lift our joyful eyes up to the courts above,
> And smile to see our Father there upon a throne of love.
> Once 'twas a seat of dreadful wrath, and shot devouring flame;
> Our God appeared "consuming fire," and Vengeance was His Name.
> Rich were the drops of Jesus' blood that calmed His frowning face,
> That sprinkled over the burning throne and turned the wrath to grace.
>
> — Isaac Watts

# The Table of Showbread

## Exodus 25:23-30

Moving eastward from the Ark in the Most Holy Place, we enter the Holy Place, which contained three furnishings. While God's holy presence above the Mercy Seat prevented man from communing with God in the Most Holy Place, every aspect of the Holy Place portrays Christ's ongoing work to enable believers to have fellowship with God.

The Table of Showbread with its twelve loaves identifies Christ as the Bread of Life, the One we must continually feed upon; He is the substance of our fellowship with God. While it is true that Christ is the light of the world, the Lampstand pertains more specifically to His revelation of truth available to the believer; that is, the light in which the believer must continue to walk in order to maintain fellowship with God. Lastly, the Golden Altar of Incense prefigures Christ as the Great High Priest who would offer up the believer's service and worship to God as a sweet-savor offering. As the Altar of Incense, Christ continues upon God's heavenly throne to intercede on the believer's behalf. Thus, every aspect of the Holy Place foreshadowed the ultimate fellowship God would enjoy with His people through Christ's ongoing ministry.

Like the Ark of the Covenant, the Table of Showbread was constructed of acacia wood and overlaid with gold. Its dimensions were to be approximately three feet long, one foot-six inches wide, and two feet-three inches high. Each Sabbath, the priests were to exchange the twelve loaves of unleavened bread that were placed upon the Table of Showbread the previous Sabbath for new ones; they were to then eat the week-old bread while in the tabernacle (Lev. 24:5-9).

The twelve loaves of unleavened bread, the *"bread of presence,"* upon the table served as a constant reminder of God's continual blessings and presence among His people. Initially, it was Moses who set the bread in order on the table: *"He put the table in the tabernacle of meeting, on the north side of the tabernacle, outside the veil; and he set the bread in order upon it before the Lord, as the Lord had commanded Moses"* (Ex. 40:22-23). The instructions concerning the showbread itself are recorded in Leviticus 24:5-7:

> *And you shall take fine flour and bake twelve cakes with it: two-tenths of an ephah shall be in each cake. You shall set them in two rows, six in a row, on the pure gold table before the Lord. And you shall put pure frankincense on each row, that it may be on the bread for a memorial, an offering made by fire to the Lord.*

The loaves symbolize the humanity of the Lord Jesus Christ. They were to be made of fine flour to picture His moral fitness, and without leaven to portray His sinless perfection. The sweet-smelling frankincense that was placed upon the loaves spoke of the Lord's complete devotion to His Father. The fact that the bread was presented seven days (seven is the number of perfection) before it was consumed by the priests typifies the perfection of the believer's enjoyment of Christ's fellowship. Although the showbread pictured Christ, the number of loaves (twelve) clearly tied it to the twelve tribes. Throughout the Bible *twelve* is the number that pertains to *governmental perfection*; there is no doubt that here it represents the twelve tribes of Israel under God's leadership. As a nation, Israel, in a future day, will enjoy full fellowship with Christ and will freely partake of His goodness.

As foreshadowed in the manna (Ex. 16), the Lord Jesus is the living bread which came down from heaven; anyone who partakes of Him receives eternal life and enjoys His abiding presence forever (John 6:35, 48). One "eats" of the Bread of Life by trusting Christ alone for salvation and then the believer continues to eat of Him (that is to feed upon His word) to grow in Him. George Rodger explains why it is important for believers to continually feed on Christ:

> Christ is the food of our love. I could never have loved God had I not seen Him in Christ. Christ is the proof and the expression of God's great love to man; and when I see this, my faith works by love and draws me to God, and I exclaim, *"I love Him because He first loved me!"* The more I meditate on Christ the warmer and purer is my love to God. I cannot love God by trying to love Him, but when I see and feel that God loves me, sinful as I am, and that, as seen in Christ, He is the most lovely and loveable being in the universe, I feel love, joy, and

> peace spring up in my heart, and I enter at once into rest. No one can be healthy and strong who does not get good food; and no soul can be truly healthy that does not feed on Jesus Christ.[1]

In the spiritual sense, eating is likened to trusting in Christ and internalizing His word (John 6:35, 40-50). These two qualities of God's blessing and fellowship are symbolized in the twelve loaves of unleavened bread, although they pertain to the nation of Israel in a future day.

During the first part of the Tribulation Period there will be 144,000 Jews (12,000 Jews from each tribe) who are sealed to be witnesses for the Lord: *"And I heard the number of those who were sealed. one hundred and forty-four thousand of all the tribes of the children of Israel were sealed"* (Rev. 7:4). After these faithful Jews have completed their ministry in the Tribulation Period, we read:

> *Then I looked, and behold, a Lamb standing on Mount Zion, and with Him one hundred and forty-four thousand, having His Father's name written on their foreheads... They sang as it were a new song before the throne, before the four living creatures, and the elders; and no one could learn that song except the hundred and forty-four thousand who were redeemed from the earth. These are the ones who were not defiled with women, for they are virgins.* ***These are the ones who follow the Lamb wherever He goes.*** *These were redeemed from among men, being firstfruits to God and to the Lamb. And in their mouth was found no deceit,* ***for they are without fault before the throne of God*** (Rev. 14:1-5).

The twelve cakes of unleavened bread upon the Table of Showbread give a prophetic foretaste of the time when Israel will be completely restored to the Lord Jesus Christ, the Lamb of power, and will ever be with Him and before Him. This will be the culmination of God's provision for His ancient covenant people to be blessed and have fellowship with Him.

> Sweet feast of love divine, 'tis grace that makes us free,
> To feed upon this bread and wine, in memory Lord of Thee.
> Here conscience ends its strife, and faith delights to prove,
> The sweetness of the Bread of Life, the fullness of Thy love.
>
> — Edward Denny

# The Golden Lampstand
## Exodus 25:31-40

The Table of Showbread was where the priests ate holy bread in God's presence. There is a similar lesson for the believer pictured in the Golden Lampstand, which was the only source of light in the Holy Place: God's people need divine light as well as divine food to remain in fellowship with Him and to be able to serve Him properly. The Lampstand was to be formed from one solid piece of pure gold that weighed one talent (about 75 pounds). It was not to be forged, but beaten into perfection; the Lampstand grew into its lovely shape under the repeated blows of the hammer. The pure gold was bruised until it was perfectly formed for service. This candelabrum consisted of a central stem with three branches springing out from each side to form a total of seven conduits through which oil could flow to the individual wicks. Each branch was to be adorned with gold flower-like cups, buds, and blossoms, all of which made the Lampstand the most elaborate of the tabernacle furnishings; sophisticated and precise craftsmanship would be required to fashion it.

Metaphorically, light in Scripture symbolizes the truth and holiness of God, and, as these are non-varying, eternal qualities, the Lampstand was always lit when the tabernacle was operational. The light of the Lampstand was not to be extinguished (except when the tabernacle was being moved); consequently, the use of consumable candles was prohibited. Accordingly, the light of the Lampstand was produced by seven ever-burning wicks; each wick drew a constant supply of fine olive oil from the Lampstand's reservoir. The priests entered into the Holy Place twice a day for the morning and evening offerings. Besides placing hot coals and specially prepared incense upon the Golden Altar the priests also trimmed the seven wicks of the Lampstand and, as needed, filled its reservoir with oil (Ex. 27:20-21; Lev. 24:4).

The number seven is God's number, and represents perfection, completeness and holiness. Through the number seven, the light of the Lampstand, which represents Christ's testimony of truth is shown to be divine in origin. Likewise, the resource enabling the seven flames to illuminate the tabernacle (the oil) is also shown to be divine in nature. As in Zechariah's vision of the two olive trees that supplied oil to a lampstand, the Holy Spirit is also in Exodus depicted in the pure oil. Speaking of the oil, the Lord told Zechariah: *"Not by might nor by power, but by My Spirit"* (Zech. 4:6). God was confirming that it would be His Spirit working in Joshua and Zerubbabel (the two trees) to accomplish His will and provide a testimony of Himself in Jerusalem. The Lampstand in the tabernacle, then, speaks of God's perfect revelation of truth in Christ through the power of the Holy Spirit.

The Lampstand draws together a type of the Lord Jesus and of the Holy Spirit to symbolically represent their distinct roles within the trinity. For example, types of Christ in the Old Testament are usually presented by people or objects: the ark, the rock, the rod, the door, the arm, the shepherd, the veil, etc. These are used to accomplish a work and to picture Christ performing the Father's will. The Holy Spirit, however, is generally depicted as an active fluid, such as flowing olive oil (Zech. 4), blowing wind (John 3), seven flames of fire (Rev. 4), or rushing water from a rock (John 7). The Holy Spirit, in these types, is not visibly seen doing the Father's will (as in the types representing Christ), but rather He enables and accomplishes the task at hand in a powerful and invisible fashion.

Types of Christ and the Holy Spirit are combined in the Lampstand. Christ is depicted as God's light to a lost world – the One who exposes the darkness of sin: *"Then Jesus spoke to them again, saying, 'I am the light of the world. He who follows Me shall not walk in darkness, but have the light of life'"* (John 8:12). The Lord Jesus was the evidence of God's truth in visible flesh, but the Holy Spirit was also working to enable the ministry of Christ to prosper. In fact, the Lord did not begin His public ministry until He had been anointed by the Holy Spirit (John 1:32; Acts 10:38). Clearly, the work of the Holy Spirit cannot be separated from the public testimony of the Lord Jesus Christ. While on earth Christ was God's Lampstand to show sinners the way to God, and the Holy Spirit worked many miracles to testify that Christ was telling the truth.

The Lampstand was to be adorned with gold almond blossoms (mentioned six times in Exodus 25 and 37). Blossoms normally occur in springtime, after the deadness of winter has passed; thus, the blossom represents new life, or, more specifically, resurrection life. This symbol of new life would later appear again when God indicated His endorsement of Aaron as His high priest by causing his dead rod to bud, shoot forth blossoms, and then yield almonds (Num. 17:8).

What application does the Lampstand have for the believer today? Putting all of these types together we understand that the resurrection life of Christ, the truth of Christ and the Holy Spirit all reside in the believer today. Consequently, as the believer remains in fellowship with Christ and chooses to live for Him, a world filled with satanic darkness becomes illuminated with divine truth. The life of Christ must be lived out and this is only possible by yielding to divine truth. Not living according to divine truth grieves the Holy Spirit and thus diminishes His supernatural enablement in our lives. Each believer is called to be a living lampstand for Christ.

Scripture affixes Lampstand responsibility on both individual believers (Matt. 5:14) and local churches (Rev. 1:20). Light testifies of divine truth and of divine power in action; thus, the Lord Jesus exhorted His disciples:

> *You are the light of the world. A city that is set on a hill cannot be hidden. Nor do they light a lamp and put it under a basket, but on a lampstand, and it gives light to all who are in the house. Let your light so shine before men, that they may see your good works and glorify your Father in heaven* (Matt. 5:14-16).

Good works that glorify God cannot be conjured up by the doings of the flesh, only as a believer is enabled by the Holy Spirit can he or she *shine out* a testimony of Christ's life within. The same is true of a local assembly. The Holy Spirit unifies and empowers believers to work together to be a testimony of Christ to their associated communities. Are you shining for Him? Is your local assembly a brilliant testimony of Christ's splendor to your community? The lamps of the Lampstand were to burn *"before the Lord continually"* in the tabernacle (Lev. 24:4). As believers continue to abide in Christ the lost cannot avoid seeing the brilliance of Christ shining out from them. What this dark world needs is a true testimony of Christ.

On Mount Sinai, Moses had the wonderful opportunity to preview *"the copy and shadow of the heavenly things"* (Heb. 8:5), but as believers in Christ, we presently walk amid the heavenly things themselves (Eph. 2:6; Heb. 9:23). May the Spirit of God illuminate our understanding concerning such glorious riches; these are things too precious, too vast, and too astonishing to keep to ourselves.

> Walk in the light, so shalt thou know that fellowship of love;
> His Spirit only can bestow, who reigns in light above.
> Walk in the light, and thine shall be a path, though thorny bright;
> For God, by grace, shall dwell in thee, and God Himself is light.
>
> — Bernard Barton

# Holy Curtains of Four Colors
## Exodus 26

One of the most outstanding lessons of the tabernacle is presented by its various coverings. The tabernacle was comprised of many coverings and was further surrounded by a wall of curtains, all of which spoke of man's separation from God. Jehovah who is holy was shut in and unholy man was shut out – this was the message of the tabernacle's coverings.

A canopy of four coverings stretched over the walls of the tabernacle. The bottom covering was composed of ten six-foot-wide linen curtains which were connected by 50 gold clasps on each adjoining edge to create a colorful sixty by forty-two foot curtain. All ten of the curtains were woven from blue, purple, scarlet, and white yarn and were embroidered with cherubim. Technically speaking, this colorful curtain ceiling was the tabernacle (vv. 1, 6). Over this curtain ceiling (referred to again as the tabernacle in verse 7) were eleven goat-hair curtains which were connected with bronze clasps. These weather-resistant curtains were six feet longer than the first colorful curtains and, thus, would reach the ground on both sides. The breadth of the eleventh curtain would hang over the door of the tabernacle and completely hide the golden hooks, and the beautiful chapiters of the five pillars at the door from all who stood outside, but not from those standing within. In fact, to anyone looking down from a hilltop, the tabernacle would not look spectacular at all, but would look like a dull-brown tent; all the color and splendor of its furnishings and tapestries were concealed within. The next two coverings were to be of ram skin and badger skin (perhaps seal skin) and were positioned over the goat-hair curtains; their dimensions are not given.

Inside the tabernacle, a four-colored veil of finely woven linen hung between the Most Holy Place and the Holy Place and between the Holy Place and the courtyard. The veil facing the Most Holy Place was also embroidered with cherubim. What did all these tabernacle coverings accomplish? Firstly, God's holiness was concealed from man's view lest he should die. Secondly, the coverings revealed a solution called blood atonement. Inside the veil, where God dwelt, sins were covered by the blood of animals. This atonement allowed God to dwell among His people, but only in a concealed fashion.

As previously stated, there was to be only one piece of furniture within the Most Holy Place of the tabernacle: the Ark of the Covenant. God would dwell above the Mercy Seat that covered the Ark of the Covenant. The unity and uniqueness of God is represented in the number one: there was *one* Most Holy Place, *one* Ark of the Covenant, and *one* Mercy Seat. However, as the reader's attention moves from God's glorious presence above the Mercy Seat to the realm occupied by men, one sees a steady presentation of the number *four* in order to symbolize earthly order, as created by God. Here are a few expressions of this use of the number four in Scripture. There are…

*Four* seasons (Spring, Summer, Fall, and Winter).
*Four* regions/directions (North, South, East, and West).
*Four* divisions of day (morning, noon, evening, and night).
*Four* phases of the moon (new, half waxing, full, half waning).
*Four* winds (from the four directions of the earth).
*Four* realms in which creatures dwell (upon the earth, under the earth, in the heaven, or in the sea).
*Four* means of dividing the human race (kindred, people, tongue, and nation).
*Four* types of soils to reflect the hearts of men (hard, stony, thorny, and good unto fruitfulness).

How is the number four incorporated into the design of the tabernacle? The ceiling tapestry, referred to as the tabernacle, was composed of four different colored threads which were woven together. Three more coverings were placed upon it to make a total of four layers over the tabernacle walls. The inner veil hung on four pillars (Ex. 26:31-32), forming a barrier between the Most Holy Place where God dwelt and the Holy Place where the priests entered twice daily. Like the ceiling tapestry, the veil was woven of the same four colors and it also displayed the figures of cherubim (note that cherubim have four wings).

Moving into the Holy Place we notice that the Golden Altar of Incense has four horns extending up from itself. Both the holy ointment, which was dabbed on parts of the tabernacle, and the prepared incense, which was placed twice daily upon the Golden Altar, were each composed of four spices.

Venturing eastward through the Holy Place into the courtyard, four more horns are noted upon the Bronze Altar. Beyond the Bronze Altar, the only entrance to the tabernacle courtyard is seen; it is formed by "hangings" upon four pillars. Like the tabernacle coverings and the inner veil, the "hangings" were also woven from four differently colored threads. Lastly, we notice that the priests offer only four types of creatures upon the Bronze Altar: the bullock, the lamb, the goat, and the turtledove. The number four pervades the journey from God's presence to man's realm of life – it is the same path the Son of God traveled to become the Son of Man.

The writer of Hebrews informs us that Christ's own flesh was a veil (Heb. 10:19-20). Coverings in Scripture both reveal and conceal things. The Lord's flesh concealed the outshining glory of God but allowed His divine moral excellencies to be viewed by all: *"And the Word was made flesh, and dwelt among us, (and we beheld His glory, the glory as of the only begotten of the Father), full of grace and truth"* (John 1:14). Furthermore, on the night before He died the Lord Jesus spoke the following to His disciples:

> *Jesus said to him, "Have I been with you so long, and yet you have not known Me, Philip? He who has seen Me has seen the Father; so how can you say, 'Show us the Father'? Do you not believe that I am in the Father, and the Father in Me? The words that I speak to you I do not speak on My own authority; but the Father who dwells in Me does the works. Believe Me that I am in the Father and the Father in Me, or else believe Me for the sake of the works themselves* (John 14:9-11).

The veil of the Lord's flesh is pictured by the inner veil of the tabernacle. This veil hung upon four pillars; each pillar consisted of wood (speaking of Christ's humanity) overlaid with gold (declaring Christ's deity). God dwelt on one side of this veil, and man dwelt on the other.

What a depiction of the Messiah – He would be both God and man! He was both the Son of David and David's Lord (Mark 12:35-37).

As previously mentioned, the tabernacle's ceiling tapestry, its inner veil, its outer curtain, and the hangings at the entrance of the courtyard were all woven of four colors. These were the basic four colors of all the coverings throughout the tabernacle, including the high priest's ephod and sash. William MacDonald comments:

> The four colors of materials in the tabernacle with their symbolic meanings also seem to fit the evangelists' fourfold presentation of the attributes of our Lord!
>
> *Purple* is an obvious choice for Matthew, the Gospel of the King. Judges 8:26 shows the regal nature of this color.
>
> *Scarlet* dye was derived in ancient times from crushing a cochineal worm. This suggests Mark, the Gospel of the bondservant, *"a worm and no man"* (Ps. 22:6).
>
> *White* speaks of the righteous deeds of the saints (Rev. 19:8). Luke stresses the perfect humanity of Christ.
>
> *Blue* represents the sapphire dome we call the heavens (Ex. 24:10), an attractive representation of the Deity of Christ, a keynote in John.[1]

C. H. Mackintosh concisely summarizes the meaning of the four tabernacle colors as they pertain to Christ:

> Here we have the different aspects of "the man Christ Jesus." The "fine twined linen" prefigures the spotless purity of His walk and character; while the "blue, the purple, and the scarlet" present Him to us as "the Lord from heaven," who is to *reign* according to the divine counsels, but whose royalty is to be the result of His *sufferings*. Thus we have a spotless man, a heavenly man, a royal man, a suffering man. These materials were not confined to the "curtains" of the tabernacle, but were also used in making "the veil," (v. 31), "the hanging for the door of the tent," (v. 36), "the hanging for the gate of the court," (Ex. 27:16) "the cloths of service and the holy garments of Aaron." (Ex. 39:1). In a word, it was Christ everywhere, Christ in all, Christ alone.[2]

Obviously, God is using the tabernacle's colors to present His Son to humanity in type, but how does the number four relate to this presentation? When the Son exited the dimensionless and timeless realm of majesty on high and descended to the earth, He willingly placed Himself under earthly order. As a man, He became subject to the natural laws of creation, even though, as God, He still maintained the order of all things (Col. 1:17). Consequently, the Lord never allowed His deity to satisfy His humanity beyond the normal scope in which all humanity experiences the daily blessings of God. Many other means are employed in Scripture to convey the nature of the Lord's condescending journey to earth for the sole purpose of suffering death that mankind might have an opportunity to be restored to a holy God. For example, the Lord Jesus referred to Himself more often by the title "Son of Man" than by the title "Son of God." In so doing, He called attention, not to His divine essence, but to His lowly position and ministry on earth. Throughout the Bible, the Spirit of God consistently employs the number four to represent four distinct glories of His Son to earth-inhabiting humanity.

Before exploring the Old Testament for such pictures, note that each of the four Gospels is written to a different audience, and upholds the brilliance of the Lord from a unique thematic perspective. The following table provides a short summary of those themes. This will assist in recognizing more clearly the same four-fold pictures of the Saviour in the Old Testament.

| **Gospel** | **Matthew** | **Mark** | **Luke** | **John** |
|---|---|---|---|---|
| **Perspective** | King | Servant | Humanity | Deity |
| **Audience** | Jewish | Roman | Greek | The World |

This explains why there are four Gospel accounts pertaining to the Lord Jesus Christ in the New Testament. God the Father described His Son's ministry on earth from four unique vantage points. As four is the number that pertains to earthly order, it is the best number to declare the "good news" message – the goodness of God to mankind. The Son willingly laid aside His outshining glory and departed from His celestial home. He became subject to creation order and took the place upon an accursed tree of every man, woman, and child that would ever live.

There, rejected and abandoned, the billows and waves of divine judgment broke upon the Saviour as every human sin was judicially accounted for. Every lie, every evil thought, every immoral act, every murder – all unrighteousness was judged by God. After the judgment was complete, the Lord committed His spirit to His Father and died. He was laid in a borrowed tomb, and on the third day, as a testimony to the Father's complete satisfaction with the work at Calvary, the Son was raised up for our justification.

In Christ, we have eternal life; apart from Him there is no life – only death (separation from God). He now sits at the right hand of God and awaits that moment in time when He will return to the air to snatch away His bride from the earth. He will then refine and restore rebellious Israel to God and establish His rightful eternal throne. The believer will co-inherit all things in Christ and co-reign with Christ forever. The Bible is really the only book of which it can truly be said that "they lived happily ever after."

In Moses' day, only those priests who entered into the tabernacle had the privilege of seeing the four-fold presentation of Christ portrayed in gold and color; those glancing at the tabernacle from the outside saw only drab animal-skin coverings. But from God's perspective within the tabernacle, the fourfold presentation of His divine Son was precious, indeed; from every viewpoint, the Gospel of Jesus Christ is "good news" indeed!

> Without a cloud between, to see Him face to face;
> Not struck with dire amazement dumb, but triumphing in grace.
>
> Without a cloud between, to see Him as He is;
> O who can tell the height of joy, the full transporting bliss.
>
> Without a cloud between, Lord Jesus, haste the day;
> The morning bright without a cloud, and chase our tears away.
>
> — Albert Midlane

# The Bronze Altar
## Exodus 27:1-8

Before discussing the pattern and purpose of the Bronze or Brazen Altar, a pertinent question must be considered: why did Jehovah, in revealing the pattern of the tabernacle and its furnishings, postpone discussing the Altar of Incense and the Laver with Moses? God began by describing the furnishings in the Most Holy Place, then detailed the Holy Place (excluding the Altar of Incense), and then continued to move eastward, ignoring the Laver, to discuss the Bronze Altar near the entrance of the courtyard. C. H. Mackintosh poses a probable answer to this puzzling order of revelation:

> He first describes the mode in which He would manifest Himself to man: and then He describes the mode of man's approach to Him. He took His seat upon the throne, as "the Lord of all the earth." The beams of His glory were hidden behind the veil – type of Christ's flesh (Heb. 10:20); but there was the manifestation of Himself, in connection with man, as in "the pure table," and by the light and power of the Holy Ghost, as in the candlestick. Then we have the manifested character of Christ as a man down here on this earth, as seen in the curtains and coverings of the tabernacle. And, finally, we have the brazen altar as the grand exhibition of the meeting place between a holy God and a sinner. This conducts us, as it were, to the extreme point, from which we return, in company with Aaron and his sons, back to the holy place, the ordinary priestly position, where stood the golden altar of incense. Thus the order is strikingly beautiful. The golden altar is not spoken of until there is a priest to burn incense thereon, for Jehovah showed Moses the patterns of things in the heavens according to the order in which these things are to be apprehended by faith. Conversely, when Moses gives directions to the congregations (Ex. 35), when he records the labours of "Bezaleel and

Aholiab," (Ex. 37 and Ex. 38), and when he sets up the tabernacle (Ex. 40), he follows the simple order in which the furniture was placed.[1]

The order of revelation, then, precisely represents Christ coming from heaven as the Light of the World and the Bread of Life and meeting the repentant sinner at the Bronze Altar, where the Lamb of God would be judged for human sin. Consequently, the location of the Bronze Altar at the entrance of the courtyard would remind the priests that before they could enter into the Holy Place to offer worship on behalf of the nation, a sacrifice first had to be placed on the Bronze Altar. Accordingly, the Ark of the Covenant and the Bronze Altar represent two complementary extremes within the tabernacle. The former symbolized the throne of God, which declared His justice and righteousness; the latter was the only place where Jehovah's mercy and truth could be received by the sinner. During the dispensation of the Law, no man dared to approach the Ark to personally meet God, for *"the way into the Holiest of All was not yet made manifest while the first tabernacle was still standing"* (Heb. 9:8). But God could approach the Bronze Altar to meet the sinner waiting there with sacrifice and atoning blood. Thus, the Bronze Altar was especially important to man, for without blood atonement there could be neither worship nor service.

Jehovah described the pattern of the Bronze Altar to Moses:

> *You shall make an altar of acacia wood, five cubits long and five cubits wide – the altar shall be square – and its height shall be three cubits. You shall make its horns on its four corners; its horns shall be of one piece with it. And you shall overlay it with bronze. Also you shall make its pans to receive its ashes, and its shovels and its basins and its forks and its firepans; you shall make all its utensils of bronze. You shall make a grate for it, a network of bronze; and on the network you shall make four bronze rings at its four corners. You shall put it under the rim of the altar beneath, that the network may be midway up the altar. And you shall make poles for the altar, poles of acacia wood, and overlay them with bronze* (Ex. 27:1-6).

Both the length and the width of the Bronze Altar were to measure approximately seven and a half feet; it would stand four and half feet tall with a bronze horn on each corner. It was to be constructed of acacia wood, which would then be overlaid with bronze. The rings for lifting and transporting the altar and all of its utensils, grates, and firepans were to be of bronze also. At this time, bronze was a forged amalgamation of copper and tin (later zinc would be used). Metaphorically speaking, bronze is used throughout Scripture to represent divine judgment, as intense heat was required to forge the alloy. Accordingly, the constant burning of sacrifices upon this altar along with its bronze construction conveyed God's righteous judgment in connection with human sin. This is why the feet of the Lord Jesus appear as flaming bronze in John's glorious vision of Christ ready to return to the earth to render judgment upon the wicked: *"His feet were like burnished bronze, when it has been made to glow in a furnace"* (Rev. 1:15; NASB). Bronze speaks of God's judgment and the Bronze Altar is where the sins of the people would be judged under the Law.

Although animal blood was sprinkled upon and before the Mercy Seat once each year on the Day of Atonement (Lev. 16), and blood was regularly applied to the horns of the Golden Altar as sin offerings were made (Lev. 4), the bulk of the blood shed was applied to the horns of the Bronze Altar or poured out at its base. The priests would then burn various portions of the animals and birds upon the Bronze Altar as a burnt offering to the Lord; their carcasses were completely consumed by fire. This indubitably speaks of Christ's future sacrifice at Calvary in which He would be completely consumed by divine wrath while being judged for all human sin. Consequently, the ever-smoking, ever-blood-stained Bronze Altar at the entrance to the tabernacle courtyard visibly announced to every Jew that the way of restoration was open.

Today, the Bronze Altar continues to symbolize that the way to God is open through the Lord Jesus Christ. This is possible because Christ was both the sacrifice and the altar; that is, He was the means of presenting Himself to God as the sin sacrifice for humanity. At Calvary, Christ was the Lamb of God who suffered for the sin of the world and the altar that sanctified the sacrifice and presented the benefit of it to God (Heb. 13:10).

O God of matchless grace, we sing unto Thy name!
We stand accepted in the place that none but Christ could claim.
Our willing hearts have heard Thy voice,
And in Thy mercy we rejoice.

— H. K. Burlingham

# A Hidden Courtyard
## Exodus 27:9-21

Besides the tabernacle's ceiling, inner veil, and outer curtain, the courtyard of the tabernacle was also composed of curtains which ensured concealment. The eastern entrance into the courtyard was created by woven tapestries which hung upon four pillars. Like the inner veil and outer curtain of the tabernacle, these hangings were composed of the colors purple, scarlet, white, and blue. Furthermore, white linen curtains hung upon 56 pillars (assuming that each side of the curtain wall shared two pillars with its adjoining sides) creating a seven and a half foot high wall around the tabernacle's courtyard. The pillars rested in sockets of brass and their hooks and tops were of silver. The courtyard measured 75 by 150 feet.

The high linen-fence about the courtyard prevented any onlooker from peeking over the top of the wall. From a natural standpoint, no one was tall enough to peer over the fence. This provided a practical object lesson to the Jews: no one measured up to God's standard of perfection and therefore His dwelling place was off limits to the people. In summary, each veil inside and outside the tabernacle declared God's holiness and man's sinfulness. Man could not casually venture into His presence and survive.

Korah's rebellion, as recorded in Numbers chapter 16, is another example of the importance of coverings. As a Kohathite, Korah was assigned the task of bearing the "covered" tabernacle furnishings from one desert campsite to another. The Kohathites were forbidden to directly gaze upon the holy furnishings; however, they were allowed to enter the tabernacle and carry the furnishings after Aaron and his sons had covered them. What an honor Korah had! However, he was lifted up with pride and rebelled against his God-appointed role; he wanted to be the high priest. Korah committed the same sin that Lucifer did – he wanted the leadership position and the glory that came with it. There was no desire to adhere to God's order. Why then did Korah and Lucifer rebel against their covering roles? Because the act of covering is a salute to God-ordained order. God judged Lucifer by casting him off God's holy mount and sentencing him to eventual suffering in the Lake of Fire for eternity. To execute judgment on Korah (who was Moses' cousin), God caused the ground to open up and swallow Korah and his family. God recompenses all rebels with justice; He will judge all those who do not follow His prescribed order.

As mentioned previously, the flesh of the Lord Jesus was called a veil (Heb. 10:20). His flesh concealed His inherent divine glory, but still revealed the righteous character of God through His humanity. Certainly, this concealing and revealing activity provides the platform for Paul's teaching on the head covering in 1 Corinthians 11. When believers gather in God presence for prayer and teaching, there is to be only one glory revealed; all other glories are to be concealed. God's glory is seen in the uncovered heads of men, while man's glory – the woman, and the woman's glory – her hair is covered.

God is pleased when created beings submit to His created order. This submission is shown in practice and in symbolism through the use of coverings. God is glorified in heaven when created beings freely choose to conceal their own intrinsic glory. In the same way, God is glorified when His divine order is seen in the local church through the use of coverings. Thus, the local church meetings are to mimic the same scene of humility that exists at all times before the throne of God. This symbolic practice ensures that only the glory of Almighty God is seen (because all competing glories are covered). Proper covering gives the visible evidence of order, both in the heavenly realms and in the assemblies of God's people on earth. Divine order is fundamental and central to the proper functioning of any local church, and it should thus be expressed symbolically in the church's public gatherings through the practice of the head covering (1 Cor. 11:3-16). This serves as a visible salute to God's authority and order.

The coverings over the three walls of the tabernacle created God's dwelling place and sanctuary. The term "house of God" occurs ninety times in the Bible; eighty-seven times it speaks of God's Old Testament dwelling place among His people – either the tabernacle or a temple. All three of the Epistles' references to "the house of God" refer to the Church. During the Church Age, God dwells in His people, not in a building (1 Cor. 6:19-20). Paul acknowledges this truth while writing to Timothy: *"But if I am delayed, I write so that you may know how you ought to conduct yourself* ***in the house of God, which is the church*** *of the living God, the pillar and ground of the truth"* (1 Tim. 3:15). Today the "house of God" is not a building, but a *household* of God's people. The NASB actually renders the expression *"house of God"* in this verse as *"household of God."*

Wrong terminology introduces an alternative and unbiblical idea of what the Church is. The Church is not a lifeless building; it is a living body. So the next time someone welcomes you to "the house of God" (speaking of a building where Christians gather), you might ask him or her, "Through what door does one gain entrance into the house of God?" The answer is the Lord Jesus (John 10:1, 14:6). He is the only spiritual entrance into the spiritual house called the Church (Eph. 2:19-22). Thus, there is a stark difference in how the term "house of God" is applied in the Old and New Testaments.

Additionally, the term "sanctuary" in the Old Testament referred to a location within the temple or the tabernacle where the priests officiated worship on behalf of the nation of Israel. In the Old Testament, access to God was limited. Only the high priest on the Day of Atonement could gain entry into the Most Holy Place (God's sanctuary), and he did so in trepidation and not without the blood of a goat and bullock (Lev. 16). In the New Testament, the term "sanctuary" is never applied to a physical room in which the Church gathers for worship, but to the abode of God, either in heaven or in the believer.

So all those "Sanctuary" signs we see in church buildings should really be turned to point up instead of down the hallway, or one might wrap a string about the sign and choose to wear it over one's own head so it points to himself – for during the Church Age, God dwells within those who have been born again (1 Cor. 6:19). Therefore, He also dwells within each local assembly (1 Cor. 3:16-17). No bricks and mortar can contain Him, but those who have responded to His invitation to be saved have His abiding presence forever. How much reverence do you place on His sacred dwelling place? Paul pleads with the believers at Corinth on this matter:

> Flee sexual immorality. Every sin that a man does is outside the body, but he who commits sexual immorality sins against his own body. Or

> do you not know that your body is the temple of the Holy Spirit who is in you, whom you have from God, and you are not your own? For you were bought at a price; therefore glorify God in your body and in your spirit, which are God's (1 Cor. 6:18-20).

The Old Testament earthly sanctuary was purified by animal blood, which allowed man limited access to God. In the New Testament, God's earthly sanctuary is those who have been redeemed and cleansed by His Son's blood. This allows every individual trusting Christ for salvation complete and full access to God. Let each believer keep short accounts with God by confessing and forsaking sin, and after Christ's blood has again fully cleansed and purified what was defiled, let us work to keep God's sanctuary glorious and untainted.

> In your hearts enthrone Him; there let Him subdue,
> All that is not holy, all that is not true;
> Crown Him as your Captain in temptation's hour;
> Let His will enfold you in its light and power.
>
> — Caroline M. Noel

# Ministering Holy Priests
## Exodus 28:1-2

Jehovah selected Aaron and his four sons Nadab, Abihu, Eleazar, and Ithamar to officiate worship in the tabernacle on behalf of the nation (v. 1). Before the Israelites moved northward from the mount, Nadab and Abihu would be fatally judged for intruding into God's presence with strange fire (Lev. 10:1-5); an event which demonstrated God's hatred of humanized religion. Eleazar and Ithamar were still teenagers at this time, but later, when the Israelites were in the Promised Land, Eleazar would replace his father Aaron as high priest. We know that Eleazar and Ithamar were not yet twenty years of age for, upon the following year, they were not judged with the adults at Kadesh-barnea (Num. 14).

After leaving Egypt, some Jewish men served temporarily as priests; perhaps these were firstborn males whom God had redeemed for service. The activities of these priests, whoever they were, had been limited; now that God would be dwelling among His people, the full attention of a sanctified priesthood would be required. The Aaronic priesthood was not perfect; in fact, its imperfections are contrasted with Christ's priesthood in Hebrews 7 to show the superior nature of the later. The Aaronic priesthood was inferior for several reasons. Firstly, it was made *"according to the law of a fleshly commandment"* (Heb. 7:16) and *"the law made nothing perfect"* (Heb 7:19). Secondly, the Aaronic priests had *"become priests without an oath"* (Heb. 7:21). Thirdly, *"they* [the priests] *were prevented by death from continuing"* (Heb. 7:23). Fourthly, the Aaronic high priest had to *"offer up sacrifices, first for His own sins"* (Heb. 7:27). With these considerations in mind, the writer then summarizes why Christ's priesthood is superior to that which had been previously established under the Law:

> *But He* [Christ], *because He continues forever, has an unchangeable priesthood. Therefore He is also able to save to the uttermost those who come to God through Him, since He always lives to make intercession for them. For such a High Priest was fitting for us, who is holy, harmless, undefiled, separate from sinners, and has become higher than the heavens* (Heb. 7:24-26).

The writer of Hebrews also acknowledges the benefit of Christ's High Priesthood to the believer-priests who compose the Church: *"Having a High Priest over the house of God, let us draw near with a true heart in full assurance of faith, having our hearts sprinkled from an evil conscience and our bodies washed with pure water"* (Heb. 10:21-22). We read of no such invitation in the Old Testament; the Levitical priests had limited access to Jehovah and could not boldly come into His presence, as the believers in the dispensation of the Church are invited to do (Heb. 4:15). Yet any allowed access before Him would require the shedding of blood and thus a fully engaged priesthood was necessary. As a result, Jehovah put order into Israel's worship and appointed the Aaronic priesthood to be responsible for ceremonial purification rites, the preparation and offering of various sacrifices, and the general care of God's tabernacle.

Throughout the dispensation of the Law, only the descendants of Aaron could serve as priests in the tabernacle (and later in the temple). Perhaps this honor was bestowed to Aaron because of his faithfulness in assisting Moses to address Pharaoh. As described in the following verses, the serving priests were not to wear common clothes, but they were to have holy and beautiful garments; this would elevate the office of priest in the sight of the people and bestow honor to the priests.

The priest's elegant attire would be woven of gold and of the same four colored thread used in the tabernacle veils and curtains. As gold symbolizes holiness and purity and the four colors picture the four Gospel presentations of Christ, the garments worn by the priests before the Lord in the tabernacle would picture our Great High Priest, who continues to minister to us upon His Father's throne. The Lord Jesus earned this official position and intercessory role by faithfully completing His earthly ministry; He did the Father's will, even though He foreknew it would cost Him His life.

The glories of the Lord Jesus are threefold: intrinsic, moral, and official. His intrinsic glory is that which is essential to Him as the Son of God – He is fully divine and an equal to the Father: *"And now, O Father, glorify Me together with Yourself, with the glory which I had with You before the world was"* (John 17:5). The Lord's moral glory consists of the perfections which characterized His earthly life and ministry: *"And the Word became flesh and dwelt among us, and we beheld His glory, the glory as of the only begotten of the Father, full of grace and truth"* (John 1:14). He was perfect in all His doings, in every circumstance, in each word spoken, and in every thought mentally conceived.

It is Christ's official glory that is typified in Aaron the high priest. Christ is the Mediator of the new covenant – He is the Great High Priest. Aaron was the high priest under the old covenant of the Law, which was put away under the new covenant through Christ. Aaron was appointed by God to the office of High Priest. Christ was also appointed by God to this office, but had to faithfully suffer to acquire the glory associated with it. Christ was rewarded and honored for finishing the immeasurable work of redemption that was assigned to Him: *"Father, I desire that they also whom You gave Me may be with Me where I am, that they may behold My glory which You have given Me; for You loved Me before the foundation of the world"* (John 17:24).

During Christ's earthly sojourn, His intrinsic glory was veiled and His official glory was not yet received. However, His moral glory could not be hidden; His character shone forth the integrity and perfections of His divine essence. Of this glory A. W. Tozer wrote, "Christ is God acting like God in the lowly raiments of human flesh."[1] It is His moral glory which was witnessed by man and which illuminates every page of the Gospel accounts.

As High Priest, Christ perfectly represents man to God. The writer of Hebrews informs us of the reason Christ had to be human in order to be our High Priest:

> *For every high priest taken from among men is appointed for men in things pertaining to God, that he may offer both gifts and sacrifices for sins. He can have compassion on those who are ignorant and going astray, since he himself is also subject to weakness* (Heb. 5:1-2).

Christ, being *holy humanity*, demonstrated compassion for others and felt the infirmities of mankind, yet, as the writer of Hebrews explains, He was sin apart: *"For we have not an high priest which cannot be touched with the feeling of our infirmities; but was in all points tempted like as [we are, yet], without sin" (Heb. 4:15)*. Note: *"we are, yet"* is not in the Greek text and distracts from the purest meaning of the text – there was nothing in Christ's members to respond to sin, though from an external point of view He was fully tested. J. N. Darby translates this passage literally, without the added words, *"For we have not a high priest not able to sympathize with our infirmities, but tempted in all things in like manner, sin apart"* (Heb. 4:15).[2]

The latter portion of this verse has been used to teach that Christ was tested and did not sin. Though this is true, it is not the direct meaning of text. The passage is highlighting, not the sinless perfection of Christ, but His inherent impeccability. Christ was tested in every way that you and I are, except in sin. He was externally solicited to sin, but in His members there was nothing to respond to it. Jeremiah bluntly summarizes our internal spiritual condition: *"The heart is deceitful above all things, and desperately wicked"* (Jer. 17:9; KJV). Our human nature is prone to sin because we are rotten to the core! Modern-day Christianity generally accepts this passage to mean else than what it says, but many older commentators rightly understood that Scripture taught that Christ was both sinless and impeccable in character:

William Newell clarifies the meaning of Hebrews 4:15:

> The word "yet" inserted in both the Authorized and the Revised versions here, "yet without sin," is an utter hindrance, instead of a true translation. The Greek reads, "tempted like as we, without sin," or, "sin apart." The Greek word for without, *choris*, signifies having no connection with, no relationship to. Temptation does not involve sin.[3]

Harry Ironside understood that Christ had no connection with sin in His human makeup. Concerning Hebrews 4:5 he writes:

> Our High Priest then is not One whose heart is indifferent to our circumstances; not One who cannot be touched with the feeling of our infirmities. He is as truly human as we, and in the days of His flesh He was tempted in all points like ourselves, though apart from sin. The expression, "yet without sin," has frequently been taken to mean,

> "yet without sinning," as though it simply implied that He did not fail when exposed to temptation, but the exact rendering would be "sin apart." That is, His temptations were entirely from without. He was never tempted by inbred sin as we are. He could say, *"The prince of this world cometh and hath nothing in Me."* When we are tempted from without, we have a traitor within who ever seeks to open the door of the citadel to the enemy. But it was otherwise with Him. If any ask, "How then could His temptations be as real as ours?" let us remember that when temptation was first presented to Adam and Eve, they were sinless beings, but being merely human, they yielded and plunged the race into ruin and disaster. Christ was not only innocent but holy, for He was God as well as Man.[4]

J. N. Darby explains the practical side of our relation with Christ as our High Priest:

> He has, in all things, been tempted like ourselves, sin apart; so that he can sympathize with our infirmities. The word brings to light the intents of the heart, judges the will, and all that has not God for its object and its source. Then, as far as weakness is concerned, we have His sympathy. Christ of course had no evil desires: He was tempted in every way, apart from sin. Sin had no part in it at all. But I do not wish for sympathy with the sin that is in me; I detest it, I wish it to be mortified – judged unsparingly. This the word does. For my weakness and my difficulties I seek sympathy; and I find it in the priesthood of Christ.[5]

How can Christ, as holy humanity and our High Priest, feel our infirmities? F. W. Bruce explains:

> How great an encouragement to know that upon the throne of God there is One who can be "touched by the feelings of our infirmities, but was in all things tempted like as we are, sin apart." Sin was to Him no temptation: there was nothing within that answered to it, except in suffering. There was and could be with Him no sinful infirmity; but He was true Man, His divine nature taking nothing from the verity of His manhood, living a dependent life as we, and, with no callousness such as the flesh in us produces, in a world everywhere racked with suffering through sin, and out of joint, the trial of which He knew as no other could.[6]

William Kelly nicely summarizes the entire matter of Christ's humanity and associated priesthood:

> We are too familiar with the human and selfish argument that He could not sympathize with us adequately if exempt from those internal and evil workings, bemoaned in Romans 7 and bitterly known by every soul born of God, at least in the early days of his awakening. But if we needed the Lord to be similarly harassed in order to feel fully with us, we should on that ground want Him to have yielded, as we – alas – have often done, in order to sympathize with us in our sad failures. No! That ground is wretchedly and absolutely opposed to Christ; and what the word reveals as the remedy for evil within and without in every form and degree is not Christ's sympathy, but His propitiatory suffering for us. He sympathizes with us in our holy, not in our unholy, temptations. For our unholiness He died; the cross alone has met it fully in God's sight. Had there been in fact the least inward taint of sin, His sensibility of evil had been impaired, his sufferings diminished, and His sympathy hindered, to say nothing of the deadly wound to His person, unfitted by such an evil nature to be a sacrifice for sin.[7]

Christ, as a man, sustained the harsh living conditions of a cursed planet, the contradiction of sinners, the opposition of Satan, and the hatred of the world. As High Priest, Christ is in no way empathizing with sin or forbidden desires but with the suffering saints of God as they endure what He already has endured – but in no way to the extent that He did. He knows all about living for God in a wicked world. In this we find a solace and comfort for our distressed souls. But there is no pity at the Throne of Grace for the lust of our flesh and the active sin of our members; these must be dealt a deadly blow from the sword of the Spirit. If it were our lust and sin He sympathized with, He would be sympathetic with all men and not just believers. Yet, only the redeemed are invited to *"come boldly,"* and only the redeemed *"may obtain mercy and find grace to help in time of need"* (Heb. 4:16).

After His resurrection, Christ experienced glorification. Presently, He is not only *holy humanity* but *glorified humanity*. The writer of Hebrews informs us that Christ presently sits at the right hand of God (Heb. 1:3) and is ever occupied with making intercession on our behalf – He is our Great High Priest (Heb. 2:17, 4:15). Having a distorted or deficient view of Christ's humanity causes a degraded view of His priestly operations and the type of sympathy that He has for suffering saints. Given that each of us has a fallen nature, it would be natural for us to approach and solicit Christ for comfort concerning depraved vexations which He cannot directly relate to. A holy God cannot endorse that which is unholy in the believer's life, though He is ever willing to assist those who want to overcome the sin that dwells within them (Rom. 7:17, 8:2-4).

Beloved of the Lord, let us not degrade Him in character or priestly office by thinking Him in some way tolerant, considerate, or sympathetic to matters that are foreign to His being and are repulsive to His holy nature! He experientially understands the consequences of our sin but not our propensity to embrace it.

When one gazed upon the Lord Jesus Christ during His earthly sojourn, all the moral perfection and splendor of the Father were seen in Him. Only the Lord Jesus could legitimately declare, *"He who has seen Me has seen the Father"* (John 14:9). Our Great High Priest is fully man and fully God and wonderfully makes intercession for us that we do not sin, and then provides ample mercy and grace when we do.

The atoning work is done, the Victim's blood is shed;
And Jesus now is gone His people's cause to plead:
He stands in Heaven their great High Priest,
And bears their names upon His breast.

He sprinkles with His blood the mercy-seat above;
For justice had withstood the purposes of love:
But justice now objects no more,
And mercy yields her boundless store.

No temple made with hands His place of service is;
In Heaven itself He stands, a heavenly priesthood His:
In Him the shadows of the law
Are all fulfilled, and now withdraw.

— Thomas Kelly

# Priestly Garb
## Exodus 28:3-29

Exodus 28 describes the priest's attire, while Exodus 29 explains the sacrifices the priests would offer. The former pertained to the needs of the people (i.e. to teach them the various duties and qualities of the priest's office). The claims of God's holy character are paramount in Exodus 29; He was and always would be in direct opposition to sin.

To serve in Jehovah's tabernacle, Aaron and his sons had to wear proper attire; failure to do so would result in death (v. 13). There were a number of spectacular garments to be fashioned for the priests: *"a breastplate, an ephod, a robe, a skillfully woven tunic, a turban, and a sash"* (v. 4). The breastplate included twelve precious stones encrusted on it (vv. 17-20). The details for the design of ephod and the breastplate are especially specific. All of Aaron's attire speaks of the intrinsic, essential, personal, and eternal qualities of Christ and His priestly ministry.

**The Ephod**

This was probably a sleeveless outer garment of two pieces (a front and a back part) that were connected by braided gold chains, which would act as shoulder straps. The ephod would slip over the priest's head to cover his torso, and would be secured by a belt about his waist (v. 8). The gold shoulder straps were to have two mounted onyx stones (one for each strap) with the names of the twelve tribes of Israel engraved on the stones (vv. 9-10). The ephod was to be made of gold thread (Ex. 39:2-3) and material of the same four colors apparent throughout the tabernacle (blue, purple, scarlet, and white).

**The Breastplate**

The breastplate was to be nine inches square and to have twelve different precious stones mounted upon it in gold settings (four rows of three stones). Each gem represented a particular tribe of Israel and was different in form, hue, and character, but each one was precious in God's sight. Each stone was to be engraved with the name of the tribe it represented. C. H. Mackintosh notes: "The people were represented before God by the high priest. Whatever might be their infirmities, their errors, or their failures, yet their names glittered on the breastplate with unfading brilliancy."[1] Of course, the shimmering nature of each stone depended predominantly upon how it was cut. When professionally cut, light illuminating a gem is refracted, reflected, and disseminated in such a way that its viewer is awestruck by its sparkling features and dazzling colors. Arthur Pink draws this application for the believer:

> Undoubtedly each one [believer] has some inherent characteristic difference, but only as the Divine hand in much patience and skill cuts and polishes the stone to catch and discover the colors of the Divine light which illuminates it doth it appear beautiful. Its beauty is not its own but it has been endowed with capacity to appreciate and reflect the beauty of Him who is light and love; and it is to reflect the beauties of the perfect One that we have been chosen – *"that in the ages to come He might show the exceeding riches of His grace in His kindness toward us through Christ Jesus"* (Eph. 2:7).[2]

The breastplate was attached to the ephod by four braided gold chains that slipped through the four gold rings mounted at each corner of the breastplate. In fact, the ephod was made specifically for the breastplate and the latter was not to be separated from the ephod (v. 28). The ephod and breastplate were an essential part of the high priest's garment for these characterized his ministry of representing the people before the Lord, while at all times having the names of God's people upon his heart. Three times Scripture states that the breastplate was to cover Aaron's heart and be a continuous memorial before the Lord.

Apparently, the breastplate had a double fold (v. 16) in which to safely carry the Urim and Thummim stones that the priest used to determine God's answers to particular questions or difficulties that occurred (Num. 27:21; Deut. 22:8-10). It is unknown how these two stones were used, but John Hannah provides the following insight:

> Apparently the Urim and Thummim were two stones. How they were used in determining God's will is unknown, but some suggest the Urim represented a negative answer and the Thummim a positive answer. Perhaps this view is indicated by the fact that Urim (*'urim*) begins with the first letter of the Hebrew alphabet, and Thummim (*tummim*) with the last letter. Others suggest that objects simply symbolized the high priest's authority to inquire of God, or the assurance that the priest would received enlightenment (Urim means "lights") and perfect knowledge (Thummim means "perfections") from God.[3]

**The Robe of the Ephod**

Under the ephod the high priest was to wear a blue sleeveless robe which hung down below his knees. Blue is the heavenly color and thus the robe expressed the heavenly nature and dwelling place of Christ. This robe would be seamless and reinforced at the collar. Pomegranates, which rattle when dried, and gold bells were to be attached to the bottom hem. As the high priest served in the tabernacle, the constant tinkling of bells and rattling of pomegranates would remind the people of God's mercy in permitting the high priest to minister before Him on behalf of the nation.

**The Tunic**

The tunic was also made of fine linen and, like the miter, was white in color. It was to be worn underneath the blue robe (Lev. 8:7).

**The Sash**

The sash was a wide belt which was to be worn about the waist of the high priest; the extra length after being tied was to hang freely. The same four colors used to create the ephod were also used in the needlework of the sash (Ex. 39:29). The sash is a symbol of service and we are reminded that our Great High Priest, the Lord Jesus, girded Himself as a servant to wash the feet of His disciples the night before His death.

**Turban**

Upon the head of the high priest was to be a linen turban (miter) with a gold plate fastened to the forefront of the miter by a blue cord. The gold plate was to be engraved with the words, *"Holy to the Lord"* and was also referred to as *"the holy crown"* (Ex. 29:6; Lev. 8:9). Paul tells us that man represents the glory of God and, consequently, his head should not be covered during times of public prayer and teaching, which would also include times of worship (1 Cor. 11:7). So why was Aaron commanded to wear a miter when offering worship to God in the tabernacle? While working in the tabernacle, the gold crown upon the high priest's head represented the glory of God in lieu of his uncovered head. Not only in the priest's headdress, but throughout the entire Jewish economy of worship the Lord intricately used symbols to represent His divine glory (and also human depravity). The gold front-piece on Aaron's miter represented God's perfection and purity; therefore, when the priest covered his head with the miter, he displayed a different symbol of God's glory which He deemed more appropriate to declare in the tabernacle.

**Other Priestly Garments**

Aaron's sons also had to wear special garments while executing the priestly office in the tabernacle. Each priest was to wear a fine linen coat, a miter, a sash, and a brief (under garment); the latter was to prevent the nakedness of the priests from being seen while they were performing their duties (v. 42).

Exodus 28 lists the garments which were to be sewed for the high priest and priests and then worn while they were before the Lord. The priests could approach Holy Jehovah only with deep reverence and respect, which meant they could not enter the tabernacle or approach the altar without the proper priestly attire; to do otherwise would result in death (vv. 35, 39). As explained later by Moses, the priests would also be required to put a sacrifice on the Bronze Altar and to ceremonially purify themselves before they could enter the tabernacle. Neglect of any of these details resulted in the death of the priest. How wonderful it is to be redeemed through the new covenant which enables and invites believers to come boldly into God's presence to receive help in time of need from our Great High Priest – the Lord Jesus Christ (Heb. 4:16)!

Yet, another contrast between Aaron's priesthood and that of the Lord Jesus reveals a deep truth. Aaron derived his *"glory and beauty"* (Ex. 28:2) from the garments he wore, but the glory of the Lord Jesus emanates from His very person. Aaron's beauty and glory only lasted as long as he lived and wore the priestly garments, but the Lord Jesus is the *"Lord of Glory"* (1 Cor. 2:9) from eternity past and will be forevermore (John 1:1, 17:1-5).

Aaron actually had two sets of priestly garments, but he was permitted to exchange his garments of "glory and beauty" for a simple white linen outfit and miter only once a year on the Day of Atonement (Lev. 16:4). This outfit is referred to as "holy," but there was no "glory and beauty" in the work that needed to be accomplished to atone for the sins of the people. Clearly, this pictures the Holy One (Luke 1:35, 4:34) who willingly put aside His glorious, beautiful appearance, left heaven, and came to earth to become holy humanity for the express purpose of suffering death to provide propitiation for human sin:

> *Christ Jesus, who, being in the form of God, did not consider it robbery to be equal with God, but made Himself of no reputation, taking the form of a bondservant, and coming in the likeness of men. And being found in appearance as a man, He humbled Himself and became obedient to the point of death, even the death of the cross* (Phil. 2:5-9).

On the Day of Atonement, Aaron wore his simple white linen coat and miter and was permitted to sprinkle the blood of a bullock and a goat on and before the Mercy Seat to atone for the nation of Israel's sin that year; this means of making atonement had to be repeated every year. But at Calvary, the Lord Jesus was stripped bare and shed His own blood to seal the new covenant forever. His loud cry, "It is finished," uttered just prior to relinquishing His life was an eternal declaration of what He had accomplished on our behalf. God's judicial wrath for human sin was appeased through His Son's sacrifice.

> *But Christ came as High Priest of the good things to come, with the greater and more perfect tabernacle not made with hands, that is, not of this creation. Not with the blood of goats and calves, but with His own blood He entered the Most Holy Place once for all, having obtained eternal redemption. For if the blood of bulls and goats and the ashes of a heifer, sprinkling the unclean, sanctifies for the purifying of the flesh, how much more shall the blood of Christ, who through the eternal Spirit offered Himself without spot to God, cleanse your conscience from dead works to serve the living God? And for this reason He is the Mediator of the new covenant, by means of death, for the redemption of the transgressions under the first covenant, that those*

*who are called may receive the promise of the eternal inheritance* (Heb. 9:11-15).

Aaron had to repeat the blood sacrifices day by day and year by year because the blood of bulls and goats could only cover sin temporarily until the ultimate solution for human sin, which the sacrifices pictured, could be accomplished. Through Christ's sacrifice, righteous justice for sin was answered, and by His blood, those who trust Him for salvation are purged from filth and guilt and become clean vessels fit for God's use. Christ has opened a way (the only way) for man to pass within the heavenly veil and enter the very place from where Christ originally came (Heb. 6:18-20).

Aaron's priestly garments strictly pertained to the dispensation of the Law; no such physical garments are commanded to be worn by believers in the Church Age. Rather, believers have received the righteousness of God positionally through Christ (Phil. 3:9); and are to continue in righteous acts to honor Him (Rev. 19:8). Unfortunately, men love to be honored by others and many in Christendom wear formal attire to elevate themselves over the "common" people. Not only does this practice supplant Christ's headship over the Church, but it also creates unbiblical classes of Christians. Christ is Head of the Church and all true Christians form one class of saints, or believer-priests (Eph. 1:22; Gal. 3:28; 1 Pet. 2:9).

There is a proclivity of men to create visual stimuli to accentuate their religious experience. Many of the religious symbols that the Church has manufactured are simply Old Testament figures of what now is reality in Christ. Judaism was full of future-related imagery which appealed to the senses, whereas the truths of Christianity are spiritual and are appreciated only by faith, not with our natural senses. Christ has come and, therefore, has replaced all the types and shadows which were the prelude of the good things to come with the spiritual realities themselves (Heb. 8:13). Unfortunately, much of Christendom is still including Old Testament symbols in religious practices; this undermines the recognition of the good things believers have actually received through Christ. Besides misusing terms, such as *the House of God* (to refer to a building) and *the Sanctuary* (to speak of a large meeting room), here are a few more examples of how Judaism is intruding into the gatherings of the Church.

The Jewish priests had ephods, and many of the clergy in Christendom today wear spectacularly colored robes. The Jewish priests burned incense and trimmed a lighted lampstand in the tabernacle; many in Christendom light candles and wave incense canisters to mimic the religious practices of old. Some call the wooden table in front of the "sanctuary" a "prayer altar." The Church has no altar but Christ (Heb. 13:10), and He is in heaven. How demeaning it is to Christ to ascribe His ministry in heaven to a piece of man-made furniture! Some bow the knee before such religious objects to extend artificial reverence to God. Through Christ – and Him alone – is the believer's worship offered to God. Using terms such as "prayer altar" or "altar calls" simply shows one's ignorance of God's dispensational economies as revealed in Scripture.

Since the first man walked upon the earth, God has shown His holiness and man's inclination for moral failure in order to emphasize that salvation is received only by divine grace through personal faith. Ignorance of dispensational theology allows Judaism to ever so quietly creep into Christian practices and to effectually mar the clear testimony of Christ. Let us not be bowing down to pieces of furniture or reverencing humans who adorn themselves in colorful robes in the guise of being religious; anything that supplants the truth is satanic and that which replaces Christ as the utmost object of our hearts is an idol!

God's order for His priests would not permit them to intrude upon His supreme position and authority, or to undermine His majesty before others. The gold plate upon the high priest's miter proclaimed "Holiness to the Lord" and this would serve as a constant reminder that man's highest occupation is to honor and worship God.

Now to the Lord, that makes us know the wonders of His dying love,
Be humble honors paid below, and strains of nobler praise above.
'Twas He that cleansed our foulest sins, and washed us in His richest blood;
'Tis He that makes us priests and kings, and brings us rebels near to God.

— Isaac Watts

# Priests Consecrated
## Exodus 29:1-25

Not only did the priests require particular garments to serve in the tabernacle, but they also had to be cleansed and consecrated for service. Moses would oversee the ceremony, which required the slaughter of one bullock and two rams and the preparation of unleavened wheat bread, which was anointed with oil (vv. 1-2). The bread and oil were to be brought in a basket with the priests to the door of the tabernacle. There, Moses was to oversee the bathing of the priests.

Next the priests were to be dressed in the appropriate attire (as described in Exodus 28), and then Moses was to pour anointing oil over the head of Aaron to consecrate him as high priest. This initial act of cleansing and anointing designated Aaron and his descendants as perpetual priests for as long as the dispensation of the Law would be administered (v. 9). Only one thing still remained before Aaron and his sons could serve before the Lord – the matter of sin had to be dealt with. For this, an unblemished bullock was to be taken for a sin offering (v. 14). Aaron and his sons were to place their hands upon the head of the bullock to symbolically show their identification with the innocent substitute, which was to take their place for the judgment in their sins.

The bullock was killed, its blood collected, and its carcass prepared for sacrifice. The fat above its liver and its two kidneys was burned on the Bronze Altar, but the remainder of the animal was burnt in a place outside the camp. Because the sacrifice symbolized the transfer of sin and judgment it had to be done outside the camp, lest there be defilement within the camp. Moses took some of the blood from the bullock and applied it to the horns of the Bronze Altar with his finger; the rest was poured out at the base of the altar. The sin offering was a non-sweet savor offering (except for the fat according to Lev. 4:31) because God demanded it in order to make atonement for the sins of the priests.

Upon the completion of the sin offering, Aaron and his sons laid their hands on the head of one of the rams before slaughtering it. Its blood was then sprinkled about the altar, and its carcass (after being washed and cut into pieces) was completely consumed by fire upon the altar as a burnt offering (v. 18). Other burnt offerings were considered sweet-savor sacrifices because they were not demanded by God, but were rather a free expression of individuals who wanted to worship the Lord. The ashes of the burnt offerings were temporarily put beside the Bronze Altar until a priest could change out of his priestly attire and carry the ashes out to a clean place (Lev. 6:9-11). The ashes would remind the Jews that God had a way of completely putting away the sting and the stain of their sins.

Jehovah appreciated the burnt offering more than the other sacrifices because it pictured the ultimate satisfaction He would have when His Son freely and wholly gave Himself as a sacrifice for sin. Consequently, the ashes from the burnt offering became the basis of acceptance for all the other offerings; ashes of the other sacrifices were piled upon the ashes of the burnt offering (Lev. 4:12). Christ's sacrifice is the basis of man's acceptance with God; it is through Him that man is fitted to serve the Lord in an acceptable manner and that his service is acceptable.

Aaron and his sons laid their hands on the head of a second ram, which served as a trespass offering. In the Levitical system, the sin offering was commanded for the *offense of sin*, but the trespass offering was required for the *damages of sin*. The sin offering deals with the guilt of sin; Christ's blood purges the believer's soul from that. The trespass offering deals with the damage that sin causes; through Christ's offering, full restoration of the sinner to God is thus accomplished. Both the sin offering and the trespass offering were not designated as "sweet savor" offerings; each was demanded by God for those who committed sins of ignorance (there were no personal offerings which atoned for willful sin). Through these two offerings, God was practically teaching His children to apologize and make restitution for wrong-doing. On a national level, all sin, including sins not done in ignorance were atoned for on the annual Day of Atonement.

Moses took some of the blood of the second ram and applied it to the tip of the right ear, the right thumb, and the right big toe of each of the priests. Some of the remaining blood was mixed with anointing oil and then sprinkled upon Aaron and sons, who were dressed in their priestly attire. This fully consecrated the priests and their garments; from that day on they were to be considered holy – set apart for God's use only.

Throughout Scripture the right side is designated as a place of honor; for example, we read that the Son sits at the right hand of God in heaven (Heb. 1:3), and that only those on Christ's right hand at the Judgment of Nations enter into His kingdom (Matt. 25:34-41). As believer-priests in the Church Age, our hearing (pictured in the ear), our service (typified by the thumb), and our walk (portrayed by the big toe) are to be consecrated for the honor and glory of God.

A fourth offering of unleavened bread, a cake, and a wafer were to be waved before the Lord by the priests and then burned upon the Bronze Altar. This type of offering would later be referred to as a meal offering. Its fine flour spoke of the superb moral character of Christ, and its lack of leaven typified Christ's sinless and impeccable nature. In the Church Age, as the believer priest is controlled by the Holy Spirit the high moral character of Christ is exhibited and ascends to God as a living sacrifice (Rom. 12:1), in much the same way as the priests waved the unleavened bread before the Lord under the Levitical system.

A portion of the second ram was also used as a peace offering, a sweet-savor sacrifice (v. 28). The peace offering spoke of fellowship and it was the only offering in which God, the offering priest, and the individual who brought the sacrifice received portions: God received the fat and kidneys, the offering priest received the breast and the right shoulder, and the priest returned the remainder of the animal to the offerer (Lev. 7:29-34). Everyone benefited from and enjoyed this offering – this portrays the fellowship that God and man are able to enjoy through Christ's past sacrifice and His present intercessory work.

Why did God demand that the fat and the kidneys from all three slaughtered animals be burned upon the Bronze Altar? Fat is where the energy of the body is stored for later use and the kidneys actively filter toxic waste from the body. The believer is, with pure motives, to dedicate his or her energy in service to the Lord. In all these offerings the central focus is upon the blood and the fat: the blood is the basis of *redemption*, and the fat speaks of the basis for *acceptance*. Through redemption, what a believer chooses to do with pure motives and as enabled by the Holy Spirit (pictured in the anointing oil) is made acceptable to God. Hence all the offerings have their center in the work and person of Christ, says Andrew Jukes:

> In the single relationship of offering, Christ is seen a Burnt-offering, Peace-offering, and Sin-offering [also a Meal-offering and Trespass-offering], each but a different view of the same one offering; each of which again may be seen in various measures, and yet the offering itself is only one. And just as in the self-same act of dying on the cross, our Lord was at the same moment a sweet-savor offering, willingly offering to God a perfect obedience, and also a sin-offering, penalty bearing the judgment due to sin, and as such made a curse for us; so in the selfsame acts of His life, each act may be seen in different aspects, for each act has a Divine fullness.[1]

The sacrifices, first mentioned in Exodus 29 and further described in Leviticus 1 through 7, present different facets of Christ's future sacrifice at Calvary: the burnt offering – the offering was totally consumed for God, the meal offering – reflected the fine moral character of Christ, the peace offering – acknowledges the communion of God with man through Christ, the sin offering – pictured God's own payment for the offense of man's sin, and the trespass offering – related to the payment for the damage that sin causes. In all of these, the person and work of Christ are presented.

The symbolism of Exodus 29 presents a significant application for the Church. Christ has already borne the judgment for the sins of humanity and the provision for redemption is available to all who want to be purchased by His blood (1 Pet. 1:19). In addition to the specific types of Christ portrayed in the offerings described in this chapter, the work of the Holy Spirit in the converting and saving of sinners is also symbolized.

First, note that Aaron and his sons willingly came to the door of the tabernacle to be cleansed by Moses; no one dragged them there; God appointed them to come and they chose to come. God forces no sinner into heaven, but, through the invitation of His Word (Rom. 10:17) and the illumination of the Holy Spirit (1 Cor. 2:14), vile sinners are made aware of their lost condition and are brought into agreement with God on the matter of sin and its only solution – Christ.

Secondly, each believer priest was regenerated and cleansed when he or she trusted Christ for salvation (Tit. 3:5) – like the Aaronic priest's initial washing at the door of the tabernacle, this act of the Holy Spirit would never need to be repeated. Later, the Laver would be used by the priests for daily purification; it was not used in their initial washing. The work of the Holy Spirit enables us to understand the ungodliness of our sinful attitudes and desires. He makes us feel their uncleanness, and leads us to repent of and repudiate them – in repentance we cry out to God regarding our need to be saved. At conversion, the Holy Spirit works to cleanse the new believer from evil bents and polluted things (though the lusting nature of the flesh remains in the new believer, he or she has a new attitude towards these and the Spirit's continuing help to repudiate them). The act of regeneration, also occurring at conversion, implants new life and a new order of living within him or her. Those who were dead are made spiritually alive (Eph. 2:1-3)!

Thirdly, just as the priests were anointed with oil at their consecration, the Holy Spirit likewise anoints the believer at his or her conversion (1 Jn. 2:20). Priests, prophets, and kings were often anointed when they were consecrated for the Lord's use. Indeed, the Lord Jesus Himself was anointed by the Holy Spirit (Acts 10:38) at the commencement of His ministry. Likewise, each believer is anointed and called to serve the body of Christ. Not only does this anointing separate out the believer for God's purpose, but the anointing actually provides divine discernment of the truth, which enables the believer to follow after God's will in his or her ministry. Through anointing, a new believer becomes part of a holy priesthood that will serve God forever. As believer-priests, it is our extraordinary privilege *"to offer up spiritual sacrifices, acceptable to God by Jesus Christ"* (1 Pet. 2:5).

Fourthly, the priests were completely equipped by the Lord with all the necessary implements and clothing to fulfill the office of priest. Similarly, the Holy Spirit distributes spiritual gifts to believers *"as He wills"* (1 Cor. 12:11). The number of gifts per believer will vary (1 Cor. 12:4), but each will receive at least one spiritual gift (1 Cor. 12:7). Also, the manner in which these gifts will be used will differ (1 Cor. 12:5), and the beneficiaries (those who receive the spiritual ministry) will vary (1 Cor. 12:6).

Fifthly, the priests were sealed by God; that is, they would be protected by Him from outside harm while fulfilling their office. Numbers

16 records a revolt against Moses, who was God's chosen leader for the nation, and Aaron, who was God's chosen high priest for the nation. Korah, Dathan, Abiram, and others sought to intrude into the priesthood – it cost them their lives. In the believer's case, the Holy Spirit Himself is the seal of God (Eph. 1:13). This eternal seal is likened to the wax seal placed on a letter or scroll in ancient times. Such a seal protected and secured the letter from being opened, and it also indicated who was the originator and owner of the letter. In some cases, seals were used to indicate approval of a contract or an agreement.

The pattern of the priesthood found in Exodus typifies with astonishing foreknowledge the eternal spiritual realities now accomplished in Christ through the power of the Holy Spirit on the believer's behalf. As each believer priest is infused by the power of the Holy Spirit and serves the Lord with pure motives, the Lord Jesus is honored and God Himself is refreshed. The sweet aroma of His Son permeates all such sacrifices that ascend to His throne, and when God breathes it in, that which was freely offered on earth reminds Him of His Son now in heaven.

Jesus, the Christ! Eternal Word! Of all creation Sovereign Lord!
On Thee alone by faith we rest, and lean our weakness on Thy breast.

Thy blood hath washed us from our sin; Thy Spirit sanctifies within;
And Thou for us in all our need, at God's right hand dost ever plead.

O keep us in the narrow way, that never from Thee our footsteps stray;
Sustain our weakness, calm our fear, and to Thy presence keep us near.

— Morshead

# The Lord's Table

## Exodus 29:26-37

The initial consecration activities for the priests were to last seven days with a bullock being slaughtered each day as a sin offering. Their blood was used to purify and sanctify the Bronze Altar. Likewise, in future generations there was to be a seven day consecration ceremony for passing down the high priest's holy garments to a successor. Only the current high priest could initiate that ceremony and the successor had to be his son.

During this seven-day consecration ceremony, the priests ate unleavened bread from the offering basket and the boiled portions of the peace offering: the ram's thigh (the heave offering), and the ram's breast (the wave offering). The priests were to assemble and eat that which had been offered to God as a sweet-savor offering at the door of the tabernacle. Because of the sacred nature of this offering, any leftovers were to be burned upon the Bronze Altar.

As previously stated, the peace offering symbolized God's fellowship with and provision for man; it was the only offering of which God, the offering priest, and the offerer all received a portion. For centuries to come, the peace offering would be God's provision for the priest's food (i.e. God shared with the priests what had been offered to Him). Consequently, in the context of the peace offering, the altar of God was also called the Lord's Table for His serving priests.

The Lord's Table is an expression that is used in both the Old and New Testaments to convey the concept of divine provision and fellowship (Ps. 23:5, 78:19; Mal. 1:7, 12; 1 Cor. 9:13, 10:18). Both Levitical priests under the old covenant of the Law (Lev. 6:16, 26, 7:6, 31-32) and believer priests under the new covenant of grace (1 Cor. 10:20-21) have been invited to abide at the Lord's Table.

The story of King David's kindness to Mephibosheth, the crippled son of Jonathan (2 Sam. 9:13), is a fitting allegory of the Lord's Table.

Normally, a new king would exterminate all remaining heirs of the previous dynasty in order to prohibit a potential takeover. However, King David, because of his love for Jonathan and the covenant he made with him (1 Sam. 18:3), set a place at his table for Mephibosheth for the remainder of his life. Mephibosheth never had to worry about where his next meal would come from, and he could enjoy daily fellowship with the king. Though once the enemies of God, believers in Christ now have the opportunity to enjoy fellowship with Him and with other believers at His table and to receive daily wherewithal to serve Him.

Often the biblical term "the Lord's Table" (which speaks of a spiritual table where believers receive blessing and fellowship in Christ – see 1 Corinthians 10) is confused with the biblical term "the Lord's Supper" (which refers to the remembrance meeting of the local church – see 1 Corinthians 11). Consequently, most of Christendom refers to the Lord's Supper by the unscriptural term "the communion service." There is *communion with Christ* at the Lord's Table, but more specifically, there is a *remembrance of Christ* at every Lord's Supper – the value of His death is proclaimed afresh. The Lord's Table is invisible and is set by Him, whereas the table at the Lord's Supper is visible and is set by us; at the former we receive provisions from the Lord, but at the latter we offer up worship to Him.

The Lord's Table speaks of the sum total of the spiritual blessings we have in Christ, while the Lord's Supper refers to the remembrance meeting of the Church. In the sense that the souls of believers are refreshed through Spirit-led worship, the Lord's Table probably includes the Lord's Supper, but the distinct terminology and significance of each should not be lost. It is a great privilege to remember and refresh the Saviour during the Lord's Supper, and it is a blessing to the heart of every believer to commune with and receive from the Saviour at His Table.

Incorrectly applying the term "Communion Service" to the Lord's Supper effectively exchanges the purpose of the meeting. At the Lord's Supper we are to give unto the Lord, rather than expecting to be served by Him. The word "service" conveys an entirely different intention of the Lord's Supper than what Scripture presents. The "Communion Service" terminology also undermines the gravity of departing from the Lord's Table to spiritually eat (partake) from *"the table of demons"* (1 Cor. 10:21). Clearly, the Church must leave the table that is set at the

Lord's Supper, but we should never forsake the Lord's Table. In consequence, the term "Communion Service" diminishes the focus of the Lord's Supper (remembering Christ) and undermines the significance of ongoing fellowship with Him at the Lord's Table.

Paul thus exhorts the believers at Corinth not to remove themselves from the Lord's table to partake of the world's resources; to do so is to fellowship with demons:

> *I do not want you to have fellowship with demons. You cannot drink the cup of the Lord and the cup of demons; you cannot partake of the Lord's table and of the table of demons. Or do we provoke the Lord to jealousy? Are we stronger than He?* (1 Cor. 10:20-22).

When ordering the priesthood and sacrifices, God wonderfully provided for the needs of His priests. While atoning blood was being applied to the altar to sanctify it, the priest also appropriated the offering by eating it. This repeats the same idea of Exodus 12 where we witnessed the blood of a victim applied to sanctify the one who ate the victim's flesh. The themes of blood atonement, substitutional death, and sanctification to God are all inter-connected in Scripture and, ultimately, have their typological climax and fulfillment at Calvary.

The Bronze Altar would be God's table to supply His priest's needs, but the priests had to eat what was provided by the Lord before Him in the tabernacle. May each believer realize the importance of eating at the Lord's Table and, accordingly, choose to abide with Him there. Failure to do so will provoke the Lord's jealousy and His chastening hand. Why would a believer ever want to leave the Lord's Table?

> The King of Heaven His table spreads, and blessings crown the board;
> Not paradise, with all its joys, could such delight afford.
>
> Pardon and peace to dying men, and endless life are given,
> Through the rich blood that Jesus shed to raise our souls to Heaven.
>
> Millions of souls, in glory now, were fed and feasted here;
> And millions more, still on the way, around the board appear.
>
> — Philip Doddridge

# The Daily Offerings
## Exodus 29:38-46

The consecration of Aaron and his sons and the cleansing of the Bronze Altar with the atoning blood from the sin sacrifices would require seven days. After that, the Bronze Altar was to be anointed and set apart for God. Having been cleansed by blood, the priest could now engage in the dauntless task of preparing animals for sacrifice, collecting and applying their blood, and then presenting portions of the animals as burnt offerings to Jehovah.

The priests could not enter the tabernacle to serve the Lord without putting a sacrifice upon the Bronze Altar, to do so would result in death. God permitted the priests to enter the tabernacle twice per day after offering a lamb each morning and evening as a burnt sacrifice. Thus, the priests and the people would be reminded each morning and again at the end of each day that without sacrifice there was no acceptance with God. The Israelites had the immense privilege of God dwelling among them, but the smoking altar testified that the entire arrangement was of a tentative nature and strictly depended upon the continuation of holy sacrifices to deal with their unholiness.

All that was consumed upon the altar ascended up to God as a sweet aroma; thus its continuous smoke was a testimony of God's utter delight and infinite satisfaction in the death of His Son in obedience to His will. It was only in this ascending fragrance that Israel had acceptance before God, and it is none the less true for the Christian today, less the fire and smoke, for now our Altar is before God in heaven and we are accepted in Him:

> *Blessed be the God and Father of our Lord Jesus Christ, who has blessed us with every spiritual blessing in the heavenly places in Christ, just as He chose us in Him before the foundation of the world, that we should be holy and without blame before Him in love, having*

*predestined us to adoption as sons by Jesus Christ to Himself, according to the good pleasure of His will,* ***to the praise of the glory of His grace, by which He made us accepted in the Beloved*** *"* (Eph. 1:3-6).

In the same way that the daily offerings of Israel were a perpetual sweet savor to God, we have been accepted in the Beloved as a continual sweet savor offering unto God. Logistically speaking, the fire on the Bronze Altar was occasionally extinguished and the sweet savor before God ceased for a time, but through Christ's redemptive work, all believers are made a sweet savor unto God forever!

There were to be two items offered with the lamb at each burnt offering: a meal offering and a drink offering. The meal offering consisted of *"one-tenth of an ephah of flour mixed with one-fourth of a hin of pressed oil,"* and the drink offering of *"one-fourth of a hin of wine"* which was to be poured out before the Lord (Ex. 29:40). Edward Dennett describes the typological representation of the meal and drink offerings in relationship to Christ:

> [The meal offering] in connection with the consecration of the priests, is an emblem of the devotedness of Christ in life, His entire consecration to the will and glory of God. The fine flour was mingled with oil (see also Lev. 2), to shadow forth the mysterious truth that Christ as to His humanity was begotten of the Holy Ghost. It represented consequently the perfection of His life below – His life of perfect obedience, every energy of His soul flowing out in this channel, finding it His meat to do His Father's will, and to finish His work. Israel was consequently before God in all the value and acceptance of His life and death – of all that He was to God, whether considered in the perfect consecration of His life, or in the highest expression of the perfection of His obedience as displayed when He was made sin on the cross.
>
> The drink-offering was composed of wine. Wine is a symbol of joy – "it cheereth God and man;" and since it is here offered to God, it speaks of His joy, His joy in the sacrifice presented. But it was offered by His people, by the priest on their behalf. It expressed on this account also their communion with the joy of God in the perfectness of the life, and the devotedness unto death, of His only begotten Son. Such is the heart of God. He would bring us into fellowship with Himself, have us feast on His own delights, that the joy of His own heart, flowing out, and filling also ours, might overflow in praise and

> adoration. Hence John says, "Truly our fellowship is with the Father, and with His Son Jesus Christ." (1 John 1: 3.)[1]

The daily sacrifices, therefore, allowed God to tabernacle among His people and to communicate His will to them through Moses. Through the daily sweet-savor sacrifices the tabernacle could continue to be "the tent of meeting." The billowing smoke was a continual testimony that their acceptance with God was due to the burning sacrifices. Unless Jehovah was moving the camp site, the absence of smoke from the Bronze Altar meant that the Israelites had no acceptance before God; the priests could not enter the tabernacle. This meant there would be no worship offered to God, and no communication or fellowship with God.

Likewise, if the cross of Christ is ignored, no relationship can be maintained with God, other than that of a guilty sinner before a holy Judge. But the moment the repentant sinner identifies with the sweet-savor sacrifice of God to God (speaking of Christ's sacrifice at Calvary), God willingly embraces the sinner with the fullness of His grace and love. How wonderful it is to be accepted by God in the Beloved! Through Christ alone can the believer enter God's presence with acceptable worship, and enjoy the benefits of divine communication and fellowship.

"In the Beloved" accepted am I,
Risen, ascended, and seated on high;
Saved from all sin thro' His infinite grace,
With the redeemed ones accorded a place.

"In the Beloved," God's marvelous grace,
Calls me to dwell in this wonderful place;
God sees my Saviour, and then He sees me,
"In the Beloved," accepted and free.

"In the Beloved" – how safe my retreat,
In the Beloved accounted complete;
"Who can condemn me?" In Him I am free,
Saviour and Keeper forever is He.

— Civilla D. Martin

# The Altar of Incense

## Exodus 30:1-10

Like the Ark of the Covenant, the Golden Altar of Incense was constructed of acacia wood overlaid with gold. Its base was one and a half feet square and it stood three feet high. The Altar of Incense, although located in the Holy Place, was really associated with the Ark of the Covenant; thus, the altar is often spoken of as being "before the Lord" (Lev. 16:12-14; 1 Kgs. 6:22; Ps. 141:2). However, the Golden Altar had to be separated from the Most Holy Place by a veil so that the priests could frequently burn special incense upon it (Ex. 30:34-38) and also so they could apply sacrificial blood upon its horns to link it with the work of atonement accomplished on the Bronze Altar. Blood from the sacrifices on the Bronze Altar was to be smeared upon its horns once a year on the Day of Atonement (Ex. 30:10), as well as whenever personal sin offerings were presented to the Lord (Lev. 4:7, 18).

This is the reason that the Golden Altar was not mentioned until Exodus 30. No priest was fit to burn incense before the Lord until his sins had been atoned for on the Bronze Altar and he had been thoroughly washed with water and purified by blood at the door of the tabernacle. The Bronze Altar had to be introduced first; this was where the righteous demands of a Holy God were satisfied for the sinner. But when the sins of the priest were judged and the ashes of his sins were carried away, the offering priest had the privilege of approaching God to serve, worship and to enjoy communion with Him; all these blessings are symbolized in the Golden Altar of Incense. On this point, C. H. Mackintosh writes:

> Thus it is ever; there must be a brazen altar and a priest before there can be a golden altar and incense. Very many of the children of God have never passed the brazen altar. They have never yet, in spirit, entered into the power and reality of true priestly worship. They do not

> rejoice in a full, clear, divine sense of pardon and righteousness; they have never reached the golden altar. They hope to reach it when they die; but it is their privilege to be at it now. The work of the cross has removed out of the way everything which could act as a barrier to their free and intelligent worship. The present position of all true believers is at the golden altar of incense.
>
> This altar typifies a position of wondrous blessedness. There we enjoy the reality and efficacy of Christ's intercession. Forever done with self and all pertaining thereto, so far as any expectation of good is concerned, we are to be occupied with what He is before God. We shall find nothing in self but defilement. … Nature can have no place in the sanctuary of God. It, together with all its belongings, has been consumed to ashes; and we are now to have before our souls the fragrant odor of Christ, ascending in grateful incense to God: this is what God delights in. Everything that presents Christ in His own proper excellence, is sweet and acceptable to God. Even the feeblest expression or exhibition of Him, in the life or worship of a saint, is an odor of a sweet smell, in which God is well pleased.[1]

What is portrayed by the burning incense upon the Golden Altar? In general, the incense offered typifies Christ's perfections and devotion to God in the believer's life. The sweet fragrance of the ascending smoke represents the offerings of believer-priests who being empowered by His Spirit worship God according to revealed truth. Only those priests having clean hands and pure hearts can engage in true worship. C. H. Bright notes that the position of the Golden Altar itself represents the believer's highest occupation – worshipping God:

> Just as the golden altar was the last object to be reached in the journey from the gate to the veil which hid the mercy-seat from view, just so is worship the highest state to be reached on earth and the object for which all other things are preparation. The Father seeks worshippers (John 4:23), and this it was that led the Lord to go through Samaria to meet that sinner, to turn her heart from her sins, by filling it with the satisfying portion of grace, that she might meet the desires of Divine love and give that praise, that worship, that only a sinner (a cleansed sinner) can give. And this it was that led the Lord to take that larger journey from the heaven of light and peace down to the cross of suffering and shame. He sought sinners, He seeketh them still; seeketh them

> that, having tasted as no angel can possibly taste, the love of God, they might then from a heart overflowing with consciousness of its indebtedness to the Saviour, and the appreciation of His own excellence, pour forth the fragrant incense of praise.[2]

Just as incense was laid upon the Golden Altar, so may the Christian offer acceptable spiritual sacrifices, including: good works accomplished with pure motives (Heb. 13:16), fervent prayers (Rev. 8:3-4), genuine praise (Heb. 13:15), and selfless giving (Phil. 4:17-18). Of course, none of these sacrifices would have any merit with God without the benefit of Christ's work at Calvary, as pictured in the Bronze Altar. Clearly, the distinct ministries of these two altars are intimately tied to the one heavenly Altar which they both picture, that is Christ. As the writer of Hebrews puts it *"we have an Altar"* (Heb. 13:10) – the believer's Altar, which both effectively restores the sinning believer to God and offers his or her personal sacrifices to God, is Christ.

The spiritual significance of these two altars for the believer is poetically expressed in Psalm 84, which was dedicated to the sons of Korah: *"Even the sparrow has found a home, and the swallow a nest for herself, where she may lay her young – even Your altars, O Lord of hosts, my King and my God"* (Ps. 84:3). After the temple was erected, it was common for sparrows and swallows to build their nests in the heights of the sanctuary and even among the altars. The priests went about their duties without discouraging the nesting patterns of these birds. The birds enjoyed rest and safety in the House of the Lord.

Two types of birds are mentioned in Psalm 84:3. The sparrow is a most worthless bird; it doesn't sing, it is not beautiful to look at, and there is very little to meat on it to eat. In the Lord's day, it was common for boys to go out and catch sparrows and them sell them to the poor who would make a little pie out of them. Two sparrows were sold for a farthing (Matt. 10:29), which was the equivalent of the two mites that the poor widow cast into the temple treasury (Mark 12:42). The sparrow was a worthless bird that found complete rest in Jehovah's presence. In Christ, poor miserable sinners also find significance before God. The second bird mentioned is the swallow, a most restless bird, yet the swallow too found rest in the house of God. Like these common birds, all believers, in the spiritual sense, were once worthless and restless, but now have found significance and rest in the refuge of Christ.

The purpose of the bronze altar was the judgment of sin; this is where the animal sacrifices were placed. The birds nested there even while the flames ascended from the inner portion of the altar; this symbolizes the believer's peace with God through the cross of Christ. No sacrifices were burned upon the Golden Altar, but sacrificial blood from the animals offered on the Bronze Altar was placed on the horns of the Golden Altar to create a connection between the two. Through Christ's blood both Altar realities are connected also for the believer. The Golden Altar speaks of Christ continuing work to perfect our worship and service and the total blessing of His intercessory ministry. This ensures that whatever Christ accomplishes within His people will be appreciated by God as the sweet smelling offering.

Contrasting types of Christ are thus pictured in these two altars. The Bronze Altar typifies Christ's death, and the Golden Altar, His life now. In the Bronze Altar Christ was judged, but in the Golden Altar Christ cares for His saints. In the Bronze Altar we gain peace with God, but through the Golden Altar the believer enjoys the peace of God. Wondrous is the typology within the Altars, but it is even greater to experience what they represent: the peace, the significance, the security of being in God's presence, and of having our sacrifices to God sanctified and presented by Christ Himself.

When it came to sacrifices upon the altar the Pharisees were quite confused about what sanctified what; they thought that the sacrifice made the altar special. The Lord Jesus corrected them with this question: *"Fools and blind! For which is greater, the gift or the altar that sanctifies the gift?"* (Matt. 23:19). The altar extended value to the sacrifice, not the other way around; it was the altar which sanctified the sacrifice that was offered on it.

The Lord Jesus used the occasion to speak of His own sacrifice to God, when He would offer Himself as propitiation for human sin. Christ was both the sacrifice and the altar that sanctified the sacrifice to God. What is the relevance of this understanding for the believer? Christ lives within all believers, and they are commanded to be living sacrifices for the Lord each and every day (Rom. 12:1-2). Christ is the altar upon which the believer offers up fragrant sacrifices to God. Just as it is the Altar that sanctifies the sacrifice upon it, it is Christ who gives value to the believer's life as it is offered unto God.

Consequently, our gifts, time, and abilities have value only when they are sanctified by Christ for God's glory. To pompously think that God would be lucky to have my intellect or skills in His service is incorrect thinking; for what we think has value to God is actually worthless until it is sanctified to God through Christ. The Lord warned His disciples, *"For without Me you can do nothing"* (John 15:5) but yet Paul states, *"I can do all things through Christ who strengthens me"* (Phil. 4:13). Apart from Christ, no one has any suitable sacrifice or service to offer God, nor any acceptable means in which to offer it. Only what is sanctified and presented by Christ, our Altar, has value to God. May we never engage in the Pharisaical sin of thinking that we have something God would be fortunate to have.

The holiest we enter in perfect peace with God,
Through whom we found our center in Jesus and His blood.
Though great may be our dullness in thought and word and deed,
We glory in the fullness of Him that meets our need.

Much incense is ascending before the eternal throne,
God graciously is bending to hear each feeble groan;
To all our prayers and praises Christ adds His sweet perfume,
And love the censer raises, these odors to consume.

— Mary Bowley Peters

# Who May Worship?
## Exodus 30:11-33

The preconditions listed in Exodus 30 address the matter of who could legitimately worship Jehovah: only the redeemed, the cleansed, and the anointed could engage in worship. The first condition applied to all of the Israelites, although the Aaronic priests would be the only ones to actually offer worship. The latter two restrictions pertained specifically to the officiating priests.

Only those Jews who were redeemed by blood could worship Jehovah; visiting foreigners were outside of that covenant relationship and, therefore, could not sacrifice to God. Although redemption is an obvious prerequisite to worship, the discussion of atonement money in verses 11-15 poses a difficulty to the human mind. Both the Old Testament and the New Testament state that material wealth regardless of its value – cannot purchase the redemption of a sinner. Peter declared, *"Knowing that you were not redeemed with corruptible things, like silver or gold, from your aimless conduct received by tradition from your fathers, but with the precious blood of Christ"* (1 Pet. 1:18-19). The prophet Isaiah foretelling of the blessings of Christ wrote: *"Everyone who thirsts, come to the waters; and you who have no money, come, buy and eat. Yes, come, buy wine and milk without money and without price"* (Isa. 55:1). Yet, Jehovah commanded Moses to tell the people that, *"every man shall give a ransom for himself to the Lord"* (v. 12). How can a man give a ransom for himself if true redemption is only through the precious blood of Christ?

The answer to this apparent contradiction is found in the specific language of the command itself: *"**When** you take the census of the children of Israel for their number, **then** every man shall give a ransom for himself to the Lord, **when** you number them, that there may be no plague among them when you number them"* (v. 12). The ransom money (a half shekel of silver) was to be paid by every adult man when the census of the people was accomplished. A census would be required before the Israelites could worship God; and then years later, a second census would be performed just before the Israelites entered the Promised Land.

Moses, picturing Christ, was God's mediator for the people; when he numbered the children of Israel he was simply appropriating to God the sum of those who had already been redeemed. By counting all of the men, God demonstrated His ownership over the entire nation. The firstborns, however, had been redeemed in Egypt by God's Passover and were thus representative of the entire nation. The act of adult men paying the ransom money showed everyone that, indeed, God had *appropriated* the entire nation to Himself, not just the firstborns. The redeemed were to stand up and be counted; the atonement money was their acknowledgment to the Lord that they had been redeemed and that He owned them. Thus, the atonement money represented what God had already accomplished, rather than actually effecting atonement itself.

When it comes to redemption, every human is worth the same to God: *"The rich shall not give more and the poor shall not give less than half a shekel, when you give an offering to the Lord, to make atonement for yourselves"* (Ex. 30:15). C. H. Mackintosh adds, "All were to pay alike. In the matter of atonement, all must stand on one common platform. There may be a vast difference in knowledge, in experience, in capacity, in attainment, in zeal, in devotedness, but the ground of atonement is alike to all."[1] This insures that there is perfect equality of all the redeemed within the body of Christ: *"There is neither Jew nor Greek, there is neither slave nor free, there is neither male nor female; for you are all one in Christ Jesus"* (Gal. 3:28-29). All believers are simply *brethren*; there are no classes of saints within the body of Christ (Matt. 23:8).

Why were pieces of silver used for ransom money? Silver symbolizes redemption in Scripture; in fact, the Lord Jesus was betrayed for thirty pieces of silver, which later the Pharisees referred to as "blood money." The pieces of silver were connected with the means of our ransom – Christ's own redeeming blood. The tabernacle consisted of a framework of forty-eight boards overlaid with gold. The bottom of each board had two tenons which stood in a silver base-plate of ninety-six sockets. The boards were then braced together by gold-covered rods of wood (five for each wall). Without the silver sockets the tabernacle would have no footing on which to erect walls. The silver to form these sockets came from the people when they were numbered and paid the ransom money. The entire activity of counting and paying the silver was God's official acknowledgment that all of the Israelites were a ransomed people. Jehovah wanted all of His people to understand that only through redemption could they offer acceptable worship to Him – the same is still true today.

The second condition for worship (vv. 17-21) was that the priests had to wash their hands and feet at the laver before entering into the tabernacle (vv. 18-19). The priests had earlier undergone a one-time complete bath at the door of the tabernacle. As mentioned before, this pictures the regeneration of a believer by the Holy Spirit. However, no priest could serve the Lord without washing his hands and feet every time he entered the tabernacle. This action typifies the believer's desire to confess sins on an on-going basis in order to be forgiven, to have his or her conscience cleared of guilt, and to be restored into fellowship with God (1 Jn. 1:9). The Laver and its application will be treated more fully later. It suffices here to say that no priest dared come before the Lord without first washing his hands and feet and no believer-priest today can be a daily living sacrifice or offer acceptable praise, service, or worship to the Lord until he or she has first stopped at the Laver, so to speak, and confessed his or her sins.

The third stipulation for worship required the high priests to be anointed with a special fragrant oil composed of myrrh, cinnamon, sweet calamus (cane), cassia, and olive oil (vv. 23-24). David identified the purpose of this fragrant mixture:

> *Your throne, O God, is forever and ever; a scepter of righteousness is the scepter of Your kingdom. You love righteousness and hate wickedness; therefore God, Your God, has anointed You with the oil of gladness more than Your companions. All Your garments are scented with myrrh and aloes and cassia, out of the ivory palaces, by which they have made You glad* (Ps. 45:6-8).

David, in announcing that God the Father would exalt God the Son, affirmed not only the deity of Christ, but also that God anointed His Son with the oil of gladness. Olive oil is often used in Scripture as a type of the Holy Spirit (Zech. 4:2-6). It is important to note that the spices produce the sweet fragrance to be enjoyed, but the oil enabled their aroma to be disseminated more powerfully. In this type, Christ in and of Himself has all the sweet moral excellencies that the Father appreciates, yet these are properly expressed and appreciated by us only through the illuminating power of the Holy Spirit.

Once produced, the holy anointing oil was used to anoint the tabernacle, all its furnishings, and all the vessels associated with the operation of the various furnishings. Last, the priests themselves would be anointed with the fragrant oil. Thus, at all times, and at all places in the tabernacle, the fragrance of the holy oil would be enjoyed. Edward Dennett summarizes the application of this reality to the believer-priest living during the Church Age:

> The fact that everything was anointed with the holy oil teaches that everything connected with the house of God, its regulation and service, all the priestly work carried on in it (see 1 Peter 2:5), must be ordered in the power of the Holy Ghost, and that when so ordered it will be expressive of the sweet fragrance of Christ to God. For indeed it is in the power of the Spirit that God reveals Himself, and it is in the power of the Holy Ghost alone that worship and service can be rendered. If therefore everything connected with the house of God were arranged even according to His own word, and yet the holy anointing oil – the power of the Holy Spirit – were lacking, it could not be acceptable to Him. Notice also the effect – everything is sanctified, becomes through the anointing "most holy," so that whatever touches anything on which the oil has been put should likewise be deemed holy (v. 29). This is the effect of the action of the Spirit of God. Whatever His power rests upon is set apart for God, and everything that comes under His action, even by contact, is also claimed as holy.[2]

As each believer is controlled by the Holy Spirit, the sweet fragrance of Christ will be powerfully disseminated to all, but as Paul notes, not everyone will appreciate the fragrance of Christ:

> *Now thanks be to God who always leads us in triumph in Christ, and through us diffuses the fragrance of His knowledge in every place. For we are to God the fragrance of Christ among those who are being saved and among those who are perishing. To the one we are the aroma of death leading to death, and to the other the aroma of life leading to life.* (2 Cor. 2:14-17).

The lost are able to witness the Lord Jesus through the selfless acts and godly character of believers. As the lost observe supernatural love, joy, peace, faith, self-control, and humility, they are prompted to take note, breathe in, and ponder the sweetness of the Lord Jesus. Some will be repulsed by what they sense, but others will be prompted to breathe again, and some will never again desire to inhale anything but Christ.

God had previously told Moses that the priests were to be anointed with olive oil when they were purified by blood and consecrated to the Lord (Ex. 29:7). This undoubtedly symbolizes the initial work of the Holy Spirit at conversion to bring a vile sinner under the power of Christ's blood. However, the priests were to be anointed a second time with the fragrant oil before serving in the Holy Place. Again, the work of the Holy Spirit is emphasized, but this time it is in the believer's life and service. It is only what God controls within us that has the potential for propagating the sweet fragrance of Christ to the world that so desperately needs to be awakened to His sweetness.

Two restrictions pertained to the anointing oil. First, it was not to be poured on man's flesh (v. 32). This reminds us that our flesh cannot work the righteousness of God; in fact, it has no capacity to please God at all. The works of the flesh are a putrid stench in the nostrils of God and cannot be tolerated (Isa. 64:6). Second, the anointing oil was not to be manufactured for private use – it was all for the Lord. It was to be applied only on the tabernacle, its furnishings, and the priest's attire; it was never to be used on a stranger; only true believers are indwelt with the Holy Spirit, and all that He does in their lives is for the glory of God (John 16:13-14).

Every child of God must remember that, though we are saved by grace through the blood of Christ, we cannot worship or serve the Lord apart from the continual energizing power of the Holy Spirit (Phil. 3:3). Reliance on human wisdom, the strength of the flesh, or vain religiosity will be futile substitutes for that real spiritual power which has the capacity to fill the world with the aroma of Christ.

> O Christ, He is the fountain, the deep, sweet well of love!
> The streams on earth I've tasted, more deep I'll drink above:
> There to an ocean fullness His mercy doth expand,
> And glory, glory dwelleth in Immanuel's land.
>
> — Anne R. Cousin

# The Lord's Incense
## Exodus 30:34-38

After God gave the instructions for anointing the priests with the holy fragrant oil, the Lord delivered further instructions to Moses concerning a unique incense that was to be burned before Him on the Golden Altar: *"Take sweet spices, stacte and onycha and galbanum, and pure frankincense with these sweet spices; there shall be equal amounts of each. You shall make of these an incense, a compound according to the art of the perfumer, salted, pure, and holy"* (Ex. 30:34-35). The same spices which formed the fragrant anointing oil were also to be combined into a special incense that was to be burnt upon the Golden Altar (Ex. 25:6, 35:8).

Although no specific measurements were given for these spices, the narrative states that equal amounts of the spices were to be *"beaten small"* and then salt was to be added the mixture. Frankincense would be placed upon the incense after it was laid upon the altar. Actually, salt was added to all the offerings, and when burned it would create a white smoke. Salt adds flavor to what is eaten, and also serves as a food preservative. This is why Paul used salt as a metaphor to speak of uncompromised truth (Col 4:6), and the Lord Jesus exhorted His disciples to have a "salty" testimony (Matt. 5:13).

The frankincense for the incense offering was not mixed in with the other spices, but rather it was kept separate until the incense was presented before the Lord. In fact, frankincense was always used this way in the Levitical offerings (Lev. 2:1; 15); it was laid upon the sacrifices. The gum from the frankincense tree is an unusual spice which does not release its aroma until it is burned. This speaks of those superb, indescribable qualities that the Father appreciates about His Son, especially those exhibited in the agony of Cavalry. Edward Dennett further explains this point:

> This being the case, there is the additional thought that the graces of Christ were brought out through the action of the holy fire; that His exposure to the judgment of God's holiness (fire) upon the cross, as there made sin, did but bring out all that was most precious and fragrant to God. He was indeed never more precious in His eyes, His perfections were never more fully displayed, than when He proved His obedience to the uttermost in the very place of sin. Hence He could say, *"Therefore doth My Father love me, because I lay down My life, that I might take it again."* It was for God's glory that He passed through the fire of judgment, and in doing so all the "sweet spices" of His moral graces and the perfection of His entire devotedness were brought out, and ascended up as a sweet savor to God.[1]

As Jehovah had inundated Moses with minute details on every other aspect of the tabernacle the lack of precise measurements for the holy perfume is conspicuous. The absence itself symbolizes something mysterious, and at the same time quite lovely. C. H. Mackintosh clarifies the meaning of the unmeasured spices:

> This surpassingly precious perfume presents to us the unmeasured and immeasurable perfections of Christ. There was no special quantity of each ingredient prescribed, because the graces that dwell in Christ, the beauties and excellencies that are concentrated in His adorable Person, are without limit. Nothing save the infinite mind of Deity could scan the infinite perfections of Him in whom all the fullness of Deity dwells; ... Every feature of moral excellence found its due place and proper proportion in Christ. No one quality ever displaced or interfered with another; all was "tempered together, pure and holy," and emitted an odor so fragrant that none but God could appreciate it.
>
> There is uncommon depth and power in the expression *"very small."* It teaches us that every little movement in the life of Christ, every minute circumstance, every act, every word, every look, every feature, every trait, every lineament, emits an odor produced by an equal proportion – "a like weight" of all the divine graces that compose His character. The smaller the perfume was beaten, the more its rare and exquisite temper was manifested.[2]

All the ingredients for the Lord's perfume had to be beaten "very small," meaning that they must be pulverized into a powder (v. 36). Spices release their maximum fragrance when crushed in this manner.

The fact that the spices of the perfume were beaten *very small* reminds us of the way that the Lord Jesus was morally tested through Calvary's fires of adversity where He endured the contradiction of sinners and the wrath of God. Yet these circumstances served only to manifest the sweet aroma of His perfections.

The fragrance of the Lord's character that was released during His sojourn on earth could not be mimicked or produced by anyone else. The outward battering of His person only further revealed the inward quality of His divine character. For this reason, the Israelites were not to try to create the perfume for themselves (v. 37). In fact, no one was even to breathe in its aroma – to do so would cause that individual to be cut off from the covenant blessings of the nation (v. 38).

Its specific ingredients and its restricted use all point to the precious nature of the perfume to God; thus, it was to have its place before Him in the Most Holy Place of the tabernacle (v. 36). The phrase *"before the testimony in the tabernacle"* is understood to refer to the Golden Altar (Ex. 40:5), but perhaps some of this *"most holy"* perfume was also placed in a golden vessel directly in the Most Holy Place. If this was the case, the perfume would have been a special memorial in the same way that the golden pot of manna and Aaron's rod were memorials to be put *"before the testimony."*

In any case, the incense was God's alone, and only God can fully appreciate the deep mystery of godliness pertaining to the Lord Jesus: *"Without controversy great is the mystery of godliness: God was manifested in the flesh, justified in the Spirit, seen by angels, preached among the Gentiles, believed on in the world, received up in glory"* (1 Tim. 3:16). There, in the utter privacy of the tabernacle, a mere two hundred twenty-five square feet of holy ground upon a minute planet within a vast universe, God the Father would breath in that sweet reminder of His Son, the love of His heart, and would be refreshed in a way that no human can fully understand. Yet, when we labor in His Word, through the illumination of His Spirit, God permits us to breathe in that sweet portion which is now ours.

> My Lord has garments so wondrous fine, and myrrh their texture fills;
> Its fragrance reached to this heart of mine with joy my being thrills.

His life had also its sorrows sore, for aloes had a part;
And when I think of the cross He bore, my eyes with teardrops start.

His garments too were in cassia dipped, with healing in a touch;
Each time my feet in some sin have slipped, He took me from its clutch.

In garments glorious He will come to open wide the door;
And I shall enter my heavenly home, to dwell forevermore.

— Henry Barraclough

# Spirit-filled Craftsmen
## Exodus 31:1-11

It is quite fitting that the discussion of Spirit-filled craftsmen directly follows the narrative that defines who may worship the Lord. In Exodus 30, we witnessed that the redeemed, cleansed, and anointed would be permitted to worship Jehovah (though only the Aaronic priests would be able to officiate worship on behalf of the people). Exodus 30 pictures completed acts of the Holy Spirit upon a repentant sinner at his or her conversion, while Exodus 31 portrays the Holy Spirit working within the believer to control his or her service to the Lord as a believer-priest. As Edward Dennett notes, it is God alone who chooses who will serve Him and how they serve Him, for without His enabling power nothing could be accomplished for Him.

> We learn then from this scripture two things. First, that God alone can designate His servants for their work; and secondly, that He alone can qualify them for the service to which they are called. Both these points deserve special attention. It will be remarked that both Bezaleel and Aholiab are divinely named. They were distinguished by name, and called. This principle runs through all dispensations. … This is a point of great moment; for it were worse than presumption to intrude into the things of God uncalled and unsent. It is true that God does not call His servants by name in this dispensation — at least since the days of the apostle Paul; but every servant should look to be divinely certified as to his work, to be undoubtingly assured that he is doing, whatever he may be engaged in, the divine will. Such a conviction is the source both of confidence and courage. … The essence of all service, indeed, lies in obedience; for if I am not doing God's will it is not service. The Lord Himself characterizes the whole of His life of service as obedience: *"I came down from heaven,"* He says, *"not to do Mine own will, but the will of Him that sent Me"* (John 6:38). It should therefore be

> our first concern to ascertain whether we have been sent by the Lord, whether we have been called to our work and service, like Bezaleel and Aholiab; and if we are found sitting at the feet of the Lord, His mind in this respect will soon be revealed.
>
> But the second thing is, that called by name they were filled with the Spirit of God, and made dependent on the Lord for wisdom and understanding, to execute the work entrusted to their care. Man's wisdom is of no avail in the service of God. ...We must begin by refusing everything that will not stand the divine test, and then we must seek, in spite of our weakness and confusion, to order everything according to the mind and will of God.[1]

The Exodus 31 text indicates that God planned how Bezaleel and Aholiab were to serve Him – they were called to create the furnishings of the tabernacle and a task they willing performed to honor God. If you are a child of God, He also has a plan for your life; in fact, He has already called you to it, though you may not yet be aware of His call and purpose. Generally speaking, our idea of "the call of God" does not correspond fully to the grammar of the Greek New Testament. It is not God's ongoing call that is the main focus of Scripture, but rather, it is the fulfillment of what He has already called us to be which is paramount.

The Greek grammar of the New Testament Epistles provides some clues to understanding the mysterious nature of God's call. Observations include:

1. The word "calling" is typically rendered from *kelsis* (a noun); the verb form is never used to speak of an active calling of God.
2. The "called" of God either refers to the *keltos* (a noun associated with those called or appointed of God for something) or *kaleo* (a verb speaking of that which God has determined to be). *Kaleo* is usually in the aorist indicative, meaning God has already called. Thus, His initial call is immutable and is affirmed in time.
3. The word "calls" occurs only four times in the epistles (Rom. 4:17, 9:11; Gal. 5:7-8; 1 Thess. 5:23-24) and relates to the believer's calling in Christ. In these instances, *kaleo* is an active verbal adjective. The rarity of an *active* divine calling seems to highlight the significances of God's sovereign purpose in time as determined by His foreknowledge.

In summary, the usage of *kaleo*, *keltos*, and *kelsis* shows the incomprehensible and timeless union of God's sovereign design and His foreknowledge in relationship with the outworking of human responsibility. Paul acknowledged the timeless aspect of God's calling by saying, *"God ...calls those things which do not exist as though they did"* (Rom. 4:17), and *"He who calls you is faithful, who also will do it"* (1 Thess. 5:24). Time does not constrain God's actions, but He does unfold His sovereign plan in time. What He has "called" is based on His foreknowledge and predetermined counsel.

Before creation, God previewed the corridors of time, considered all the possible permutations of natural cause and effect as well as the future choices of cognitive beings, and made sovereign choices to bless humanity and glorify His name throughout time and eternity. Only a triune God existed when the plan of redemption was devised, therefore, the plan is solely His – it originated in His mind and He deserves all the glory for it. God's choices ensure, in the end, that humanity will receive the greatest possible blessing and He will obtain the greatest glory.

The apostles wrote of God's timeless call and our responsibility to obey it. Here are some examples:

**Paul writes:**

The divine call: *"For we are His workmanship, created in Christ Jesus for good works, which God prepared beforehand that we should walk in them"* (Eph. 2:10).

Human responsibility to answer the call: *"I, therefore, the prisoner of the Lord, beseech you to walk worthy of the calling with which you were called"* (Eph 4:1).

**Peter writes:**

The divine call: *"Elect according to the foreknowledge of God the Father"* (1 Pet. 1:2).

Human responsibility to answer the call: *"Therefore, brethren, be even more diligent to make your call and election sure, for if you do these things you will never stumble"* (2 Pet. 1:10).

**John writes:**

The divine call: *"I have set before you an open door, and no one can shut it"* (Rev. 3:9).

Human responsibility to answer the call: *"Hold fast what you have, that no one may take your crown"* (Rev. 3:11).

These seemingly contradictory aspects of God's call intentionally create a dichotomy in the human brain. Incomplete answers to our inadequate questions do not satisfy our searching minds, but these perplexing aspects of God's calling do inspire awe of God and humility before Him. There are some matters that man is not expected to understand; in these abstruse areas, being dumbfounded is the expected and God-honoring outcome (Deut. 29:29). Logically speaking, a time-dependent being cannot fully understand time-independent truth – the tie between creation order and the ultimate eternal order of things rests solely in God's resolve to complete His predetermined counsel.

Concerning our divine calling, one cannot read Scripture without marveling at God's wisdom and design, yet each of God's calls must be personally obeyed. In a manner that we cannot fully understand, human responsibility and sovereign design are intimately connected in God's plan for our lives. Such a realization is proof that we cannot obtain divinity, nor should we seek to. Unfortunately, the systemization of Scripture in these perplexing matters has caused some Christians to overstate what Scripture actually teaches, others to superficially accept God's Word, and many more to just ignore the matter of God's calling altogether. The best response is to state what Scripture says and leave the unrevealed details with the Lord.

Man has no choice in being a part of God's plan, but as a moral and a conscious being, he has every choice in how he will answer God's call and be used within God's unfolding design. Whether or not we yield to His call, God will be glorified through our choices; He will use us either as vessels of mercy prepared for glory, or as vessels of wrath fit for destruction (Rom. 9:14-23). God prepares yielded vessels for glory and rebellious vessels to receive His wrath.

For example, God did not force Pharaoh to worship Egyptian gods, but on certain occasions He did intervene to harden Pharaoh's heart to accomplish the release of His people from Egypt. The fact that Pharaoh hardened his own heart afterwards demonstrates that he still had a free choice in the matter. God would have been perfectly just to destroy a pagan like Pharaoh, but instead He designed ten specific plagues to prove to Pharaoh that He was superior to a number of specific Egyptian gods. Pharaoh rejected this revelation and hardened his own heart against the Lord – he prepared himself to be a vessel of wrath fit for destruction. Yet, in honoring Pharaoh's decision, God brought glory to His name, which was a foreknown conclusion of Pharaoh's decision. This example shows how human responsibility and sovereign design ensure that God receives all the glory in every situation.

Is God calling you? Absolutely. His personal call for you was initiated long before your conception; in fact, God was mindful of you before the foundations of the world were laid. While commissioning young Jeremiah as a prophet, God said, *"Before I formed you in the womb I knew you; Before you were born I sanctified you; I ordained you a prophet to the nations"* (Jer. 1:5). Jeremiah, after hearing these words, asserted that he was too young to fulfill God's calling for his life. But after further divine encouragement, Jeremiah chose to obey God's call and became an emboldened mouthpiece for God during one of the most distressing eras of Jewish history. And, in the autumn years of his life, he penned the second longest book in the Bible.

The profound nature of God's call for each life demands our utmost reverence and respect as we seek to know and obey His will. His ways are above our ways. His thoughts are above our thoughts. The ultimate experience in life is to know God and to serve Him in the way He has deemed best. Only then does the spirit of man find what it longs for – joyful fellowship with God.

In the harvest field now ripened there's a work for all to do;
Hark! The voice of God is calling, to the harvest calling you.
Does the place you're called to labor seem too small and little known?
It is great if God is in it, and He'll not forget His own.
Are you laid aside from service, body worn from toil and care?
You can still be in the battle, in the sacred place of prayer.
Little is much when God is in it! Labor not for wealth or fame.
There's a crown—and you can win it, if you go in Jesus' Name.

— Kittie L. Suffield

# A Sign from God
## Exodus 31:12-18

God gave three signs to the Jews which marked them as a distinct, peculiar people among humanity. The first sign was male circumcision, which from the days of Abraham, physically marked them as God's covenant people (Gen. 17:9-14). The Passover feast was the second sign; it was given to the Jews as a memorial celebration of their redemption (Ex. 12:13). The third sign was the Sabbath day, which God originally sanctified at the end of the creation week (Gen. 2:1-3), but now confirmed to Moses as a distinct ordinance for the Jews to obey: *"Speak also to the children of Israel, saying: 'Surely My Sabbaths you shall keep, for it is a sign between Me and you throughout your generations, that you may know that I am the Lord who sanctifies you"* (Ex. 31:13). The Sabbath would serve as a constant reminder that they were a sanctified people.

The Jews were given (and commanded to keep) these three specific signs as tokens of God's love for them. The repetitive nature of the three signs would work conjunctly to remind them that they were a special people to God. They were Jehovah's covenant people who had been redeemed by blood and had been set apart to be a testimony of His glory on earth. Those who did not adhere to male circumcision or participate in the Passover feast were to be cut off from God's commonwealth blessings to the nation (Gen. 17:14; Ex. 12:14, 19). The penalty for failing to keep the Sabbath Day holy was even more severe: *"You shall keep the Sabbath, therefore, for it is holy to you. Everyone who profanes it shall surely be put to death; for whoever does any work on it, that person shall be cut off from among his people"* (Ex. 31:14). God considered each of these signs important and the punishment for ignoring them was severe.

These three signs relate only to the nation of Israel. Even though many Christians continue to circumcise their male children during the

Church Age, it is water baptism that marks those who have trusted Christ for salvation (Matt. 28:19-20). The one-time act of water baptism publicly identifies a believer as a Christian, just as the one time act of physical circumcision identified a Jewish male for life. Also, though some Christians still celebrate the yearly Pascal (Passover) Feast (inappropriately called *Easter*), this was never commanded of them by the Lord. Rather, He asked Christians to remember him by frequently keeping of the Lord's Supper. The Lord's Supper reminds Christians of their redemption (Luke 22:19-20), just as the Passover Feast reminded the Jewish people of their redemption out of Egypt. The Sabbath Day was never to be a holy day observed by Christians. Instead, the Church set aside Sunday, Resurrection Day, as the Lord's Day: a time of worship and service to God (Acts 20:7; Rev. 1:10). C. H. Mackintosh compares the various distinctions between the Sabbath of the Old Covenant and the Lord's Day of the New Covenant:

> There is a great deal more involved in the distinction between "the Sabbath" and "the Lord's Day" than many Christians seem to be aware of. It is very evident that the first day of the week gets a place, in the Word of God, which no other day gets. No other day is ever called by that majestic and elevated title, "the Lord's day." ... The believer is delivered, most completely, from the observance of "days and months, and times and years." Association with a risen Christ has taken him clean out of all such superstitious observances. But, while this is most blessedly true, we see that "the first day of the week" has a place assigned to it in the New Testament which no other has. Let the Christian give it that place. It is a sweet and happy privilege, not a grievous yoke. ... I shall close ... by pointing out, in one or two particulars, the contrast between "the Sabbath" and "the Lord's Day."
>
> 1. The Sabbath was the *seventh* day; the Lord's Day is the *first*.
> 2. The Sabbath was a *test* of Israel's condition; the Lord's Day is the *proof* of the Church's acceptance, on wholly unconditional grounds.
> 3. The Sabbath belonged to the old creation; the Lord's Day belongs to the new.
> 4. The Sabbath was a day of *bodily* rest for the Jew; the Lord's Day is a day of *spiritual* rest for the Christian.
> 5. If the Jew worked on the Sabbath, he was to be put to *death*: if the Christian does not work on the Lord's Day, he gives little

proof of *life*. That is to say, if he does not work for the benefit of the souls of men, the extension of Christ's glory, and the spread of His truth. In point of fact, the devoted Christian, who possesses any gift, is generally more fatigued on the evening of the Lord's Day than on any other in the week, for how can he rest while souls are perishing around him?

6. The Jew was *commanded* by the *law* to abide in his tent; the Christian is *led* by the spirit of the *gospel* to go forth, whether it be to attend the public assembly, or to minister to the souls of perishing sinners. The Lord enable us, beloved reader, to rest more artlessly *in*, and labor more vigorously *for*, the name of the Lord Jesus Christ! We should *rest* in the spirit of a *child*; and *labor* with the energy of a *man*.[1]

The three signs given to the Jews to mark them as God's covenant people have been replaced by three new signs for the Christians during the Church Age. Baptism replaces circumcision as a sign of the New Covenant. The Lord's Supper replaces the Passover Feast as a memorial of the believer's redemption. The Lord's Day (Sunday) replaces the Sabbath (Saturday), as a day to worship and serve God. Each sign distinctly marks the Church as a "called out company" of people upon the earth. May the Church do what the nation of Israel failed to do and be a godly people who testify of the Lord's goodness.

To be a "Christ-one" and to be a part of Christ's "called out company" is a great privilege and a high honor. May every believer understand that his or her identity in Christ conveys the strictest charge to honor Him in word and in deed. If you are a Christian, why not surround yourself with daily reminders of your eternal calling in Christ. For example you could wear clothing that displays scriptural messages and decorate the walls of your home with Scripture texts. These will be helpful reminders of the sanctified life that we ought to live.

Everyone who comes in contact with you should become aware of your association with Christ. Your modesty, humility, speech, and genuine concern for others should testify of your intimate relationship with Jesus Christ. For example, the Pharisees understood by the bold and wise behavior of the disciples *"that they had been with Jesus"* (Acts. 4:13). Believers are called to bring Christ into every situation of life – not to do so is to neglect His Lordship.

Again the Lord's own day is here, the day to Christian people dear.
As week by week, it bids them tell how Jesus rose from death and hell.

For by His flock their Lord declared His resurrection should be shared;
And we who trust in Him to save with Him are risen from the grave.

And therefore unto Thee we sing, O Lord of peace, eternal King;
Thy love we praise, Thy Name adore, both on this day and evermore.

— Thomas a` Kempis

# God's Anger Burns Hot
## Exodus 32:1-10

Moses had been in the Lord's presence for forty days. In Scripture, *forty* is the number of *probation* and *testing*. For example, the Israelites were tested forty years in the wilderness, Jonah preached of coming judgment forty days to the city of Nineveh, and the Lord Jesus was tested forty days in the wilderness after His baptism. Moses' stay on Mount Sinai provided an opportunity to test the Israelites - would they obey God's Law?

As Moses lingered on the mountain the Israelites grew restless; they feared that something had happened to Moses and that they were now without a leader. They murmured: *"as for this Moses, the man who brought us up out of the land of Egypt, we do not know what has become of him"* (v. 1). The people turned to Aaron for leadership and requested that he provide visible gods for them to follow. Aaron fashioned a golden calf and presented it to the people, who then declared to one another, *"This is your god, O Israel, that brought you out of the land of Egypt!"*

Though the word "gods" is mentioned twice in this chapter (five times in the KJV), it is not likely that the people were asking to replace Jehovah with other gods, for surely Aaron would not consent to that. Rather, they wanted an image of Him to worship. The Hebrew word *elohim* rendered "god" in verse 4 and "gods" in the KJV can have a plural or plural intensive meaning as based on context. *Elohim* may mean gods, something god-like, or speak of the one true God (who has a triune nature).

The Jews already knew the one true God and His name – Jehovah. It is not likely that they were rejecting the existence of Jehovah, but rather incorporating Him into an Egyptianized form of worship. Thus, Aaron makes *"a feast to Jehovah"* (v. 5) the following morning. On this point, William MacDonald summarizes: "They [the Israelites] professed to be worshipping the Lord (v. 5) by means of a calf."[1]

God's pattern for the tabernacle and His order of worship had not yet been delivered to the people, for Moses was still receiving it on the mount; however, the people did know that creating images to worship was against the second of the Ten Commandments. Despite this, Aaron, unaware of Moses' well-being, succumbed to the demand of the people and agreed to form an image for them to worship. Aaron chose to create the image of a calf for the people. He requested the gold earrings which they had acquired the day they departed from Egypt, and the people readily provided Aaron the materials to create a golden calf.

The following day, Aaron built an altar, proclaimed a festival, and presented burnt offerings to Jehovah (as likely represented in the golden calf). *Apis,* the bull-god of Egypt, was not worshipped as an image, so the golden calf could not have represented him; rather, it was Aaron's concept of Jehovah. However, *Apis* represented fertility and strength, and based on the people's lewd behavior the following day, the pagan attributes of *Apis* were still reflected in the golden calf. Singing and dancing soon led to revelry and lascivious behavior (vv. 18-19). The Israelites joyfully violated several of the Ten Commandments which they had agreed to obey just days earlier.

God was fully aware of what the people were doing below; in fact He told Moses what they had done (v. 8), and how they had corrupted themselves (v. 7). He then characterized them as a stiff-necked people (v. 9). God's anger burned hot towards the Israelites because of their offenses. Consequently, He informed Moses that He would wipe them out in judgment and make a new nation unto Himself through Moses. Jehovah told Moses: *"I will make you into a great nation"* (v. 10). Of course, this was not Jehovah's plan, but the statement was necessary to arouse Moses to offer intercession for the people in order to avert God's threatening judgment upon the Israelites.

God was very angry with His people, and rightly so, they had broken their covenant with Him. Obviously, sin angers God, but it may be observed that Scripture does not mention God's anger at the rebellion of Lucifer or at the fall of man. We know that God is unchanging in every aspect of His essence and character (Mal. 3:6). He, therefore, had the capacity to be angry before He created anything, but there would have been no reason for His anger to exist. Adam was fashioned in the "likeness" of God (Gen. 1:26) and, thus, had the inherent capacity to experience anger immediately after God breathed life into his inert form. While man was in Eden, anger was dormant, unneeded and unwelcome.

Man had been created in God's image to visibly represent God's authority over His creation; thus, he was God's crown to creation (Heb. 2:7-8). As long as upright and innocent man maintained a pure testimony of God's authority in creation, a state of felicity existed in Eden for there was nothing present to provoke anger. We may conclude, therefore, that righteousness or unrighteousness anger manifests itself as a result of sin. Sin provokes anger and, if it is not rightly managed, anger incites more sin – it is a vicious cycle that ensures much suffering and pain. However, since God can become angry there must be a proper way for anger to be used. This can only be understood by examining what God has revealed in Scripture regarding His own anger.

The Lord's anger is always perfect and in agreement with His divine character. God is not motivated to action by one particular emotion in such a way that any part of His perfect character is compromised. Love, grace, mercy, justice, righteousness, long-suffering, purity, etc. are always satisfied in every divine action. This is why Paul speaks of the *"fruit of the Spirit"* in Galatians 5:22-23 and not the "fruits of the Spirit." All God's character is homogeneous and reflects His holiness.

Yes, God is a God of love (1 Jn. 4:8), but He could not justly save mankind by love alone – His sense of justice demanded that sin had to be judged. Yet, it was God's love which supplied the solution by which mankind could be saved: *"But God demonstrates His own love toward us, in that while we were still sinners, Christ died for us. Much more then, having now been justified by His blood, we shall be saved from wrath through Him"* (Rom. 5:8-9). Thus, God's love found a way to righteously offer salvation by judging His Son for human sin. He can legally offer the gift of eternal salvation to *"whosoever will"* (John 3:16). Those who reject His gracious offer will spend an eternity in the lake of fire, *"for the wages of sin is death"* (Rom. 6:23). "The eternity of punishment is a thought which crushes the heart," said Charles Spurgeon, "The Lord God is slow to anger, but when He is once aroused to it, as He will be against those who finally reject His Son, He will put forth all His omnipotence to crush His enemies."[2]

God so loved us that He sacrificed His own Son that we might be saved by Him from wrath and be conformed to His moral image – God wants the redeemed to be like His Son. Perhaps the reader has heard the parental instruction as a child, "Do what I say, not what I do." Our heavenly Father can truly charge us to "Do what I say and do what I do." In Him the two are perfectly consistent. God longs for His children to be like Himself in thought and deed (Rom. 8:29). *"Be ye holy; for I am holy"* (1 Pet. 1:16; KJV).

How is it possible to morally behave as God does? Paul informs us how: *"But we all, with unveiled face, beholding as in a mirror the glory of the Lord, are being transformed into the same image from glory to glory, just as by the Spirit of the Lord"* (2 Cor. 3:18). We can keep our faces unveiled before God by confessing and forsaking sin. We gain a greater understanding of righteousness as we behold the mirror, the Word of God (Jas. 1:23-25), and see ourselves in contrast to God's holiness. By yielding to divine truth, the believer is transformed into deeper shades of Christ-likeness.

Occupation with the splendor and glory of Christ and submission to the control of the Holy Spirit will truly usher holy living into our lives. H.A. Ironside explains this concept in his book, *Holiness – The False and the True*:

> I have been learning all along my pilgrim journey that the more my heart is taken up with Christ, the more do I enjoy practical deliverance from sin's power, and the more do I realize what it is to have the love of God shed abroad in that heart by the Holy Spirit given to me, as the earnest of the glory to come.[3]

Learning to behave in different situations as Christ would is especially important when we experience anger. Believers must learn the characteristics of God's anger and pray for grace to conform the outworking of our anger to His. Living a Christ-centered and disciplined life will reduce the number of occasions in which we inappropriately or unnecessarily feel angry. When we are in close fellowship with the Lord, the power of the Holy Spirit will effectively control and mold our anger so that we behave in a God-like way. A brief review of the characteristics of God's anger is necessary in order to learn the right pattern to follow.

Firstly, God is slow to anger: *"The Lord is gracious and full of compassion, slow to anger and great in mercy"* (Ps. 145:8). God is slow to anger and we should be as well. The fact that God's anger is not quickly kindled does not mean He is negligent to act. His slowness to anger ensures a deliberate response at the appropriate time. By His own character, God demonstrates that anger is to be a secondary emotion, not a primary one. If anger were a primary emotion, it would rule our lives with a heavy hand. Anger is not to be a quickly-triggered emotion that abruptly enters and exits our daily routine. God desires that we have a long-suffering attitude, which allows anger to deliver a calculated response at the most advantageous time (Prov. 14:17; Tit. 1:7; Prov. 16:32).

Secondly, God is provoked to anger. Moses foretold how the future idolatry of the Israelites would provoke God to anger: *"When you beget children and grandchildren and have grown old in the land, and act corruptly and make a carved image in the form of anything, and do evil in the sight of the Lord your God to provoke Him to anger"* (Deut. 4:25). The Lord is not a furious God, but He can be provoked to anger. Likewise, we should not be an angry people, but rather be provoked to anger by some appalling event in order to equip the body to act in extraordinary way to face the challenge. Anger heightens the body's physical capability to respond in a way it would not normally be able. Obviously we don't want to act in a powerful manner in all situations, but rather for only those righteous causes for which it is appropriate for us to respond and with appropriate force. The Lord Jesus warned that, *"Whoever is angry with his brother* ***without a cause*** *shall be in danger of the judgment"* (Matt. 5:22). When we first sense a surge of anger, we should ask ourselves if we have a righteous cause for being angry. If we act in anger when the situation does not call for such measures, we have been wrongly provoked to anger (Eph. 4:26-27).

Thirdly, God's anger is kindled. For example, *"So the anger of the Lord was kindled against Moses, and He said: 'Is not Aaron the Levite your brother? I know that he can speak well. And look, he is also coming out to meet you'"* (Ex. 4:14). The Hebrew word translated as "kindled" in this verse is *charah* (khaw-raw'), which means "to grow warm." It is normally applied in a figurative sense, "to blaze up." The word describes the ignition of combustible materials and the nursing of the initial spark into the desired conflagration. God is not only slow to become angry, but even when provoked He takes time to fully develop His anger before rendering any action. His anger requires sufficient kindling before flaming vengeance is invoked. As the writer of Hebrews reminds us, *"our God is a consuming fire"* (Heb. 12:29; KJV) when His anger is provoked and fully kindled. Both a righteous provocation and a period of development are necessary before acting in anger.

Fourthly, God's anger does not endure: *"He will not always strive with us, nor will He keep His anger forever"* (Ps. 103:9). If anger does not have an immediate God-honoring purpose, it is to be released (i.e. dismissed without action). This is a fundamental rule of anger management – anger must have a **present righteous purpose,** or it must be dismissed until such a time as it can immediately and righteously serve God. Once righteous anger has served its purpose, it also must be relinquished. Anger is too strong an emotion to contain or control for a long period of time. If we hold on to it, we will eventually serve the flesh, and in so doing, we sin against God (Ps. 37:7-8; Eccl. 7:9).

Fifthly, God's anger prompts His secondary work: *"For the Lord will rise up as at Mount Perazim, He will be angry as in the Valley of Gibeon – that He may do His work, His awesome work, and bring to pass His act, His unusual act"* (Isa. 28:21). Isaiah calls our attention to the fact that God's anger and subsequent wrath are not part of His primary work. God's anger, leading to judgment and destruction, is a necessary aspect of God's sovereignty, but His normative work arises from His gracious loving nature. Although Scripture frequently speaks of God's wrath and anger, it is His actions of mercy, love, and grace which are His normal, usual work. It is not that righteous wrath is less noble than divine love, for each necessitates the other. J. Oswald Sanders explains:

> It was Jesus' love for the man with the withered hand that aroused His anger against those who would deny him healing. It was His love for His Father, and zeal for His glory, that kindled His anger against the mercenary traders who had turned His house of prayer for all nations into a cave of robbers (Mt. 21:13, Jn. 2:15-17).[4]

Warren Wiersbe concisely contrasts God's righteous anger with our natural propensity to sin when angry:

> In the Garden, Peter was slow to hear, swift to speak, and swift to anger – and he almost killed a man with the sword. Many church fights are the result of short tempers and hasty words. There is a godly anger against sin (Eph. 4:26); and if we love the Lord, we must hate sin (Ps. 97:10). But man's anger does not produce God's righteousness (Jas. 1:20). In fact, anger is just the opposite of the patience God wants to produce in our lives as we mature in Christ (Jas. 1:3-4).[5]

May the Lord give each one of us grace and wisdom to use anger to glorify Him and to edify others. If anger does not have a present righteous purpose it must be extinguished or it will lead to sin – it is too powerful an emotion to control for long. Secondly, as we learn to immediately release offenses to the Lord we will ensure a better opportunity to think objectively and to use our anger to serve others and glorify God. No child of God should ever be given over to rage or resentment; these are unbiblical, ungodly recourses of mismanaged anger.

Jesus, my Saviour, let me be more perfectly conformed to Thee;
Implant each grace, each sin dethrone, and form my temper like Thine own.
To others let me always give what I from others would receive;
Good deeds for evil ones return, nor when provoked, with anger burn.

— Benjamin Beddome

# Moses the Intercessor
## Exodus 32:11-14

Besides the intercession of the Lord Jesus there are at least two other marvelous examples in Scripture of a mediator standing in the gap between a holy God and rebellious sinners. In Genesis 18, we observe Abraham interceding for Sodom; in Exodus 32, we find Moses engaged in the same ministry for the Israelites. A brief review of the past and present intercessory work of the Lord Jesus will better enable us to understand what important work Moses accomplished by being a mediator for the nation of Israel.

One of the present ministries of Christ in heaven is to be our legal representative or advocate before the Father (1 Jn. 2:1). This is a special comfort for all believers, especially knowing that Satan slanders us before God's throne day and night (Rev. 12:10). Although the English word "advocate" is translated only once from the Greek New Testament, the same Greek word *parakletos* is often rendered "comforter," as in the references to the Holy Spirit in the Gospel of John. The role of an advocate or a comforter is to plead the case of another person in a court of law – to be a legal intercessor. As pertaining to Christ, *Thayer's Greek Dictionary* defines the meaning of *parakletos* as "Christ's pleading for pardon of our sins before the Father." When does Christ plead our case? Is it when we acknowledge and confess our sins? No, 1 John 2:1 affirms that Christ's advocacy occurs *if* we sin, not *when* we confess our sins, even though we certainly should confess them. In other words, Christ is our Advocate at all times, not just when the believer fails. It is our Advocate's presence in heaven and not His plea per se that provides every believer with assurance of their positional standing before God. S. Emery further explains the Lord's ministry of advocacy for believers when they do sin:

> His valid ministry, therefore, on our behalf, is not on the basis of an effective, verbal and persuasive pleading before the Father, but on the basis of a perfect satisfaction for all our sins ever before the Father's face. He is our propitiation of undiminishing value. ... His very presence before the Father is the plea. Continuance in the family of God is never in question, but forgiveness of our sins, and cleansing from all unrighteousness, is experienced only when we make confession (1 Jn. 1:9).[1]

James Gunn further explains why the Lord Jesus can righteously plead for every child of God to be judicially acquitted for the sins he or she commits.

> Christ is not a mere suppliant petitioner. He pleads for us on the grounds of justice, of righteousness, of obedience to the law, and endurance of its full penalty for us, on which He grounds His claim for our acquittal. The sense therefore is, "in that He is righteous."[2]

When a believer sins, Satan may abruptly call God's attention to the despicable deed. However, Christ being at the right hand of His Father (Heb. 1:3), is able to promptly proclaim that the penalty of the unrighteous act, though offensive to God, has already been paid for at Calvary. In this way, all heavenly hosts, powers, and principalities will see that God is righteous and that He has justly accounted for every wrong the believer commits. God hates sin, but because He judged Christ for it, He can extend the repentant sinner a full pardon and family status as His adopted child (Rom. 8:15). Though the believer does not need to worry about God's judicial wrath, he or she should pursue holy living to stay in fellowship with God and to avoid provoking His chastening hand. Our souls have been liberated through the work of Christ to serve God out of love, not out of the fear of judgment, for the judgment of our sins has been accomplished and true love does not fear (1 Jn. 4:18).

Understanding that our accuser constantly levies charges against us and that our faithful Advocate continually defends us should prompt the believer to keep "short accounts" with God. As soon as one is conscious of sin, the sin should be confessed to God as wrong, and all reveling in it should cease. Bible commentator J. V. McGee tells the following story to illustrate this point. The great preacher, C. H. Spurgeon, was once walking across a dangerously busy street with another Christian man. Spurgeon stopped in the middle of the street, bowed his head momentarily, and then proceeded to walk across the street without saying a word. The man reproved him for stopping, exclaiming, "You could have been run down by a carriage! What were you doing? It looked like you were praying." Spurgeon replied, "I was praying." The man asked, "Was it so important?" "Indeed it was," Spurgeon answered, "a cloud came between me and my Saviour, and I wanted to remove it before I got across the street."[3] God desires that His children do not sin (1 Jn. 2:1). But when we do sin, *"If we confess our sins, He is faithful and just to forgive us our sins, and to cleanse us from all unrighteousness"* (1 Jn. 1:9). May every child of God stay in active fellowship with God Father by living righteously and confessing sin the moment he or she stumbles.

In Exodus 32, Moses stood in the gap for sinful Israel. They were dancing naked around an idol, and God was ready to destroy them and to make a nation out of Moses. But Moses interceded, and the King James Version of the Bible reads that *"The Lord repented of the evil which He thought to do unto His people"* (Ex. 32:14). Whose "will" was accomplished that day – Moses' or God's? It is suggested that both Moses and God received what each desired; certainly God's will was fully achieved that day. God did not change His mind in the way He planned to punish Israel, but rather, it was the will of God for Moses to intercede for His wayward people so that He could extend them mercy. God longs for a person with a righteous standing to stand in the gap between Himself and the unrighteous in order to plead for grace and mercy on their behalf. God really did not change His mind, but from man's perspective, it seemed as though He did. Both the declaration of God's anger over sin and the punishment deserved by the offenders were stated before Moses was given the opportunity to make intercession. Contemplate for a moment the matter from Moses' perspective as he, years later, recalls that dark day as he warns a new generation of Israelites of God's holiness:

> *And I fell down before the Lord, as at the first, forty days and forty nights; I neither ate bread nor drank water, because of all your sin which you committed in doing wickedly in the sight of the Lord, to provoke Him to anger. For I was afraid of the anger and hot*

> *displeasure with which the Lord was angry with you, to destroy you. But the Lord listened to me at that time also. And the Lord was very angry with Aaron and would have destroyed him; so I prayed for Aaron also at the same time. Then I took your sin, the calf which you had made, and burned it with fire and crushed it and ground it very small, until it was as fine as dust; and I threw its dust into the brook that descended from the mountain. ...*
>
> *Thus I prostrated myself before the Lord; forty days and forty nights I kept prostrating myself, because the Lord had said He would destroy you. Therefore I prayed to the Lord, and said: "O Lord God, do not destroy Your people and Your inheritance whom You have redeemed through Your greatness, whom You have brought out of Egypt with a mighty hand. Remember Your servants, Abraham, Isaac, and Jacob; do not look on the stubbornness of this people, or on their wickedness or their sin, lest the land from which You brought us should say, 'Because the Lord was not able to bring them to the land which He promised them, and because He hated them, He has brought them out to kill them in the wilderness.' Yet they are Your people and Your inheritance, whom You brought out by Your mighty power and by Your outstretched arm"* (Deut. 9:18-29).

Intercession for those in sin is hard work; Moses prostrated himself for forty days before the Lord while pleading for mercy for the Israelites. He called God's attention to His promises to the patriarchs and to how He would be ill-perceived by the local pagans if He destroyed His people in the wilderness. God's intention all along was to show mercy, but a holy God cannot wink at sin; it must be identified and punished. The Israelites did receive Jehovah's forgiveness, but their sin cost them dearly – thousands of Israelites died by the sword and by pestilence. Two facts are apparent from God's dealings with the Israelites in the aftermath of their sin. First, anytime an individual chooses to sin, he or she chooses to suffer. Second, those who choose to sin, soon learn that God alone chooses the consequences of his or her sin. Sin's consequences are generally tempered with mercy, but on some occasions, God does not grant the rebel any more opportunities to repent. For example, in the case of Moses' defiant uncle Korah, the ground opened up and swallowed him and his family alive (Num. 16).

That event effectively ended Korah's rebellion – God's patience had run out and His judgment was swift, complete, and final.

God is long-suffering and slow to judge, and He desires that someone plead the case of the guilty so that He may show mercy upon them. Isaiah 59:16 reads, *"And He* [God] *saw that there was no man, and wondered that there was no intercessor; therefore, His arm brought salvation unto Him, and His righteousness, it sustained Him."* When it came to ultimately finding someone to stand in the gap for all mankind, there was no one who could righteously plead man's case. Therefore, God sent His own Arm (His Son) to mediate for us. The mediator had to be God Himself in order to be the perfect sacrifice and to be able to sustain the judgment of a holy God for all man's sin. The Lord Jesus was that mediator and successfully pleaded our case by His own blood. At present, the Lord Jesus is our heavenly Advocate who continues to intercede at the throne of grace for every straying believer.

Almighty God, whose only Son over sin and death the triumph won,
And ever lives to intercede for souls who of God's sweet mercy need;

In His dear Name to Thee we pray for all who err and go astray,
For sinners, wheresoever they be who do not serve and honor Thee.

And many a quickened soul within there lurks the secret love of sin,
A wayward will, or anxious fears or lingering taint of bygone years.

O give repentance true and deep to all Thy lost and wandering sheep,
And kindle in their hearts the fire of holy love and pure desire.

— Samuel Webbe, Sr.

# God Judges Sin
## Exodus 32:15-29

In receiving the Law, Moses had been alone with God for forty days on the mount. Below Mount Sinai, the children of Israel had become anxious about Moses' welfare, and apparently presumed him dead (vv. 1, 23). There was no way to send out a search party for Moses, for only he was allowed to venture into God's presence on the mount. Rather than waiting any longer for information about Moses' wellbeing or instructions on how to properly worship Jehovah, the people coerced Aaron into creating a golden image of Jehovah for them to worship. The One who had brought them out of Egypt was now epitomized as a golden calf. Why would the Jews liken the self-existing God of the universe to an animal, especially since His Law (which they had already agreed to obey) prohibited the creation and worship of images? The event exposes the utterly depraved nature of the human heart; left to himself, man will always turn aside from the path of righteousness and go his own way.

God was furious over the Israelites' offense and instructed Moses to immediately return to camp (vv. 7, 15). Joshua, who had been faithfully waiting part of the way up the mount for Moses' descent, greeted him with these words: *"There is a noise of war in the camp"* (v. 17). Joshua had remained on the lower part of the mountain and was completely separate from the depravity of the Israelites. In fact, he was not even aware of it and suggested to Moses that the camp was under attack. But Moses, who already knew of the Israelites' rank debauchery, clarified Joshua's statement: *"It is not the noise of the shout of victory, nor the noise of the cry of defeat, but the sound of singing I hear"* (v. 18). In Exodus 17, Joshua pictured Christ among His people as he led them to victory over the Amalekites, but now, Joshua is seen apart from the Israelites. Christ cannot have any fellowship with or victorious power among His people while they are in sin – He will not reside with the rebellious.

Moses had instructed all of the seventy elders to wait upon the lower part of the mountain until he returned after his meeting with God (Ex. 24:14). Perhaps some waited for Moses a day or two, perhaps others a week; in any case, only Joshua remained until the coming of Moses. In so doing, Joshua was kept undefiled by the sin of the people below. Likewise, the Lord Jesus, in a general sense, exhorted His disciples to faithfully watch, wait, and be ready for His coming (Matt. 24:42-44). John understood the benefit of living each day as if the Lord could return for the Church at any time: *"Beloved, now we are children of God; and it has not yet been revealed what we shall be, but we know that when He is revealed, we shall be like Him, for we shall see Him as He is. And everyone who has this hope in Him purifies himself, just as He is pure"* (1 Jn. 3:2-3). If Israel's leadership had been expecting fresh revelation from God through Moses, they would have remained on the mount and the opportunity to create a golden calf would have been avoided. Likewise, believers living with the hope of the imminent return of Christ are prompted to live purely before God. They desire to be found undefiled and faithful when they are suddenly brought into the Lord's presence and are examined by Him.

Exodus 32:19 recounts Moses' entrance into the camp: *"So it was, as soon as he came near the camp, that he saw the calf and the dancing. So Moses' anger became hot, and he cast the tablets out of his hands and broke them at the foot of the mountain."* Moses had a good reason to be angry – the children of Israel had committed a grievous sin against the Lord (idolatry). But why did he break the stone tablets upon which the Law of God was written? C. H. Mackintosh responds to this question:

> When we read of "the ark of the covenant," we are led to believe that it was designed of God to **preserve His covenant unbroken**, in the midst of an erring people. In it, as we know, the second set of tables were deposited. As to the first set, they were broken in pieces, beneath the mount, showing that man's covenant was wholly abolished — that his work could never, by any possibility, form the basis of Jehovah's throne of government. … Man might fail to fulfill his self-chosen vow; but God's law must be preserved in its divine integrity and perfect-

> ness. If God was to set up His throne in the midst of His people, He could only do so in a way worthy of Himself. His standard of judgment and government must be perfect.

The children of Israel had broken their covenant with God; if Moses had brought the Law of God into the camp at that moment, swift judgment would have been executed. Therefore, in breaking the tablets, Moses anger served the people in that it presented to them the possibility of repentance and restoration with God, rather than immediate and fierce judgment. No system had yet been established to atone for the sins of the people, and no one can stand against God's justice for sin unless God's grace presents a means of pardon which does not affront His righteous character. This is why the blood of an innocent substitute was required upon the Mercy Seat, which rested upon the Ark of the Covenant. The ark contained the righteous Law of God, which presented the only means of escaping God's judgment. The Mercy Seat was the only place on earth where God's righteousness and His grace cooperated as one for the good of man: for *"it is God who justifies"* and Him alone (Rom. 8:33).

Moses, who as an intercessor had pleaded that his people not be destroyed, now took on the role of judge, executing punishment upon them so that they might be made to feel the bitterness of their sin. He burnt the golden calf, ground it into power, scattered it over the camp's drinking water, and then made the people drink it. This was a humiliating end to their supposed "god" that brought them out of Egypt; however, it was only the beginning of God's disciplinary judgment on His people. Their **relationship** with God was sealed by God's covenant with Abraham, but their **fellowship** with God would depend strictly upon their obedience to His laws.

This distinction in terminology is thoroughly upheld in the New Testament. Believers must understand the difference between relationship and fellowship or they will misunderstand the reason for God's disciplinary judgments. Relationships are established through acts (e.g. marriage, birth, and adoption), but fellowship between these parties is contingent upon proper behavior. For example, the birth of a baby establishes the relationship between the parents and a child forever; but, as he or she matures, fellowship between the parents and their progeny is contingent on appropriate behavior. Because of offenses, there may be times that fellowship does not occur in a relationship, but the opposite can never be true – fellowship cannot exist without relationship.

The same is true in God's family. In the Church Age, one becomes a member of God's family by spiritual birth (John 1:12-13, 3:3; Gal. 4:6), and this relationship is eternally secure. However, God cannot have fellowship with His erring children (1 Jn. 1:6). Instead, He promises to chasten them in order to restore them into communion with Himself; He does this as a proof of His love (Heb. 12:6), and because He knows His children will be most joyful and most fruitful when they abide in Him (John 15:4-11).

Under the dispensation of the Law, the Israelites as a nation were collectively adopted as God's people. Thus, God's *parental* judgment was always national in its application, though indeed particular offenders were punished also. Those who have no relationship with the Lord must be dealt with on a *judicial* rather than a *parental* basis (Rom. 6:23; Rev. 20:15; 1 Tim. 1:15). Until an individual accepts by faith God's remedy for sin, he or she remains under the wrath of God. Though the payment for all human sin was accomplished at Calvary by Christ, the merit of that work cannot be applied to an individual's account unless he or she wants to receive it. Thus, God will judge those who reject salvation through Christ, but will be a Father to those who receive salvation through Christ.

Moses rebuked Aaron for leading the people into such a grievous sin. Aaron's response was quite pathetic:

> *Do not let the anger of my lord become hot. You know the people, that they are set on evil. For they said to me, "Make us gods that shall go before us; as for this Moses, the man who brought us out of the land of Egypt, we do not know what has become of him." And I said to them, "Whoever has any gold, let them break it off." So they gave it to me, and I cast it into the fire, and this calf came out* (Ex. 32:22-24).

Aaron blamed his own failure on the waywardness of the people. He then distorted the facts about the construction of the golden calf by asserting that he had merely thrown gold earrings into the fire and that the golden calf had jumped out of the flames. Instead of confessing his sin and taking responsibility for his actions, Aaron compounded his sin through deception and arrogance. The ancient Roman philosopher

Cicero concedes that this is foolishness of the worst kind: "It is the nature of every man to err, but only the fool perseveres in error."[1] Alexander Pope wrote concerning the wisdom of acknowledging one's mistakes: "A man should never be ashamed to own he has been in the wrong, which is but saying that he is wiser today than he was yesterday."[2] It is not falling that makes one a failure, but rather it is wallowing in self-pity and not learning from one's mistakes: *"For a righteous man may fall seven times and rise again, but the wicked shall fall by calamity"* (Prov. 24:16).

The Israelites had gone wild in their revelry before the golden calf. Paganism often incorporates lascivious practices within its worship rituals; it is Satan's way of striking a blow against God's order for marriage. It is a marriage covenant which sanctifies the sexual relationship between a husband and wife – all other physical unions are a violation of God's order for marriage (1 Cor. 6:16-18; Heb. 13:4). Apparently, Aaron had led, or at the very least had not prevented their wild frenzy of dancing, nudity, and promiscuity. When Moses saw that the people were naked and had broken God's seventh commandment, he was moved to issued a challenge to all of them. The golden calf was a direct challenge to the supremacy of Jehovah; thus, a call of separation was given: *"Whoever is on the Lord's side – come to me!"* (v. 26). Moses, fresh from God's presence, was altogether on the Lord's side in this controversy. The Israelites had been dancing around the golden calf, but if they wanted to be identified with Jehovah they must gather with Moses. Only the sons of Levi responded to the call (v. 27). After the opportunity of separation had past, Moses pronounced judgment upon the unrepentant rebels:

> *Thus says the Lord God of Israel: "Let every man put his sword on his side, and go in and out from entrance to entrance throughout the camp, and let every man kill his brother, every man his companion, and every man his neighbor." So the sons of Levi did according to the word of Moses. And about three thousand men of the people fell that day. Then Moses said, "Consecrate yourselves today to the Lord, that He may bestow on you a blessing this day, for every man has opposed his son and his brother"* (Ex. 32:27-29).

The gross nature of the sin demanded swift judgment. The Israelites were now under the Law, and *"the Law brings about wrath"* (Rom. 4:15). By responding to the call of separation, the sons of Levi cleared themselves of wrong-doing and were thus chosen as Jehovah's instrument to execute justice upon those still gathered about the golden calf. Their action of putting three thousand men to death that day was a token of the judgment deserved by the entire nation.

Jehovah is a holy God. To be associated with Him, His people must be holy too – the Law was rigid on this matter and offered no mercy for shortcomings. The Israelites had agreed to follow Jehovah's commandments, and yet within a few days of their agreement, they had broken their covenant with Him. Perhaps no stronger contrast between the dispensational realities of the Law and Grace are found in the Bible than in Exodus 32 and Acts 2. On the day that Moses brought the Law to the Israelites on stone tablets, three thousand souls perished in judgment; but, on the day that the Holy Spirit baptized believers into Christ to form the Church, about three thousand souls were saved. The Law brought condemnation and death because no one could keep it, but Christ brought acquittal and life. God's grace delights to do what man cannot do for himself.

Saviour, lead us by Thy power safe into the promised rest;
Choose the path, the way whatever seems to Thee, O Lord, the best:
Be our guide in every peril, watch and keep us night and day,
Else our foolish hearts will wander from the straight and narrow way.

In Thy presence we are happy, in Thy presence we are secure;
In Thy presence all afflictions we can steadfastly endure.
In Thy presence we can conquer, we can suffer, we can die.
Wandering from Thee we are feeble, let Thy love then keep us nigh.

— William Williams

# God's Book of Names
## Exodus 32:30-35

The next day Moses reminded the people that they had committed a great trespass against God, and, that he would return to Mount Sinai to intercede on their behalf and to learn from the Lord how atonement could be offered for their sin. God already knew all about the people's offense against Him, but because Moses had descended that mount and confirmed the specific nature of the sin he was better equipped to plead for mercy on their behalf. Sins should be specifically confessed to reaffirm proper behavior and to show sorrow for improper conduct.

Like Paul centuries later (Rom. 9:3), Moses pled for God to condemn him so that mercy could be granted to the Israelites. These were hypothetical prayers, for both men knew their divine callings, but they do demonstrate the supernatural compassion of these men for their countrymen. Evidently, Moses knew that God kept a roster of the names of everyone He would create in a book entitled *The Book of the Living* (including those who perish in the womb). David refers to this same book in Psalm 69:28. Psalm 139:15-16 confirms that this book contains the specific details of each person prior to that individual's conception.

Moreover, Revelation 3:5 also speaks of *The Book of the Living* and verifies that the names of faithful (true believers) are not blotted out of this book. At death, the unbeliever's name is blotted out of *The Book of the Living*, so that when it is reviewed at the Great White Throne Judgment (after the earth's destruction), it will contain only the names of the righteous. The Lord Jesus told His disciples (see Matt. 10:20) to rejoice because their names were written in heaven; this statement may refer either to *The Book of the Living* or to *The Lamb's Book of Life*, which is a timeless roster of the redeemed. The Greek verb translated *"written"* is in the perfect tense, which means it can be rendered as

Kenneth Wuest does in his expanded translation: *"your names have been written in heaven and are on permanent record up there."*[1]

*The Book of the Living*, though written before time, has its fulfillment in time. *The Lamb's Book of Life*, also written before creation, has its verification at the Great White Throne judgment. The former book has names blotted out of it as the lost die, while the latter remains unaltered – only the names of those who would come to salvation are written in it. Revelation 13:8 and 17:8 speak of *The Lamb's Book of Life*, which contains the names of all the redeemed of God throughout time. Whereas *The Book of Life* (or *The Book of the Living*) initially contained the names of all those who would ever live, those not coming to salvation never had their names written in *The Lamb's Book of Life*. Because the names of the lost when they die are blotted out of the former book, both books will be in perfect agreement at the Great White Throne Judgment. The one shows God's foreknowledge, and the other, His record of human responsibility.

Because of Moses' great love for God's people, he was willing to be blotted out of *The Book of the Living* in order to secure forgiveness for the Israelites. Moses was willing to suffer in the place of sinners. God's sixth dispensation of working in human affairs would be characterized by a similar message: The Lord Jesus willingly took the place of condemned sinners at Calvary in order to secure the opportunity for them to be forgiven and restored to God. It is interesting that during Moses' sixth visit to the mount that he freely offers himself to God in place of the sinner in order for God's mercy to be extending to the Israelites.

Although Moses pictures the Lord Jesus' willingness to take the place of the condemned, Moses himself was a sinner and, therefore, could not suffer for the sins of others – he was under judgment for his own sins. Only through a righteous substitute could an unrighteous person be justified before God. Even though Moses himself was a sinner, F. B. Hole explains why Moses could successfully intercede on behalf of the people:

> Only in Galatians 3:19 is Moses spoken of as a mediator, yet in verse 30 we see him formally taking his place as such. In consequence we see at once the contrast between him and the Lord Jesus, who is "the Mediator of a better covenant" (Heb. 8:6). Moses realized that nothing

> short of an atonement for the sin was needed, and he proposed to go up to the Lord and offer himself; such was his fervent love to his erring people. His plea was for the forgiveness of the sin, and if not that he instead of the nation might be blotted out of the Divine Book. But he was only able to undertake the office with "Peradventure" on his lips. How great the contrast between this and what we have in 1 Timothy 2:5-6.
>
> Moses, though so eminent and faithful a servant, was not a perfect man, but himself a sinner. The words of the Lord, which are recorded in verse 33, reminded him that consequently he himself was liable to be blotted out of the book and hence he could not stand as a ransom for anybody else. The true Mediator, "the Man Christ Jesus," has given Himself a ransom, not merely for the one sin of one people but for "ALL." The efficacy of His ransom is guaranteed by the fact that He is God as well as Man.[2]

Though Moses was not a perfect man his intercession pictured what would be perfectly accomplished through Christ in the future and therefore was accepted by Jehovah. After Moses pled for mercy for the people, God informed him that He would soon be leading the nation to another location in the wilderness, and that His angel would show them the way. He also promised to *"visit punishment upon them for their sin"* (v. 34). The following verse confirms that *"the Lord plagued the people because of what they did with the calf which Aaron made."* No details are given concerning the plague, but the Israelites learned that, although sin could be atoned for and forgiven, its consequences never made it a worthwhile proposition (Gal. 6:7-8).

> John in vision saw the day when the Judge will hasten down;
> Heaven and earth shall flee away from the terror of His frown:
> Can I bear His awful looks? Shall I stand in judgment then,
> When I see the opened books, written by the Almighty's pen?
>
> But the book of life I see, may my name be written there!
> Then from guilt and danger free, glad I'll meet Him in the air:
> That's the book I hope to plead, 'Tis the Gospel opened wide;
> Lord, I am a wretch indeed! I have sinned, but Thou hast died.
>
> — John Newton

# God Outside the Camp
## Exodus 33:1-11

Because Jehovah had promised Abraham that He would bring his descendants back to Canaan (regardless of their failures), Moses was commanded to follow His Angel, which would lead the Israelites from Mount Horeb to Canaan, a land flowing with milk and honey. He also told Moses to inform the Israelites that He would not travel in their midst, lest they sin again and be consumed in His anger (v. 3). The point of this dialogue was to ensure that the Israelites keenly felt the break in fellowship their sin had caused, and to move them to humility and brokenness before Him.

Moses understood that Jehovah could not dwell in the midst of a camp that had been defiled by the presence of the golden calf and, therefore, he erected a temporary tent far apart from the Israelite camp. He called it the *"tabernacle of the congregation"* (v. 7). This was not the official tabernacle in which the priests would minister, for in that tabernacle God spoke with Moses in the Holy Place, not at its entrance, as with the temporary tent. Every time Moses went to the tent to speak with God, the pillar of cloud descended to the doorway of the tent. The descending cloud upon the tent located outside of camp served as a visual reminder to the Israelites that their sins had caused a separation between themselves and God. Jehovah now dwelt outside their camp; He was not among them. Therefore, *"everyone who sought the Lord went out to the tabernacle of meeting which was outside the camp"* (v. 7).

To further prompt brokenness before Him, Jehovah commanded the children of Israel to strip themselves of their ornaments (or decorations); this would test their disposition towards Him on the matter of reconciliation. Awareness of their separation from God and the removal of their ornaments had a positive effect on the people: *"And when the people heard this bad news, they mourned, and no one put on his ornaments"* (v. 5). As J. G. Bellett, explains this was an appropriate response of a remorseful nation that desired restoration with Jehovah, but had neither the means nor the knowledge of how it could be accomplished:

> Israel had destroyed themselves under the Law, under their own, or the old, covenant. Having made the golden calf, they broke the first article of the Law, and were to be cut off from the land. But the mediator stays the execution of righteousness; and under his words (brought to them from the Lord) they take a new place, they assume a new character; they strip themselves of their ornaments, and seek the Lord in the place to which He had retired outside their camp. This was, by conviction, taking the place of sinners in the sight of God. And this was a new thing. But this was the only thing that the Lord could possibly accredit. It was the only true thing, the only real place; for they were sinners, and they must be as sinners before Him. But being convicted, they let the mediator know, that he was all their confidence. They look after him as he enters the place to which God had come down, they leave their tents, they stand, every man at his door, and from thence, as convicted and humbled, while bowing and worshipping, they look towards the mediator.
>
> This was beautiful – the second step in the path of a convicted sinner. As stripped of their ornaments, they go outside the camp, as though they were unclean, and let the mediator know that he is all their confidence. And he does not, he could not disappoint them. The earnestness with which he pleads with the Lord that He would own Israel as His people, and give them the benefit of the grace in which he himself was standing, it is beautiful to see – and we know in all this he [Moses] represents One greater than himself, that he [Moses] is but the shadow or reflection of the true and only Mediator.[1]

Perhaps it was the utter failure of the people which prompted Moses to refer to Mount Sinai as Mount Horeb in verse 6. Although the meaning of "Sinai" is difficult to assert, "Horeb" means "to dry up, to be in ruins, or to lay waste." This appropriately describes the Israelites' spiritual condition after breaking their covenant with Jehovah. Yet God's ultimate solution for their failure had been previously conveyed to Moses' during his sixth visit the mount (Ex. 32:30-33:3). As previously noted, the sixth trip to the mount aligns with God's sixth dispensation of human responsibility (i.e. the Age of Grace). This is further explained in the New Testament and may be prefigured by God's revelation to Moses at this time. The writer of Hebrews explains that during the Church Age, the Jews must come out of the camp of Judaism and receive Christ as Saviour by faith:

> *We have an altar from which those who serve the tabernacle have no right to eat. For the bodies of those animals, whose blood is brought into the sanctuary by the high priest for sin, are burned outside the camp. Therefore Jesus also, that He might sanctify the people with His own blood, suffered outside the gate.* ***Therefore let us go forth to Him, outside the camp, bearing His reproach.*** *For here we have no continuing city, but we seek the one to come* (Heb. 13:10-15).

Shortly after Christ's resurrection, Jerusalem was destroyed, the temple was laid bare, and the Levitical sacrifices were stopped. Since that time, all Jews who want to be reconciled with God must humble themselves (remove their ornaments, so to speak), come out from their dead traditions, and receive the Lord Jesus Christ as Saviour. The system of the Law, which pointed the way to salvation in Christ, has been replaced with a New Covenant sealed by His own blood (Heb. 8:8). No type of Christ will do; those who want to be restored to God must trust the antitype of the Horeb scene – Christ Himself.

When Moses went outside the camp to speak with God at the tent of meeting, the glorious cloud concealing His presence visibly descended to the entrance of the tent. All of the Israelites had rushed to the doors of their tents to watch Moses walk to the tabernacle, and when the pillar of cloud descended, they bowed in worship. They knew they were in trouble and they also knew that Moses was the only person who could request mercy on their behalf. Their isolation from Jehovah's presence was keenly felt by His people, and their remorse over the matter was evident.

After returning from the mount the seventh time (Ex. 34:34), each time Moses spoke to the Lord at this tent, he brought back two things; the glory of God upon his face (Ex. 34:29-35), and the patterns of what he had seen on the mount, which were the shadows of the good things to come in Christ (Heb. 10:1-7). Although the Israelites didn't understand the latter item, their humility and reverence before Jehovah was an acknowledgment that the good to come was God's provision of grace to sinners. What was then only a foreshadowing pattern is the reality today – it is only through Christ that men and women are prepared for God's indwelling. Only within the cleansed and regenerate vessel will God abide; He must dwell apart from all others. God can do nothing for man until man takes the place of a convicted sinner and receives by faith God's provision for his guilt and judgment; then, and only then, will personal offerings of service and worship be accepted.

Moses went back and forth to the tent, but young and faithful Joshua *"departed not out of the tabernacle"* (v. 11). Joshua had led the people in the victorious battle against the Amalekites. He had also waited for Moses to return from Mount Sinai with the Law of God. Perhaps Joshua had been asked to maintain the tent of meeting in good order. He had demonstrated faithfulness to Jehovah and was, therefore, rewarded with God's presence also. We may not have much to give to the Lord, but faithfulness to Him and to His Word is the most fragrant of all the offerings to God.

Throughout Exodus, Joshua's ministry is intimately tied to the ministry of Moses: they battled the Amalekites together (Ex. 17), they confronted the sinning Israelites together (Ex. 32), and together they apparently offered intercession on behalf of the people in the tent of meeting (Ex. 33:8-11). When the Israelites were obedient Joshua was victoriously among them; yet, when they were sinning, he was completely separated from them. The ministry of Joshua typifies the work of the Lord Jesus Christ among His people as they engage the enemy in spiritual warfare. The lesson is clear: if we want Christ and His power among us, then we must remain faithful and obedient, for without Christ we can do nothing to please Him. The Lord Jesus said, *"Abide in Me, and I in you. As the branch cannot bear fruit of itself, unless it abides in the vine, neither can you, unless you abide in Me. I am the vine, you are the branches. He who abides in Me, and I in him, bears much fruit; for without Me you can do nothing"* (John 15:4-5).

When we see Thy love unshaken, outside the camp,
Scorned by man, by God forsaken, outside the camp.
Thy loved cross alone can charm us, shame need now no more alarm us,
Glad we follow, nothing can harm us, outside the camp.
Thy reproach, far richer treasure, than all Egypt's boasted pleasure;
Drawn by love that knows no measure, outside the camp.

— Elizabeth Dark

# "Show Me Your Glory"
## Exodus 33:12-23

Moses enjoyed full fellowship with God. When they met together, Jehovah spoke to Moses *"face to face, as a man speaks to his friend"* (v. 11). This is not a literal statement, for no one in his or her natural state can look upon God's face and live (v. 20); rather, it is a figurative expression used to convey blessed intimacy. As Moses demonstrated, one of the great privileges of being in intimate fellowship with God is the opportunity to seek His assistance during troubling times. Moses understood this and used prayer to intercede on behalf of the people. But first, Moses petitioned the Lord on his own behalf:

> *See, You say to me, "Bring up this people." But You have not let me know whom You will send with me. Yet You have said, "I know you by name, and you have also found grace in My sight." Now therefore, I pray, if I have found grace in Your sight, show me now Your way, that I may know You and that I may find grace in Your sight. And consider that this nation is Your people* (Ex. 33:12-13).

God had commissioned Moses to lead the people, but if God were not with them, it didn't matter where they went. So, while in the spirit of prayer, he reverently reminded God what He had previously promised to do. Though God had told Moses that He would send His Angel before him (v. 2), Moses had limited knowledge of "God's way" in the matter (v. 13). This sincere prayer of Moses was offered on the sole basis that God personally knew him by name (i.e. that Moses belonged to God) and that he had found grace in God's sight (v. 12).

The answer to Moses' prayer is brief, but tremendously consoling: *"My Presence will go with you, and I will give you rest"* (v. 14). God's response was a solace to Moses' soul, for he knew that he could do nothing apart from Jehovah and that there was no reason for the nation to exist apart from its connection with Him. Moses' reason for living and his strength for living came from the abiding presence of Jehovah. This was "God's way," and would be sufficient for the desolate path ahead. This is true for every Christian also; the indwelling presence of the Holy Spirit enables the believer to overcome difficulties and to commune with God.

Next, Moses immediately offered intercession for the people, saying *"Consider that this nation is Your people"* (v. 13). Moses' intercession for the Israelites was also successful; the Lord responded, *"I will also do this thing that you have spoken; for you have found grace in My sight, and I know you by name"* (v. 17). The Israelites will be restored to Jehovah; they will again be His people, and will again be put under the covenant of the Law, the very covenant they broke (Ex. 34; Jer. 31:32). By this act, God demonstrated that though the Law revealed sin and condemned the sinner, His overall plan of salvation included the possibility of receiving grace. However, this merciful aspect of salvation was not fully explained (in fact, it was deliberately concealed) until after Christ's resurrection (1 Cor. 2:7-8).

Another example of this truth is found in the life of David, a man after God's own heart. David partly understood that God's salvation had to be more than what was revealed in the Law. In Psalm 51, he pleads for the Lord to forgive his transgressions and to cleanse him of his guilt, though the Law demanded death for the sins of adultery and murder, and David had committed both.

Moses was elated over the demonstration of God's grace and mercy in forgiving and restoring the Israelites to Himself. Edward Dennett describes the effect this had on Moses:

> Every successive display of grace does but elicit larger desires; and Moses therefore now longs for himself that he may see God's glory. *"And he said, I beseech Thee, show me Thy glory"* (v. 18). Such is ever the action of grace upon the soul. The more we know of God, the more we desire to know. But this very petition of Moses affords a contrast with the place of the believer. Now we behold with unveiled face the glory of the Lord; here Moses prays that he may see it. The holy longing, however, which he thus expresses, shows the effect of intimacy with God, and the consequent energetic action on the soul of the Holy Ghost.[1]

The Lord responded to Moses' prayer to see His glory with a warning: *"You cannot see My face; for no man shall see Me, and live"* (v. 20), and then answered his prayer to the degree possible without harming Moses in the process. No human in his or her natural state can look upon the full goodness and glory of God and live, so the Lord tucked Moses into a cleft of a rock and allowed Moses to view His "afterglow" as He passed by. How are we to understand what Moses saw? It is like the light of the sun: our eyes cannot stare at the sun in its full strength without being damaged, but yet we are able to enjoy beautiful sunsets. Likewise, Moses could not look upon God's full glory and live, but he could appreciate God's afterglow after He passed by him.

Moses was extended a great privilege, but in this present dispensation, the humblest Christian is brought nearer to beholding the glory of God by viewing Christ through Scripture than Moses was when he was in the cleft of the rock. Paul, speaking of the transforming power of God's Word, puts it this way: *"But we all, with unveiled face, beholding as in a mirror the glory of the Lord, are being transformed into the same image from glory to glory, just as by the Spirit of the Lord"* (2 Cor. 3:18). As we peer into the Holy Page, the Spirit of God shows us the glory of Christ in God and to the extent that we desire to behold His glory, we are changed into the same image. Every believer should long to see Christ's glorious appearing, but while waiting for that day, may each of us earnestly beseech the Lord, as Moses did, *"Please, show me Your glory."*

> Face to face with Christ, my Saviour, face to face—what will it be,
> When with rapture I behold Him, Jesus Christ Who died for me?
> Face to face I shall behold Him, far beyond the starry sky;
> Face to face in all His glory, I shall see Him by and by!
> Only faintly now I see Him, with the darkened veil between,
> But a blessed day is coming, when His glory shall be seen.
>
> — Carrie F. Breck

# New Tables and New Vision
## Exodus 34:1-9

After Moses saw the afterglow of God's glory from the cleft of the rock, he was instructed to hew out two new tablets of stone similar to the ones that he had previously been given. He was to do this task immediately, so as to be ready with two tablets in hand to ascend Mount Sinai in the morning. Moses would again receive the Law of God.

The next morning, Moses ascended the mount for the seventh and final time. Jehovah, faithful to His promise, descended in the familiar cloud near where Moses was standing and proclaimed the glory of His own name:

> *The Lord, the Lord God, merciful and gracious, longsuffering, and abounding in goodness and truth, keeping mercy for thousands, forgiving iniquity and transgression and sin, by no means clearing the guilty, visiting the iniquity of the fathers upon the children and the children's children to the third and the fourth generation* (Ex. 34:6-7).

Jehovah declared Himself as the Holy God who had entered into a special relationship with Israel, His covenant people. In this proclamation, God highlights certain aspects of His character which relate directly to His governmental authority over Israel. He would be merciful, gracious, longsuffering, and patient with them, but His holy nature cannot clear the guilty – sin must be judicially punished. God had clearly expressed His love for His people, and they would learn that their sins must be atoned for in order to receive the fullness of His love; full restoration can not precede reconciliation.

From Sinai to Calvary, blood atonement would be God's means of restoring wayward Jews to Himself. Only after full propitiation was completed through Christ's work at Calvary could the floodgates of God's heart fully open to overwhelm the redeemed sinner with His irresistible and matchless love (John 17:26). While Israel honored God as their Ruler, Christians may enjoy Him also as their heavenly Father. Consequently, the Israelites were never referred to as "the children of God," though collectively they were God's firstborn son, that is, the first nation that He chose to provide a testimony of Himself to the world.

Jehovah's proclamation to Moses had a humbling effect on him: *"Moses made haste and bowed his head toward the earth, and worshiped. Then he said, 'If now I have found grace in Your sight, O Lord, let my Lord, I pray, go among us, even though we are a stiff-necked people; and pardon our iniquity and our sin, and take us as Your inheritance'"* (Ex. 34:8-9). We see this principle throughout Scripture: when God connects with humanity and reveals His character to them, those desiring to be restored to God respond by worshipping Him. For example, after God revealed Himself to Abram (Gen. 12:7), Isaac (Gen. 26:25), and Jacob (Gen. 28:18), each one erected an altar or pillar and worshipped God. As believers are consistently in the Word of God, they receive fresh illumination of who God is; this in turn prompts consistent worship of God. Those who neglect the Word will not grow in knowledge of God. As a result, their appreciation and reverence for Him will wane over time. Moses was constrained to worship because he had become overwhelmed by the revelation of God's glory.

With his soul prostrated before the Lord, Moses seized the privilege that had been extended only to him (v. 3), that is, offering intercession on the behalf of the people. True worshippers of God will be prompted to pray to Him for the good of others. Who else can one go to for help? Who other than Almighty God can resolve hopeless matters to the utmost blessing? Moses could not plead for the people on the grounds of justice, for that would serve only to condemn the Israelites. There was only one course of action to be taken: Moses reminds God of His unconditional promise to manifest His glory through His people.

Moses was a righteous man and he had found grace in the eyes of God. However, he was also fully identified with the sinful nation of Israel. As such, he was the only one who could stand in the gap between Jehovah and Israel. He pled with God, *"If now I have found grace in Your sight ... pardon our iniquity and our sin"* (v. 9). His petition was based on the concern that God's glory would be diminished if He did not perform His covenant with the children of Abraham. Of course, God did what He had always purposed to do – He restored and blessed His people. But this could not have been accomplished without a righteous intercessor. John Darby wrote on this matter:

> Moses does not speak of governmental mercy, but goes above to God's own glory, and to the unconditional promises of His own purpose; but he associates, as often remarked, the people with it, which is faith as to this. But there is progress – his intercession at the door of the tabernacle is upon the general ground that they are God's people. Faith and the Lord's thoughts meet – God retreats into His own sovereignty, does not go on the ground yet of governmental mercy, for indeed they had cast Him off. But when God has revealed His goodness – Himself, as far as was possible – then Moses goes further, and begs God to go amongst them – puts himself as one of the whole company in God's revealed presence, and prays Jehovah as Adonai to go amongst them, because it is a stiff-necked people; he is amongst the people, but this is very holy boldness – and we know we need God's doing so, or how should we get through – and very beautiful, but founded on revealed grace. But in all this Moses shines greatly through grace; he is there – God revealing Himself – yet not confounded, or as dumb before Him; there is a just demand suited to God's glory – suited to the people's state and want.[1]

The principle typified here is of great importance in understanding the work of prayer that believers in close fellowship with the Lord can accomplish on the behalf of others, especially those who are not enjoying the nearness of the Lord. It is the Christian's identification with those who have failed and the Christian's privileged position in Christ that enables the righteous man or woman of God to have an effectual prayer life. As witnessed in the life of Moses, those who practice righteousness and have found grace in the eyes of God will be prompted to identify with others who need God's grace. James puts the matter this way: *"Confess your trespasses to one another, and pray for one another, that you may be healed. The effective, fervent prayer of a righteous man avails much"* (Jas. 5:16). May every true worshipper of God engage in the important work of interceding for others!

Moses, a righteous man who had received the grace of God and basked in His glory, made effectual intercession to God on behalf of people who desperately needed His help. Moses, Daniel, and Nehemiah are also examples of righteous men who, after coming in contact with God, were prompted to pray for others. True worshippers of God, then, will be marked as men and women who are compelled to prayer for others. Those who are content to know the Lord superficially will not be burdened to pray for others.

> Prayer is the soul's sincere desire, unuttered or expressed;
> The motion of a hidden fire that trembles in the breast.
> Prayer is the Christian's vital breath, the Christian's native air,
> His watchword at the gates of death; he enters Heaven with prayer.
> No prayer is made by man alone, the Holy Spirit pleads,
> And Jesus, on the eternal throne, for sinners intercedes.
> O Thou by Whom we come to God, the Life, the Truth, the Way,
> The path of prayer Thyself hast trod: Lord, teach us how to pray.
>
> — James Montgomery

# A Renewed Covenant

## Exodus 34:10-28

The seventh and final divine dispensation is called the Kingdom Age. Paul describes the future, earthly reality of this stewardship in this way: *"That in the dispensation of the fullness of the times He* [God] *might gather together in one all things in Christ, both which are in heaven and which are on earth – in Him* (Eph. 1:10). During this thousand-year period, Christ will reign over the nations with a rod of iron (Rev. 12:5, 20:6), His glory will fill the earth (Isa. 60:1-2; Ezek. 42:3), and the Jews will acknowledge and worship Him as their Messiah (Zech. 12:10).

Interestingly, Moses' seventh appearance before God on Mount Horeb seems to picture Christ's future Kingdom in two ways. First, the Jewish nation will be refined and restored to Him at this time. Second, the glory of God, as seen in the face of Moses, is witnessed among the people for the first time (Ex. 34:29-35). During the millennial kingdom the glory of God will be among His covenant people and, in fact, fill the earth. Scripture does not mention whether or not Moses' face radiated God's glory after previous visits with Jehovah, but it certainly did after the seventh visit. Exodus does not record Moses visiting the mount again, instead, the book concludes with God's glorious presence having descended upon the tabernacle. This symbolizes God's future spectacular presence among His people. Twice the Holy Text reads, *"The glory of the Lord filled the tabernacle"* (Ex. 40:34-35). In the Kingdom Age, God's glory will fill the earth as Christ reigns over the nations with power, justice, and righteousness. One of the main outcomes of the seventh dispensation is the restoration of the Jews to God through Christ. And during the seventh visit to the mount, Moses' intercession typifies Christ's future mediatory work of restoring Israel to God.

As previously stated, Moses identified with Jehovah's people. Knowing he had found grace in Jehovah's eyes, he asked God to pardon and restore them. Moses includes himself with the group of people needing to be forgiven, knowing full well that he was secure in God's grace. Jehovah's response to Moses' prayer was immediate and comprehensive:

> *Behold, I make a covenant. Before all your people I will do marvels such as have not been done in all the earth, nor in any nation; and all the people among whom you are shall see the work of the Lord. For it is an awesome thing that I will do with you. Observe what I command you this day* (Ex. 34:10-11).

Notice the phrases, *"all your people," "all the people among whom you are,"* and *"it is an awesome thing that I will do with you."* Moses had identified himself with the Israelites and God was willing to forgive and bless the people because of that identification. Although animal sacrifices were required to atone for the Israelite's sin, they were not the sole basis of God's pardon. The real reason God was inclined to return to His people was because Moses numbered himself with the repentant rebels and had asked Him to forgive them.

Through Moses' intercession, God renewed His covenant with His people. He promised to go with them and before them to the Promised Land and to drive the inhabitants of Canaan out of the land. However, God also issued a stern warning to His people:

> *Take heed to yourself, lest you make a covenant with the inhabitants of the land where you are going, lest it be a snare in your midst. But you shall destroy their altars, break their sacred pillars, and cut down their wooden images (for you shall worship no other god, for the Lord, whose name is Jealous, is a jealous God)* (Ex. 34:12-14).

The Israelites had learned from the golden calf incident that their God was a jealous God and that He would not tolerate idolatry. Although God had forgiven them and had renewed His covenant with the Israelites, He also warned them not to play the harlot again by embracing the false gods in Canaan (v. 14). Whether it is the veneration of an idol, being given over to temporal thrills, being controlled by human relationships, or being ensnared in worldliness, God views all of it in the same light – it is spiritual adultery and He hates it (Jas. 4:4). Anything that robs our affection for the Lord and hinders us from fully pursuing Him is idolatry. It grieves His heart and He will chasten all who do such things against Him, for He is a jealous God!

To prevent the Israelite's love for Him from growing cold, Jehovah instituted several reminders for them to observe: annual feasts (vv. 18, 22-23), redemption of the firstborn (of man and beast; vv. 19-20), and the Sabbath Day (vv. 21, 35:1-3). Although all of these had been previously mentioned on earlier visits to the mount, in this encounter, more details were given concerning the Feasts of Jehovah. Three seasons of festivals, including a total of seven feasts, were to be observed by the Israelites. Every Jewish male was required to present himself before Jehovah three times a year at the Feast of Unleavened Bread (which included the Passover and First Fruits; v. 18), the Feast of Weeks (v. 22), and the Feast of Ingathering (v. 23). This last feast was also called the Feast of Booths.

The Passover Feast and the Feast of Unleavened Bread, which were both instituted in Exodus 12, are explained more thoroughly in Leviticus 23, which identifies all seven of the Feasts of Jehovah. These seven feasts provide an exceptional prophetical blueprint of God's means of reconciling the nation of Israel to Himself forever. Every aspect of this blueprint centers in the work of Christ (timing has been converted from the Jewish to Roman timetable beginning with the fourteenth day of the first month):

**Passover** (14$^{th}$ day of 1$^{st}$ month) pictures Christ on the cross on Friday; this was the day the Passover lambs were slain and was also the day when the Lamb of God was slain for the sins of the world (1 Cor. 5:7).

**Unleavened Bread** (15$^{th}$ day of 1$^{st}$ month) speaks of Christ in the grave on Saturday; like the bread, Christ's body had neither life while in the grave nor had it been previously influenced by sin (i.e. Christ lived an unleavened life).

**First Fruits** (16th day of the 1st month) typifies Christ's resurrection on Sunday; He was the first fruits from the dead (1 Cor 15:20).

**Pentecost** (fifty days after First Fruits) pictures the formation of the Church (Christ's body of believers) fifty days after Christ's resurrection. The events at Pentecost conveyed a final ultimatum to Israel (Acts 2).

Note: The Church Age is represented by the gap between the Spring and Autumn feasts (this also relates to the interval between Daniel's 69th and 70th week; Dan. 9:24-27). The Autumn feasts speak of Israel's future acknowledgement of Christ as Messiah, their restoration to Him, and the blessings of His Millennial Kingdom.

**Trumpets** (1st day of the 7th month) refers to the time when Christ will gather all the Jews back to Israel and under His rule (Matt. 24:29-31; Ezek. 39:28-29).

**The Day of Atonement** (10th day of the 7th month) pictures the future event when the Jews will repent and receive Jesus Christ as their Messiah (Heb. 9:28; Zech. 12:10).

**Tabernacles** (15th day of the 7th month) announces the future release of the Jews from the Antichrist's rule during the Tribulation Period, and the blessings of Christ's rule during His Millennial Kingdom.

God indeed has a wonderful plan for the nation of Israel. Prophetically speaking, the spring feasts are completed, while the fall feasts are yet to be fulfilled, though certainly the current ingathering of Jews back to the land of Israel is a preface to the fulfillment of the Feast of Trumpets. When the last trumpet of the Tribulation Period is heard, every Jew will be gathered out of the nations back to the land of Israel; this refined remnant will then receive the Holy Spirit (Ezek. 39:28-29). Each feast prophetically presents a portion of God's plan to fully restore the Jewish nation to Himself once and for all during Christ's

Millennial Kingdom. As previously mentioned, this ultimate restoration is pictured in the events of Exodus 34.

Jehovah pardoned the Israelites and renewed the covenant of His Law with them; it is the same covenant that they previous violated by worshiping the golden calf (v. 27). Moses wrote down God's Law, the Ten Commandments, upon two stone tablets. He was with Jehovah for forty days and nights on the mountain, and he did not eat bread or drink water during that time (v. 28).

The Bible records a few occasions when individuals went forty days without food or drink through the supernatural care of God: Elijah during his wilderness experience (1 Kgs. 19:8), Moses before Jehovah on Mount Horeb (Ex. 34:28), and Christ during His testing in the wilderness (Matt. 4:2). How was this possible? Once, the disciples observed that the Lord Jesus had not eaten for an extended period of time, and they encouraged Him to eat something. He responded:

> *"I have food to eat of which you do not know." Therefore the disciples said to one another, "Has anyone brought Him anything to eat?" Jesus said to them, "My food is to do the will of Him who sent Me, and to finish His work"* (John 4:32-34).

From this and the previous examples it would seem that there are times in which God supernaturally sustains an individual's body for the purpose of accomplishing His work. The application for the believer is that doing God's will should be the primary objective of one's life and though the temporal facets of life, such as food and drink are necessary, one should not be ruled by them.

Why forty days of fasting and not thirty or fifty? The number forty is used in Scripture to represent *probation* and *testing*, which explains its frequent occurrence. At times, God extended the nation of Israel forty-year probationary periods to test or prove them: the Israelites were tested in the wilderness forty years (Deut. 8:2-5), delivered and had rest during the forty years that Othniel, Barak, and Gideon judged Israel (Judg. 3:11, 5:31, 8:28), and enjoyed dominion during the forty-year reigns of five kings: David, Solomon, Jeroboam, Jehoash, and Joash (2 Sam. 5:4; 1 Kgs. 11:42; 2 Kgs. 12:17, 12:1; 2 Chron. 24:1). Another demonstration of forty as the number of probation and testing is found in God's dealings with Nineveh; the prophet Jonah preached that, unless the inhabitants repented, God's judgment would fall on them in forty days (Jon. 3:4).

The first time Moses spent forty days on the Mount Sinai served not only as an opportunity for him to receive the Law, but was also a time of testing for the Israelites: would they be faithful to their newly-affirmed covenant with Jehovah? They failed the test and were judged. However, the second time Moses was before the Lord for forty days, the Israelites remained repentant and faithful. They patiently waited for Moses (the only one who could make intercession for them) to descend the mountain and tell them whether or not they had been forgiven.

When Moses did return, with God's covenant in hand, the news was most welcome – God had pardoned their transgressions, He would remain among them, and He would go with them to the Promised Land. The Israelites had come to realize that life has no meaning unless God is at the center of it. Whether that be for forty seconds or forty days, or forty years, every believer will experience seasons of probation and testing. Our failures should lead to personal brokenness, which should then cause us to cast ourselves upon the Lord in a way that we were hesitant to do beforehand. Our victories, won by His grace, prompt us to praise His name! The outcome of testing, then, is that the believer knows and trusts the Lord with a greater patience and confidence than he or she had before.

> God of our fathers, the strength of our people and nation,
> Gladly we come to Thy presence with true adoration.
> Seeking Thy face, trusting Thy love and Thy grace,
> Thou art our health and salvation.
>
> God of all mercy, for pardon and peace we implore Thee,
> Humbly confessing our faults and our failures before Thee.
> Children of men, falling and rising again,
> Still give us grace to adore Thee.
>
> — Winfred E. Garrison

# The Dispensational Significance of Moses' Trips to Sinai

| Visit to Sinai | Dispensation Represented | Ex. Ref. | Circumstances of Visit/Dispensational Overview |
|---|---|---|---|
| 1st | Innocence | 19:3-8 | *"If"* the Israelites obeyed the Lord's voice they would be a holy nation. They said *"all that the Lord has spoken we will do."* Likewise, as long as Adam did not eat from the forbidden tree he would remain in fellowship with God in Eden. |
| 2nd | Conscience | 19:9-19 | The quaking mount caused the people to fear God; later they stood afar off from the mount. Adam hid from God after becoming aware of his sinful condition. |
| 3rd | Government | 19:20-20:17 | Moses was command to put boundaries about the base of the mount to protect and control the people. After the flood God ordained human government to further teach man the importance of submission to His authority. |
| 4th | Promise | 20:18-23:33 | Aspects of the Law are verbally given on the 3rd trip, but the provision for worship was revealed during the 4th trip; blood sacrifices upon God-approved altars. Abraham was commanded to walk rightly before the Lord; he built at least five altars to offer animal sacrifices to God. |
| 5th | Law | 24:1-32:29 | The Law, fully revealed and written in stone, demanded the guilty Israelites be judged. The purpose of the Law now and then is to show man his sin (Rom. 3:20). |
| 6th | Grace | 32:30-33:23 | Moses makes intercession for the people, who have humbled themselves before the Lord. Grace is conferred and Moses gets a glimpse of the glory of God. In the Church Age those who repent and trust Christ as Saviour receive grace; Christ becomes their intercessor and by the Holy Spirit's illumination of Scripture believers get a glimpse of God's glory. |
| 7th | Kingdom | 34:1-40:38 | The Jews are restored to God and the fading glory of the Law seen in Moses' face is replaced by the glory of God which filled the tabernacle. In the Kingdom Age the Jews are completely restored to God; His glory fills the earth. |

# Moses' Face Shines
## Exodus 34:29-35

After being alone with God forty days, Moses returned to camp carrying the two stone tablets of the Law. There was no need to break these tablets as he entered the camp for the people were patiently waiting for his return. Moses did not realize it at first, but he soon learned from the reaction of others that his countenance shone brightly – his face had remained illuminated after coming in contact with God's glory. Consequently, the people, and even his own brother Aaron, were afraid to come near him.

To dispel their fears, Moses called Aaron and the elders of the congregation to him. After they approached (without any ill-consequence), the rest of the people were also obliged to come near to Moses to listen to him. After that, when Moses was among the people he covered his face (perhaps his entire head) with a veil, but whenever he went to the tent of meeting to speak with God he removed the veil. It would seem that a human face shining with the glory of God would have been an excellent reminder to the people of Jehovah's glory; one then wonders why Moses covered his face with a veil. Was it to settle Israelite anxiety? Paul addresses this question in a letter to the Church at Corinth:

> *Unlike Moses, who put a veil over his face so that the children of Israel could not look steadily at the end of what was passing away. But their minds were blinded. For until this day the same veil remains unlifted in the reading of the Old Testament, because the veil is taken away in Christ. But even to this day, when Moses is read, a veil lies on their heart. Nevertheless when one turns to the Lord, the veil is taken away* (2 Cor. 3:13-16).

Paul explains that the reason Moses covered his face with a veil was not to make the Israelites more comfortable in his presence, but rather so they would not notice that the brilliance of his face diminished over time. Why was this important? Moses brought the Israelites the Law, but though it reflected God's righteous character, it did not convey the full measure of God's goodness in resolving man's problem of sin. The Law showed sin, but did not provide power to overcome it – it only condemned the sinner. Just as the reflected glory of God faded from Moses' face, the Law also had a diminishing glory.

In time, the Covenant of the Law would be replaced with the New Covenant, which was sealed with Christ's own blood. However, this truth was not conveyed to the Jews until the Lord Jesus Christ personally presented Himself to them as their Messiah. Christ was God's glorious solution to what the Law had thoroughly proven to be true: every child of Adam was separated from God by sin.

When Christ sojourned among the Jews, He removed the veil that was over the Law in order to show its fading glory. However, instead of trusting Christ, the Jews covered their own hearts with the same veil; nationally speaking, they remain blind to the truth of the gospel message unto this day. Paul explained their willful blindness to the Church at Rome:

> *I do not desire, brethren, that you should be ignorant of this mystery, lest you should be wise in your own opinion, that blindness in part has happened to Israel until the fullness of the Gentiles has come in. And so all Israel will be saved, as it is written: "The Deliverer will come out of Zion, and He will turn away ungodliness from Jacob; for this is My covenant with them, when I take away their sins"* (Rom. 11:25-26).

Ultimately, during the latter days of the Tribulation Period, Christ will remove this veil of deception from their hearts. The nation of Israel will be converted and restored to God at Christ's second coming. Then they will understand that though the Law was good and holy, it had a limited glory associated to it. Its sole purpose was to make them aware of their sin and point them to the solution – Christ (Gal. 3:24)!

> All glory, laud and honor, to Thee, Redeemer, King,
> To Whom the lips of children made sweet hosannas ring.
> Thou art the King of Israel, Thou David's royal Son,
> Who in the Lord's Name comest, the King and Blessed One.
>
> — Theodulph of Orleans

# Gifts from Willing Hearts
## Exodus 35:1-29

After again reminding them to sanctify the Sabbath day, Moses announced that a collection would be taken for the Lord (v. 5) for the purpose of constructing the tabernacle and its furnishings (vv. 10-11). The following items were to be collected: precious metals, gems, olive oil, and various fabrics and skins. Three important points are noteworthy at this juncture. First, though Moses mentioned the tabernacle (vv. 11, 21) and its various furnishings (vv. 12-19), he did not tell them what the tabernacle was for, though he knew that the collected resources would be used to construct and equip God's dwelling place among them. Second, giving was not compulsory; only those who wanted to give were to contribute. Moses declared, *"Take from among you an offering to the Lord. Whoever is of a willing heart, let him bring it as an offering to the Lord"* (Ex. 35:5). Third, an invitation to construct the articles of the tabernacle was offered, but only those who were willing and wise-hearted could participate (v. 10).

The people, still rejoicing in their pardon, gave generously to the Lord, even though they did not completely understand what the collection was for. An opportunity to show their appreciation for Jehovah had been extended, and the people quickly took advantage of it. Even after the collection was complete, Moses did not tell the congregation exactly what was to be constructed with it. J. G. Bellett explains:

> Look at Israel in Exodus 35 - 39, bringing their gifts to the Sanctuary, and making the materials for it. Did they know what was to come forth out of it all? No. All that Moses told them was, what they were to bring, and then what they were to make, and that the result would be a Sanctuary. But how each thing was to be disposed of, what place each was to fill in relation to the rest, and what the general effect of the whole was to be, they know not. But this did not hinder them *offering* and *working*. The great result lay in Moses' hand. And accordingly,

> when they had made all, Moses arranged all (Ex. 40). The confusion ceased and the heaps of things made by them, strewn under their eyes, were reduced to most perfect order, and not only to order, but made to disclose the most precious mysteries and secrets of Divine counsel and grace. They gave in faith, and laboured in faith. They knew but little. But they trusted. And the end so vindicated all their confidence, that they fell down and shout in holy triumph (Lev. 9: 24.).[1]

The people's response to Moses' call to contribute and to labor was overwhelming. Two aspects of their giving are stressed: First, that they were willing to donate their possessions, skills, and time to the construction of the tabernacle (vv. 21-22, 29), and second, that everyone was involved with the activity. The Bible specifically states who participated: *"everyone"* (v. 21 {twice}, v. 24), *"both men and women"* (vv. 22, 29), *"every man"* (vv. 23, 24), and *"all the women"* (v. 26). The contributions and the labor needed to construct the tabernacle, its furnishings, and the priestly attire were given by the entire assembly – everyone chose to be involved with the work!

How wonderful a scene this is – God's people jointly giving of themselves for the work of the Lord, not knowing the end result, but yet willing and obedient to what they understand is required of them. If brethren today could recapture this enthusiasm, the Church would be transformed from a superficial religious facade into a vibrant, living testimony for Christ. Giving to the Lord brings joy to the heart, and laboring together with like-minded believers for the cause of Christ builds unity, strengthens the Body of Christ, and accomplishes what individual efforts could never do. If the Church were busy giving to and laboring for the Lord, its members would have neither energy nor resources to attack, backbite, and wound one another.

This historical scene is a bright spot in Israel's history. May Christians learn from their example and endeavor, in our remaining time on earth, to have willing hearts and laboring hands for the cause of Christ.

> Take my lips and let them be, filled with messages for Thee;
> Take my silver and my gold, not a mite would I withhold,
> Not a mite would I withhold.
> Take my love my God I pour, at Thy feet its treasure store;
> Take myself and I will be, ever only all for Thee,
> Ever only all for Thee.
>
> — Frances R. Havergal

# Work from Wise Hearts
## Exodus 35:29-36:2

Willing hearts contributed resources to the work of the tabernacle; and wise hearts offered time, skills, and energy to accomplish the work. The phrase "wisehearted" is employed several times in this chapter to describe the people who constructed the tabernacle and its furnishings (vv. 10, 25, 35). The construction of the tabernacle involved sewing, weaving, forging, carving, pounding, cutting, forming, polishing, etc.; the Israelites were a ready workforce.

However, the natural abilities of the people were not sufficient to accomplish the work of the Lord; it required individuals that were filled, gifted, and controlled by the Holy Spirit. Bezalel, the son of Uri, the grandson of Hur (v. 30), and Oholiab, the son of Ahisamach of the tribe of Dan (v. 34), were specifically named as the individuals whom the Lord had prepared with wisdom, knowledge, and workmanship to lead and achieve *all* of the tasks related to the construction project. Apparently, these men were to lead the effort, guiding others who had also been given wisdom in some particular aspect of the work (Ex. 36:1-2).

This chapter emphasizes a number of New Testament truths concerning the work of the members within of the Church, the body of Christ. First, note that giving to the work of the Lord was engaged by all the Israelites. Years later, Paul would exhort the Church at Corinth, *"On the first day of the week* ***let each one of you*** *lay something aside, storing up as he may prosper, that there be no collections when I come"* (1 Cor. 16:2). All believers are to regularly give to the work of the Lord, as they have been prospered by God (i.e. as God has provided the wherewithal to give back to Him). Believers are not instructed how much to return to the Lord, nor will believers contribute the same amount, but they should give to the work of the Lord willingly and regularly.

The second truth that is seen in Exodus 35 and reiterated in the New Testament for the Church is that everyone was given an opportunity to serve God and everyone was expected to fulfill their assigned ministry. This same truth is affirmed in the Church Age. The Lord Jesus gave individuals, such as evangelists and teachers, as gifts to the Church for a particular reason: *"for the equipping of the saints **for the work of ministry**, for the edifying of the body of Christ"* (Eph. 4:12). Every believer in the Church has a work to engage in, which in turn, in one way or another, blesses the entire body of Christ.

The third truth portrayed in Exodus 35 is that the Holy Spirit gifts, equips, and enables God's people to serve the Lord in a way that would not be naturally possible. Bezalel and Oholiab used their God-given wisdom and skills to assist others to accomplish the work of the Lord. As believers correctly use their spiritual gifts, they equip others in the body to minister as well. This passes the original blessing along to still more believers, further edifying the Church. Individuals are enabled to reach their full potential in Christ and to fulfill God's sovereign purpose for their lives. An example of this process can be seen in the work of the evangelist. Though he or she is skillful in reaching the lost for Christ, this ministry within the Church is to stir up others within the Body to evangelize wherever God has placed them as a testimony. The result is that, in a collective sense, the Church is stimulated and equipped to obey the great commission (Matt. 28:19-20).

Beneficial Church life is enjoyed as each member practices sound doctrine while also learning how to properly use his or her spiritual gifts. Paul puts it this way: *"All Scripture is given by inspiration of God, and is profitable for doctrine, for reproof, for correction, for instruction in righteousness, that the man of God may be complete, thoroughly equipped for every good work"* (2 Tim. 3:16-17). Scripture supplies a foundation of truth for all believers; as we yield to the truth and live it out, practical sanctification occurs. All believers will need the conviction, correction, and reproof of which Paul speaks, for none of us is perfect in any service we render. The Holy Spirit and other believers will be involved in this ministry, and will provide further *training in righteousness* to enable the one who stumbled to walk more successfully in the future. The prospect of God-honoring service becomes increasingly feasible with spiritual maturity.

Thus, to be thoroughly equipped unto every good work, a believer will rely on the Word of God, the guidance of the Holy Spirit, and the mentoring of spiritually-minded believers as he or she matures in Christ. Believers will accomplish their ministries within the Body as they continue to grow spiritually, and develop their spiritual gifts. The world is God's classroom, not the believer's playground! Believers are called to maturity and service – the two cannot be separated. Scripture testifies to the fact that God grows ministries as He grows people.

You have longed for sweet peace, and for faith to increase,
And have earnestly, fervently prayed;
But you cannot have rest, or be perfectly blest,
Until all on the altar is laid.

Is your all on the altar of sacrifice laid?
Your heart does the Spirit control?
You can only be blest, and have peace and sweet rest,
As you yield Him your body and soul.

— Elisha A. Hoffman

# Tabernacle Construction
## Exodus 36:3-38

The response of the people in both giving and laboring for the work of the Lord was incredible. The resources collected to construct the tabernacle and its furnishings were so plentiful that the craftsman told Moses that they had more than enough materials to accomplish the work; in fact, they had *"too much"* (v. 7). Based on this information, Moses issued a decree to prevent the people from giving more:

> *Then all the craftsmen who were doing all the work of the sanctuary came, each from the work he was doing, and they spoke to Moses, saying, "The people bring much more than enough for the service of the work which the Lord commanded us to do." So Moses gave a commandment, and they caused it to be proclaimed throughout the camp, saying, "Let neither man nor woman do any more work for the offering of the sanctuary." And the people were restrained from bringing, for the material they had was sufficient for all the work to be done – indeed too much* (Ex. 36:4-7).

When God's children are free from idols, are brokenhearted before Him, and rejoicing in God's forgiveness, they will be prompted to give back to the Lord out of what He has so generously given to them. God could certainly accomplish His will without our gifts, but then we would miss out on the joy of being a part of His work. Giving to the Lord is an opportunity to show our appreciation for Him; as stated earlier, a lack of giving is a spiritual problem, not a financial one.

Exodus 36, 37 and 38 describe how the children of Israel, under Moses' leadership and through the guidance of Spirit-controlled craftsmen, constructed all the items associated with the tabernacle. The specific pattern which Moses received on the mountain was followed in every detail. This is the main point of these chapters – the Israelites willingly did what they were told to do, and as a result, they learned that God would dwell among them in the tent they had constructed – the tabernacle would be their place of worship.

One of the furnishings addressed in Exodus 38 must be addressed, as it has scarcely been mentioned in Scripture up to this point – that is, the Bronze Laver. It was constructed of polished bronze and filled with water so that it was highly reflective in respcct to a downward glance. Concerning its part in the pattern of heavenly things, the Laver may have represented the sea of glass before the throne in heaven (Rev. 4:6). We learn from Exodus 38:8 that the Laver was actually made from women's looking-glasses (i.e. their polished bronze mirrors). C. H. Mackintosh draws an application from this:

> The laver, with its foot, was made "of the looking-glasses of the women assembling, which assembled at the door of the tabernacle of the congregation" (Ex. 38:8). This fact is full of meaning. We are ever prone to be *"like a man beholding his natural face in a glass; for he beholdeth himself and goeth away, and straightway forgetteth what manner of man he was."* Nature's looking-glass can never furnish a clear and permanent view of our true condition. *"But whoso looketh into the perfect law of liberty, and continueth therein, he being not a forgetful hearer but a doer of the word, this man shall be blessed in his deed"* (Jas. 1:23-25). The man who has constant recourse to the word of God, and who allows that word to tell upon his heart and conscience, will be maintained in the holy activities of the divine life.[1]

The significance of blood and water are set forth in the pattern of the Bronze Altar and the Bronze Laver; in the former, blood cleanses sin, and in the latter, water washes away defilement. The blood upon the Altar flowed from smitten animals and the water in the Laver came from the smitten rock. Both the animals slain and the rock struck are types of Christ (1 Cor. 10:4; John 7:37-39). Through His blood alone is the sinner cleansed and only through the washing of His Word by the power of the Holy Spirit is the saved soul purified (John 15:3). The blood was needed to justify, and the water was needed to sanctify the soul. These two agents of blessing are put forth in plain view at Calvary, for when the soldier's thrust his spear into the Lord's side both blood and water poured out (John 19:34). In the shed blood we see the sacrificed life of Christ (for the life of the flesh is in the blood), and in the water we see the Word and Spirit of Christ. Thus, only through Christ is the sinner cleansed of sin and purified for service.

The Bronze Laver was located in the courtyard directly in front of the entrance to the tabernacle. It was necessary for the priests to wash their hands and feet before coming into Jehovah's presence to worship and to serve. Likewise, every believer must petition the Lord Jesus for cleansing from the filth of the world that we accumulate on our hands (i.e. from what we did outside of God's will), and on our feet (i.e. from where we ventured beyond God's will). Christ symbolically signified the need for believers to repeatedly be cleansed from that which defiles them by washing the dirt of the world from His disciples' feet. Christians have the opportunity to come to Christ and be continually cleansed from the guilt and stain of sin (this benefit was obtained at the Bronze Altar, which pictures the work at Calvary). Just as no priest dared to enter the tabernacle without first washing his hands and feet at the Laver, no child of God should attempt worship or service without first confessing his or her transgressions and being restored to full fellowship with God. To this end, Christ continually labors as our High Priest and Advocate.

The instructions for the Bronze Laver were the concluding portion of the pattern for the tabernacle that God gave to Moses (Ex. 30:28); and apparently, the Laver was the last of the furnishings to be fabricated (Ex. 38:8). As shown in the following diagram of the tabernacle, the order in which the furnishing were revealed and their layout beautifully portray Christ's divine mission to save sinners. Departing eastward from God's heavenly dwelling place (the Ark of the Covenant), Christ came to the Earth as the Bread of Life (the Table of Showbread) and the Light of the World (the Golden Lampstand) to become the sacrifice for humanity's sin at Calvary (the Bronze Altar); this is the only place Christ can accept a repentant sinner. Those who trust His gospel message are spiritually united with Him. This necessitates ongoing cleansing from the sin and guilt in the believer's life (the Bronze Laver) in order to enter the Holy Place to serve and worship God (the Golden Altar of Incense). Each aspect of Christ's ministry on our behalf is an antitype of what is portrayed in the specific tabernacle furnishings.

The Holy Place typifies the communion between the Lord and His saints during the interim between their rebirth and either their death or glorification. While waiting to be brought into God's intimate presence (the Ark of the Covenant), believers will continue to feed upon Christ (the Table of Showbread), and to learn of Him and be a testimony of truth for Him (the Golden Lampstand). Christ's journey to save sinners began at the Ark of the Covenant, and there it will end. As the diagram of the tabernacle shows (i.e. by the outline of an imposed cross), it is only the cross of Christ which can enable sinful people, living outside of God's habitation, to be restored to God and to dwell with Him forever.

> When I saw the cleansing fountain, open wide for all my sin,
> I obeyed the Spirit's wooing, when He said, "Wilt thou be clean?"
> I will praise Him! I will praise Him! Praise the Lamb for sinners slain;
> Give Him glory, all ye people, for His blood can wash away each stain.
> Blessed be the Name of Jesus! I'm so glad He took me in;
> He's forgiven my transgressions; He has cleansed my heart from sin.
>
> — Margaret J. Harris

# Diagram of the Tabernacle

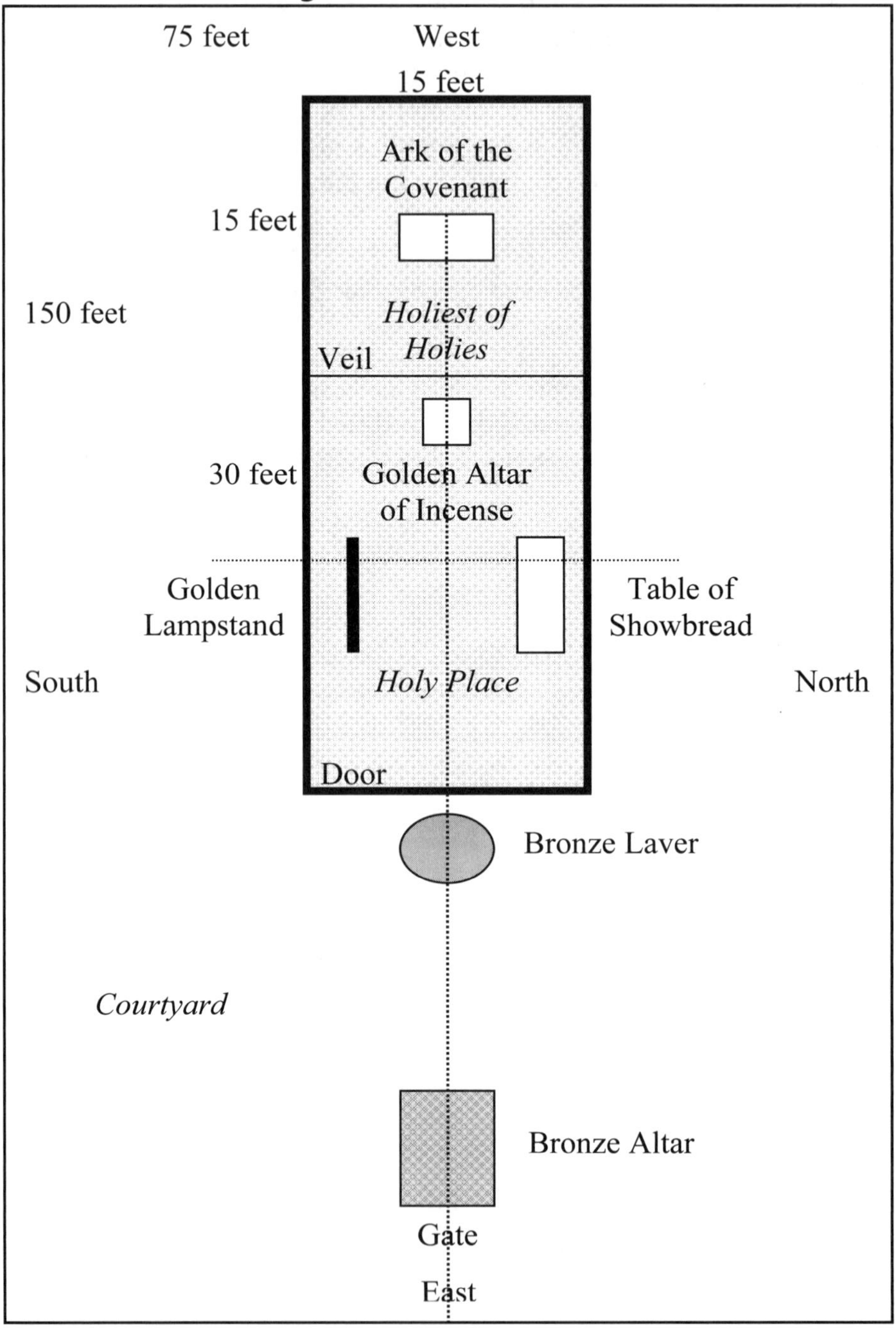

# Reflections of Christ
## Exodus 39

In Exodus 39, Moses reviews all the previous instructions concerning the fabrication of Aaron's holy garments. Aaron was to be the high priest and, as before mentioned, typifies Christ's heavenly priesthood for believers. Accordingly, the typology of this chapter provides us with wonderful reflections of Christ.

For example, the four colors in the high priests garments (purple, scarlet, white, and blue) remind us of the Father's fourfold presentation of Christ in the gospels: Christ as the King of the Jews (Matthew), Christ as the Servant of Jehovah (Mark), Christ as the sinless man (Luke), and Christ as the incarnate God (John). The pure gold crown upon the high priest's miter speaks of Christ's deity and holiness. The crown was to be engraved with this signet: *"Holiness to the Lord"* (v. 30). The pomegranates and the gold bells around the hem of Aaron's blue robe speak of Christ's continual intercessory work before the Throne of Grace on the believer's behalf. This ministry enables believers to be fruitful (as typified in the pomegranates which were full of seeds) and to have a clear testimony of Him in the world (as pictured in the pure gold bells).

When the children of Israel had finished all the work that they had been given to do, we read that *"Moses looked over all the work, and indeed they had done it; as the Lord had commanded, just so they had done it. And Moses blessed them"* (Ex. 39:43). Moses' action foreshadows the time when Christ will review all of our earthly labor. There is a coming day in which every believer must stand before the Lord Jesus and give an account of his or her works (2 Cor. 5:10). This event is called the Judgment Seat of Christ (Rom. 14:10). What was done in the strength of the flesh or for selfish motives or not as the Lord commanded will be consumed by His presence; what has eternal value will be rewarded by Christ Himself.

Although Scripture contains the stories of many godly men and women, the emphasis in each life is the manifestation of God's glory and the receipt of His goodness. God has chosen to manifest His glory and goodness through His Son the Lord Jesus Christ. Thus, it is His personage, character, and attributes which are of a primary focus in Scripture. Consider Scripture's threefold presentation of the glories of the Lord Jesus Christ: intrinsic, official, and moral glory.

His intrinsic glory is that which is essential to Him as the Son of God – He is fully divine and equal to the Father. As such, He prayed, *"And now, O Father, glorify Me together with Yourself, with the glory which I had with You before the world was"* (John 17:5). In His essence, Christ is divine (i.e. one with the Father), always has been divine, and always will be divine.

Christ's official glory is that which pertains to Him as the Mediator of the New Covenant – He is the Great High Priest. The Lord acquired His official glory; it is His reward for finishing the immeasurable work of redemption assigned to Him. This is the glory He was referring to when He said, *"Father, I desire that they also whom You gave Me may be with Me where I am, that they may behold My glory which You have given Me; for You loved Me before the foundation of the world"* (John 17:24).

The Lord's moral glory relates to the perfections which characterized His earthly life and ministry. John writes, *"And the Word became flesh and dwelt among us, and we beheld His glory, the glory as of the only begotten of the Father, full of grace and truth"* (John 1:14). As the Lord Jesus walked upon the earth, He completely reflected the full and perfect character of His Father. He, as God, behaved in the way God would in every circumstance, in every action, in every word spoken, and in every thought.

During the Lord's earthly sojourn, His intrinsic glory was veiled and His official glory had not yet been received. However, His moral glory could not be hidden; the integrity and the perfections of His divine essence shone forth in His character. Of this glory, A. W. Tozer wrote, "Christ is God acting like God in the lowly raiment of human flesh."[1] The various glories of Christ were represented to the Jews in the high priest's attire (as well as various Levitical offerings), and were later witnessed by Jews during His sojourn on earth. In fact, the moral glory of Christ illuminates every page of the Gospels, and indeed, all of Scripture.

O Lord, when we the path retrace which Thou on earth hast trod,
To man Thy wondrous love and grace, Thy faithfulness to God;
Thy love, by man so sorely tried, proved stronger than the grave;
The very spear that pierced Thy side, drew forth the blood to save.

Unmoved by Satan's subtle wiles, or suffering, shame and loss,
Thy path, uncheered by earthly smiles, led only to the cross.
We wonder at Thy lowly mind, and fain would like Thee be,
And all our rest and pleasure find, in learning, Lord, of Thee.

— James Deck

# The Tabernacle is Erected
## Exodus 40:1-33

Although the children of Israel had greatly grieved God after Moses first brought the Law to them, the Israelites did not repeat their mistake when Moses appeared the second time with the tablets. They labored diligently to complete all that God had given them to do: *"Thus all the work of the tabernacle of the tent of meeting was finished. And the children of Israel did according to all that the Lord had commanded Moses; so they did. And they brought the tabernacle to Moses"* (Ex. 39:32-33). The entire episode demonstrates how much better it is for God's people to work together for the honor of God than to sit idly about. Many personal failures could be avoided if believers would stay busy in the work God has given them to do.

With all the various components of the tabernacle complete, God instructed Moses to erect it on the first day of the first month. This means that the children of Israel, having left Egypt on the fourteenth day of the first month, had been in the wilderness with Jehovah for nearly a year (vv. 2, 17). Exodus 40 records how the Israelites set up the tabernacle for the first time and how God then adopted it as His dwelling place among His people.

After the tabernacle was erected, its various furnishings were put in their specific places according to the pattern God gave Moses on the mount – Moses was responsible for its initial setup. The Ark of the Covenant was covered and was the first article placed in the tabernacle; it would be the sole furnishing in the Most Holy Place. Afterwards, the furnishings of the Holy Place (the Golden Lampstand, the Table of Showbread, and the Golden Altar) were arranged accordingly. Although the hanging veil provided a barrier between the Most Holy and the Holy compartments, God considered the Golden Altar of Incense immediately before Him, though it was actually located just on the eastern side of the veil in the Holy Place (v. 5). Recall that the Golden

Altar represents the lovely aspects of Christ's character and His faithfulness to His Father, while the Ark represented God's dwelling place. The tie between the two tabernacle furnishings speaks of the Father's affection for the Son and the Son's love and faithfulness to the Father. The physical arrangement of these articles was necessary to allow the priests to offer incense twice a day on the Golden Altar without being consumed by God's glory (i.e. they didn't have to enter the Most Holy Place).

Moses did all that God had commanded regarding the construction, and set up of the tabernacle. This fact is recorded in verse 33, which states, *"Moses finished the work."* In the final verses of Exodus 40, we read of the Shekinah glory filling the tabernacle as Jehovah took up residence there. This scene, as J. G. Bellett suggests, marvelously pictures the then future event of Acts 2, when, as promised by our Lord, the Holy Spirit came, and took up residence within another house, a living house – that is the Church:

> The Tabernacle is set up in Exodus 40, the Old Testament house of God. The Lord enters it and adopts it. The Cloud rests on it, and the Glory enters into it. So is it, though in another form, in the New Testament house of Acts 2. The Holy Ghost, as a rushing mighty wind, enters into it, and cloven tongues like as of fire sit upon it. This is the Lord, (though again I say in another form), adopting this latter house, as He had adopted the former. The house was now a living house, and the Lord *personally* enters it, bringing with Him His gifts, symbolized by the cloven fiery tongues. The house of old had been a material, and thus but a *shadowy,* house, and the Lord had entered it as the Glory, the *expression* or effulgence of the Divine presence.
>
> We have, however, in connection with these things that are kindred in the two houses, to mark a strong contrast. As soon as the Lord had seated Himself in the Old Testament house, He speaks – as we find in the opening chapters of Leviticus, which immediately follow Ex. 40. But He speaks as One that was seated there to be worshipped or to be reconciled. If His people apprehended Him in any measure of His divine worthiness, they might accordingly bring Him a burnt or a meat offering. If they valued communion with Him, they might bring Him a peace offering. If they found their conscience defiled by reason of any transgression or short-coming, He was there to receive a sin or a

> trespass offering, that the breach might be repaired, and atonement or reconciliation perfected.
>
> From the New Testament house, the Spirit speaks, in like manner, as soon as He has entered it. Through the vessels which He had now filled, He speaks – as the Lord God, of old, had spoken from the tabernacle of the congregation. (Lev. 1:1) But here is the contrast. He speaks of "the wonderful works of God." It is not again of what man was required to do, either as a worshipper or a confessor; as when the Lord had spoken from the former house; but of what God had already done on behalf of man. Peter's words are a sample of this – and they rehearse God's wonderful works in Christ.[1]

Moses conducted an audit of all the work that the children of Israel had accomplished and found that it had been completed accurately in every aspect: *"According to all that the Lord had commanded Moses, so the children of Israel did all the work. Then Moses looked over all the work, and indeed they had done it; as the Lord had commanded, just so they had done it. And Moses blessed them"* (Ex. 39:42-43). The work that the Israelites accomplished was done according to God's revealed truth and through the wisdom and power of the Holy Spirit – all such service has the approval of God and will be rewarded.

After Moses finished reviewing and inspecting all the work, he proceeded to commend the people for a job well done. Moses' action pictures a future day when the Lord Jesus Christ will judge His saints and reward them for their honorable service to Him. Besides those resounding words that every believer longs to hear, *"Well done, My good and faithful servant,"* there are various rewards that believers will receive at the Judgment Seat of Christ. These rewards are called crowns, and though there are likely many other types of crowns, five are mentioned in Scripture:

The Crown of Glory will be given to church elders who shepherd well (1 Pet. 5:4).

The Crown of Life will be given to those who endure trials because they love the Lord (Jas. 1:12).

The Crown of Rejoicing will be given to those who were soul-winners for Christ (1 Thess. 2:19; Phil 4:1); this crown may be more encompassing – such as reward for spiritual growth.

The Crown of Righteousness will be given to those who long for His appearing (2 Tim. 4:8).
The Incorruptible Crown will be given to those who control fleshly desires through the Holy Spirit (1 Cor. 9:25).

The rewards that are earned during this lifetime provide the believer with a greater appreciation for the Lord, a greater capacity to worship Him throughout eternity, and indeed, a greater capability to enjoy heaven (Rev. 4:11). Paul clearly taught that some believers will shine more brightly (this is an earned reflective glory of Christ) than others in their eternal glorified bodies (1 Cor. 15:40-42). What is truly done for Christ now translates into an eternal weight (or measure) of glory (2 Cor. 4:17). It is a common axiom, but believers should never grow weary of it: "Only one life and 'twill soon be past; only what's done for Christ will last." Believer, will your life count for eternity?

Only one life to offer – take it, dear Lord, I pray,
Nothing from Thee withholding, Thy will I now obey.
Thou who hast freely given, Thine all in all for me,
Claim this life for Thine own, to be used, my Saviour,
Every moment for Thee.

— Avis B. Christiansen

# God's Glory
## Exodus 40:34-38

Jehovah had given Moses the pattern of the heavenly things, and Moses faithfully completed all of God's instructions (v. 33). After the tabernacle and its furnishings were constructed and arranged, only one thing remained: *"Then the cloud covered the tabernacle of meeting, and the glory of the Lord filled the tabernacle. And Moses was not able to enter the tabernacle of meeting, because the cloud rested above it, and the glory of the Lord filled the tabernacle"* (Ex. 40:34-36). Note that the manifestation of God's glory to the Israelites followed their obedience to God's directions.

Apparently, the glory of God filled the tabernacle in such a fabulous way that even Moses was not able to enter it. Because the tabernacle had been constructed according to divine revelation, it could be filled with divine glory. C. H. Mackintosh draws a practical application from this fact:

> We are too prone to regard the Word of God as insufficient for the most minute details connected with His worship, and service. This is a great mistake, a mistake which has proved the fruitful source of evils and errors, in the professing Church. The word of God is amply sufficient for everything, whether as regards personal salvation and walk, or the order and rule of the assembly. *All Scripture is given by inspiration of God, and is profitable for doctrine, for reproof, for correction, for instruction in righteousness, that the man of God may be perfect, thoroughly furnished unto all good works* (2 Tim. 3:16, 17). This settles the question. If the Word of God furnishes a man *thoroughly* unto "*all* good works," it follows, as a necessary consequence, that whatever I find not in its pages, cannot possibly be a good work and, further, be it remembered, that the divine glory cannot connect itself with ought that is not according to the divine pattern.[1]

Several historical narratives within Scripture demonstrate an intimate tie between the visible glory of God and human obedience to revealed truth. If Christians want to witness the glory of God in their homes, church gatherings, and indeed in their daily lives, obedience to God's revealed truth is crucial; otherwise, our lives become marked by mundane affairs rather than the supernatural handiwork of God.

The same cloud that was witnessed above the tabernacle the day that God filled it with His glory would remain a continual testimony of His abiding presence among the Israelites. The cloud illuminated the camp at night (by fire), and shaded it each day. Furthermore, God used the pillar of cloud to guide His people in all their wilderness journeys (v. 38). When the cloud of God's presence was taken up, the children of Israel packed up and moved with it. Accordingly, the children of Israel learned to look heavenward to determine God's direction to them; whether night or day, the fire and the cloud clearly revealed God's will to the entire camp.

In this way, the Lord was a shepherd to His people. He had heard their cries in Egypt and had visited them in their affliction. He had delivered them out of bondage and *out of Egypt* with His outstretched arm; He had led them through the Red Sea and vanquished their enemies. And now, He would guide them day by day through the wilderness, as they pressed ever forward to their hope of inheritance in the Promised Land.

The book of Exodus concludes with this dazzling scene – the glory of God visibly displayed in the midst of His people as, together, they venture through the wilderness. It is a spectacular vista; God surrounds Himself with His redeemed people in a solitary place, apart from the world. Yet this is but a foretaste of that which is to come:

> *Now I saw a new heaven and a new earth, for the first heaven and the first earth had passed away. Also there was no more sea. Then I, John, saw the holy city, New Jerusalem, coming down out of heaven from God, prepared as a bride adorned for her husband. And I heard a loud voice from heaven saying, "Behold, the tabernacle of God is with men, and He will dwell with them, and they shall be His people. God Himself will be with them and be their God. And God will wipe away every tear from their eyes; there shall be no more death, nor sorrow, nor*

> *crying. There shall be no more pain, for the former things have passed away* (Rev. 21:1-4).

The end of Exodus portrays that future time when God will dwell among His redeemed people forever! Yet this scene will be far better for there will not be any sin, wickedness, ill-thoughts, or adversaries. The believer will bask in the glory of God and forever contemplate the goodness of His grace (Eph. 2:7).

The glory of God is witnessed in creation, in miracles which confound the laws of science and human reasoning, and in the regeneration of lost souls. God's glory serves as a beacon for all humanity to consider not only what He does, but who He is. To this end, Scripture supplies man with incredible insights into the character and attributes of God. This provokes our respect and reverence. The outshining of God's glory beckons us to consider our own frail existence and our accountability to *Him with whom we have to do* (Heb. 4:13). His glory is paramount in all things, in all places, and for all of time and eternity.

> Everlasting glory unto Jesus be!
> Sing aloud the story of His victory!
> How He left the splendor of His home on high,
> Came in love so tender on the cross to die.
>
> Christ is Lord of Glory, sing we now today;
> Tell abroad the story, own His rightful sway!
> Sing aloud and never cease to spread His fame,
> Triumph now and ever in the Saviour's name.
>
> — Hannah K. Burlingham

# End Notes

**Types**

1. J. F. Walvoord, R. B. Zuck, & Dallas Theological Seminary, *The Bible Knowledge Commentary : An Exposition of the Scriptures* (Victor Books, Wheaton, IL; 1983-1985), p. 172
2. Ibid., p. 172
3. F. W. Grant, *Genesis – In the Light, The Serious Christian Series* (Loizeaux Brothers, Inc., Neptune, NJ), pp. 6-7

**"These are the Names"**

1. Arthur W. Pink, *Gleanings in Exodus* (Moody Press, Chicago, IL; no date), p. 9
2. http://www.bible.org/page.php?page_id=41

**Oppressed in Egypt**

1. J. F. Walvoord, R. B. Zuck, & Dallas Theological Seminary, op. cit., pp. 104-108
2. http://www.cresourcei.org/exodusdate.html

**The Birth of the Deliverer**

1. http://education.yahoo.com/reference/factbook/countrycompare/pg/1a.html

**Rescuing the Deliverer**

**Rejected by Egypt**

1. C. H. Mackintosh, *Genesis to Deuteronomy* (Loizeaux Brothers, Inc., Neptune, NJ; 1972), p. 145
2. J. N. Darby, *Synopsis of the Books of the Bible Vol. 1* (Stow Hill Bible and Tract Depot, Kingston, ON: 1948), p. 7

**The Burning Bush**

1. William Kelly, *Lectures on the Pentateuch* (Heijkoop, Winschoten/Netherlands: reprinted 1970), pp. 133-134

**"Come"**

1. Edward Dennett; http://stempublishing.com/authors/dennett/EXODUS1.html
2. J. F. Walvoord, R. B. Zuck, & Dallas Theological Seminary, op. cit., p. 112

**A Forever Name**

1. P. P. Enns, *The Moody Handbook of Theology* (Moody Press, Chicago, IL; 1989 – electronic copy)
2. C. H. Mackintosh, op. cit., p. 157

**"Go"**

1. F. W. Grant, *Lessons from Exodus – The Serious Christian Series* (Loizeaux Brothers, Inc., Neptune, NJ), p. 44

**The First Objection**

1. Edythe Draper, *Draper's Quotations from the Christian World* (Tyndale House Pub. Inc., Wheaton, IL – electronic copy)
2. F. W. Grant, op. cit., pp. 35-36
3. C. I. Scofield, *The New Scofield Study Bible* (KJV) (Oxford University Press, NY; 1967), p. 74

**More Objections**

1. Edward Dennett, http://stempublishing.com/authors/dennett/EXODUS1.html
2. Arthur W. Pink, op. cit., p. 39
3. C. H. Mackintosh, op. cit., p. 162

**Returning with Peace**

**Lessons on the Way**

1. James Vernon McGee, *Thru the Bible* Vol. 1 (Thomas Nelson Publishers, Nashville, TN; 1981), p. 215
2. William Kelly, op. cit., p. 146

**Bricks without Straw**

**Suffering in the Will of God**

1. Edward Dennett, op. cit.
2. Edythe Draper, *Draper's Quotations from the Christian World* (Tyndale House Pub. Inc., Wheaton, IL – electronic copy)
3. Ibid.
4. Warren Wiersbe, *Be Patient: An Old Testament Study – Job* (Victor Books, Wheaton, IL; 1994 – electronic copy)

**An Outstretched Arm**

1. J. N. Darby, http://stempublishing.com/authors/darby/NOTESCOM/41019E.html
2. John Hannah from J. F. Walvoord, R. B. Zuck, & Dallas Theological Seminary, op. cit., p. 1121

**Go Again**
1. C. I. Scofield, op. cit., p. 79
2. Arthur W. Pink, op. cit., p. 62
3. J. F. Walvoord, R. B. Zuck, & Dallas Theological Seminary, op. cit., p. 120

**"I AM the Lord"**

**A Sign of Authority**
1. C. H. Mackintosh, op. cit., p. 174
2. Watchman Nee, *Love One Another*, (reprinted by Christian Fellowship Publishers; Richmond, VA; 1975)

**The Sway of Imitation**
1. C. H. Mackintosh, op. cit., p. 174
2. Edward Dennett, op. cit.

**A River of Death**
1. F. B. Hole, http://stempublishing.com/authors/hole/Pent/Exodus.html

**Too Many Frogs**

**Life from Dust**
1. Edward Dennett, op. cit.

**Swarms of Flies**
1. Arthur W. Pink, op. cit., p. 72

**Livestock Smitten**

**Boils and Ulcers**
1. Arthur W. Pink, op. cit., p. 66

**Hail Fire**

**The Plague of Locusts**
1. Edward Dennett, op. cit.
2. Arthur W. Pink, op. cit., p. 73 (quoting C. H. Mackintosh)
3. C. H. Mackintosh, *The Mackintosh Treasury* (Gute Botschaft, Dillenburg, Germany; reprinted by Loizeaux Brothers, Inc., Neptune, NJ; 1972), p. 500

**Darkness in the Land**
1. Arthur W. Pink, op. cit., p. 67
2. Ibid., p. 74

**A Great Cry**

1. J. F. Walvoord, R. B. Zuck, & Dallas Theological Seminary, op. cit., p. 126
2. Edythe Draper, op. cit.
3. Ibid.

**The Passover Lamb**

**Worthy is the Lamb**

1. J. N. Darby, *The Holy Scriptures: A New Translation from the Original Languages* (Logos Research Systems, Oak Harbor; 1996), electronic copy – 1 Timothy 3:16
2. Edythe Draper, op. cit.

**The Passover Feast**

1. Arthur W. Pink, op. cit., p. 82
2. Ibid., p. 90
3. A. W. Pink, *Gleanings in Genesis* (Moody Press, Chicago: 1922), p. 108 – quoting William Lincoln

**Sweep Your House Clean**

1. Henry M. Morris, *The Genesis Record* (Baker Book House, Grand Rapids: 1976), p. 347
2. Alexander Hislop, *The Two Babylons* (Loizeaux Brothers, Neptune, NJ; 2nd ed. - 1959), p. 103
3. Ibid., pp. 93-94
4. *The Unwrapping of Christmas: It's History, Myths and Traditions* (Jeremiah Films, Inc.; 1990)
5. Ibid.

**Redeemed by Blood**

1. Arthur W. Pink, op. cit., p. 93
2. Ibid., p. 78

**Egypt Despoiled**

**The Exodus Begins**

1. C. I. Scofield, op. cit., p. 86
2. Edythe Draper, op. cit.

**A Circumcised People**

**The Firstborn is Sanctified**

1. Oswald Sanders, Spiritual Lessons, (Chicago, IL: Moody, 1975), pp. 112-113

**The Long Way Home**

1. C. H. Mackintosh, op. cit., pp. 198-199

**Guided by a Cloud of Fire**

1. Warren Wiersbe, *The Bible Exposition Commentary, Vol. 1* (Victor Books, Wheaton, IL; 1989), p. 416
2. Edythe Draper, op. cit.

**Fear Not, Stand Still**

1. Arthur W. Pink, op. cit., pp. 107-108
2. A. W. Pink, *Gleanings in Genesis*, op. cit., p. 273 (quoting J. N. Darby)
3. Edward Dennett, op. cit.

**A Way of Escape**

1. C. H. Mackintosh, op. cit., p. 204
2. J. N. Darby, *Synopsis of the Books of the Bible Vol. 1*, op. cit., pp. 60-61

**The Redeemed Sing**

**A Wilderness Experience**

1. Arthur W. Pink, op. cit., p. 120
2. http://www.bible.ca/ef/topical-robbed-broke-but-thankful.htm
3. Arthur W. Pink, op. cit., p. 122

**More Lusting and Complaining**

1. P. L. Tan, *Encyclopedia of 7700 illustrations* (Bible Communications, Garland TX; 1996, c1979); Complaining

**Bread from Heaven**

1. C. H. Mackintosh, op. cit., pp. 214-215
2. Partially derived from Arthur W. Pink, op. cit., chps. 22 & 23

**No Lack and No Hoarding**

1. Arthur W. Pink, op. cit., p. 124
2. F. W. Grant, op. cit., p. 114
3. Ibid. p. 115
4. William MacDonald, *The Discipleship Manual* (Gospel Folio Press, Port Colborne, ON; 2004), p. 287

**Remember the Sabbath**

1. William MacDonald, *Believer's Bible Commentary* (Thomas Nelson Publishers, Nashville: 1989), p. 109

**Water from "the Rock"**

1. C. H. Mackintosh, op. cit., p. 219
2. John Walvoord, *The Bible Knowledge Commentary* (Victor Books, Wheaton, IL; 1985), p. 301
3. George Rodgers, *The Gospel According to Moses: The Tabernacle and Its Services* (Morgan and Scott, London, England; 1880), p. 117

**Heavy Hands**

1. F. C. Cook, *Barnes' Notes – Exodus to Esther* (Baker Book House, Grand Rapids, MI; reprint 1879), p. 47
2. F. W. Grant, op. cit., pp. 126-128

**Reunion at the Mount**

1. Arthur W. Pink, op. cit., pp. 146-147
2. William Kelly, op. cit., pp. 177-178
3. C. H. Mackintosh, op. cit., p. 223

**Working too Hard?**

1. Arthur W. Pink, op. cit., p. 149
2. Edward Dennett, op. cit.
3. Ibid.
4. C. H. Mackintosh, op. cit., pp. 225-226

**A New Age Dawns**

1. L. Laurenson, *Classic Christian Commentary* (Books for Christians, Charlotte, NC; no date), p. 60
2. C. H. Mackintosh, op. cit., pp. 228-229

**Ascending the Holy Mount**

1. F. W. Grant, op. cit., p. 133

**A Peculiar Treasure**

1. William Kelly, op. cit., p. 181
2. Edward Dennett, op. cit.

**God Speaks from the Darkness**

**The Ten Commandments**

1. C. H. Mackintosh, op. cit., p. 229
2. Ibid., pp. 232-233

**Worshipping a Holy God**

1. C. H. Mackintosh, op. cit., p. 234
2. Edward Dennett, op. cit.
3. J. N. Darby, op. cit., p. 65

**Social Regulations**
1. C. H. Mackintosh, op. cit., pp. 236-237

**I Will Not Go Out free!**
1. J. F. Walvoord, R. B. Zuck, & Dallas Theological Seminary, op. cit., p. 120
2. F. B. Hole, op. cit.
3. C. H. Mackintosh, op. cit., p. 237

**An Eye for An Eye**
1. Edward Dennett, op. cit.

**Righting Wrongs**
1. Edward Dennett, op. cit.

**Riots, Bribes, Lies and Rest**

**Feasts and Conquest**

**Thrones and Altars**
1. C. H. Mackintosh, op. cit., p. 238
2. Ibid.
3. F. B. Hole, op. cit.

**Materials for the Tabernacle**
1. Arthur W. Pink, op. cit., p. 181
2. Edythe Draper, op. cit.
3. Warren Wiersbe, *Be Joyful: A New Testament Study – Philippians* (Victor Books, Wheaton, Il; 1996 – electronic copy)

**The Pattern**
1. C. H. Mackintosh, op. cit., pp. 239-240
2. Arthur W. Pink, op. cit., p. 187
3. Edward Dennett, op. cit.

**The Ark of the Covenant**
1. C. H. Mackintosh, op. cit., pp. 242-243

**The Table of Showbread**
1. George Rodgers, op. cit., p. 67

**The Golden Lampstand**

**Holy Curtains of Four Colors**
1. William MacDonald, op. cit., p. 1198
2. C. H. Mackintosh, op. cit., pp. 242-243

**The Bronze Altar**

1. C. H. Mackintosh, op. cit., pp. 250

**The Hidden Courtyard**

**Ministering Holy Priests**

1. Edythe Draper, op. cit.
2. J. N. Darby, *The Holy Scriptures*: A New Translation from the Original Languages (Logos Research Systems, Oak Harbor; 1996), electronic copy Hebrews 4:15
3. William Newell, *Hebrews Verse by Verse* (Moody Press, Chicago, IL; 1947), p. 148
4. H. A. Ironside, *Hebrews* (American Bible Conference; Philadelphia, PA; 1932), p. 67
5. J. N. Darby, *Synopsis of Books of the Bible Vol. 5,* op. cit., p. 179
6. F. W. Bruce, *The Serious Christian, Notes on Hebrews* (Books for Christians, Charlotte, NC; no date), p. 26
7. William Kelly, *The Serious Christian, Hebrews* (Books for Christians, Charlotte, NC; no date), p. 49

**Priestly Garb**

1. C. H. Mackintosh, op. cit., p. 252
2. Arthur W. Pink, op. cit., p. 187
3. John Hannah from J. F. Walvoord, R. B. Zuck, & Dallas Theological Seminary, op. cit., p. 152

**Priests Consecrated**

1. Andrew Jukes, *Four Views of Christ* (Kregel Publications, Grand Rapids, MI; 1966), p. 15

**The Lord's Table**

**The Daily Offerings**

1. Edward Dennett, op. cit.

**The Altar of Incense**

1. C. H. Mackintosh, op. cit., p. 257
2. C. H. Bright, quoted by Arthur W. Pink, op. cit., p. 284

**Who May Worship?**

1. C. H. Mackintosh, op. cit., p. 261
2. Edward Dennett, op. cit.

**The Lord's Incense**

1. Edward Dennett, op. cit.
2. C. H. Mackintosh, op. cit., p. 257

**Spirit-filled Craftsmen**

1. Edward Dennett, op. cit.

**A Sign from God**

1. C. H. Mackintosh, op. cit., p. 264

**God's Anger Burns Hot**

1. William MacDonald, op. cit., p. 124
2. Warren Wiersbe, *Be Satisfied: An Old Testament Study – Ecclesiastes* (Victor Books, Wheaton, IL: 1989), electronic copy: Eccl. 12:14
3. H. A. Ironside, *Holiness – The False and the True* (Loizeaux, Neptune, NJ: 1912), p. 33
4. J. Oswald Sanders, *Spiritual Leadership* (Moody Press, Chicago, IL: 1980), p. 96
5. Warren Wiersbe, op. cit., Vol. 2, James 1:19

**Moses the Intercessor**

1. S. Emery, *Treasury of Bible Doctrine* (Precious Seed Magazine, UK: 1977), p. 210
2. James Gunn, *Christ The Fullness of the Godhead* (Loizeaux Brothers, Neptune, NJ: 1982), p. 167
3. James Vernon McGee, *Thru The Bible Commentary Vol. 5*, (Thomas Nelson Publishers, Nashville, TN; 1983)

**God Judges Sin**

1. Edythe Draper, op. cit.
2. Ibid.

**God's Book of Names**

1. Kenneth S. Wuest, *The New Testament: An Expanded Translation* (Eerdmans Publishing Co., Grand Rapids, MI; 1989), Matthew 10:20
2. F. B. Hole, op. cit.

**God Outside the Camp**

1. J. G. Bellett, (Article 26 of 47 Short Meditations; Cavenah; 1886): http://stempublishing.com/authors/bellett/MED16.html

**"Show Me Your Glory"**

1. Edward Dennett, op. cit.

**New Tables and New Vision**

1. J. N. Darby (chp. 34): http://stempublishing.com/authors/darby/NOTESCOM/41019E.html

**A Renewed Covenant**

**Moses' Face Shines**

**Gifts from Willing Hearts**

1. J. G. Bellett, (Article 15 of 47 Short Meditations), op. cit.

**Work from Wise Hearts**

**Tabernacle Construction**

1. C. H. Mackintosh, op. cit., pp. 259-260

**Reflections of Christ**

1. Edythe Draper, op. cit.

**The Tabernacle is Erected**

1. J. G. Bellett, (Article 17 of 47 Short Meditations), op. cit.

**God's Glory**

1. C. H. Mackintosh, op. cit., p. 270

# Bibliography


J. G. Bellett, (Article 26 of 47 Short Meditations; Cavenah; 1886): http://stempublishing.com/authors/bellett/MED16.html

F. W. Bruce, *The Serious Christian, Notes on Hebrews* (Books for Christians, Charlotte, NC; no date)

F. C. Cook, *Barnes' Notes – Exodus to Esther* (Baker Book House, Grand Rapids, MI; reprint 1879)

J. N. Darby (Exodus 34): http://stempublishing.com/authors/darby/NOTESCOM/41019E.html

J. N. Darby, *Synopsis of the Books of the Bible Vol. 1* (Stow Hill Bible and Tract Depot, Kingston, ON: 1948)

J. N. Darby, *The Holy Scriptures: A New Translation from the Original Languages* (Logos Research Systems, Oak Harbor; 1996)

Edward Dennett; http://stempublishing.com/authors/dennett/EXODUS1.html

Edythe Draper, *Draper's Quotations from the Christian World* (Tyndale House Pub. Inc., Wheaton, IL)

S. Emery, *Treasury of Bible Doctrine* (Precious Seed Magazine, UK: 1977)

P. P. Enns, *The Moody Handbook of Theology* (Moody Press, Chicago, IL; 1989)

F. W. Grant, *Lessons from Exodus – The Serious Christian Series* (Loizeaux Brothers, Inc., Neptune, NJ)

F. W. Grant, *Genesis – In the Light, The Serious Christian Series* (Loizeaux Brothers, Inc., Neptune, NJ)

James Gunn, *Christ The Fullness of the Godhead* (Loizeaux Brothers, Neptune, NJ: 1982)

Alexander Hislop, *The Two Babylons* (Loizeaux Brothers, Neptune, NJ; 2nd ed. - 1959)

F. B. Hole, http://stempublishing.com/authors/hole/Pent/Exodus.html

H. A. Ironside, *Hebrews* (American Bible Conference; Philadelphia, PA; 1932)

H. A. Ironside, *Holiness – The False and the True* (Loizeaux, Neptune, NJ: 1912)

Andrew Jukes, *Four Views of Christ* (Kregel Publications, Grand Rapids, MI; 1966)

William Kelly, *Lectures on the Pentateuch* (Heijkoop, Winschoten/Netherlands: reprinted 1970)

William Kelly, *Hebrews – The Serious Christian,* (Books for Christians, Charlotte, NC; no date)

L. Laurenson, *Classic Christian Commentary* (Books for Christians, Charlotte, NC; no date)

William Lincoln quoted in A. W. Pink, *Gleanings in Genesis* (Moody Press, Chicago: 1922)

William MacDonald, *The Discipleship Manual* (Gospel Folio Press, Port Colborne, ON; 2004)

William MacDonald, *Believer's Bible Commentary* (Thomas Nelson Publishers, Nashville: 1989) C. H. Mackintosh, *Genesis to Deuteronomy* (Loizeaux Brothers, Inc., Neptune, NJ; 1972)

C. H. Mackintosh, *The Mackintosh Treasury* (Gute Botschaft, Dillenburg, Germany; reprinted by Loizeaux Brothers, Inc., Neptune, NJ; 1972)

James Vernon McGee, *Thru the Bible* Vol. 1 (Thomas Nelson Publishers, Nashville, TN; 1981)

Henry M. Morris, *The Genesis Record* (Baker Book House, Grand Rapids: 1976)

Watchman Nee, *Love One Another*, (reprinted by Christian Fellowship Publishers; Richmond, VA; 1975)

William Newell, *Hebrews Verse by Verse* (Moody Press, Chicago, IL; 1947)

Arthur W. Pink, *Gleanings in Exodus* (Moody Press, Chicago, IL; no date)

George Rodgers, *The Gospel According to Moses: The Tabernacle and Its Services* (Morgan and Scott, London, England; 1880)

J. Oswald Sanders, *Spiritual Leadership* (Moody Press, Chicago, IL: 1980)

C. I. Scofield, *The New Scofield Study Bible* (KJV) (Oxford University Press, NY; 1967)

P. L. Tan, *Encyclopedia of 7700 illustrations* (Bible Communications, Garland TX; 1996, c1979)

J. F. Walvoord, R. B. Zuck, & Dallas Theological Seminary, *The Bible Knowledge Commentary : An Exposition of the Scriptures* (Victor Books, Wheaton, IL; 1983-1985)

Warren Wiersbe, *Be Joyful: A New Testament Study – Philippians* (Victor Books, Wheaton, Il; 1996)

Warren Wiersbe, *Be Patient: An Old Testament Study – Job* (Victor Books, Wheaton, IL; 1994)

Warren Wiersbe, *Be Satisfied: An Old Testament Study – Ecclesiastes* (Victor Books, Wheaton, IL: 1989)

Warren Wiersbe, *The Bible Exposition Commentary, Vol. 1* (Victor Books, Wheaton, IL; 1989)

Kenneth S. Wuest, *The New Testament: An Expanded Translation* (Eerdmans Publishing Co., Grand Rapids, MI; 1989)

**Other Sources**

http://education.yahoo.com/reference/factbook/countrycompare/pg/1a.html

http://www.bible.ca/ef/topical-robbed-broke-but-thankful.htm

http://www.bible.org/page.php?page_id=41

http://www.cresourcei.org/exodusdate.html

*The Unwrapping of Christmas: It's History, Myths and Traditions* (Jeremiah Films, Inc.; 1990)

# HALLOWED BE THY NAME

## Revering CHRIST in a casual World

Is scriptural terminology important? Does wrong terminology tend to lead to erroneous Church practices? Do I ignorantly show disdain for the Lord's name by the way in which I address Him or speak of Him to others? What is the sin of blasphemy? Can a Christian blaspheme God today? These are some of the questions *Hallowed Be Thy Name* examines in detail. Our speech and behaviour reflect our heart's adoration for the Lord Jesus and, thus, directly affect our testimony of Him to the world. May God bestow us grace to *"buy the truth, and sell it not"* (Prov. 23:23), and may each one be subject to the *"good, and acceptable, and perfect, will of God"* (Rom. 12:2).

**Binding:** Paper

**Size:** 5.5" X 8.5"

**Page Count:** 160 pages

**Item #:** B-7450

**ISBN :** 1-897117-45-0

**Genre:** Christian Living

**Warren Henderson**

An aerospace engineer, who now serves the Lord with his wife Brenda in "full time" ministry. They are commended by Believers Bible Chapel in Rockford, Illinois. Warren is an itinerant Bible teacher and is involved in writing, evangelism, and church planting.

GOSPEL FOLIO PRESS
I WILL PUBLISH THE NAME OF THE LORD
304 Killaly St. West | Port Colborne | ON | L3K 6A6 | Canada | 1 800 952 2382 | E-mail: info@gospelfolio.com | www.gospelfolio.com